THE
EAST INDIA TRADE

THE EAST INDIA TRADE

IN THE XVII TH CENTURY

In its Political and Economic Aspects

SHAFAAT AHMAD KHAN

GYAN

Published by

GYAN

Gyan Publishing House
5, Ansari Road
Daryaganj, New Delhi-110002
Phone: 011-47034999, 9811692060
E-mail: books@gyanbooks.com

Distribution Network
gyanbooks.com
India, USA, Canada, UK, Australia, France

ISBN: 978-81-212-9344-0 (PB)
First Published, 1923

2nd Impression 2023

Printed at: Gyan Press, Delhi.

THE EAST INDIA TRADE

AUTHOR: SHAFAAT AHMAD KHAN

EAST INDIA TRADE
In the XVIIth Century

THE EAST INDIA TRADE IN THE XVIIth CENTURY

In its Political and Economic Aspects

BY

SHAFAAT AHMAD KHAN
LITT.D., F.R.HIST.S.
UNIVERSITY PROFESSOR OF MODERN INDIAN HISTORY, ALLAHABAD

OXFORD UNIVERSITY PRESS
LONDON: HUMPHREY MILFORD
1923

PREFACE

THE East India Trade in the seventeenth century has exercised a strange fascination on the minds of many of the most erudite and conscientious historians. The pioneering work of the Company's factors, the administrative mechanism evolved by the supple and shrewd Directors of the English East India Company, the plantation of English factories in the heart of India, and the interesting problems that developed inevitably out of their contact with the Moghuls, have all been discussed by previous writers. Mr. William Foster's monumental work on the *English Factories in India*, Sir William Hunter's *History of British India*, and Professor W. R. Scott's *Constitution and Finance of English etc. Joint-Stock Companies*, have thrown a flood of light on the leading events in the early history of the East India Company. Of the earlier writers, it is sufficient to mention the works of Bruce and Macpherson.

The present work deals with the subject from a different standpoint. I have traced the history of the East India Trade in the seventeenth century, and estimated its influence on the foreign, no less than the economic, policy of England during the period. The question, How far and to what extent was the English economic and foreign policy affected by the East India Trade? could be answered only after a thorough and careful study of the data for the period. I tried to utilize the essential data preserved in the British Museum Library, the Bodleian Library, the India Office Library and Record Department, and the Public Record Office. Those who take an interest in the bibliography of the subject are referred to my articles in the *Journal of Indian History*, founded and edited by me, and published by the Department of Modern Indian History, Allahabad University. I hope to be able to reprint them next year.

Chapter I traces the history of the East India Trade, and discusses the action and reaction of political and economic theories and foreign policy during the years 1600–1660. For this purpose a number of MSS., rare economic tracts, and important pamphlets have been utilized. Chapter II deals with the effects of the Restoration on the Company. Foreign policy now becomes a principal instrument in the hands of enterprising merchants, and nowhere else is the intimate connexion between the growth of commerce and foreign policy so well illustrated. In Chapter III the economic policy of Sir Josiah Childe is discussed. I have attempted to estimate the influence of his economic theory and principles of administration on the development of the East India Company. The last Chapter exhibits the interdependence of economic theory and commercial growth. The East India Company advocated Free Trade mainly for the reason that the prohibition of the importation of Indian manufactures into England, and of the export of bullion to the East, would have totally destroyed the foundations upon which the Company had been so laboriously built up. The Free Trade theories, so lucidly sketched by Sir William Ashley, would be inexplicable to us without a thorough knowledge of the causes that brought them forth. Of these, the most important was the unusual progress of Indian manufactures in England. I am convinced that the study of the actual movement of commerce, coupled with a thorough knowledge of the political history of the period, will remove many of the errors into which students of the period have fallen. Adam Smith's strange ignorance of the causes that brought Thomas Mun's Mercantilism into existence is a case in point. Chapter I attempts to show that Mun, and other economists of the period, were influenced mainly by the Anglo-Dutch rivalry, and their theories received a specific mould from a struggle that threatened to destroy the entire future of commerce. *The book deals with the East India Trade only in so far as it affected the economic and political policy of England in the seventeenth century.*

Further information on various aspects of the East India Trade will be found in my book, published by the Oxford University Press, in the 'Allahabad University Studies in History', entitled 'Anglo-Portuguese Negotiations relating to Bombay, 1660–1677'. I am engaged on the critical study of the sources for seventeenth century British Indian History, and hope to be able to publish the results of my study by the end of 1923.

In the arduous task of writing and publishing this work I have received constant aid and active encouragement from Mr. William Foster, C.I.E., Superintendent of Records, India Office, Professor Sir Charles Firth, Regius Professor of Modern History, Oxford, and the late Archdeacon Cunningham, D.D. I should have found it impossible to prosecute my researches without the deep interest, invaluable advice, and ungrudging aid rendered by them. Without the keen and sustained interest of these scholars the book would not have been printed. Mr. A. Yusuf Ali, I.C.S. (Retired), Revenue Minister, Hyderabad State, Dr. Hubert Hall, Assistant Keeper of Records, Public Record Office, Chancery Lane, and Professor F. J. C. Hearnshaw, Professor of History, King's College, Strand, have taken a keen interest in the work, and their advice has proved of inestimable value.

Finally, I have to thank His Majesty's Secretary of State for India for sanctioning a grant in aid of the publication of this book.

SHAFAAT AHMAD KHAN.

Department of Modern Indian History,
University of Allahabad, India.

CONTENTS

I

THE EAST INDIA TRADE UP TO 1660[1]

THE foundation of the East India trade was mainly an expression of the growing national desire for commerce. The national self-consciousness awakened by the conflict with Spain had roused the dormant energies and half-articulate longings of the Englishmen under Elizabeth. The struggle was at bottom an economic one, and though it assumed a religious character in the conflict with the Spaniards, the main cause was the desire to partake in the trade and to share in the wealth of the Spanish colonies. The union of Portugal with Spain in 1580; the defeat of the Armada, and the determination of Philip to convert the Mediterranean into a Spanish lake intensified the latent desire of the Englishmen to take part in the rich trade to the Indies. The Venetians, who had long served as intermediaries between Europe and the East, and punished with death the revealer of a maritime route,[2] sent their last argosy to Southampton in 1587. The loss of their ship put an end to their trade. The consequent demand for the spices and other products of the East increased. The union of Spain with Portugal seemed to bar effectively the entry of the English into the East Indies. The desire had led John Cabot to try to reach Asia by the North Atlantic, as Columbus was supposed to have reached it by the South, and to make London a greater entrepôt

[1] This sketch of the East India trade is confined mainly to the commerce carried on by England with the East Indies. Barbosa, De Laet, Faria y Sousa, Maffeius, Major, Monserrate, Pyrard, Father Hosten, Maclagan, Yule, Varthema, Bernier, Sewell, Della Valle, Hawkins, Peter Mundy, Roe, Coryat, and John Marshall are known to all students of seventeenth century Indian history, and the writer has derived considerable help from the priceless information contained in their writings; but his object in writing this essay is not so much to sketch the organization of Indian industry as to trace the course of English commerce with India, and estimate its effect on the economic and foreign policy of England. Hence, these writers occupy only a subordinate place in the development of this essay.

[2] Monson's *Naval Tracts*, printed in Churchill's *Collection of Voyages*, vol. iii, p. 408.

for spices than Lisbon.[1] The voyages of Cabot, Burrough, and Frobisher, in search of a passage to the Indies, testified to the universal desire for participation in the rich traffic with them.[2] Their complete failure did not daunt the spirits of the heroic pioneers; and the gleam of the wealth of the Indies never faded from their sight. No sooner was the country freed from the danger of foreign invasion than some of the merchants memorialized the Queen for permission to send ships to trade in the Indies. Ralph Fitch and Stephens had no doubt led the way, but they do not seem to have exercised the influence with which Sir William Hunter[3] has credited them. The Queen's Council was at the time engaged in negotiations for peace with Spain, and the petition of the merchants was not, therefore, given a favourable hearing. The remarkable success of the Dutch Company, however, precipitated matters. They memorialized again, and this time they were favourably listened to. The sum of £30,133 had already been subscribed by 101 merchants. The Charter granted for 'the Honour of our Nation, the Wealth of our People, the Increase of our Navigation, and the Advancement of lawful traffick'[4] invested the Company with the exclusive monopoly of trade to the East Indies, and provided for its government by a Governor and twenty-four Committees. Full powers were given to the freemen to meet as often as necessary to 'make reasonable laws, Constitutions, Orders, and ordinances, necessary and convenient for the good government of the Company'. Breaches of such laws were punishable both 'by imprisonment of body, or by fines and amercements'.[5] The essential feature of the Company was foreshadowed in the petition of the merchants to Elizabeth, praying her to incorporate them into a Company, 'for that the trade of the Indies, being so far remote from hence, cannot be traded, but in a joint and a united stock'.[6] It is no doubt true, as pointed out by Hunter

[1] Weare's *Cabot's Discovery of North America*, pp. 144-50.

[2] *Narratives of Voyages*, by Rundell; Sainsbury, vol. i, Introduction i–xxxiv, passim; *The Three Voyages of Frobisher*, by Collinson.

[3] *History*, vol. i, p. 236.

[4] Bruce, vol. i, pp. 136–9; Shaw's *Collection of Charters granted to the East India Company*; *Letter Book*, pp. 163, 189; Anderson's *Annals of Commerce*, vol. ii, pp. 196–7; Sainsbury, vol. i, pp. 115–18.

[5] Shaw, *Charters granted to East India Company*, pp. 1–26.

[6] Sainsbury, vol. i, no. 258; Bruce, vol. ii, pp. 112–13.

and Dr. Scott,[1] that the terminable stock of this Company was a transition between the Regulated and Joint Stock Company. It did not acquire the latter character till 1613. Yet it is apparent from their petition that they intended it to become ultimately a Joint-Stock Company.

The original aim of the East India merchants was the acquisition of a part of the spice trade in the East Indies. But it was quickly discovered that English commodities were in small demand in the East India islands, while the products of India, specially calicoes and saltpetre, were very profitable commodities. Hence the establishment of English factories in India. The Company's sphere of activity was considerably narrowed through financial difficulties. Capital was scarce; the trade was depressed on account of the plague;[2] and some of the adventurers paid their shares only after a threat of imprisonment from the Privy Council. The nominal capital of the First Voyage (1601) was returned at £57,473.[3] The stock of the voyage was not wound up, but was transferred to the account of the Second Voyage. According to Sambrooke[4] the capital of the Second Voyage was £71,350. This was added to the First, and divisions were paid on the total of £128,823. The dividends on the total amount were £195 per cent. But as they were not fully paid till 1609, the average rate of profit on the total amount was about 21 per cent. The Third Voyage began before all the money necessary had been paid by the adventurers.[5]

There was a loss on the Fourth Voyage, owing to the wreck of the two ships employed. The Fifth Voyage proved, however, the most profitable of the Twelve Voyages, and yielded a return of £334 per cent. on the combined capital of the Third and Fifth Voyages. The average rate of profit seems to have been about £101 per cent. The profits of the last Seven Voyages were on the same magnificent scale. The total capital of the First Joint Stock was £418,691. The general rate of profit on the

[1] *Constitution and Finances of the Joint Stock Companies*, pp. 96–7.
[2] London's *Lord Have Mercy Upon Us*, in Somers' Tracts, vol. vii, p. 54.
[3] Sambrooke's *Report on the Progress of the East India Trade*, printed in Sainsbury, vol. ix, pp. 360–3.
[4] In Sainsbury, ib.
[5] Court Book, vol. ii, 27th February 1607.

First Joint Stock and the Voyages, arrived at after deducting the insurance, seems to have been 31 per cent. The existence of separate stocks produced the usual consequences of disorganization. The maintenance of separate factories in Bantam had resulted in constant bickerings. Sambrooke's account is significant. 'The Twelve Voyages drawing towards an end, and in regard of the inconveniencies which befell the trade by having several factories in Bantam for several accounts, each endeavouring to prefer the interests of their distinct employments, they grew up to such an height of difference that they became as enemies one against another, making protests each against the other, which was a great disturbance to the benefit of the trade; to remedy which the then adventurers took it into consideration how to prevent the like in the future, who in conclusion resolved themselves into a Joint Stock, raising a subscription amounting to £418,691.' This characteristic account throws much light on the organization of Companies. The inherent drawbacks involved in the maintenance of separate voyages could be removed only by the creation of a permanent stock, guaranteeing a continuity of policy, permanence of regulations, and rigid regulation of trade for national interest. The coherent and vigorous policy and constitution of the Dutch East India Company supplied a fresh motive for the conversion of a semi-regulated into a purely Joint-Stock Company. Up to 1617 the Dutch Company had divided its profits at an average annual rate of 25 per cent., while the dividends of English undertaking on the capital actually employed came to over 31 per cent. on the Voyages and Joint Stock. The lower return of the Dutch Company was due to its expenditure of considerable sums on the building of forts, &c. The advantages of a permanent capital were not unknown to the directors of the English East India Company. The replacement of uncoordinated voyages by a permanent capital, with a centralized machinery for the regulation of trade, and the enforcement of regulations necessary for its existence, embodied in a concrete form the inner changes that had taken place in the original design of the Company. The regularization of its machinery, and the consequent acquirement of a definite corporate character, facilitated its transition from a purely private Company, formed for the specific purpose of benefiting private traders, into a semi-national institution carrying on a most important trade for the benefit of the nation.

The whole conception of the original functions and constitution of the English Company was ultimately modified. It justified its existence on national grounds. The East India trade was claimed by Mun to be the 'principal instrument' whereby 'foreign treasure' could be acquired. The Company, argued Mun, did a national service by 'counterpoising the greatness of the Hollanders'. It was upon this ground that the Company insisted on the absolute importance of safeguarding the interests of the English Company. This could be effected by the Central Government alone. A private Company was powerless against an institution that was armed with all the authority of the State. Hence the necessity of constant support on the part of the State.

It is interesting to compare the two Companies with regard to the amount of support received by each from the State. The first fifteen voyages undertaken by the Dutch had brought large profits to the adventurers. The average annual rate seems to have been about £5 per cent., and, though this was not so high as that of the English East India Company, it may be regarded as very satisfactory, in view of the fact that a considerable amount of money had been spent on the construction of forts in the East. This proved a source of great strength to the Dutch Company. The organization of the disconnected, unorganized, and, in many cases, antagonistic Companies and Copartnerships trading to the East into one strong and completely centralized Company was effected only after the serious drawbacks of this method of carrying on commerce had been recognized. The merchants were not slow to realize its benefits. The Portuguese and Spaniards could never be driven out of their commercial strongholds under the Equator except by a concentration of the private strength and wealth of the merchants. Hence the formation of one East India Company, and hence, moreover, the identification of the Dutch Company with the Central Government. As the State undertook the defence of the Company, it followed that greater power would be conferred on it. Again, as all the authority of the State was exercised by the Dutch East India Company in the East Indies, the quarrels of the latter were taken up by the States-General with a vigour and energy that have hardly been surpassed. All the Chambers of the United Provinces were represented on the Directorate. All the inhabitants of the provinces had the right within a certain time to take shares in the Company. It could make treaties with the East Indian powers, in the name of the States-General of the United Provinces; it could build fortresses, appoint generals, and levy troops. The generals had command over all its forces by land and sea, and exercised undisputed control over its finances. The Company was, therefore, a thoroughly national institution, wielding enormous powers, and exercising all the rights of sovereignty over a large tract of land.[1]

This close connexion between the Dutch Company and the States-General differentiates the former completely from the English Company. The latter was no doubt given wide powers. These were subsequently enlarged. The Charter granted by James in May, 1609, conferred on the Company the benefits of the 'whole, entire, and only trade and traffic to the East Indies' for ever. This was a considerable improvement on that of Elizabeth. The latter had limited the privileges of the Company to fifteen years. Moreover, James's Charter prohibited all persons from trading within the Company's limits except by licences obtained from them under their Common Seal.[2] It could invoke the authority of the Crown for enforcing obedience, punishing interlopers, and protecting its commerce. Yet the lack of support on the part of the Crown, combined with the paucity of its resources, produced difficulties from the outset. It was never identified with the State; its factors were insulted in the East through its weakness at home; and the

[1] There is not a single exhaustive treatise in English on the subject. George Edmundson's article on the subject (*Cambridge Modern History*, vol. v, pp. 510–14) is very valuable, but it does not give us sufficient information. Motley's *United Netherlands* contains acute remarks on the subject, and is indispensable (vol. iii, p. 652; vol. iv, pp. 148–51). Hunter's *History of British India* (vol. i) has a valuable chapter on the subject. Professor Egerton's chapter in the *Cambridge Modern History* (vol. v, chap. xxv, pp. 729–46) is useful and accurate. The most trustworthy information is, however, to be sought in the dispatches of the factors and Court Minutes of the English Company.

[2] Sainsbury, vol. i, no. 440; *Court Minutes*, Book II. 125–7; Shaw, *Charters, &c.*, pp. 27–53.

Dutch were enabled to expel its factors from many a fair and fertile isle. This is the main feature that distinguishes it from the Dutch Company. The Company could demand support only on the ground that it ministered to the needs of the nation, and carried on the trade, not so much for private as for public benefit. Hence, an entirely new development of the original design. The perfectly rounded unity and harmonization of the various elements that were engendered by the existence of the seemingly contradictory principles—public and private benefit—were not impossible of achievement. The Company could show, and, as a matter of fact, did show, later on, that the sole criterion of any trade is the *res publica*. 'If', asserted the champions of the Company, 'the East India Trade cannot be carried on by it with advantage to the nation, then its dissolution would be justifiable.' But they denied the validity of the minor premise from which this conclusion was deduced. They went farther. They adduced proofs to show that the East India trade was the most national of all the trades, and that only a Joint Stock Company, viz. the existing East India Company, could carry it on.

It is totally immaterial, from our present standpoint, whether the statements of the East India Company were well founded. What is really of importance is the fact that the evolution of the idea was productive of far-reaching consequences. As the Company justified its existence on national grounds, it expected the Central Government to adopt its quarrel as that of the State, to support it against all its rivals, and ultimately to wage war for the recovery, or maintenance, of its rights. The State was now called upon to exercise functions which had hitherto been left to the initiative of private merchants. This had other consequences. The defence of its rights, and the support of its subjects' privileges in the East, logically involved regulation. The two—regulation of commerce, and the maintenance and extension of the commercial and colonial rights and privileges—constitute Mercantilism. Both these elements are essential to a right understanding of that tendency. This will be explained and elucidated in the following pages.

The chief articles of export from India were calicoes, indigo, cotton, raw cotton, raw silk, saltpetre, and spices.

The importance attached by the Company to the spices can hardly be exaggerated. Before the establishment of the East India Company, the main source of supply was Antwerp. Here more than 20,000 persons are said to have been employed by the English merchants. Spices were, and remained for a time, the most important article of export from the East. It was not till after the English had been expelled from the East Indies that the trade declined. Sir Dudley Digges reckoned that the smallest quantity of pepper that the kingdom was esteemed to spend was 1,500 bags, containing 400,000 lb. Mun, however, thought that about 250,000 lb. were consumed in 1620.[1] The price of pepper is differently given by three writers. Sir Dudley Digges makes it 4*s.* a lb. Mun, however, says that it was sold in England at 1*s.* 8*d.* a lb. This is, perhaps, a more correct estimate. As the price of the pepper in the East was usually 2½*d.* a lb., there was thus a considerable profit on this article. The price seems to have fluctuated considerably. This was due mainly to the monopoly exercised by the Dutch. In the Moluccas to such a pitch was the spirit of monopoly carried that the quantity of spice grown was carefully restricted in order to keep up the price. Particular spots were selected suitable for the purpose, and elsewhere, as far as possible, the trees were destroyed.[2] It is instructive to compare the price given by the redoubtable Malynes in his ponderous *Lex Mercatoria.*[3] The pepper of Calicut, Malabar, and the island of Sumatra was sold at ten ducats the hundred bought by the bahar of four quintals. From the value of the ducat as given in L. Roberts's *Merchant's Map of Commerce*[4] we deduce the conclusion that the price of pepper was 6*d.* the lb. It is, however, highly probable that the Malabar pepper was not in great demand at the time. The other variety of pepper given by Malynes is called long pepper. It was at twenty-five ducats the hundred, or 15*d.* the lb.[5]

[1] It is instructive to compare the amount given by Dudley Digges in his *Defence of Trade*, pp. 43–4, with those in Mun, vol. v, pp. 276–7.

[2] George Edmundson, op. cit.; Sainsbury, vol. ii, nos. 268, 463, 666; vol. iii, nos. 156, 267, 370; Bruce, vol. i, p. 155. The figures given by Mun have been verified by comparison with those in Sainsbury.

[3] Brit. Mus. 509. h. 4, 1686, pp. 53, 54.

[4] Ib. 522. m. 20, 1700, pp. 18–24.

[5] Ib. 509. h. 4, p. 54.

The next important spice is cloves. Not more than about 50,000 lb. of cloves seem to have been consumed in 1614. In 1620, however, the amount was greatly increased, and reached the figure of 150,000 lb. This seems a really large amount when we consider its price. Before the interruption of this trade by the Dutch,[1] its price was about 4*s.* a lb. The profits reaped by the East India merchants were large. It was bought in the East for 9*d.* a lb., and sold here (in 1620) for 6*s.* a lb. The most famous variety seems to have grown in the islands of Moluccas. It was bought at 27*d.* the lb. Another 'leaner sort' of cloves deserves mention. It was sold at 13½*d.* a lb.[2]

Next to cloves comes nutmegs. The price in 1614 was 2*s.* 8*d.* a lb. Before that time it was 5*s.* a lb. In 1620 the amount seems to have been 150,000 lb. The price in the East was 4*d.* the lb. In England, in 1620, it was 2*s.* 6*d.* a lb. Malynes, however, estimates it at 8*d.* a lb.

Next to nutmegs comes mace. The price of mace was 10*s.* a lb. before 1614, but it was lowered to 6*s.* a lb. in that year. In 1620 it was 8*d.* a lb. in the East, and 6*s.* a lb. in England. It is remarkable that Malynes gives the price of mace as 40*d.* or 3*s.* 4*d.* a lb. The enormous difference between the two varieties can hardly be adduced as the main cause.

The popularity of the spices did not show any sign of diminution. The eagerness of the Dutch to acquire the monopoly of all the spices in the East can be accounted for by this cause. The conquest of Constantinople by the Turks had affected the overland trade, and the amount of benefit derived by the East India merchants from the voyages to the East was considerable. The main varieties of spices were very dear at Aleppo. The cost of pepper there was 2*s.* a lb.; in the East it was only 2½*d.*; the cost of cloves at the former place was 4*s.* a lb.; in the Indies it was only 9*d.* a lb. If the total amount exported from the East Indies had been exported through Aleppo, the loss would have been serious. They cost not more than £511,458. 5*s.* 8*d.* At Aleppo, however, the price would have been £1,456,001. 10*s.*[3] This shows the extent of the

[1] Dudley Digges, op. cit., p. 44.
[2] Malynes, op. cit., p. 54.
[3] Mun, *Discourse of Trade,* Purchas, vol. v, pp. 268–9.

benefit derived by the East India Company from trade in the Indies. Nor was it the only advantage. It was evident that the large amount of pepper exported to England could not all be consumed in England. It was, therefore, sent 'abroad into Germany, the Netherlands, France, Spain, Italy, Turkie and other places'.[1] Consequently, 'out of Spices only, about £200,000 was added to the stock of the Kingdom'.

The Venetian ambassador testifies to the popularity of the spices in England. 'Ships have arrived from the East Indies with the value of 1,400,000 Crowns at least, in diverse kinds of drugs and a quantity of diamonds. They are accustomed to draw supplies from these countries, and there is enough to supply both the State and the rest of the world.' This is significant. It confirms the impression produced by the study of the Company's Court Minutes and the reports of the factors from the East. The next entry is from the same series, but of a different date.[2] 'From the Indies', says the Venetian, 'they generally bring pepper, cloves, indigo, things which previously came through Venice, and were distributed through Holland, and Low Germany, France and England, but now with this navigation, the English and Dutch have absorbed all this trade.' This was perfectly true. Venice was eliminated altogether from a share in the East India trade, though she still continued to trade in the Levant.

The importation of spices was not accorded a general approval in England. There was a considerable opposition to the trade, and Mun found it necessary to defend the amount spent on their purchase.[3]

The other article that acquired importance later on was calico. There does not seem to have been an active demand for calico

[1] Digges, p. 43. Later on the Company, to avoid seizure of its merchandise by the State, sold its pepper at Genoa, and other Italian towns. See below. Sainsbury, vols. vii, viii, passim.

[2] *Venetian Calendar*, 1613–15, p. 160. Compare Piero Contarini's dispatch, in volume dealing with 1617–19. The number of articles desired by Chamberlain was seventy. The list in Macpherson, vol. ii, p. 131, is large enough. Compare p. 106. Mun's list is by far the most accurate and concise, pp. 265–6. Sainsbury, vols. i–v, passim. The references to spices in the Court Minutes, &c., are so frequent that I have deliberately left them unnoticed. It would have considerably increased the bulk of this essay. Only the most important are given below.

[3] See below.

goods at first. They, however, soon replaced the linens imported. It could not be denied by the East India Company that the commodity was not 'profitable for the state of Christendom in general'.[1] But it was of 'singular use'. It not only increased the foreign trade of the kingdom, but also abated the excessive prices of 'Cambricks, Holland, and other Sorts of Linnen Cloth, which daily are brought into this Kingdom for a very great sum of money'.[2] The amount of calicoes bought in 1620 seems to have been 50,000 pieces of several sorts, rated at 7*s.* a piece. They were sold in England at 20*s.* a piece, for £50,000. This leaves a handsome margin of profit. The cheapness of the articles and the fact that they were re-exported ensured them a steady market.[3]

Raw silk was another article of importance. The Company's efforts to import large quantities of raw silk into England may seem inexplicable to us at the present day. The importance of the industry had, however, been borne in upon James I, and considerable progress had already been made. The Italian States were the pioneers of that industry in Europe. The States of Genoa, Florence, and Lucca provided raw silk out of Sicily to the value of £500,000 per annum.[4] The East India Company could procure a sufficient supply of silk from Persia alone. There were, however, various difficulties in the way. It was not till 1618 that the Company's factors were enabled to make a contract with the Shah for 8,000 bales of silk, of 180 lb. per bale. They declared that the silk made in Persia would yearly amount to a million pounds. The Company hoped to sell English commodities of the same value. It sold seventy-one bales of raw silk in September 1619.[5] It is instructive to notice

[1] Mun, p. 266. [2] Ib.

[3] The first mention of the name in the East India Company's records occurs under date August 1602: 'Book Calicoes, bought in certain Junks near Socotra at 4*s.* a piece. They are worth here at 12*s.* a piece': Sainsbury, vol. i, nos. 309, pp. 135, 271. 'Inquiry to be made how Calicoes and Pinlathoes will sell in England, that directions may be given to factors in the East Indies to buy and send them over': p. 317. 'Indigo, Calicoes, &c., the Chief Commodities in Surat': ib., p. 328, nos. 776, 792; vol. ii, p. 73, nos. 88, 608, 750; Mun, op. cit., pp. 265–80. Sainsbury's *Court Minutes*, vols. vi to x, show the increasing popularity of the calicoes. There was a reduction in demand owing to the Civil War, the Interlopers, and the famine in India in 1630. After 1657 we find a noticeable change.

[4] Mun, op. cit., p. 272.

[5] *Court Minutes*, 22–25th Sept. 1619, Book IV; Sainsbury, vol. ii, pp. 155–9. A very accurate account of the Persian trade.

that Sir Thomas Roe had advised the Company to pay as much as *7s. 6d.* per lb. for the Persian silk.[1] The price of China raw silk, however, was slightly lower. It seems to have been *7s.* a lb.; the total amount bought by the Company in 1620–1 was 107,141 lb.

Bengal raw silk had not yet acquired the popularity which it subsequently attained. It was not till the establishment by the East India Company of factories in Patna, &c., and the instruction of Indian weavers by the English 'artists' expressly sent from England, that Bengal silk became a serious competitor in the English market. We find only occasional references to the Bengal silk in the early records of the Company. The fluctuations of trade in Persia, the disorders of the Civil War, and the weakened position of the Company produced fluctuations in the demand for silk. There were consequent fluctuations of price, silk selling as high as *28s.* a lb. between 1652–4, and falling as low as *18s. 6d.* a lb. in 1636. The Company, writing to Surat in March 1657, declared that 'Raw Silk was in small demand'.

Indigo was another article imported. It was in great demand in Europe, and early attempts had been made to acclimatize it in England. The imports from the East were for a long time confined to indigo. In 1615 a single ship took home from Surat over 1,000 bales of indigo.[2] The quantity of indigo purchased by the Company in 1620–1 seems to have been 200,000 lb. The price in the East was *14d.* a lb. It was sold here at *5s.* a lb. Malynes[3] says that the indigo of the better sort, called Carquez, and the common sort, called Aldcas, were sold for *22d.* and *18d.* a lb. respectively. The West Indian islands proved very serious competitors. The East Indian indigo was, however, much better in quality than the West Indian, and Malynes[4] remarks that 'this rich Indigo'—from the East—'is better than Laurea, or Lahora, coming from the said West Indies'. The popularity of the article was, however, steadily maintained. The Surat factors wrote, in 1652, 'that Indigo has hitherto been the most gainful commodity'.

[1] Sainsbury, vol. ii, p. 156.

[2] Foster, op. cit.; Sainsbury, vol. i, nos. 840–2, 859, 865, 921, 922; vol. ii, pp. 44, 45, 55, 57, nos. 403, &c.; Mun, op. cit., p. 269.

[3] *Lex Mercatoria*, p. 54. [4] Ib., p. 54.

Saltpetre was another useful commodity imported by the Company.[1] The importance of saltpetre in the seventeenth century can hardly be exaggerated. At that time powder-making depended on the obtaining of earth from the floors of buildings that had been used for stables.[2] The earth required to be put through certain processes in order to extract the saltpetre. The operations of digging and extracting it have been graphically described by the writer of the article on saltpetre.[3] The only means whereby the State could supply itself with a sufficient amount was by the grant of patents. The holders were allowed to dig for peterish earth in grounds not only of the meaner sort, but 'also of the better sort, which had not been entered previously'. The cancellation of the patent was not an effective remedy for the due supply of the Government.[4] The Company secured a licence from the Crown for the manufacture of gunpowder; but the venture proved a total failure and the loss sustained thereby was serious. The Civil War in England increased the demand for gunpowder, and, consequently, saltpetre. At the same time fresh sources of supply were opened up in Behar. The utility of the article, combined with its scarcity, made its importation a matter of national importance, and the Company became the sole provider of it to the Crown. The Company brought forward the importation of saltpetre as a justification for the maintenance of its privileges, and after recounting all the benefits of that article, triumphantly asked, 'Now, who will supply the Crown with this article, if the Company is dissolved?' The argument was irresistible.

The chief articles of export from England to the East were woollen goods, lead, tin, and coral. The Company was hopeful of supplying English commodities to Persia to the value of a million pounds. They encouraged all their factors to increase the sale

[1] Sainsbury, vol. iv, nos. 10, 12, 18, 25, 69, 110, 314, 315, pp. 172, 173; vol. vi, p. 140. 'Saltpetre, of which there are about 50 or 100 tons to be sold at £4. 10*s.* per cwt.' In February 1611 it was sold at £40 a cwt., pp. 149, 164. The price varied from £4 to £4. 10*s.*, pp. 221–2, 232, 253–5; vol. viii, pp. 325, 346, 350.

[2] Scott, op. cit., p. 113.

[3] *Dictionarium Rusticum*, 1717. Compare H. Townshend, *Historical Collections*, p. 251, 1680.

[4] D'Ewes, *Journals*, p. 653, &c. A very vivid account of the patents granted by the Queen.

of woollen goods in the East. But the high price rendered it impossible for the poorer classes to use the broad-cloth exported from England.[1] As a factor remarked in 1605, the Indians could make three suits of clothes for the price of one yard of English cloth.[2] Only the Emperor and his courtiers could afford it. The Dutch cloth competed here as elsewhere, and as the Dutch could easily undersell, the competition was severely felt. These causes rendered its sale extremely difficult. The Directors tried in every way to increase its sale. Their efforts were in vain. Though a large amount was exported it found few buyers.[3]

The other important article of export, iron, suffered in the same way. It could not compete with the cheaper Indian iron, and its export was consequently restricted. We have a very interesting account of the quantities, &c., of English goods exported in 1614.[4] The Company sent 'Bayes, Kersies and most broad clothes dyed and dressed to the Kingdom's best advantage' to the value of £14,000; lead, iron, and foreign merchandise to the value of £10,000, 'ready money in all the ships but £12,000'.

Another article that yielded large profits was coral. It was procured from the Mediterranean, and sold at a great profit. The other articles exported—copper, tin, vermilion, and quicksilver—never achieved any prominence. They figure in the later lists of practically all the cargoes, but it appears that their sale was considerably limited. The shrewd Roe had warned the Company that 'these people are very curious, and can judge of workmanship well'. He advised them therefore to 'fit them with variety, for they are soon cloyed with one thing'. The advice was not neglected by the Company.

From 1609 to 1617 the Company's trade expanded rapidly. The Dutch interferences did not begin to be felt excessively until 1617. Up to that time its progress may be considered

[1] Sainsbury, vols. ii and iii, passim.

[2] Ib., vol. ii, p. 159, nos. 339, 753. See the price of wool on p. 65 of vol. iv, and nos. 230, 767, 803. Ib., vols. vi to x contain many references to wool.

[3] See Sir Thomas Roe's Advice to the Company about the proper articles to be exported to India, Sainsbury, vol. ii, nos. 316, 317, 402, pp. 145–6.

[4] Digges, *Defence of Trade*, p. 46.

phenomenal. The Company, during the period of the four voyages, sent out a considerable number of ships. It sent out five ships in 1613, nine in 1614, eight in 1615, and seven in 1616. This does not include many of the ships built and maintained by the Company. In 1614 it possessed twenty-four ships. The total tonnage of the ships was 10,259 tons.[1] As, however, two more ships were being built at Deptford in 1614, we come to the conclusion that the total tonnage of the Company's ships, in 1614, was 12,259. This was not an inconsiderable amount in those days. The largest ship in the kingdom, the *Trade's Increase*, belonged to the Company. Her tonnage was 1,293 tons and she was the 'largest merchant ship'. King James signified his intention to be present at the launch, and named her the *Trade's Increase*. The ship was, however, very unfortunate, being wrecked on her second voyage with Sir Henry Middleton, who died on board.[2] The Company's shipping showed no signs of decline. The magnificence of its ships excited the admiration of the Venetian ambassador, who wrote in 1618: 'The East India Company have 45 galleons, of more than 2,000 tons each, built for war; and so well constructed and armed as to cause amazement. They usually make the return voyages in the third year, taking all the provisions they need for the 200 men carried by each ship.'[3] Linello, the Venetian secretary in England, testified to the excellent workmanship of their ships. 'Seven ships, all new, have been got ready by the merchants in the river here for the East Indies. They are the finest that have ever been seen at sea.'[4]

The Company had at first exported English products worth only £6,860. The amount of bullion exported in the same year —1601—was £21,742. In 1614 'ready money in all the Ships' was no more than £12,000.[5] The amount rose to £52,087 in 1616. The English exports also showed an increase, viz. £16,506, while the capital invested was £109,000.[6] The total amount spent on the buying of East India commodities in 1620 was no more than £100,000. This does not include the cost

[1] By adding up the amounts of tonnage in Digges, pp. 19–22.
[2] Sainsbury, vol. i, nos. 474, 476, 730, 731, 862.
[3] *Venetian Calendar*, vol. xv, p. 415. Compare vol. x, pp. 237, 394.
[4] Ib., vol. xiv, p. 443.
[5] Digges, p. 46.
[6] *Abstract of Stock*, Marine Records.

of victualling, &c. We know that the charges were excessive. A concrete example will help to show the amount of money expended by the Company in the East. The charge for the fleet of 1614 amounted to £100,000. Of this amount ships and 'their Furniture' cost £34,000; victuals, £30,000; English articles exported, £26,000. Only £12,000 was exported in ready money. The cost of ships and victualling for 1613-16 was £272,544.[1]

From a letter of Mr. Skrine,[2] it is apparent that the shipping of the Company had maintained its reputation. 'Four ships have lately arrived from India belonging to the East India Company, with cargoes on board which are said to be worth £400,000.'

Another evidence of the Company's progress is to be found in the increase of customs. Under the Queen 'Mr Customer Smith had farmed the customs at £1,200'. In 1613 they were £13,000. They were considerably increased in 1615. The customs for the two ships returned in 1615 were £14,000. In 1622, however, they were more than trebled. The exact sum paid in 1622 for customs was £40,000. This shows an unprecedented rise. This was not all. Two years later another £10,000 was added to the King's customs, and the total amount paid by the Company in 1624 was £50,000.[3] In 1622-4 twelve ships were laden by the Company with English goods, consisting chiefly of broadcloths, kerseys, quicksilver, lead, tin, and Spanish ryals, as much as 200,000 ryals being sent out to Surat for the purchase of Indian commodities, and arrived safely in the East Indies.[4] The Company ordered for the Christmas fleet of 1624, 600 butts of cider, 500 oxen, and 1,500 hogs to be bought for provisioning.[5] In the same three years thirteen ships laden with spices, indigo, sugar, rice, diamonds, silks, Persian carpets, and cotton yarn arrived in England.[6] During the same period four of the Company's ships were wrecked.

The total amount of bullion exported by the Company in the twenty years ending July 1620 was £548,090 in Spanish ryals,

[1] *Abstract*, op. cit.

[2] *Historical MSS. Commission*, Report II, Part I, p. 91, 6th November 1626.

[3] Sainsbury, vol. i, no. 1021; ib., vol. iii, nos. 165, 570.

[4] Ib., vol. iii, no. 347.

[5] Ib., p. 412.

[6] Ib., nos. 51, 351, 640.

although they might have exported £720,000. In the same period they had exported to the value of £292,286 in broadcloths, kerseys, lead, and tin. The goods which had been bought in India for £356,288 had produced in England no less a sum than £1,914,600. These extraordinary profits throw a flood of light on the state of the East India trade.[1]

The trade maintained about 10,000 tons of shipping, and employed 1,500 mariners and as many artisans in 1622–4. The savings to England were not negligible. Commodities from the East Indies were brought to England at a quarter of the price hitherto paid in Turkey and Lisbon. Pepper alone to the value of £200,000 was imported into England in 1623, nine-tenths of which was exported within twelve months.[2]

It will be apparent from the above that the East India trade had made considerable progress up to 1620. It had greatly increased the King's customs, and it had provided the country with a number of ships, completely armed, and efficiently organized.

The Company's trade would have been impossible if the natives had refused to deal with them. There is no direct evidence to prove that they did so. On the contrary, we may say that the Company could not carry on its trade without the permission of the natives. This permission was readily granted, and a series of factories was built in the most important parts of Asia. The increased activity of the Company was the result of increased intercourse with the peoples of the East Indies. The latter preferred them to the Portuguese, and were not sorry to see one European power pitted against the other. In India the centralized government was too powerful to be trifled with, while the infraction of its laws was visited with condign punishment. The chief advantage possessed by the Mogul Government was its unity of action. It was not liable to be turned away from the path chosen by itself; nor could its subjects be ill-treated with impunity. The treatment meted out to the Portuguese by the Mogul Government has been described to us in a series of letters from the Company's factors.[3] It testified to the vigour of the

[1] *Public Record Office*, C.O. 77, vol. ii, nos. 24, 25.
[2] Sainsbury, vol. iii, nos. 165, 540.
[3] Ib., vol. i, nos. 763, 768.

Mogul's policy. It showed, moreover, that there was one sovereign authority in India which could enforce its decrees rigorously. The English Company were, therefore, very desirous of establishing factories in India. The Mogul's pharmaund did not, of course, settle everything, and we have evidence of the provincial governors' defiance of the Emperor's orders. This was, however, the characteristic of the later age of the Mogul Empire. At that time its pharmaunds were laws, and its laws could not be violated with impunity. The Company's efforts in this direction were crowned with success. It was less difficult to negotiate with the natives of the East India Islands. The latter were totally disorganized and thoroughly demoralized. The Portuguese had been the dominant European power for over a century, but their days of glory had departed. The hideous barbarity which characterized the actions of even the most eminent men of the later stage of the Portuguese Empire, and the terrible sufferings which the subjects of that empire had to endure, have been vividly described to us in a series of papers.[1] It was inevitable that the advent of two European powers in the Eastern seas should be followed by a struggle with the Portuguese. The latter refused to allow them a share in the spices of the East Indies. A conflict between the Catholic power and the Protestant poachers on the reserved traffic of the East was unavoidable. It ended with the crushing defeat of the Portuguese in the East. A 'very hot fight' had already taken place between the Dutch and the Portuguese; though the former lost upwards of 600 men, they were bent on expelling the Portuguese as well as the Spaniards from their strongholds in the Indies. They were joined in this desire by the English.[2] Captain Downton engaged the Portuguese fleet, consisting of nine ships, two galleys, and fifty-eight frigates. The English were victorious. Many of the Portuguese were killed, 'besides above 300 men carried in the frigates to Damaun to be buried'.[3]

The series of factories established by the East India Company testified to its astonishing progress. Captain Lancaster had

[1] Practically all the accounts of the Portuguese falling under the dates 1550–1660 are unanimous on the above points. The most remarkable account is in Danvers' *Portuguese Empire in India*, vol. ii.

[2] Sainsbury, vol. i, nos. 350–1, 369.

[3] Ib., nos. 931, 935, 946.

settled factories at Acheen and Bantam, and obtained favourable privileges from the King of Acheen for the English merchants.[1] Articles were afterwards concluded by Captain Best, and confirmed by the Great Mogul, for permission to trade and settle factories in Surat, Cambaya, Ahmedabad, Goga, 'or any other parts of the country within the Great Mogul's dominions'.[2] Besides Surat, there were English factories at Agra, Ajmere, and Broach.

Nor were the important islands in the Indian Ocean overlooked. In Sumatra the Company had trade with seven of the chief cities or ports, in Borneo with four; and in Java likewise with four principal towns. In Macassar, in the Celebes, a factory had been established. They also plied more or less regular trade with Acheen, Baros, Passaman, Pedir, Priaman, and Jambee.

The English vessels resorted to almost every place where there was the least likelihood of obtaining trade with the natives. On the Eastern coast factories were established at Masulipatam and Pettapoli.[3] In Landak a factor describes the savagery of the people of Dyaks 'who lie in the rivers on purpose to take off the heads of all they can overcome'.[4] The Company's agents were well received at Bangkok, and the Company determined to settle more factors to 'beat out a trade' at Siam, Patani, and other places. The attempt to establish a factory in Cochin China ended in the English and the Dutch being 'killed in the water with harping irons like fishes'.[5]

In Persia the conclusion of a contract for the supply of silk attended the extension of the English trade there. Ormuz was captured by the combined forces of the English and Persians, and the Portuguese were completely defeated.

With China also trade was attempted by means of junks plying between the English factories at Siam, &c. The sanguine Cocks,[6] the Company's factor in Japan, fed the East India Company with false hopes regarding the Chinese trade,

[1] Sainsbury, no. 314. Bruce's *Annals*, vol. i, p. 252, October 1602.
[2] *Cal. State Papers, Domestic, Jac. I*, vol. lxxv, nos. 31, 38, p. 214.
[3] Sainsbury, vol. i, nos. 596, 662; *Roe's Journal* in Churchill's Collection; Sainsbury, vol. ii, no. 750; Foster's *Embassy*.
[4] Sainsbury, vol. i, no. 760.
[5] Ib., p. 309, nos. 751, 753, 804, 823.
[6] Ib., no. 1180; vol. ii, nos. 963 and p. 461.

but the inborn conservatism of the Chinese was proof against all seductions, and it was never really established until the middle of the seventeenth century. The same fate befell the trade with Japan. Adams's heroic efforts were attended with some measure of success, but the trade to Japan was never really prosperous, and the death of the Emperor of Japan led to the persecution of Europeans there, which ended only with their expulsion.[1]

The Dutch had not been idle in the East. They, too, had been consolidating their conquests, building a line of forts to keep down the natives, and extorting treaties from them. The treaties took the form of a guarantee to defend their territory against the Portuguese attack, in exchange for the right to erect forts, establish factories, and enjoy the exclusive privilege of trade.[2] After the overthrow of the Portuguese in the Spice Islands, the Dutch, by means of treaties with the native powers, obtained complete commercial control over Amboyna, Ternate, Tidor, Banda, and the smaller islands. The destruction of the old Javanese town of Jacatra was followed by the establishment of a Dutch factory at Batavia. The latter became the capital of their empire. Gradually, the neighbouring States were subdued, and the Dutch Governor-General exercised undisputed sway over the most flourishing and celebrated islands in the East Indies.

Dutch supremacy in the East would have been tolerable if they had allowed foreign nations to trade with the natives. The English had fought with the Dutch against their common enemy, the Portuguese, and there was no reason why this friendship between the two Protestant powers should not continue. They expected some return for the services which they had rendered to Holland in her war against Spain, and they were in

[1] Sainsbury, vol. i, nos. 779, 789; vol. ii, nos. 313, 819, p. 495; nos. 105, 315, 930.

[2] Compare the extracts from the Hague Archives in the India Office. They are quoted by Hunter, vol. i. The treaties of December 1605, 17th May 1606, 3rd July 1596, June 1607, in the Java MSS., show the leading features of the Dutch policy in the East. Mr. Edmundson, *Cambridge Modern History*, vol. v, p. 710, gives a clear, though necessarily brief, account of that monopoly. Compare also, p. 732, ib. Motley calls it 'a Mighty Monopoly', *United Netherlands*, vol. iii, pp. 651–2. This is, perhaps, the truest description of the Dutch Company.

hearty sympathy with her, so far as the treatment of Spaniards and Portuguese in the East Indies was concerned. They were speedily undeceived. The Dutch were not reluctant to utilize the services of the English in the East for their own benefit. They found the English Navy indispensable for their operations in the East, but they were not ready to allow them freedom of trade with the natives. The monopoly which they had so laboriously built up would, in their opinion, have been absolutely useless if other European nations had been allowed to trade with their allies. Their main object was the establishment of a monopoly of all the spices in the East, and the consequent exaction of high prices from the buyers in Europe. Competition would destroy all prospects of the realization of this desire. Hence, the bitter rivalry between the two Protestant nations in the East. It took place in almost every important factory there. At Jambee the Hollanders vilified the English; they allowed no communication between the natives of the Moluccas and the English merchants. When the latter were well received by the natives, the Hollanders, 'with one overwhelming force compelled the English to depart'. As early as 1602–5, we hear of differences between the two nations.[1] Honest William Keeling asserts that when he went to 'Comby the Dutch did us much wrong'. They tried to drive the English from Banda, and offered '12,000 Dollars among the country, to make their peace', but the natives refused. The same thing happened in other parts of Banda. William Keeling was obliged to complain to his masters of the behaviour of the Dutch.[2] Peter Williamson Floris was stopped at Pulicat, and told that 'it should not be lawful for any that come out of Europe to trade there, but such as brought Prince Maurice his Patent, and therefore desired our departure. We answered we had commission from His Majestie of England, and would therefore doe what we could'.[3]

In the Moluccas the Dutch forbade the natives 'to bring us any more spices'. They were not content with mere words. They dismantled 'their forts and caused two great ships to ride by the English merchants'.[4] At Bantam they threatened (1616) to pull the English factors out of the factory 'by the

[1] Purchas, vol. ii, pp. 456–62.
[2] Ib., pp. 523–49.
[3] Ib., pp. 320–1.
[4] Ib., pp. 422–3.

ears'. Sometimes they quarrelled with them in the street, at other times they imprisoned them. 'At Poulaway', an island with which the English Company had made a treaty, 'they abused our people, putting halters about their necks, and leading them through the town with an hour-glass before, publishing that they should be hanged so soon as the glass was run.'[1] In Java the English and Flemings fought in 1605 in earnest with their muskets. In the evening Mr. Scot put them in mind that 'if it had not been for the English, they must have been the most contemptible nation in Europe. Their answer was that Times and Seasons had changed'.[2]

In Japan the English were much molested by 'the unruly Hollanders, who, by sound of trumpet, in the harbour of Ferando, proclaimed open war against the English nation both by land and sea, with fire and sword, to take our ships and destroy our persons to the utmost of their powers'.

In India the same tale was repeated, the Hollanders intriguing with the Mogul Governors against the English. In Malacca, owing partly to the dealings of the Dutch, no factory could be established. At whichever of these islands the English went, they were 'beaten away by superior force', and 'the natives threatened with the loss of their heads, if they dealt with the English'.[3]

It is not too much to say that every factory in the East India Islands was a scene of bitter strife between the two nations.[4]

The maintenance of the East India trade on the part of the Company could hardly be effected without the support of the Central Government. The successes of the Dutch were due to

[1] Walter Peyton's Second Voyage, Purchas, vol. iv, pp. 302–3.

[2] *Collection of Voyages and Travels.* Printed by Thomas Astley, vol. i, p. 301. In 1605 there was a dispute with the Dutch in Java. 'The Flemings were drubbed home to their very gates.' Ib., p. 304.

[3] Sainsbury, no. 609. The Hollanders used every possible endeavour to debar the English from trade with Acheen, 'but the more they sought, the less they prevailed'. Nos. 671, 673. 'The island of Machian was offered to Sir Henry Middleton; the inhabitants expected his return for three years, when they were forced to yield to the Flemings.' No. 630. William Adams's letter from Japan, pp. 231–2. The fifth volume of Purchas, pp. 1–232, is full of 'Dutch force and fraud', 'their lying devices', 'their cruelties', 'the base dealings of the Dutch', 'their cunning tricks in Banda'.

[4] The Journals of Captain Pring (Purchas, vol. v, chap. vii), of Master Nathaniel Courthop, chap. ix, and of other travellers in the East, teem with details of the Anglo-Dutch rivalry in the East.

the wonderful organization of their Company in the East. This had become possible only through the support of the State. The Company symbolized all the authority of the State, and the East India Islands formed part of the Dutch Empire. These two features of the Dutch Company were lacking in its English rival. It had insufficient capital at its disposal. More serious still, while the Dutch Government lent all its support to its Company in the East, the Executive in England exhibited the characteristics to which James's vacillating personality gave fitful expression in its dealings with foreign powers. The ultimate realization of the material interests of the English people in the early seventeenth century could be effected only by the increased support on the part of the Crown. The Executive alone could maintain the privileges of the English in foreign parts. This is the chief reason for the insistence of most of the economists of the first half of the seventeenth century on the absolute importance of safeguarding the commercial privileges of Englishmen, not only in the East, but also in Greenland and in Russia. In Russia, in Greenland, in India, in Persia, in Japan, in China, wherever, in short, the English merchants went, they were met by the Dutch, who opposed them by every means they could devise.

The importance of the East India trade in the seventeenth century lay in the fact that it was one of the most important causes of the development of what I may call Later Mercantilism. It is distinguished from the old by its insistence on the necessity of the protection of English commerce against foreign enemies. The Government is now called upon to defend the right of Englishmen to the East India trade, the herring fishery, and the Russian trade. This is the most important feature of the commercial activity of the seventeenth century. The merchants take the lead and demand armed support on the part of the Crown. The latter is now expected to play a new rôle. It has to develop the English industries by a series of laws, having for their object the exclusion of, first, the Dutch manufactures, and then, from about 1675, the French manufactures from England. This was only one phase of that policy. The other phase of the policy assumed the form of commercial warfare against the rival power. The combination of these two elements resulted in what may be termed the Later Mercantilism. It was the logical deduction from the theories that animated the conduct of the chief commercial nations in the seventeenth century. The main safeguard against 'the mighty monopoly' of the Dutch in the East lay in the prompt and energetic support of the Company by the Executive. The same applies to the other scenes of commercial warfare. This support took the form of various 'prohibitive laws', and, later on, of actual war against its rival. The movement was due to the agitation of the merchants, and was not imposed from above. It was the result of the interaction of a multiplicity of phenomena.

The commercial rivalry was not confined to the East Indies, but extended to Europe, America, and Africa. A most important feature is its intimate connexion with the naval rivalry. It would be completely meaningless without a due understanding of the naval rivalry between the two nations. Dr. Cunningham's[1] lucid account of the part played by the navy in the development of commerce and the functions it performed under Elizabeth has hardly been surpassed.

I have come to the conclusion that the same tendency was operative throughout the seventeenth century. In my opinion the influence of the East India trade on the development of a naval policy was felt during the whole of that period. The three forces that moulded the economic thought of the seventeenth century—East India trade, herring fishery, and the dominion of the seas—acted and reacted on one another. They were indissolubly blended. One led imperceptibly into another. The herring fishery could hardly be secured to the English nation unless their dominion of the seas was recognized by the Dutch. But the freedom of the seas, which the Dutch claimed, logically involved freedom of trade. This had been foreseen by Grotius, and defended by him in his *Mare Liberum*. If so, then the Dutch monopoly of the spices in the East ought to have been destroyed. The Dutch could hardly claim the freedom of the seas in the English Channel and deny the same freedom to the English merchants in the Spice Islands. It is surprising that Grotius neglected the force of these arguments. This may be due to the fact that he wrote primarily against the Portuguese

[1] *English Industry*, vol. ii, p. 1.

pretensions, and at a time when the Dutch power in the East was comparatively insignificant.

The Dutch fishery was another cause of the commercial rivalry. The early history of that rivalry throws a flood of light on the subsequent proceedings of the English Government. We find the earliest expression thereof in a letter of Chamberlain to Carleton.[1] Chamberlain is discussing the advantages of peace with Spain. 'One of the chiefest reasons I can have for it is a kind of disdain and envie at our neighbours (the Dutch) well doing in that we, for their sake and defence entering into this war, and being barred from all commerce and intercourse of merchandise, they in the meantime thrust us out of all traffick, to our utter undoing if in time it be not looked into, and then our own advancement.' This is a characteristic utterance. It sums up in a short sentence the gravamen of the charge against the Dutch. The English factors and sailors who wrote a number of dispatches to the Company termed them 'ungrateful Hollanders'. They regarded their state as a creation of their own Queen, and they naturally expected that the Dutch would requite them with kindness. The grievances voiced by Chamberlain found an echo in the writer of a remarkable pamphlet entitled 'Observations made upon the Dutch Fishing, About the Year 1601', by John Keymers.[2] It is perhaps the earliest tract on the herring fishery in the British Museum. The number of fishing boats maintained by the Dutch seems to have been 4,100. It is essential to distinguish cod and ling fishery from herring fishery. Some of the seas where the cod fishery was carried on were totally unsuitable for herring fishery. The coasts of England and Scotland seem to have been the best adapted for the purpose. 'And every one of them do set on work on other vessels to fetch salt and transport fish into other Countries after they are brought into their own Countries out of His Majesty's Seas.' The number of busses employed in 1601 seems to have been 2,000. All of them were restricted to 'Herring only, about Baughamess in Scotland, all along the coasts of England to the Thames mouth' for above twenty-six weeks.[3]

[1] Camden Society, *Letters of John Chamberlain*, edited by Sarah Williams, 1861, p. 12 et passim. There are a number of references to Holland.

[2] Brit. Mus. 103. l. 20, 1751.

[3] Ib., pp. 5–6.

One Dutch buss usually took eight, ten, or twelve lasts of herrings at a draught in one night. Contrast this with the English fishery of the time. 'Our fishing continues but 7 weeks, with small cobbles from 5 to 10 tons.' 'When the Herrings came home to our own Roadstead, we take one, two, or three lasts a night.' The total amount of lasts taken by the Hollanders was about 300,000.[1] They were sold to the merchants at £10 or £12 the last. The total amount was therefore £3,300,000. The merchants transported and sold them into Pomerania, Poland, Denmark, and even England, at from £16 to £36 the last more.[2] This was a handsome profit, and we are therefore not surprised to find the writer complaining of the impudence of the Dutch and the improvidence of the British race in general. 'The people of Ireland, and round about the coasts of England, after they have been at Sea, and brought home their vessels full of Fish, will not go to Sea again for more till those be spent and they in debt, so that necessity compels them.'[3] Owing to this cause, 'We are eaten out of Trade and the bread taken out of our own mouths in our own seas, and the great custom carried to foreign states'. The author therefore urged the Englishmen to devote more attention to that industry, owing to the advantages it possessed. It would give employment to mariners, spinners, and hemp winders to make cables and cordage, likewise yarn, twine, and thread, for the making of nets, &c.[4]

The author of *Trade's Increase*[5] urged his countrymen to persevere in that industry. 'As the havens be open to us, as the seas be our own, and as we have all things almost fitting for such a business at home, and naturally.... Here then we may get treasure in abundance.'[6] The author then replies to the usual arguments: the incapacity of the English sailors, the lack of funds, &c. The connexion between the fishery and the Navy is well brought out, and means are suggested whereby the obstacles could be removed. The author is not original in the treatment of the subject. He copies extensively from Tobias Gentleman. This work exercised great influence on the later plans whereby the industry could be utilized by English fishermen.

[1] 12 barrels to the last.
[2] Brit. Mus. 103. l. 20, p. 7.
[3] Ib., pp. 19–22.
[4] Ib., p. 17.
[5] *Harleian Miscellany*, 1615, pp. 224–7.
[6] Ib., p. 226.

He gives an admirable list of the chief places where English fishermen could ply their trade. This is followed by an account of the methods employed by the Dutch. Their industry, frugality, &c., are highly praised and are contrasted with the sloth of England. 'Shall we neglect so great blessings, O slothful England, and careless Countrymen? Look on but these fellows, that we call the plump Hollanders; behold their diligence in fishing, and our own careless negligence.' The writer then urges Englishmen to take a share in an industry in which they ought to be the predominant partner. Their sloth has deprived them of the fairest parts of their seas, and reduced many to beggary. It is unfortunate that we cannot rely on his calculations. His statement that the Dutch maintained 2,000 busses may readily be accepted, as it agrees with those of Keymour and De Witt. It is more difficult to accept his statement that the whole charge for keeping a buss for the whole summer 'was no more than £335'.[1] It was certainly more than that amount. His importance lies in his attempt to deduce the consequences of the maintenance of the industry by England on a large scale. 'The industry will breed Masters, pilots, Commanders, and sufficient directors of a Course',[2] but now 'there is a pitiful want of sufficiently good men.'[3]

Sir Walter Raleigh's 'Selected Observations relating to Trade and Commerce'[4] are based on well-authenticated facts, and were relied on by De Witt in his pamphlet on fishery.[5] Raleigh's analysis of the causes that produced the unexampled prosperity of Holland is wonderfully acute. He shows how the Hollanders 'glean the wealth and strength from us'. Their 'Liberty of Traffick', the small duties levied upon their merchants, their grant of free 'Customs inwards and outwards for any new erected Trade',—all these, and many other reforms of the like nature, made them the 'Carriers' of the world. In a year and a half they carried away from Southampton, Bristol, and Exeter nearly £200,000. This was not all. What grieved Raleigh was the fact 'that the greatest fishing the world has produced is on the coast of England, Scotland, and Ireland', and

[1] Ib., p. 405. [2] Ib., p. 407.

[3] A copy of this pamphlet is among the invaluable tracts relating to trade, Brit. Mus. 712. m. 1 (8).

[4] Brit. Mus. 712. m. 1 (17). [5] See below.

that the 'subtle Hollanders' had robbed honest Englishmen of all that treasure. They sent into Russia nearly 1,500 lasts of herrings, and sold them for £27,000; 'while we but 20 or 30 Lasts'. They carried 'Fish and Herrings' to Hamburg, Bremen, and Emden, and sold them for £100,000. To Gelderland, Artois, Zutphen, &c., were carried between 15,000 and 16,000 lasts, and sold for about £300,000.[1] They were supreme, not only in the herring fishery, but also 'in corn trade'; they have the 'great vintage and staple of salt'. While we sent only 'rough, undressed, undyed cloth' 'there is an exceeding manufactory and Drapery in the Low Countries'.[2]

While England's trade in the Baltic countries depended upon three towns, Elbing, Königsberg, and Dantzig, and while she sent only 100 ships a year, 'the Low Countreys sent into the East Kingdoms yearly about 3,000 ships, trading into every city and port town'.[2] They traded with every British port town with 500 or 600 ships, 'and we chiefly but to three towns in this country, and but with 40 ships'. Raleigh's pamphlet gave expression to a widely-felt grievance. The commercial rivalry of Holland seemed to presage the economic downfall of England. England possessed 'all things in super-abundance to increase traffick and timber to build ships and commodities of our own to lade about 1,000 ships and vessels at one time'. The main bulk and mass of herrings from which the Dutch raised so many millions yearly 'proceeded from English seas and Lands'. Yet 'all the amends they (the Dutch) make us is, they beat us out of Trade in all parts with our own commodities'.

There was another danger to which Raleigh referred. The employment of 20,000 ships and vessels and 400,000 people, with sixty ships of war, upon the coast of England, Scotland, and Ireland 'may prove dangerous'. Not all were employed upon the English coasts, however. The exact number seems to have been 3,000 ships. The number of persons employed on the British coast alone was 50,000. These 3,000 ships, however, employed 9,000 other ships and 150,000 men by sea and land.[3] The only remedy was the organization of industry by the Crown. The whole trend of the seventeenth century economic thought

[1] Brit. Mus. 712. m. 1 (17), pp. 3–4. [2] Ib., p. 4.
[3] Ib., p. 7.

lay in the same direction. As the danger to commerce became manifest, protection by the State was regarded as the sole means whereby the danger could be averted. Sir Walter Raleigh was not alone in this view. It was held by all the merchants of the time, and passionately advocated. The rivalry between the English and the Dutch in Spitzbergen is apparent in Conway's *Early Voyages to Spitzbergen*.[1] The English claim that Sir Hugh Willoughby had discovered and found the 'big island of Spitzbergen'[2] was no less preposterous than the Dutch claim to the whole trade of the spices in the East.

In 1610 and 1613 ships had been sent to Spitzbergen. After the Dutch had been sent away by the English they attempted exploration northwards.[3] But the success of the English in 1613 was far from conclusive. In 1615 the Dutch were again aggressive, and settled by force at Fairhaven, Bell, and Horn Sound.[4] The English confined themselves to the south, near the harbour of Fairhaven, Foreland Sound, and Ice Island. Owing to the high-handed action of Heley, the commander of the *Dragon*, the Dutch determined to make reprisals in 1618. On the 19th July 1618 they forcibly set upon the English 'Vice-Admiral', 'used the English very unkindly', and, in fact, utterly overthrew the English voyage that year.[5] The next year, 1619, the East India and Muscovy Companies sent out nine ships and two pinnaces under the famous Captain Edge. Again the old story was repeated. 'Divers Hollanders being in the Northernmost Harbour in the Country, employing great quantity of Boats in chasing the Whale there, off into the sea', so that five of the Company's ships were disappointed of their voyage. 'The voyage was greatly hindered, to the Company's exceeding great loss.'[6] In 1620 seven ships were sent, but again by reason of 'great store of Flemmings and Danes', the venture was not successful. 'They returned home half laden, with 700 tons of oil.' The next year, 1621, eight ships were hired, but 'their voyage was overthrown by reason of the foresaid Flemmings and Danes'.[7]

The disasters of the Company and the ill-success of the whale

[1] Hakluyt Society, series II, vol. xi.
[2] Conway, op. cit., pp. 35–41.
[3] Ib., p. 4.
[4] Ib., p. 40.
[5] Purchas, vol. xiii, pp. 1–31.
[6] Ib., p. 24.
[7] Ib., p. 25.

fishermen recurred with a frequency that is monotonous. All had their origin in the insecure protection against the Dutch. We find the merchants demanding redress and protection against them, not only in the East Indies, but also in Greenland.[1] Though this referred primarily to whale fishery, herring fishery fared no better. There was, however, a widespread belief that the herring fishery would hinder the cloth trade. Malynes replies to this argument in his own incomparable way.[2] The cloth trade and the herring fishery produced two distinct commodities. 'One serveth for the Belly, the other for the Back, and both are sold by us and other nations in one or more places, and we both make our returns homewards by commodities, money and Exchange for money by Bills.' Again, it had been urged that other nations were more 'painful' and industrious, and that Englishmen, as Mun said, 'besotted themselves with Pipe and Pot'. Malynes does not deny the force of the argument, but thinks that the 'same may be amended by use and custom, seeing our people can endure all climates and hardiness as well as others'.[3]

It is interesting to compare the views of John De Witt on the subject. There is nothing original in the great statesman's *Account of the Dutch Fishery*.[4] He relies on Sir Walter Raleigh, Malynes, and Aitzma for the accuracy of his figures. Far more important is the view he takes of the functions performed by the industry in that Dutch national life which he moulded for over a quarter of a century.[5] De Witt admirably shows the vital importance of commerce to Holland: 'The greatest difficulty for so innumerable people has proved the most powerful means to attract all foreign wares into Holland, not only to store them up there, and afterwards to carry them up the country to very many cities, towns, and People lying in the side of them. No Country has so many artificers, and rivers, and canals for the purpose.' This extract is significant. It throws a searching light on the character and policy of De Witt. The geographical position of Holland determined her commercial position in the world. The

[1] There are numerous references to it in Conway's *Early Voyages to Spitzbergen*, Hakluyt Society, vol. xi, series ii.

[2] *Lex Mercatoria*, p. 1.

[3] Malynes quoted Tobias Gentleman's pamphlet, and his whole chapter is merely a summary of that writer's most forcible arguments.

[4] Brit. Mus. 103. i. 20, pp. 33–9.

[5] De Pontalis, *De Witt*, Eng. trans.

apprehension of this fact resulted in an entire modification of the economic theories of the times. The Dutch trade would have been totally impossible without free trade. She was compelled to grant in Europe free trade, to impose low Custom duties, to establish a State bank, and to institute various other economic reforms, because she was the carrier of the world, and any other policy would have been suicidal. De Witt apprehended this simple fact. He calculated that 1,000 busses took 40,000 lasts of herrings. Counting them 'at least' 200,000 guelders per last, they would yield in Holland more than a million of guelders.[1]

What is of far more importance is his account of the Dutch trade in 1667. He says that from 1618 to 1667, or about half a century, the Dutch trade had increased to one-third more. The herring fishery is included in the list. We are not, therefore, surprised to find De Witt defending the Dutch fishery. It employed hundreds of thousands of men, and upon it depended the maintenance of a great part of the Dutch commercial supremacy. It was a matter of life and death to the fishermen, and they were not likely to respect the 'sanctity' of English waters. While the Dutch were determined to maintain their hold upon the herring fishery, intense feeling had been aroused in England. The agitation begun by Keymers[2] did not die down. They were accused of 'engrossing the universal trade, not only of Christendom, but indeed of the greater part of the known world'.[3] The author charged them with beating out the 'English in all place of Trade'.[4] He is intensely indignant at their treatment of the English in the East Indies, whereby 'they monopolized 3 sort of spices almost to the whole world, as Cloves, Nuts, and Mace, and, lately, Cinnamon'. Their herring fishing, which employed upon the coast of this land only above 2,000 sail of shipping, was nothing else but poaching upon English preserves. The means they employed were, however, worthy of being imitated in England. The author recounts all the methods employed by the Dutch.

Raleigh's analysis[5] is, however, deeper than De Witt's. He is not slow to point out the obvious advantages of the Convoy

[1] Ib., p. 34. [2] See above, p. 25.
[3] *The Advocate*, Brit. Mus. 712. m. 1 (1), 1651. [4] Ib., p. 2.
[5] See above.

system introduced by the Dutch; the absurdity of encumbering an exclusively merchant ship with a number of guns for defence; the cheapness of their freights, &c.[1] The result was that they engrossed the whole trade of all the 'Bulkie Commodities', as timber, clap-board, masts, &c. They got the preference of the market of us in other countries. The consequences to England were, in the opinion of the writer, disastrous. Whereas formerly 200 sails of shipping used to be sent, now 'only 16 sails are sent. The Hollanders send 600 a year'. The Dutch were in the proportion of twenty to one. 'In Spain, Canaries, and Levant, where they formerly rarely laded one ship of Goods, they have lately laded more than one.' Another writer thought that the English 'were so near pinched, that it had been very hard fairly to have wrested ourselves out of the Nets of our Neighbours, had Sweden been as much shut to us as Denmark'.[2] The English would be 'straitened and subjected unless either the Dutch are debarred the course of some necessary Commodities and obstructed in the sale or vent of the native commodities, or their shipping is weakened'. The author points out, in justification of this new policy, that it is by a knowledge of trade and commerce and the course of it, that one Nation or State knows 'perfectly how to pinch another'. This passage is interesting though not novel. It is but an application of Mun's vigorous doctrine. The pamphlet was written on the eve of the First Dutch War, and heralded the future commercial and colonial wars waged by the chief European powers during the last two centuries. It throws a searching light on the policy of the statesman who brought about that war. The three questions—East India Trade, Shipping, and Herring Fishery—are now fused into one, the question of commercial victory or defeat. It is simpler, however, to analyse all the causes that brought about the First Dutch War. The analysis yields the above three causes as by far the most important.[3]

De Witt's pamphlet on Fishery had emphasized the importance of that industry to Holland. R. L'Estrange's *Discourse of the Fishery*[4] showed the benefits that would accrue to England from the industry. He valued the herring, cod, and

[1] Brit. Mus. 712. m. 1 (1), pp. 3–5. [2] Ib., p. 12.
[3] See below. [4] Brit. Mus. 103. l. 20, pp. 45–73.

ling taken in 'His Majesty's seas' by the turbulent Dutch at ten million pounds per annum. Again, England can carry on the trade much more easily because it is nearer, and, in case of storms, the fishermen are seldom above four or five hours' sail, whereas the Dutch have usually 200 leagues to sail. England possessed, moreover, abundance of tackle, salt, casts, and victuals.[1] Everything, except pitch and tar, could be procured in England.

With regard to the alleged sloth of the Englishmen, the author has no difficulty in showing that the 'English do daily run greater Hazards and suffer hardships'.[2] The only way whereby the industry can be carried is by the imposition of a general tax and the institution of staple. Creeks and wharfs should be speedily built. The charge of herring busses of eighty tons, furnished at all points for the fishery, together with victuals and wages, was rated by L'Estrange at £900. The trade will ease the kingdom of at least £300,000 per annum by employing all sorts of people, &c.[3] Moreover, 'Fishery will relieve us too by planting a Trade there, which draw on Commerce, and consequently repeople and strengthen us'. The passages quoted are interesting as they show the vital connexion between the Navy and Commerce in the seventeenth century. Moreover, the tendency to the nationalization of that industry is latent in the pamphlets dealing with the subject.

The above sketch of the herring fishery in England has been attempted with a view to pointing out and emphasizing the main causes which, in my opinion, shaped the economic policy and the theories of political economy in the seventeenth century.

Another important cause was the intense naval rivalry. It has been assumed hitherto that the three causes were mutually exclusive, and that there was no connexion whatsoever between the East India trade and the naval war. In my opinion, such a theory is indefensible. The naval rivalry was intense, partly because the naval supremacy was threatened, and partly because commerce, upon which depended ultimately the growth of the Navies of the two rival powers, was the bone of contention. The dominating motive that underlay the actions of the Dutch statesmen was commerce. The Navy itself was regarded simply as

[1] Ib., p. 47. [2] Ib., p. 48. [3] Ib., pp. 68–9.

an instrument whereby the Dutch commerce could be expanded. Ultimately, therefore, the naval rivalry resolves itself into a commercial rivalry. The methods employed by the Dutch in the First Dutch War will illustrate this. The Dutch State was mainly a commercial State, and the Navy was fostered because upon it depended the safety of their East India and other trades. Hence, we cannot draw a hard and fast line between naval and commercial rivalries. In England, the case was not very different. There too, commerce was the end, and Navy the means. But the commercial advantages of a powerful Navy were not really perceived in England till the time of Charles II. This was due partly to the fact that the foreign trade of England was much more limited than that of Holland, and partly to the fact that her geographical position rendered her completely dependent upon her Navy. Consequently, the dominion of the seas was at first much more highly prized than the dominion of commerce. The relative positions of these two factors was reversed from the time of Charles II onwards. Grotius's *Mare Liberum* was written in the winter of 1604–5,[1] and was directed primarily against the Portuguese. It is perhaps the best exposition of the theory which was universally held in Holland. The whole theory is based really upon a rigorous interpretation of the Roman law of Possession. The Law of Nature, which was to perplex the political philosophers for over two centuries and to undergo various forms through the hands of Hobbes, Locke, and Rousseau, is sandwiched in here, as elsewhere. But the shrewdness of Grotius saved him from resting his argument upon such a slender foundation. It is to *Ius Gentium* that he appeals, and the verdict of history is decisive on the point. Grotius did not wear his learning lightly, and his whole book is sprinkled over with a number of quotations. The scriptural authority seems to him decisive on this point, while the Roman legists seemed to have propounded the doctrines which he advocates. He starts with a 'primary rule or first principle, the spirit of which is self-evident and immutable; to wit: Every nation is free to travel to every other nation, and to trade with it.'[2] He

[1] See the admirable translation of the book in Professor Magoffin's volume, published in 1916 by the Carnegie Endowment for International Peace.

[2] Grotius, p. 7.

has no difficulty in showing that nature has given to all peoples a right of access to all other peoples.[1] Chapter ii is interesting, because in it Grotius analyses the Portuguese conception of Sovereignty. He has no difficulty in showing that 'they lied, both in law and in fact', if they said that those lands came under their jurisdiction as the reward of discovery. 'For to discover a thing is not only to seize it with the eyes, but to take possession thereof.' The force of Grotius's argument depends mainly upon this vital difference between discovery and possession. It was to this argument that the Dutch appealed in the seventeenth century. Nor have the Portuguese any right of Sovereignty over the East Indies by virtue of title based on the Papal Donation; nor can they be said to have conquered India. The sea is *res communis*, or *res nullius*. He distinguishes between Sovereignty in its strictest term from 'Common possession'. The distinction is not really scientific, and his book suffers from the lack of a clear demarcation between 'Occupation' and 'Sovereignty'. The two are with him convertible terms, and though the early history of Sovereignty was, in his opinion, totally different from its later developments, his main argument rests upon the Roman law of possession. He thinks that 'that which cannot be occupied, or which never has been occupied, cannot be the property of anyone, because all property has arisen from occupation'. Moreover, 'all that which has been so constituted by nature that although serving some one person it still suffices for the common use of all other persons, is to-day and ought in perpetuity to remain in the same condition as when it was first created by nature'.[3]

The air belongs to this class of things, because it is not susceptible of occupation; and secondly because its common use is destined for all men. For the same reason the sea is common to all, because it is so limitless that it cannot become a possession of any one, and because it is adapted for the use of all, whether we consider it from the point of view of navigation or of fisheries.[4] Hence, navigation and fishing ought to be free.[5]

The conclusions that Grotius deduced from the premises lead to startling results. The freedom of the seas was deduced from

[1] Ib., p. 8. [2] Ib., chap. iii. [3] Ib., p. 27. [4] Ib., p. 28. [5] Ib., p. 32.

the Roman law of property, and throughout his argument he constantly appeals to the Roman jurists. But freedom of the seas was meaningless unless it involved freedom of trade. The former was advocated only because it would lead to freedom of trade with the Spice Islanders. The freedom of trade was based on a primitive right of nations which has a natural and permanent cause.[1] Commerce was born out of necessity for the commodities of life, but, after immovables also began to be recognized as private property, the consequent annihilation of universal community of use made commerce a necessity, not only between men whose habitations were far apart but even between men who were neighbours. Consequently, the universal basis of all contracts, namely exchange, is derived from nature.

Consequently, no one nation may justly oppose in any way two nations that desire to enter into a contract with each other.[1]

Freedom of seas led naturally to freedom of trade, because it was upon the former that the latter was based. Grotius's book has had a permanent effect on International Law.[2] But it is important to notice that it was aimed primarily against the Portuguese. It was soon apparent, however, that it was applicable to England. The Dutch fishermen justified their title to the herring fishery on the British coast upon this ground. The seas were not the exclusive property of any one nation, but the common heritage of all.[3] Hessel Gerritsz, in his *Description*

[1] Grotius, p. 64.

[2] Grotius's *Mare Liberum* was published anonymously in November 1608. It formed the twelfth chapter of his work, *De Iure Praedae*, which was written in 1604–5. The manuscript of this work, written when the author was only twenty-one years of age, was not discovered till 1864, and was published in 1868. Walker (*History of the Law of Nations*, pp. 278–83); Hall, *International Law* (6th edition), pp. 140–51, and Oppenheim, *International Law* (1905), pp. 300–8, have treated this subject lucidly. It is interesting to note that William Wellwood anticipated some of the arguments of Selden in his *Sea Law of Scotland* (Bodleian Library, Oxford), and an *Abridgement of all Sea Laws*, and subjected Grotius's book to keen criticism. He appeals to the Scriptures; quotes the Roman lawyers; and has frequent recourse to history to prove his points, and to demolish the foundations of Grotius's arguments. But he lacked the charm of his style, and the width of his intellect, and though the comparative failure of his book was due to the elaborate and eminent work of Selden, the faulty arrangement and the scholastic pedantries which disfigure his chapter on 'the Community and propriety of the Seas' contributed to their failure. (See also Fulton, *Sovereignty of the Seas*.)

[3] Walker's *History of the Law of Nations*, vol. i, pp. 278–83, 1899. The case of the *Louis*, decided by Lord Stowell, in 1817.

of Spitzbergen,[1] relied upon this argument when he replied to the claim of the English merchants to all the islands situated in the North, not only those islands which have been discovered up to now, but also those which may be discovered hereafter, as follows: 'Why then, should not the islands of Faroe, Friesland, and Greenland belong to His Majesty?' His reply is: 'The navigation of the sea and fishing are, according to the universal rights of all peoples, common to all and freely permitted.' This passage brings out the importance of Grotius's theory. If the dominion of the seas were denied, and the Dutch prohibited from fishing on the English coast, the Dutch would have been deprived of one of the most ancient and fruitful means of subsistence. De Witt had asserted that the industry had existed for 250 years[2] and that it supported about 400,000 people. This accounts for the importance attached by the Dutch to Grotius's *Mare Liberum*. It became popular, not because it advocated freedom of trade, but because it was the most successful defence of the right of the Dutch to the freedom of the seas. Again, it became popular, not because it was directed against the Portuguese, but because it could be applied to England.

Selden's *Mare Clausum* can hardly be called a successful defence. He has much clearer notions of Dominion, Law, and Sovereignty. Grotius had based his argument mainly upon the universal validity of International Law. Selden opposed Positive Law to the *Ius Gentium*. The one is permissive and possesses no sanctum; the other 'relates not to all nations, but only to some particulars thereof'.[3]

It is interesting to compare Selden's conception of 'positive law' with the Austinian theory of law and sovereignty. Another interesting point is Selden's foundation of his argument on the vexed 'Original Contract'. While Grotius asserted that the sea was common to all, Selden went back to the original contract theory, and derived 'dominion' therefrom. As for the rest, 'which neither are possessed in several, nor expressly held in

[1] Ib., p. 38, ed. Conway.

[2] De Witt's *Account of Dutch Fishery*, Brit. Mus. 103. l. 20, p. 34.

[3] *The Dominion of the Seas*, translated by the notorious henchman Marchmont Needham, and published in 1652 'by the special Command', presumably of the Council of State. Brit. Mus. 502. f. 12, chapters i–vii.

common, and have continued vacant', they were seized by the different claimants, and the latter were confirmed in their possession by an agreement, which applied not only to the things which were at first assigned, but also to those which were occupied.[1] The effects of private dominion were immediately felt. There was first the inevitable appropriation of 'the same territories, or Field, whose Use before was free for all men in Tillage, Building, Pasturage, &c.' This was inevitable. What is more difficult to understand is Selden's attempt to prove 'that from the same original contract there springs a private Dominion of the Sea, as well as of the land'.[2] He does not wear his learning lightly, and the treatise is overweighted with unnecessary quotations and references. The second book is far more interesting.

The first book is deductive, and contains not a few mistakes. The second traces the claim of England to the dominion of the seas. His attempt to prove that the ancient Britons did enjoy and 'possess' the seas of the same name before they were brought under the Roman yoke, and his statement that the southern and eastern seas were an appendage of the British Empire, from the time of Constantine till the Romans quitted England, may seem fantastic to us now.[3] He is on firmer historical ground when he asserts that the dominion had been acknowledged by many foreign nations. This had not always been the case. But generally, the English coast had been regarded as 'the exclusive property of England'.[4] Selden's book cannot be compared with the production of Grotius. The latter was the expression of a long-felt grievance; the former was aimed primarily at the maintenance of a privilege which, if allowed, would have considerably hampered the colonial and commercial progress of the European countries. Again, it has been thought that Selden was the only writer who replied to Grotius, and that his defence was successful. These suppositions seem to me to be groundless. We find a succession of writers asserting the dominion of the seas, pointing out the connexion between the Navy and Commerce, and far more successfully than Selden's ponderous folio.

[1] The influ nce of sixteenth-century political thought on Selden is remarkable. See Dr. Figgis's chapter in vol. iii; also his *Gerson to Grotius*.

[2] Selden, Book I, chap. v.

[3] Chapters ii and vi.

[4] Book II, chapters xxvii, xxix.

John Hagthorpe, Gent., brought out the importance of the Navy to England. The glory and sovereignty of the sea had, said the writer, three competitors, the English, the Dutch, and the Spaniards.[1] With regard to Spain, her neglect of industry had left her destitute of any power; but with the Hollanders the case was different. 'They have many good ships, good ordinance.' Their State was, however, exhausted by long wars, and it seemed to the writer that England should be the most able of all the rest.[2] He then brings out the importance of the Navy. 'It seemed as needful as ever to seek the increase and augment of shipping, by reviving trades decayed, finding out new, and cherishing the Plantation.'[3] The East India, the West India, and the Russian trades are fully represented. If a stock of £200,000 or £300,000 could be contributed by the people, England could furnish 2,000 sail of good ships of '300 ton apeece, with munition and ordinance fitting'.[4] This naval strength would enable England 'to propagate her religion, the Navy strengthened, and this our fruitful mother unburthened of her many, many children, by transporting yearly thither 10,000 people' besides volunteers, to the Plantations. The Navy becomes the means whereby colonies are planted, commerce expanded, and England defended. Mun had pointed out that the East India trade was a means 'to counterpoise the Hollanders' swelling greatness by Trade', and to keep them from being absolute lords of the seas, if they drove us out of this traffic.[5]

Mun's statement is significant, as it brings out the dependence of commerce upon the Navy. Far more important was the argument employed by Malynes in his *Lex Mercatoria.* It is quite possible that Selden borrowed many of Malynes's arguments. There is a striking similarity between the two. Malynes admits that, according to *Ius Gentium*, the navigation through all the world is no less free and open to every one than the use of the air.[6] He is careful to point out that the main great seas 'do not belong to any one nation'. They are *res nullius.* But besides these seas, there are 'distinct Dominions upon the

[1] *England's Exchequer*, or *A Discourse of the Sea and Navigation.* Brit. Mus. 533. d. 2 (1), p. 7, 1625.
[2] Ib., p. 8. [3] Ib., p. 13. [4] Ib., p. 26.
[5] *Petition of the East India Company*, Brit. Mus. 1029. c. 30, p. 17, 1628.
[6] *Lex Mercatoria*, chap. xxxiii.

sea'. He has in view, of course, the English Channel, and that part of the English coast where the Dutch used to fish. There may be visible marks of dominion. All the sea within 100 leagues from the coast may be termed the dominion of a country. Malynes then shows that the English kings did possess the ancient right. 'In those days there was no fishing in the Low Countries.'[1] It dated only from the time of one Violet, when he and others procured inhabitants to fish for them 'in His Majesty's Seas, Streams and Dominions'. Malynes then shows how 'that noble King', Henry VIII, used the invention of the 'Sign of the Portcullis'. Nor is this claim confined to England. The kings of Denmark, Sweden, Russia, and the princes and states of Italy have all claimed the dominion of the seas.[2] He therefore concludes that the Dutch had no right to fish in English waters. The controversy did not die down. The quarrel over the dominion of the seas was one of the most important causes of the First Dutch War. The last great tract on this controversy is by Sir John Boroughs.[3] Sir John quotes many of the ancient records in the Tower of London. His contention is that the kings of England had been in peaceable possession of the dominion of the English seas by immemorial prescription, and that this was acknowledged by most of the Christian powers. There is really nothing original in this argument. Far more effective is his appeal to the English people to bestir themselves, and to take a share in the rich treasure which they allowed the Dutch to steal. He has no difficulty in showing that the Hollanders had increased in shipping, the total number of ships and busses plying the Herring Fair being 6,400. We get also a remarkably good account of the extent of the Dutch fishery in 1686. The total number of mariners and fishers is put by the author at 112,000; while double or treble the number of women and children were maintained through that industry. He shows that the Dutch trade had increased, and that this had led to the increase of their power. All these benefits were filched from England because the latter allowed her rival to fish in her own waters. The pamphlet was written in 1686. It shows that

[1] *Lex Mercatoria*, p. 134.
[2] Ib., p. 137.
[3] *The Sovereignty of the British Seas, proved by Records, History, &c.*, Brit. Mus. 509. h. 4, 1686.

the controversy had not died down, and that the herring fishery was still regarded as the preserve of the English nation. The controversy is not over even yet, but is, in some respects, as acute in the twentieth century as it was fierce in the seventeenth.

It was these causes that led ultimately to the First Dutch War. There were, of course, a number of others, but they were of comparatively little importance besides the more general causes described above. It is not difficult to estimate the relative importance of each. The English fishermen could not compete with the trained Dutch fishermen. They were handicapped by the failure of the Crown to render any aid to its subjects in their quarrel with the Dutch. James I might get intensely indignant at the outrages committed by the Dutch, but his anger went no farther,[1] and the Dutch sailors continued to enjoy the right. Moreover, the herring fishery never assumed the importance that the East India trade did. It does not seem to have been properly organized in the seventeenth century. The tract of Sir John Boroughs shows[2] that the Dutch were masters of the situation as late as 1686. Again, no comparison is possible between a thoroughly organized trade, having ramifications in nearly every part of Asia, holding more than two million pounds worth of stock, and owning many forts and places in the East, and an ill-equipped, ill-directed, and ill-protected industry.

I think, therefore, that the herring fishery did not assume the same importance as the East India trade in the seventeenth century. The remaining cause mentioned above, viz. the naval rivalry, was operative in practically every quarrel in the seventeenth century, but it would be a mistake to suppose that the freedom of the seas was claimed by the Dutch as an end in itself. It was because their commerce was dependent upon the allowance of that freedom, that supreme importance was attached to it. If England were allowed to exercise her dominion of the sea, and if the Dutch were prohibited from fishing in 'His Majesty's Oceans and Streams', widespread misery would have stalked through the homes of hundreds of thousands of Dutch. It was upon this account that the Dutch passionately insisted upon the right to which they thought they were entitled, not

[1] Gardiner, vol. v, chap. xliv, pp. 78–88.

[2] Op. cit.

only by the Law of Nature, but also by International Law. In England, the commercial aspect of this question did not become prominent till the time of Charles II. Though this is so, the writers of the Ante-Restoration did not neglect it. There is really not a single English writer who forgot to point out the significance of the right claimed by England. The Navy would be the means whereby the English plantations would be made populous and English commerce expanded. Nearly every writer cited above treats of it. Some of them show the importance of the Navy to the plantations, but none of them forget to emphasize the connexion between commerce and the Navy. Hence we cannot separate by watertight compartments purely commercial questions from those exclusively naval. All naval causes ultimately resolved themselves into commercial causes. This tendency is manifest in the writings of Sir Josiah Childe. He asserted that 'though the Dominion of the sea may be obtained by Arms and fortunate battles at sea, it can never be retained, preserved, and maintained, but by the excess and Predominancy of foreign trade'.[1] Childe admirably describes the interaction of the various elements of national life. 'Advance in Trade and Navigation; the increase of Trade and Navigation is a great means to secure our Protestant Religion. Foreign Trade produces Riches, Riches produce Power, Power preserves our Trade and Religion. They mutually work upon, and for the preservation of each other.'[2] 'All tyrannies in the world are supported by Land Armies. A Naval power never affrightens us. Seamen never did, nor ever will, destroy the liberty of their own Country.'[3]

Childe was not the only writer who traced the connexion between the Navy and commerce. Davenant showed the benefits that England would derive from the policy. 'Our inclinations to sea', said Davenant, 'fitted us as well as the Dutch for the

[1] Childe, *The East India Trade is the most National of all the Foreign Trades*, Brit. Mus., pp. 1–4.

[2] Op. cit.

[3] Compare Pollard, *Factors in Modern History*, Julian Corbett's two books, *Successors of Drake* and *England in the Mediterranean*. Chapters xiv, xv, xix, xx of the latter bring out the importance of this dependence of commerce upon the Navy. Admiral Mahan's *Influence of Sea Power upon History* is less satisfactory from this point of view. It is indispensable for the eighteenth century. For the seventeenth century, chapters i and ii are useful. Oppenheim's *Administration of the Royal Navy* is well known.

traffic of carrying goods from one country to another. The English ports are safer and fitter than the Dutch ports.' Nothing is so advantageous as the carrying trade of which the Dutch had then the monopoly. 'Hence', concluded Davenant, 'England should imitate the Dutch, buy goods in one country and sell them in another. It breeds seamen, increases Shipping, and improves shipping.'[1] Sir Dudley North carried the idea to its logical conclusion.

Of the commercial causes, the East India Trade was one of the most important. The various fishery societies founded in the seventeenth century have been described exhaustively by Professor Scott.[2] None of them proved successful. Nor did any one of them assume the importance which the East India trade attained in the same period. Hence its importance in the seventeenth century. The fierce rivalry of the Dutch in the East had been transformed into an armed conflict with the English merchants. This rivalry brought out the insecure foundations on which the English Company rested. It could achieve success only through the help of the State. The latter alone could carry into effect all the measures necessary to the maintenance of the English trade. This was rendered inevitable by the fact that the Dutch East India Company had the complete support of the States-General. The latter had invested the Company with unlimited power, and regarded 'their East India trade as more precious than a gold mine'. It is for this reason that we find the merchants insisting again and again on increased State support, and that Mun and others advocated measures which were denounced by Adam Smith.

The Anglo-Dutch rivalry affected not only the foreign policy, but also the economic theories of the seventeenth century. The State alone could devise measures for the due protection of English interests abroad. Private merchants were helpless in the face of the Dutch competition, and English trade could not be maintained without the support of the Crown. The State is now regarded as the sole means whereby the interests of the English merchants could be maintained. Hence, a totally new

[1] *Essay on the East India Trade*, see the last chapter, pp. 35–8.
[2] *Constitution and Finances of the Joint Stock Companies*, vol. ii, Division III, pp. 361–79.

significance is attached to the functions that the State was called upon to perform. It now becomes a 'Commercial State', imposing a series of restrictive measures against the principal commercial rivals, Holland and France, planting colonies, extending commerce, and utilizing the Navy as a means whereby every one of these functions could be performed. Hence the significance of the Anglo-Dutch rivalry in the seventeenth century.

Nearly every important seventeenth-century tract on the East India trade refers directly or indirectly to Holland. It is this intense rivalry in the East that helps to explain not only the theories of Mun, but also the importance which the later economic writers attached to those theories. He exercised a permanent influence on the seventeenth-century economic thought because he gave the clearest expression to the opinions which were held by nearly every merchant of his day. He merely expressed in lucid and forcible language what others had been feeling for a long time.

Another aspect of the East India trade was now brought under discussion. The extraordinary growth of the East India trade and shipping was not likely to escape the vigilant eyes of the critics. The Company's ships involved the cutting down of timber and employment of a large number of men on a dangerous undertaking. More serious was its exportation of bullion and importation of East Indian commodities. 'Our woods', exclaimed the author of *Trade's Increase*,[1] 'are extraordinarily cut down, in regard of the greatness of shipping, which doth devour our timber since the Indian Trade, and merely through their building of the ships of so great burthen, and their repairing timbers raised with land 5*s*. and more on the load. Nay, almost not to be had for money, which the Company seek to avoid by building in Ireland.' The policy of Burleigh, and the vigilant care exercised by the Queen as regards the preservation of timber for the Royal Navy [2] seemed to have been completely reversed by the Company. 'If in 5 years, their building beget such a scarcity, what will a little continuance bring forth? A priva-

[1] *Harleian Miscellany*, vol. iv, p. 218.

[2] See Burleigh's letter to the Marquis of Winchester, *State Papers, Domestic, Elizabeth*, vol. vii, nos. 11, 21 (October 1559); vol. cxxxvi, nos. 6, 8, 9, 22, 33, 65, 71, 79.

tion will follow, even of all our own timber.' 'We must then trade without shipping, or make ships without timber.'[1] A far greater harm was done, however, by the exportation of bullion to the 'heathens'. 'Let the Comon people say that their commodities are unnecessary. Ask the tradesmen, nay, all men, what they have cheaper. Look into the price of victuals, how it riseth out of their great provisions. Let the whole land murmer at their transport of treasure, and bring in Charles Vth's opinion to the Portuguese of their East India Trade that they were enemies to Christendom, for they carried away the treasures of Europe to enrich the Heathens.'[2] Again, hundreds of men had been 'consumed' in the dangerous voyages of the Company. Nor should the other Englishmen be barred from the East India trade. 'We are all Britons, all subjects to one Royal King, all combined together in one national League, and therefore not to be barred from trading equally to all places, which the King, with the whole assent of the High Court of Parliament, openly professeth.'[3]

This vigorous onslaught on the East India Company combined in a few sentences the various grievances which were to harass the Company throughout the century, and nearly to bring about its fall. Its importation of Indian commodities into England, its exportation of bullion, its exclusive monopoly—all these were attacked, and all had to be defended. The defence involved the advocacy of Free Trade on the part of the Company. The crude 'bullionism' of the day was intensely hostile to the exportation of money. Nor was the 'natural right of Englishmen to trade', asserted repeatedly by Burleigh and championed fervently by Sandys,[4] compatible with the practical exercise of a monopoly granted by the Crown itself. Hence, in defending its monopoly, the Company was obliged to defend it upon higher grounds than those of private interest. It was now regarded as the only body that could carry on the East India trade. The trade itself was now claimed to be 'the most national of all the Foreign Trades'.[5] Moreover, the importation of Indian commodities was justified on the ground that England should buy in the cheapest market

[1] Ib. [2] Ib. [3] Ib.

[4] *Journals of the House of Commons*, vol. i, pp. 218–21.

[5] Childe, *The East India Trade is the most National of all the Foreign Trades*, 1681, India Office Tracts, vol. lxxxiii.

and sell in the dearest. Consequently, all restrictions of trade were injurious. The Company's advocacy of freedom of trade was, therefore, the result of its importation of large quantities of Indian goods into England. This argument was developed to its logical conclusion by Childe, Davenant, and Sir Dudley North.[1] The attacks made on the Company were greatly resented by the Directors, and the latter commissioned Sir Dudley Digges to reply to the author of *Trade's Increase*.[2]

Digges can hardly be regarded as an ideal controversialist. His personal abuse of the author of *Trade's Increase* is paralleled only by the wealth of his arguments and the vigour of his criticism. He has no difficulty in showing that the loss of men was greatly exaggerated. 'The East India ships come home so strong and serviceable, that without cost of Plank or Timber, they have been found fit to send out again into the Indies.'[3] No doubt four ships were lost at sea, but 'is the loss of 4 ships, so long at sea, so great a loss, especially in 14 years, of our yet infant and discovering Trade, while we seek for Traffick with Strange Nations'?[4] Men were, no doubt, killed on the voyage, though the 'malice of this man has killed many that came home in safetie, and some that were never there'. 'With regard to the "consumption of timber", what are they (woods) good for, if not for building ships?' 'The Providence that bids us go and plant commands us to use our well-grown timber ere it rot, as that would soonest that is fittest for great shipping. His Majesty was loth to have our timber spent on Beggars' Nests, new tenements, whose rotten rents make many gentlemen before their time, or that our woods should be consumed on Fir and Furness for glasses and such trifles when God hath blest us with a Fuell in the bowels of the earth, the waft whereof can do no hurt.'[5] Digges's chief merit lay in his disposal of the crude arguments with which the Company was assailed. He was not so successful with regard to the importation of Indian commodities, and exportation of money to India. Nor could the exportation of bullion be viewed with indifference by the mercantilists of the day. The East India Company had been authorized to export foreign coin to the value

[1] See below, chapter iv.

[2] Sainsbury, vol. i, pp. 381, 385, nos. 902, 912.

[3] *Defence of Trade, from one of that Societie*, Brit. Mus. 1029. c. 19, 1615.

[4] Ib.

[5] Ib., pp. 23–6.

of £30,000. This had increased to £60,000, and later still to £100,000.[1] In four years, 1613–16, they had exported £111,499.[2] During the first twenty years of the Company's existence £548,000 had been exported in Spanish ryals.[3] From March 1620 to March 1624 the Company exported bullion to the value of £264,516.[4] The total amount exported by the Company (£812,516) in twenty-four years may not seem large at the present time, but to a generation which identified money with wealth, and regarded all exportation of money as so much loss of wealth, the continued increase in the Company's imports of Indian products, and exports of bullion, seemed highly dangerous. It conflicted with the fundamental tenets of Protectionism, and it seemed to prepare the way for the inundation of English markets with useless Indian products. The author of *Trade's Increase* had but echoed a common complaint, and, with the growth of the trade, the complaints became louder. Yet the fallacy of unalloyed bullionism was patent both to the practical merchant and the theoretical economist. As early as 1601 Malynes had exposed the fallacy.[5] In his opinion, the wealth of nations cannot decrease but by three manners of ways: (1) 'by the transportation of ready money or bullion out of the country; (2) by selling of our home commodities too good cheaper; (3) by buying the forreign commodities, wherein chiefly consists the aforesaid overbalancing, which is the cause of inequality, the giving in effect both money and commodities to have forreign money for them.'[6] Yet if more money can be obtained by the exportation of a smaller amount, its exportation ought to be permitted. This conception of money as, and its complete identification with, wealth was modified by him on a closer scrutiny of the nature of money itself. Hence, 'in countries where we have no ordinary exchanges, neither the exportation of our money is prejudicial to the realm, if we bring

[1] Sainsbury, vol. iii, p. 267.

[2] Abstract of Stock, Marine Records, op. cit.

[3] Sainsbury, vol. iii, p. 267. Compare Mun, *Discourse*, who puts the figure at £100,000 a year, p. 277.

[4] Macpherson, *History*, p. 107. I have compiled this list from the Abstract laid before the Parliament in 1624. Compare also Sainsbury, vol. iii, p. 267.

[5] *Canker of England's Commonwealth*, Brit. Mus. 1391. a. 15, 1601.

[6] Ib., p. 3.

for it again needful and necessary wares for the same, being both a kind of permutation or barter'.[1] This extension of the prevailing conception of the functions of money had a permanent effect upon the fortunes of the Company. It was developed by Digges and Mun into a consistent and cogent plea for the exportation of money. It was transformed by Sir Dudley North and Davenant into a powerful argument for the freedom of trade, and the abolition of obnoxious restraints on it. Again Malynes's statement 'that the plenty of money maketh generally things dear, and scarcities of money maketh likewise generally things good cheaper' contains the germ of the Quantity Theory of money.[2] The 'over-balancing' on which he insisted so much was incorporated by Mun in his treatise, and developing gradually into the well-known 'Balance of Trade' was observed with sedulous care throughout the century. Nor was his theory of Foreign Exchanges so fantastic as may appear at first. It, no doubt, deserved all the castigation it received at the hands of Mun and Misselden.[3] Mun found no difficulty in exposing the fallacies underlying Malynes's argument, and, taking up each of the 'Feats' which Malynes had attributed to the Exchangers, showed the true nature of the Exchanges. Nor was Misselden far wrong when he asserted [4] that 'it is not the rate of exchanges, whether it is higher or lower, that maketh the prices of commodities dearer or cheaper, but it is the plenty or scarcity of commodities, their use or non-use, that maketh rise or fall in prices'.[5]

The theory tentatively put forward by Malynes was extended by Digges. 'The importation of East India Commodities had broken the monopoly of the Hollanders; had saved the nation £69,666. 13*s*. 4*d*.,[6] and had cheapened the articles.' Moreover,

[1] *Canker of England's Commonwealth*, p. 76.

[2] Laughlin's treatise on Money, in the *History of Quantity Theory of Money*, ignores Malynes, Mun, and other seventeenth-century economists, who anticipated Hume in his formulation of the theory.

[3] Mun, *England's Treasure by Forraign Trade*, India Office Library, 1664, chapters xii–xiv, pp. 94–142; Misselden, *The Circle of Commerce*, 1623, Brit. Mus. 1029. b. 2, pp. 20–1; *Free Trade*, 1622, Brit. Mus. 712. c. 2; Malynes, *The Maintenance of Free Trade*, a reply to *Free Trade*, 1622, Brit. Mus. (1622) 712. c. 30.

[4] *Circle of Commerce*, pp. 20–1.

[5] Compare also pp. 37–8, part ii, of the Treatise.

[6] Ib., p. 43.

the exportation of English products to the East Indies had considerably increased. 'While the exportation of English cloth, tin, &c., amounted to £24,000, that of bullion (in 1614) was only £12,000.' There was, moreover, the benefit derived by the nation from the employment of men, construction of ships, and increase of customs.[1] Nor were the benefits derived from the importation of 'Comfortable Spices' to be despised, for who had not heard of the healing powers of 'Drugges and Spices'?

If the nation gained so many advantages from the exportation of bullion, it was absurd to complain of the exportation of money. For how can the nation get money except by the exportation of money? If the exportation of a smaller amount result in the importation of a much larger amount, then the exportation ought rather to be encouraged than discouraged. Digges had pointed out the advantages thereof. Mun began where Digges had ended. The defence put forward by Malynes, and extended by Digges, was not only developed into a clear-cut and well-reasoned principle, but was connected with his theory of foreign trade. It is here that the East India trade becomes of such paramount importance in the right understanding of the economic theories of the period. He can hardly be called the founder of the Mercantile system. Nor was he the first English writer who emphasized the importance of foreign trade. In the pamphlets written by Misselden, Malynes, Digges, Tobias Gentleman,[2] and the author of *Trade's Increase*, the supreme importance of foreign trade was clearly pointed out. The due recognition of this was the characteristic feature of the seventeenth century. The impetus thereto had been given by the rivalry with Spain. After the destruction of the Armada, the wonderful national revival under Elizabeth increased commercial and colonial activity. Foreign trade acquired a new significance. It became a chief, and, with Mun, the sole means of acquiring the treasure so much valued at the time. The author of *Trade's Increase* had pointed to its importance; Raleigh had remarked upon the activities of the Dutch and the negligence of the Englishmen in that respect; Digges had pointed to the enormous profits secured through the East India

[1] Ib.

[2] *England's Way to Win Wealth.*

trade. Mun's chief merit consists in systematizing the various views on foreign trade into a coherent and consistent whole. Money was, no doubt, the object of foreign trade. Yet this was not the sole object. 'The ordinary means to increase the wealth and treasure is by Foreign Trade, wherein we must ever observe this rule: to sell more to strangers yearly than we consume of theirs in value.'[1] But money is not treasure in every case. 'Neither is it said that money is the Life of Trade, as if it could not subsist without the same. For we know that there was great trading by way of commutation or barter when there was little money stirring in the world.'[2] That money may be dispensed with is proved by the fact that the 'Italians and some other nations dispense with the actual use of money by assigning their credits from one to another daily for very large sums, with ease and satisfaction by writings only'.[3] Mun himself recognized that his advocacy of the exportation of money is so contrary to the common opinion, 'that it will require many and strong arguments to prove it, before it can be accepted of the Multitude'.[4]

Money is not valued in and for itself, for 'plenty of money does not improve our lands. For when the merchant hath a great dispatch beyond the sea, he doth presently return to buy up the greater commodities which doth improve the Land Rent, and enables many men to buy land, which must make them dear.' Yet all this is mainly dependent upon foreign trade, for if 'the Foreign Trade come to a stop or declination by neglect at home, or injury abroad, whereby the merchants are impoverished, then all the said Benefits, and our Lands fall in pieces'.[5] Hence the supreme importance of foreign trade. Treasure can be acquired only through foreign trade. The conception of treasure too undergoes a change. It becomes the medium whereby the land is improved in value, the price of wool rises, and other benefits are conferred. As foreign trade is the only means whereby we can acquire this treasure, so the East India trade is the 'Principall Instrument' therein, because it has so much increased the traffic of the nation.[6] The trade gives

[1] Mun, op. cit., p. 11. [2] Ib., p. 42. [3] Ib.

[4] *Treasure*, p. 34, chap. iv. Compare the *Petition of the East India Company*, 1628, Brit. Mus. 1029. c. 30, p. 32.

[5] *Petition of the East India Company*, op. cit., p. 3. [6] Ib., p. 13.

employment to 12,000 men. Of the £208,000 worth of pepper imported in 1627, no less than £180,000 was re-exported to foreign states. The Company, moreover, had become a defender of the Commonwealth 'to counterpoise the Hollanders' swelling greatness by trade, and to keep them from being Absolute Lords of the Seas'.[1]

Nor were the drugs of the East unnecessary. 'Who is so ignorant in any commonwealth which will not consent to the moderate use of wholesome Druggs and Comfortable Spices?'[2] Nor should the prohibition of the exportation of bullion be allowed, for, though the Company yearly export £100,000, the money exported brings in commodities which are sold here for £494,223. 6*s.* 8*d.*[3] Nor is it the keeping of our money in the kingdom which makes a quick and ample trade, but 'the necessity and use of our wares in foreign countries, and our want of their commodities which causeth the vent and consumption on all sides'.[4] 'For if we only behold the actions of the husbandman in the seed-time when he casteth away much good corn into the ground, we will rather accompt him a madman rather than a husbandman; but when we consider his labours in the harvest, which is the end of his endeavours, we find the worth and plentiful increase of his action.'[5]

Mun's thoroughgoing plea for the exportation of money essentially fixed the circle of seventeenth-century economic thought. The chief defenders of the East India Company under William, North, Davenant, Childe, utilized his arguments to prove the necessity of exportation.

It does not, however, seem to have had immediate effects. Popular opinion, against which Mun had railed, still attributed the scarcity of money in 1622 to the drain of money by the Company. As early as 1615 the author of *Trade's Increase* had voiced their opinion. James I had felt compelled to assure the Company by Proclamation, in 1619, that 'it was not his intention to revoke or discharge any liberty which the East India Company had, or ought to have, by the lawful use and exercise of their charter'.[6] Nor did the clamour die down. In the

[1] Ib., pp. 13, 17, 19, 22, 24, 25.
[2] *Discourse of Trade*, p. 265.
[3] Ib., pp. 276-7.
[4] *Petition of the East India Company*, pp. 27-8.
[5] Mun's *Treasure*, op. cit., p. 50.
[6] Ruding's *Annals of Coinage*, vol. ii, p. 216.

Parliament of 1621 'the scarcity of money was represented to be so great that the tenants gave up their farms, and land had fallen from 20 years' purchase to 19, 18, and even to 13 years'. Some ascribed this to the East India's Company's patent to carry out coin; while the Committee of Grievances appointed by Parliament attributed the scarcity of coin to the unequal balancing of trade, and to the East India Company.[1] Even the King was obliged to investigate the point, and among the instructions to the Standing Commission of 1622 we find the following: 'To inquire whether the East India Company do justly and truly perform their contract with us concerning the exportation of money, because they have been much taxed by men for exporting the coin and treasure of this realm to furnish their trade withal, or that would otherwise have come in hither for the use of our subjects, and that they do not return such merchandise from India as doth recompense that loss into our Kingdom.' The Parliament of 1624 returned to the charge. Buckingham, unable to extort money from the East India Company, moved in the House of Lords for stay of the Company's ships. Others cried out, 'Stay the money that they send out of the land', which some reported to be £80,000 this year. There was intense excitement. There was a motion 'to search the books'. 'Mr. Deputy, hearing the motion, grew hot, stood up' and explained the advantages that the country derived from the trade. As there is no further mention of the matter, it presumably dropped.[2]

The Parliament merely reflected the opinion of the majority of the people. The Venetian ambassador, writing in 1618, has the following: 'From England they take away gold and silver. Thus this trade is not of great use to the kingdom, as, although some individuals make large profits, they introduce into England

[1] Ruding's *Annals of Coinage*, vol. ii, p. 225; *Proceedings and Debates of the House of Commons*, 1620 and 1621, Oxford, 1766, vol. i, pp. 17, 239.

[2] This is taken mainly from the Court Minutes of the East India Company, 8th March 1624. The only reference to the above debate in the *Commons' Journal* is to the following effect: 'Sir Thos. Estcourt moveth to search the East Indian ships for money', p. 678. The above circumstances were, however, reported to the House of Commons by Mr. Wandesford, in the Parliament of 20th April 1626, as 'exactions by the Duke of Buckingham'. *Commons' Journal*, pp. 846, 847. Compare also Sainsbury, vol. iii, pp. 256–7, no. 425.

things which are not necessary for them, and many men are lost on the voyage.'[1] There is no change four years later. 'It (the East India trade) brings them nothing but exaction and hard knocks, and absorbs a large quantity of gold which does not return, in return for spices, and causes great waste among the sailors, eight dying out of 10.'[2] Nor were they guiltless of the scarcity of money at the time. The same ambassador, writing on 16th December 1622, thus describes the scarcity: 'This Kingdom has never been so short of gold. They attribute it to exportation of gold to the East Indies and Flanders, where its value is increased. His Majesty is desperately in need of it. Payments are made only to few, and with great difficulty.'[3]

Misselden ascribed this want of money to the East India Company.[4] 'It was the special remote cause of our want of money.' The greatest drawback, however, was the want of an East India stock. 'This causes the body of the commonwealth to be wounded sore, through the sides of the particular members thereof. For the Stock of the East India Company being of great value, and collected and contracted from all other particular trades of the Commonwealth, and a great part thereof being enlarged and detained now for more than 5 years past, the Commonwealth hath lost the value of the Stock itself, and all the increase of Trade which might have been produced in the several trades of the subjects, whereby abundance of treasure might have been brought into this land in all this time.'[5] 'The money that is traded out into those parts is continually issued out, and never returneth.'[6] Moreover, the Commonwealth was deprived of the use of many of its principal members, 'by whose industry, art, and action the Commonwealth might wonderfully have been increased.' The loss is 'sensible in the drapery of the Kingdom, whereby the poor are set on work, and in all the other trades of the Kingdom; and hath begot that Dampe and Dearness in all the Trades of the Kingdom which we unhappily feel at this day'.[7]

Misselden's indictment of the East India trade was answered by his lifelong opponent, Malynes. The influence of Mun is

[1] *Venetian Calendar*, vol. xv, p. 415. [2] Ib., vol. xvii, p. 423.
[3] Ib., p. 524.
[4] *Free Trade*, 1622, Brit. Mus. 712. c. 2, p. 13.
[5] Ib., p. 14. [6] Ib., p. 20. [7] Ib., p. 29.

apparent on every page dealing with the East India Company. Leaving aside his mystery of Exchange, which he inserted in every discussion, and to which he referred nearly all the prominent economic phenomena of the day, the main argument is a mere repetition in different words. There is the same outlook upon, and the same radical changes in the conception of, the functions of money. 'When the said Indian Commodities are sent from England into Turkey, Leghorn, Genoa, the Low Countries, Marseilles, and other places, and are sold for ready money, the same is employed again upon Currants, Wines, Cotton Wool and Yarn, Galls, and divers other Commodities, wherewith the ships being reladen, yet a great proportion remaineth to be brought over in moneys.'[1] The chief causes, as usual with him, were the narrow policy of the Merchant Adventurers, and the frauds of the Exchangers. Misselden's sudden change of his opinion may be due to the fact that the East India Company had appointed him their Commissioner for Holland.[2] The benefits to the nation are again estimated at £100,000. There, however, is a wider conception of the East India trade. It not only yields £500,000, but also employs '10,000 Tons of Shipping, and 3,000 Mariners, Carpenters, and other artificers'.[3] 'Moreover, the King's Customs will be greatly increased by the Trade.'[4] The adoption of Mun's arguments by Malynes and Misselden showed the influence of the former on the evolution of the chief argument for the existence of the East India Company.

Both the critics and the defenders of the East India Company were, however, unanimous in regarding the foreign trade as the chief means of securing treasure. As England possessed no gold mines, said Mun, the only means whereby the treasure could be acquired was foreign trade. As treasure was identified with foreign trade, all the means whereby the latter could be secured were to be utilized and efficiently employed. The chief commercial rivals were to be removed by the State itself, and their commodities prohibited. Hence the connexion of foreign trade

[1] *Maintenance of Free Trade*, 1622, Brit. Mus. 712. c. 30, pp. 27, 28.

[2] Compare Sainsbury, vol. iii, nos. 331, 665, 682; vol. iv, no. 729, 'Will not have any further dealings with the East India Company's affairs'.

[3] *Circle of Commerce*, by E. M. (Misselden), Merchant, 1623, Brit. Mus. 1029. b. 2. Compare also Malynes's *Centre to the Circle of Commerce*, a reply to the above.

[4] Ib., p. 38.

with Protectionism. A Company that had the organized will and unlimited support of the State at its back was a far more serious rival than a number of private merchants without any adequate authority from the Government. The theory of the State is completely transformed by the rivalry of the merchants of two commercial powers. The State is no longer the passive spectator of its people's activities, but an active asserter of their rights to the East India trade, the Greenland fishery, and other trades. Hence the importance of Mun in the history of economic thought. A clear recognition of the importance of foreign trade went hand in hand with a bitter hatred of the Dutch. This was due mainly to the fact that they were the most determined opponents of the English merchants in the East Indies, in Russia, and in Greenland. It is instructive to trace the stages through which these quarrels passed before they became 'matters of state'.[1] At first, the East India merchants bear all the troubles meekly, and though they complain, the complaint is not addressed to the King. It is still regarded as a quarrel among merchants, and the State is not called upon to redress their grievances. At length, the East India Company, 'having long endured notorious injuries', were, in 1611, 'enforced to break silence, and complain of their griefs'.[2] In their petition they implored the 'Lord Treasurer's assistance and mediation with the States for redress'; the petition described how Captain Middleton was forcibly put from all trade at Banda, and went on to narrate other injuries committed by the Dutch. Winwood's reply to Salisbury's dispatch about the Company's petition is striking. The Dutch Company, he asserted, is a body by itself, high and mighty, and will not acknowledge the authority of the States-General more than shall be for their private interest.[3] At last three Commissioners, accompanied by Hugo Grotius, arrived in London in March, 1613.[4]

The first memorial of the Dutch brought out the essential differences between the two parties. The Dutch asserted that they had spent large sums in maintaining their trade, and they thought it very hard that the King's subjects should trade in

[1] Downing's expression.
[2] *Public Record Office, East Indies*, vol. i, no. 34.
[3] Winwood to Salisbury, Sainsbury, vol. i, p. 234.
[4] Ib., no. 641.

those parts. The English Commissioners, on the other hand, maintained their right to trade there, and justified it by appealing to the *Ius Gentium* which Grotius had so forcibly defended.[1] The real aims of the Dutch were not hidden from the shrewd English merchants. Sir Thomas Smythe's letter to Winwood shows plainly the effect produced by the meeting. 'We have treated all along', says Smythe, 'with no other benefit, but only that we now know that they endeavour to seclude us from trading in those parts; where hitherto we have had it from fear of the Portuguese, and with the good affection of the country people.'[2] The Dutch Commissioners had many conferences with the English, but were unable to settle the differences. The King at last advised that these should be referred to a future treaty. He expressed his willingness to depute Commissioners for that purpose. The Conference, which had lasted two months, broke up without effecting any settlement. Meanwhile, the quarrels in the East increased in intensity. The Company had dispatched a vessel to Bachian, one of the Moluccas, early in 1613, but the factors could get no trade there, 'because of the sway of the Flemings'. They were forced to yield the island of Machian, which had been offered to Sir Henry Middleton, 'to the Flemings'. The people desired to trade with the English, 'but the Flemings sent great ships to prevent it, and threatened the islanders with punishment'.[3] The Company's factors might hope that their masters would 'not put up with such insupportable injuries', but they were powerless for the time.

The following year Caron, the Dutch Ambassador, made for common action on the part of the two Companies 'in a loving and friendly trade'. The Dutch were to make use of trading to Cambaya, while the English Company was to be admitted to the Moluccas, but in such a manner 'that no places may be overlayed'.[4]

This was certainly a considerable improvement upon the former proposals, but it left the original problem unsolved. There was no guarantee that the two powers would cease their

[1] *Public Record Office, East Indies*, vol. i, nos. 38, 39.

[2] Smythe to Winwood, 16th May 1613. *Historical MSS. Commission*, MSS. of the Duke of Buccleuch at Montagu House, vol. i, p. 132.

[3] Sainsbury, vol. i, 2nd Dec. 1613.

[4] *Court Minutes*, Book III, pp. 28–34, 8–11th Feb. 1614.

rivalries upon the assignation of their respective spheres. The proposal merely expressed the leading ideas of the Dutch on the freedom of commerce in the East. They were determined to maintain a monopoly, even though the monopoly might be exercised by them in parts alone, and not in all the East India Islands. This was made clear at the meeting of the Commissioners in 1615. The English merchants desired nothing more than the removal of all interruptions to free trade to all parts of the East Indies, especially to the Spice Islands.[1] The Dutch, however, desired no competition in the East. At the first meeting they brought forward two propositions to which they adhered throughout the seventeenth century. They refused the English Company all share in the East India trade because (1) they had, at great expense and danger, established their trade in the East Indies, by 'taking, supervising, and building of many forts; and (2) because they had contracted amity with diverse kings there, and therefore do not think it reason that any man should go about to deprive them of those benefits and advantages, which they expect and look for, after much effusions of blood, great charges, travails, and perils'.

It cannot be denied that the Dutch had expended large sums in the East, and that they were entitled to the rewards to which they looked forward, and which they ultimately obtained. But they claimed much more than a proportionate reward for all their expenses. They claimed a right to expel every other power from the Spice Islands, and to monopolize the whole commodity in the East. The English Commissioners, on the other hand, rested their claim for 'free trade into the East Indies, and every part thereof, as well by the Law of Nations, as by the admittance of Kings and Princes'. The free trade, which they claimed, had been advocated by Grotius, and they pertinently asked the countrymen of Grotius whether they were ready to deny freedom of trade and to advocate freedom of the seas. The Dutch reply was ingenious. They now threw away the Laws of Nature and Nations to which they had appealed in their advocacy of freedom of the seas, styling them as 'indefinite in themselves', and informed the English Commissioners that 'they were limited by the Municipal laws and institutions of

[1] Sainsbury, vol. i, no. 860.

people and governments, whereby it is evident in all Kingdoms that it is not lawful for every man to buy every commodity of every person, in every place, and at all times'. Moreover, every person was at liberty to 'tie himself, and since certain Indians have done that by promising the sale of Spices unto the Hollanders, there is nothing more agreeable to natural equity, and Law of Nations'.

The English pointed to the earlier treaty made by Sir Francis Drake with the ruler of Ternate, and claimed that the contract entered into in 1579 should have precedence of all later agreements. The English claim was not really very sound. Sir Francis Drake's treaty could hardly be relied upon by the Company. It certainly had no such wide effects as the Company attributed to it.[1] They were on firmer ground when they asserted that the Dutch were claiming precisely that which the Spaniards had claimed in the West and East Indies, and that, in some respects, the Dutch monopoly was more galling than the Spanish monopoly. The Dutch retorted that they were claiming monopoly of only a part of Asia. To this the English rejoined that it made no difference. Both 'used the same reasons to keep others from commerce in those parts, which they would exempt from the Common Right and Law of Nations'. Throughout all these negotiations, the English insisted upon 'the Law of Nations', 'primitive law', and 'law of nature'. Their deduction of the right of trade from the law of nature may appear illogical to us, but the universal major premise upon which it was based had not only been assumed by Grotius, but also defended, and expanded into a fervent plea for the freedom of the seas. Throughout the century the same question recurs with almost mechanical frequency. The English Company in their petitions, manifestoes, &c., to James I, Cromwell, and Charles II demand freedom of trade to the East Indies. We find the old words as late as 1680. The Dutch, on their side, claim freedom of the seas, and as vehemently deny the right of the English to freedom of trade with the Spice Islands. Neither party conceded what the other demanded, and both of them utilized the law of nature for their own benefit. The history of these theories is a melancholy commentary, not only on the *Mare Liberum* of

[1] See Corbett, *Drake and the Tudor Navy*.

Grotius, but also on the *Leviathan* of Hobbes, and the *Social Contract* of Rousseau.

The result of these academic discussions was foreseen by the shrewd English merchants. They concluded thus: 'It appears that their purpose and intent is to exclude His Majesty's subjects from the trade of the Spices in the East Indies and to engross the same wholly to themselves.'[1] Though there was no prospect of settlement on these lines, the differences might have been removed by the union of the two Companies. As early as 1610 it had been suggested by Holland.[2] But the English ambassador rejected the proposal, as he thought the smaller English Company would have been swallowed up by the larger body. The idea was eagerly adopted by James I. He urged upon the Company the necessity of union with its Dutch rival. He 'disliked the Company refusing to join with the Dutch if they should fall upon a Joint Stock'. The reasons adduced by the Company were intelligible enough. It urged in defence of its conduct, that 'the Dutch maintained their merchandise with their state, and had made no dividends but small matter'. This was really the crux of the situation. The liberty of trade which the Company desired ought to be supported by all the resources of the State, and the privileges enjoyed by the English merchants ought to be maintained by all the power at its disposal.[3]

The English merchants were naturally apprehensive of the Dutch plans. The Commissioners informed the Company that the Dutch Company had fifty-one ships in the East Indies and a Stock of £900,000, and owed £400,000 at interest, which, they added, 'is a great discouragement to their adventurers'.[4] The veteran Caron was not, however, dismayed. He knew the advantages of the union to the Dutch Company, and he required the help of the English navy in a possible war with the Spaniards. He proposed that each Company should put

[1] *Historical MSS. Commission.* MSS. of the Duke of Buccleuch at Montagu House, vol. i. *A Brief of the Proceedings which have passed betwixt His Majesty's Commissioners, and those others of the States touching the Trade into the East Indies*, pp. 166–70. Sainsbury, vol. i, nos. 854, 855, 860, 874, 976.

[2] Winwood, *Memorials*, vol. iii.

[3] *Court Book*, vol. iv, 3rd Jan. 1615, pp. 328–31.

[4] *Court Minutes*, Book III, pp. 419–22, 5th May 1615.

£1,100,000 or £1,200,000 into the Stock.[1] The Company's reasons for its refusal to unite were clear. They could derive no advantage from the union. The special place for which the English strove did not yield sufficient to counteract the excessive charges; they suspected the designs of the Dutch, whom they accused of endeavouring to draw the English Company to participate in their charges in the Indies against the Spaniards and the Portuguese, and so 'to help themselves out of the gain made by the English'. Nor were they afraid of the Spaniards of the East. They thought that 'in time they will eat him out of that trade, only by underselling him in all parts of Christendom'. Accordingly, 'finding the resolution of the Hollanders to keep the English away where they can, by forts, ships, or soldiers', it was thought fit to return no answer to Caron's proposal.[2] The Company acted very prudently on this occasion. They saw the inevitable drawbacks of the union of a weaker with a powerful body, and instinctively shrank from the desired combination. Meanwhile, the rivalry in the East had not ceased. At whichever of these islands the English went they were 'beaten away' by superior force, and the natives threatened 'with the loss of their heads if they dealt with the English'.[3]

The commercial rivalry in the East had developed into an armed struggle. In 1617 the complaints against the Dutch became incessant. From almost every factory in the East the same account is repeated. 'The Flemings thunder it most terrible in these parts,' wrote the President of the English factors in January. 'Their untruths are daily more discovered, and they are rather feared than respected by their brutal carriage,' wrote another factor. A third factor declared that 'the Hollanders are mortal enemies to the English in their trade'. Poulaway was reduced by the Dutch, and the heroic Courthope was struggling against overwhelming odds. By 1620 eleven laden English sail had been captured by the Dutch, while the English Company had only taken the *Black Lion*,

[1] *Court Minutes*, Book III, pp. 419–22, 28th June 1615.

[2] *Court Minutes*, *Court Book*, vol. iii, 28th June 1615, pp. 432–8; *Public Record Office*, *East Indies*, vol. i, no. 48; *Court Book*, 18th Aug. 1615, pp. 463–7.

[3] Sainsbury, vol. i, nos. 1004, 1006, 1023.

worth 71,000 ryals. Almost all the captured English ships were laden with goods and bullion.[1]

It would be tedious to go through the complaints of every English factor in the East Indies. They are universal, and the letters and dispatches of the period teem with references to the 'bloody', 'insolent', 'cruel', 'ungrateful' Hollanders.[2] The Company was obliged to draw the attention of the King to this state of affairs, and drew up two sets of complaints.[3] In these documents the Company complained of 'the efforts of Hollanders to dispossess them by force' of many places in the East Indies; of their most outrageous behaviour, as any mortal enemies could do; of the unjust seizure of the Company's ships, 'and keeping their men prisoners in irons', and declaring they will take from the English all the trade in the East Indies.[4] The negotiations with the Dutch Commissioners were several times broken off. On one occasion the Lords, taken by surprise at the Dutch deputies' preparations for departure, professedly entreated Caron to stay them; but the King directed for answer that if they will be wilful to go, it was their own fault, and His Majesty would not stay them. There were loud complaints on both sides.[5] James I seems at this time to have been dominated by his ruling passion, that of peace. It was utterly distasteful to him that two Protestant powers should haggle over points, the importance of which he did not know at the time. He therefore urged upon the Company the expediency of arriving

[1] Ib., vol. ii, pp. 384-6.

[2] The whole volume of *State Papers, East Indies*, 1617-21, is full of them. So is Purchas, vol. v, op. cit.

[3] *Public Record Office, East Indies*, vol. i, no. 7; *Domestic, Jac. I*, vol. civ, no. 62, p. 607.

[4] James's foreign policy has been exhaustively dealt with by Professor Gardiner in his first five volumes of the *History of England*. It is evident, however, that the Anglo-Dutch struggle in the East has not received the same attention that he devoted to James's policy towards Spain and the Palatinate. Though he refers to the struggle in chap. xxvi, the account he gives of it is not completely satisfactory. Again, though he mentions the East India papers calendared by Sainsbury in the preface to vol. iii, it does not appear that all the voluminous material collected therein was thoroughly digested. He relies greatly upon the Add. MSS. 17677. The transcripts from the archives of the Hague are undoubtedly important; but the study of the original correspondence of the Company's factors and the Court Minutes of the East India Company are of no less importance. I find him deficient in the latter.

[5] Chamberlain to Carleton, 30th Jan. 1619. Sainsbury, vol. ii, no. 572.

at a settlement with the Dutch Commissioners. His Majesty expressed his determination to effect it, and to be 'no more partial to either side than if they were both of his own subjects'.[1] This was, no doubt, a lofty ideal, and would have been worthy of imitation if either party had conformed to it. There is ample evidence to convince us that neither party did. At a meeting held on 21st May, the Committee of the East India Company were of the opinion that 'this treaty was but a colour to give time to work all the insupportable wrongs against them, and therefore fit to press it home unto His Majesty'.[2]

The main points of difference between the two Companies were the maintenance of forts and the division of spices in the East India islands. The article of the contemplated treaty stipulated that the existing fortifications should remain in the hands of the original owners. This was disliked by the Company on the ground that 'having one fort at Pooloroon, the Company conclude that they should demand the right to build others at Ternate, Motir, and Poolaway'.[3] The Company knew that their safety depended ultimately upon their forts in the islands, and that if they allowed the Dutch to keep more than four times the number of their forts, they would be overwhelmed in a short time.

Another question that gave some trouble was the division of the spices. The Company accepted the share allotted them by the Dutch.[4] Nor did they object to pay for the defence of the islands out of a fund to be raised by a duty on exports. The treaty provided for the maintenance of a combined English and Dutch fleet, consisting of four representatives from each Company. The King's eagerness to conclude an agreement could not be repressed by the English Company's protests, and the Company at length referred the vexed question of fortifications to James. The King's decision was not delayed long. 'He dissolved the difficulties of the East India business and by his own wisdom and authority brought them to accord.'[5] The

[1] Doncaster to Carleton, 12th May 1619. Sainsbury, vol. ii, no. 665.
[2] *Court Book*, vol. iv, pp. 347–50, 21st May 1619.
[3] *Court Minutes*, vol. iv, pp. 345–7, 14–17th May 1619.
[4] Viz. one-third of all the spices in those parts, and all the pepper at Bantam, *Court Minutes*, ib.
[5] Chamberlain to Carleton, 31st May 1619. Sainsbury, vol. ii, no. 677.

States-General were delighted. They said 'how honourable and just the King was, and all honour and thanks was by them wholly ascribed to His Majesty'.[1] The impartiality shown by James, and praised by the Venetian ambassador,[2] had a very unhappy effect on the Company's fortunes in the East. While the States applauded him and while he himself posed as a peace-maker who had conferred peace on the three kingdoms,[3] the English statesmen and the English Company were of a different mind. Chamberlain acknowledged that 'things are passed as the others would have it, which makes the world suspect that they (the Dutch) have found great friends, and make much use of their wicked mammon'.[4] Carleton himself admitted that the treaty might have been more advantageous to us 'in point of fortifications', but, he added, 'these are stiff not to quit the prize'.[5]

Another design of the Dutch had fortunately been frustrated by the shrewd common sense of the English Company. They had asked for the union, not only of the East Indies, but also of the Virginia Company, as early as 1610.[6] Their aims were clear. By uniting with the English Companies they would be able to partake of a share in the English plantations, and to hold complete sway in the Eastern seas. They could, moreover, ask James for help against Spain in their impending war against the latter. Caron now again brought forward the proposal, and asked for a meeting of Commissioners on both parts to treat of the settling a Joint Stock between the two Companies.[7] The King, as usual, favoured the idea.[8] The Company was in a very difficult position. They could not refuse the King's request without incurring his displeasure. Nor could they commit suicide by uniting with an unprofitable undertaking. Roe

[1] Sainsbury, vol. ii, nos. 668, 673.

[2] 'There can be no better moderator than James I, who, after hearing the Ambassadors of the States and his Council, decided absolutely in favour of the Dutch.' *Venetian Calendar*, vol. xvii, p. 465.

[3] See James's *Peacemaker*, British Museum, 1618.

[4] Chamberlain to Carleton, *Domestic Correspondence, Jac. I*, vol. cix, no. 75, p. 51. Compare also the petition of the English Company 'touching questions of forts' immediately after the conclusion of the landed treaty, *Public Record Office, East Indies*, vol. i, nos. 77–8.

[5] Carleton to Chamberlain, 16th June 1619.

[6] Winwood, op. cit.

[7] Sainsbury, vol. ii, nos. 238, 443.

[8] *Court Minutes*, Book IV, 14–15th Dec. 1618.

strongly advised the Company 'never to join Stock with the Dutch to profit and loss, for their garrisons, charges, and losses by negligence would', he said, 'engage the English Company to bear part of their follies for no profit'. His representation to 'Mr. Secretary and some of the Lords' had the desired effect, and the project dropped. James I's policy towards the East India Company illustrates in a special manner the effect exercised by the Anglo-Dutch struggle in the East. The quarrel between the English and Dutch Companies is treated by him merely as a dispute between two private Companies, who were foolish enough to disturb the peace. The representations of Carleton to the States-General are cautiously worded, and there is no sign of the treatment of the quarrel as a matter of State. James was genuinely desirous of removing all grievances, and used his authority so impartially as to decide all questions in 1619 'absolutely in favour of the Dutch'. Of the real nature of the dispute he seemed to be totally unconscious.

After the conclusion of the treaty we notice, however, a distinct change. A series of battles in the East Indies convinced him of the hollowness of the ground on which he was treading. It was not by ejaculating pious expressions in his *Peacemaker*,[1] but by maintaining the privileges of the English merchants in the East Indies by force of arms, and employing all the resources of the State against the most serious commercial rivals in the East, that he could represent the nation. The rivalry in the East had not ceased in the meanwhile. The Dutch had been defeated in a 'cruell bloody fight' in 1619. In October the English squadron in Sumatra met with a serious defeat.[2] The great Dutch Governor-General, Coen, made the expulsion of the English from the islands the corner-stone of his policy. He advised his successor 'not to trust the English and French any more than open enemies, and give no way to the shortening of sovereignty. Everything ought to be done to obtain prerogative over the English.'[3]

Commerce now becomes the prize for which wars are waged and colonies planted. It was this intense rivalry with the Dutch in the East Indies that helps to explain not only the economic

[1] British Museum, 1618.
[2] Sainsbury, vol. ii, nos. 529, 547, 609, 733, 761, 767.
[3] *Coen's Instructions*, Sainsbury, vol. iii, no. 243.

writings but also the foreign policy of the period. All the economists of the period were eminently practical, and were connected either directly or indirectly with commerce. This applies to Mun, Roberts, Robinson, Malynes, Digges, Raleigh, and a host of other writers. It seemed imperative to them that the State should carry out its policy in accordance with the material interests of the people by giving increased support to their claims. These representations seem to have had no effect on James I till 1619. After that date, we notice a very remarkable change. The discontent of the merchants had not been removed, and there were loud complaints of the treaty. The King was obliged to assure 'the Company that he esteems the East India Company a great ornament and strength unto his kingdom, whom he hath and will maintain'. More significant still were the following words:—'He doubted not to procure them in some convenient time their own desires in the Indies, which if the Dutch should deny, that quarrel should be no longer the Company's but of the State, and that if the Dutch hold not good correspondency with his subjects beyond the Line, he will not hold any with them here.'[1] James had at length become conscious of the difficult situation in which the Company had been placed through his lack of support. Unless he was able to adopt the cause of the Company as the cause of the State, and to render effectual aid to the Company in all its quarrels with the Dutch, the dissolution of the Company was certain. Hence this modification of his original policy. The increasing bitterness engendered by the rivalry in the East led to increased support of the East India Company on the part of the Crown.

The treaty of 1619 was to remain in force twenty years, but in less than twenty months both English and Dutch were compelled to open fresh negotiations. The same disputes continued to arise between the two Companies, and the same complaints were made by the English Company. The causes of the quarrel would have been foreseen by any capable negotiator. The English Company had promised to maintain ten ships in the Spice Islands, and their neglect to maintain them was a breach of the treaty. There were other causes. The Dutch charged the English Company with refusal to pay their part of the

[1] *Court Minute Book*, vol. iv, p. 379, 2nd July 1619.

charges in keeping soldiers there. The Company's factors alleged, however, that the object of the Dutch was to impose such heavy charges upon the English as would ultimately compel them to relinquish their trade in the Spice Islands, and that then the Dutch would remain the sole European masters of this most remunerative commerce.

The negotiations of 1622 were as tedious as those of 1619. The English and Dutch Commissioners held many conferences, but the 'wayward proceedings' of the Commissioners made most of the Lords careless to meet, and the negotiations were broken off more than once.[1] An intercepted letter of the Spanish Ambassador to Gondomar tells us that the 'controversy between the English and the Dutch concerning their business increases daily, and were it not that the King favours the rebels to the prejudice of his own subjects, the treaty would have been broken, for they have proclaimed there that they have no greater enemies than the Dutch'.[2] 'Scandalous words' passed between the merchants on both sides, and on one occasion the papers laid before the Lords Commissioners were torn up. Calvert told Carleton that the Dutch had with much art made many offers, varied and gilded over, and 'because we will not swallow the gudgeon they grow angry'. The Lords Commissioners believed that the Dutch had no intention to come to any reasonable terms. After the lapse of about a month, points of accommodation were again debated, and the negotiations renewed. The most important of the points that required settlement was the *règlement* of trade in the East. This was really the crux of the situation, and was the subject of the Company's petitions to the Crown throughout the century.[3] Its settlement would have prevented most of the subsequent quarrels. The Lords Commissioners had pointed out that this was the most important point, and that if it were settled both Companies might be made happy enough. In their Second Report they again pointed out the necessity of this.[4] The King, however, was of a different mind. In spite of the advice of the Commissioners, he granted the Dutch a private audience and recommended the Lords Com-

[1] Sainsbury, vol. iii, pp. 13, 29, 32, 64.
[2] 19th July 1622. Sainsbury, vol. iii, no. 114.
[3] See next chapter.
[4] *Public Record Office, East Indies*, vol. ii, nos. 26, 28.

missioners 'to keep themselves to the treaty, and not give way to any novelty'.[1] Hence, the most important point was left over by the Commissioners, who stated that 'as the King commanded, to keep themselves to the treaty and not give way to any novelty, so they think the point touching *règlement,* which merely concerns trade, may as well be agreed upon amongst the merchants themselves'. A treaty was at length signed in January, 1623.[2] It was as worthless as that of 1619. John Chamberlain echoed the universal complaint when he asserted that 'whatever they are, our East India Company will never be the better for them'.[3] James's treatment of the East India Company can hardly be reconciled with his promises. It was due in a great measure to the complications on the continent. The treaties between England and the United Provinces then fighting against the Spanish dominion no doubt greatly influenced the King in his dealings with the States-General and the two Companies.[4] This was only a phase of the situation, but it showed the dangers of dependence upon the promises of James. The Massacre of Amboyna was, however, too terrible a calamity to be lightly passed over. It produced immediate effect. The King's eyes were opened to the serious nature of that event, and we find the clearest expression of his indignation in his dispatches to the Ambassador at the Hague. The negotiations that ensued are interesting, as they enable us to explain the strange proposals of the King to partition the United Provinces.

The acute commercial rivalry between the two countries was nowhere better displayed than at Amboyna, and the King's foreign policy underwent considerable modification. He proposed to partition the United Provinces, and the Spanish Ambassador sent a series of dispatches on the project. Dr. Gardiner has supplied us with valuable extracts from those dispatches,[5] but he

[1] Ib., nos. 27, 32.

[2] See a copy of the Treaty in the *Calendars of State Papers, East Indies*, 1622–4, pp. 106–7.

[3] Sainsbury, vol. iii, no. 233. The Secretary of State himself told Carleton that 'we had at last made an end and parted good friends, though with much loss and disadvantage to the English Company as was conceived'. Carleton's dispatch of 5th Feb. 1623 shows that the Dutch were elated by the 'favourable usage' received from James. Sainsbury, vol. iii, no. 257.

[4] They have been exhaustively dealt with by Gardiner, in vols. iv and v of his *History of England*.

[5] *History*, vols. iv and v.

has failed to account for this aberration of James. Really it was due to the clamours aroused by the English merchants. The massacre produced a deep impression.[1] Carleton made vigorous protests to the States, and demanded immediate satisfaction for the injuries done to the East India Company. James's conduct was admirable throughout. He lent all his support to the representations of the Company; promised to exact damages from the Dutch, and to seize the Dutch ships in the Narrow Seas. The whole volume of documents, calendared by Sainsbury,[2] shows clearly the change that had been brought about in the King's policy. The commercial rivalry in the East had now developed into an armed conflict. Mr. Secretary told the East India Company that 'the King's present force in the Narrow Seas was small; that the Dutch were strong and resolute to fight, and for setting out any present force, the King wanted money, but that he intended to arm both by sea and land, and was resolved to buoy up the reputation of the Kingdom, and in the doing of that would have the means to right all'.[3]

The whole volume of Calendars (1622–4) shows the overwhelming effect produced by these events. The *Court Minutes* of the period show the various stages through which the proposal to 'make this a business of the State' passed. They show, moreover, the main thing that the merchants desired. Again and again we find the merchants saying 'that unless protected they must leave the trade'.[4] James's policy in 1624 is in curious contrast with his policy in 1619. Then he desired the composition of these disputes, and the union of the two Companies. Now, in 1624, he is ready to back the Company by arming 'both by sea and land'. It is nothing else but a recognition of the claims of the East India merchants and the carrying out of that policy which had been recommended by a number of economists. The East India trade, therefore, plays a new rôle. As foreign trade

[1] Sainsbury, vol. iii, nos. 511, 524, 534, 574. Copies of the pamphlet published by the Company were presented to the Lords of the Council and the principal nobility. The Venetian Ambassador in England testified to the intensity of hatred against the Dutch, *Venetian Calendar*, vol. xviii. The pamphlet was dispersed in all parts of England, as well as in the Netherlands, ib., pp. 463, 660, 688. Copies were much asked after by Members of Parliament, ib. 544.

[2] *East Indies*, 1622–4.

[3] *Court Minutes*, 22–24th Nov. 1624.

[4] Ib. 22–24th Nov. 1624.

was regarded as the chief means of obtaining the treasure and as the East India trade was regarded (by Mun and others) as the 'Principal Instrument' whereby the foreign trade could be obtained, the East India trade becomes the principal cause of the seventeenth-century mercantilism. The State is now conceived as the chief agency by which the protection of the merchants' interests may be effected. James I descends from his lofty heights, and agrees to adopt 'their business as the business of the State', and foreign policy is regulated in accordance with the wishes of the merchants. Hence, the importance of the East India trade for a right understanding of the economic and foreign policies of the Government in the seventeenth century.

It is instructive to contrast the policy of Charles I with that of James. While the latter was genuinely anxious for the progress of the East India Company and rendered considerable help towards the end of his reign, the former utilized the misfortunes of the Company for his own benefit. Though, on the representation of the East India Company, three Dutch ships from Surat was stayed by Charles at Portsmouth,[1] they were unexpectedly released, and the Company justly characterized it as a 'discouragement to their trade'.[2] The reason given by the King for their release did not satisfy the Company, and they justly suspected Charles of sacrificing their interests for his own benefit. This was proved by Charles's reply to a letter from Josias de Vosherghen, the Resident and Councillor of Denmark, about the business. In this the King promised to release the Dutch ships in case the Resident came to an agreement with the Dutch Company to raise money on certain jewels equivalent to the arrested goods.[3] Subsequently he obtained three tons of gold for the release of the Dutch ships.[4]

The Company's petition to the Privy Council on this subject was remarkably candid. It referred to the promises of support made to the Company and went on to state the grounds on which it was obliged to asked for the support of the King. The attempts of the committees of the Company to raise a stock of £600,000 to be adventured in four years, or £150,000 for one year, were fruitless. The discouragements of the Company were

[1] Sainsbury, vol. iv, pp. 503–8.
[2] Ib., nos. 701, 706.
[3] Ib., nos. 640, 641.
[4] Ib., no. 719.

increased daily by reports given out by the 'Hollanders that the ships have been released for money given underhand, concerning which 3 tons of gold have flowen'.[1] The petition brings out the low state into which the Company had fallen, mainly through the conduct of Charles. The negotiations in reference to the Amboyna massacre slowly drag their course in the documents of the time.[2]

Charles I's accession had not improved the prospects. While James had manifested considerable theoretical interest in the fortunes of the Company and had negotiated on its behalf, Charles I utilized the negotiations in his own interests, created a rival body with coequal powers, and ensured its complete decline by pursuing the fitful, vacillating policy which was ultimately to prove his own ruin. As we have seen, the ships arrested by him, on the representation of the English Company, were returned to the Dutch, on receiving a bribe of three tons of gold.[3] The Bewinthebbers gave out that they had 'already obtained a grant of their release on condition to redeem His Majesty's Jewels'.[4] The Company were quite justified in regarding him as 'a great discouragement' to their trade.[5] Nor could his requests for the loan of £10,000 from the Company be complied with. The Company might cheerfully grant more than double that to Charles II. It was not prepared to lend the father even half that amount.[6]

Nor was Charles bound by the Charter which had been granted by James. As early as 1630 Captain Quail had been sent to the Red Sea to capture the ships and goods of Spaniards. On the strength of this authority, he made prize of a Malabar junk. As the Company had granted passes to the ship it was held liable for the outrage.[7] Endymion Porter, the courtier and favourite, taking advantage of the licence to Quail, obtained a licence to fit out two ships as privateers. The funds necessary were obtained by taking certain London merchants into partner-

[1] *East Indies*, vol. iv, nos. 51 and 51. I.

[2] Sainsbury, vols. v, vi. The usual petitions by the East India Company for redress and satisfaction. The King promises but never performs.

[3] Ib., vol. iv, p. 555, nos. 640, 641, 719.

[4] Ib., no. 612.

[5] Ib., nos. 701, 706.

[6] Ib., p. 521.

[7] See *Court Minutes*, vols. vi and vii, with a masterly Introduction by William Foster.

ship, amongst whom were Kynaston and Bonnell. The latter was closely connected with Courteen, one of the prominent capitalists of the period. The venture developed into a Company, invested with considerable powers, and patronized by the King. Charles himself held stock to the extent of £10,000.[1] Courteen provided £120,000,[2] the Earl of Shrewsbury adventured £2,500, and Sir Paul Pindar £36,000.[3] The successes of these voyages emboldened the adventurers, and they now wanted the grant of such privileges as would place their undertaking on a more permanent basis. The King acceded to their request, and authorized the adventurers to Goa and other parts to trade at all places in India where the Company had not settled factories prior to 12th December 1635.[4] Charles justified the permission on the ground that the East India Company had 'neglected to plant and settle trade in those parts, and had made no fortifications to encourage any in future times to adventure thither, contrary to the practice of the Dutch and Portuguese'.[5] But these mistakes could not be repaired by the creation of a rival Company, with equal powers, and greater financial support. The King did not make his position quite clear to either of the rivals, though he assured the old Company that no hindrance was intended to the Company's trade, and that ships would not go near the Company's factories, but were meant only for a voyage of discovery.[6]

The Company can surely be excused if it placed little faith in the King's promise. He ignored the Company's protests, released Kynaston, when the latter was prosecuted in the Admiralty Court by the East India Company, and expressly ordered the Company to send out directions that their servants were not to trade at Bhatkal or at any other place where Courteen and his associates had settled factories.[7] He ought either to have suppressed the

[1] Ib., vol. vi, p. 188.

[2] Darrell puts his share at £150,000. *Strange News from the Indies*, Brit. Mus. 1029. g. 20, p. 5.

[3] *Lex Talionis*, Brit. Mus. 712. g. 18 (2), *Dedication*, p. 19; *A brief Narrative of the Cases of Sir William Courteen and Sir Paul Pyndar*, by E. Graves, 1679, Brit. Mus. 515. k. 21 (5), p. 3. Compare also *Mr. Courteen's Catastrophe*, 1652, Brit. Mus. 1029. g. 19, which describes the wretched state of Courteen's factors in India, and estimates their whole loss at £50,000.

[4] Sainsbury, vol. vi, pp. 127, 274–5, 282–3, 294–5, &c.

[5] Ib., *Preamble to the grant.*

[6] Ib., vol. i, p. 157.

[7] Ib., vol. vi, pp. 219, 220, 294, 295, 337.

old Company, after giving it three years' notice, or to have prohibited the formation of a rival Company. He did neither, and instead of pursuing a clear policy, he played a part which made him a just object of suspicion to both parties. The existence of two English Companies, each vested with great privileges, and each competing with the other, could lead only to one thing—the expulsion of the English from Asia. The King was probably not aware of the danger. His support of the new Company encouraged them in their efforts, and ensured them financial support among the influential men of the day. Yet the old Company had to pay for the piracies they committed in the Indian Ocean, and, as the Indian Government could hardly distinguish between the two English Companies, the former held the Company responsible for the damages sustained by their subjects, imprisoned their factors, and confiscated their goods. Nor were the Dutch idle. They tightened their grasp on commerce, captured several ships of the new association, and consolidated their former gains.[1]

The King was at last aroused to the gravity of the situation, and appointed a strong committee of the Privy Council to discuss the question. The opponents of the old Company attributed the decline in the trade to the mismanagement of the Company, advocated the plantation 'of Colonies in India after the Dutch model', and desired a Regulated rather than a Joint-Stock system. The chief profits, it was asserted, 'were taken up by some of the merchants, while the rest suffered more'.[2] The opponents agreed, however, upon the importance of the East India trade. The trade, says a writer, had continued for 35 years, and had profoundly modified the commerce of Europe; for whereas formerly England received East India commodities from the Mediterranean, the reverse was now the case.[3] If this trade were deserted, it would enrich the Hollanders, and make them 'very proud neighbours'.[4] Nor could the trade be thrown open, for no individual could afford the expense of sending out a ship and awaiting its return.[5] The only way out of the difficulty was the disavowal of the inter-

[1] Sainsbury, vol. vi; see fears of the East India trade being monopolized by the Dutch, pp. 139, 271, 272, 273 295, 303, 336, 341, &c.
[2] Ib., *passim*.
[3] Ib., pp. 270-4.
[4] Ib., p. 272.
[5] Ib., p. 273.

lopers, combined with the active support of the East India Company by the King. This had been suggested by the writer of a memorandum on the East India trade.[1] Nor did the intended plantations of Madagascar and Mauritius tend to end the dispute.[2]

The Committee presented its report in December, 1639.[3] The King, at last, threw over Courteen's Association; promised to revoke all the patents granted to it; to negotiate with the Dutch with regard to the reparation claimed by the Company; and, finally, to renew the Company's Charter as soon as a sufficient sum was subscribed.[4]

All these causes combined to make its position extremely difficult. The growth of the Company's trade up to 1624 has been traced above. From 1624 till the grant of a new Charter by the Protector, the Company was harassed by a series of misfortunes.

The competition of a rival Company, the lack of Charles's support, the divisions amongst the shareholders and the Civil War, all combined to reduce it to an extremely low condition. We get, in 1629, a valuable account of the Company's affairs in its Answer to Smethwick.[5] It appears that since their new Joint Stock the Company had sent out fifty-seven ships, containing 26,690 tons, besides eighteen pinnaces to be worn out by trading from port to port in the Indies. For relading these ships they sent in money and goods £1,145,442, and there had been raised in the Indies £289,643, in all £1,435,085. Again, the Company proved that 'a few months before', or about 1628, they had in Jacatra £1,100,000 ryals of 8, which, besides the stock sent afterwards, would have laded home 15 of their greatest ships and yielded here at least £1,100,000. Yet the difficulties they had to face were enormous. Their factors in the East could never employ more than 150,000 ryals in a year, owing to the siege of Bantam by the Dutch; their fort and house at Lagundy were so unhealthy that the Company were obliged to abandon them after the loss of 120 men; their house and warehouse at

[1] Ib., pp. 273-4.
[2] For Mauritius and Madagascar see Sainsbury, vol. vi, pp. 322, 323, 330, 338, 340.
[3] See the Report in Sainsbury, vol. vi, pp. 31-2.
[4] See the document in Sainsbury, vol. vi, p. 352.
[5] *Public Record Office, East Indies,* vol. iv, no. 65.

Batavia had cost 40,000 ryals. Moreover, the generality had not paid in above £40,000 per annum, whereas in former years they paid in £200,000 per annum. Consequently they had not only been forced to continue great sums at interest, but their credit failing upon the Company's seal, they had been forced to supply on their particular credit and bonds £80,000, whereby they were in debt £70,000 more than they had in England to pay. Their debt at interest in June 1628 was £230,000. In March 1629 it had increased to £300,000.[1] They had, moreover, £20,000 per annum interest to pay. Their Stock had fallen 20 per cent., and was not then worth more than £80.[2] During 1625–9 twenty-eight ships were laden by the East India Company and arrived in the East Indies. The Company built and purchased twelve ships to replace those which had been lost or laid up as unserviceable.[3]

The position of their factors was becoming intolerable. At Bantam the English were for a long time debarred from trade by the Dutch; at Batavia they had to spend 40,000 ryals in buying a house and building warehouses, which were afterwards ransacked, pulled down, and fired by the Dutch. They were also compelled to buy pepper and commodities at exorbitant prices.[4]

The Company's factors were insulted not only by the Dutch, but also by the Indian rulers. At Masulipatam the English factors protested against the conduct of the Indian Governor, and were eventually obliged to leave that place, and take all their goods with them.[5] At Surat the Company's factors were all imprisoned in irons 'to be the shameful subjects of daily threats, revilings, scorns and disdainful derisions of whole rabbles of people'.[6]

It is not therefore surprising that the Company, harassed by so many misfortunes, resolved to dissolve itself. Charles told them that if they would go on stoutly, like honest and worthy merchants, he would leave nothing undone that might encourage and countenance them. So they resolved to proceed in their

[1] *Court Minutes*, 5th June 1628; Sainsbury, vol. iv, p. 637.
[2] Sainsbury, vol. iv, nos. 283, 444, 555, 688.
[3] Ib., p. 730.
[4] Ib., pp. 500, 616, nos. 656, 693–5.
[5] Ib., no. 716.
[6] Ib., no. 56.

trade, and thereupon ordered that six stout ships be prepared, richly laden, to be set forth with all expedition.[1]

There is only one gleam that relieves the all-pervading gloom. The representations of the Company's factors in Persia had the effect of turning the attention of the Company to trade in that country, and of inducing many members to underwrite for large sums of money to furnish ships for voyages thither. The Shah's firmaund and contracts for silk, for which the Company were to deliver three parts in merchandise and one part in money, were the chief inducements to undertake these voyages.[2] It was resolved, moreover, that the ships should trade at Surat and Bantam, as well as in Persia. The total subscriptions for the new Stock amounted to £125,000.[3]

The hopes of the Company were at this time directed to Persia, where a profitable trade in silks had been promised. The Company devoted its energies to encouraging this great industry, and spent large sums in fitting out voyages to develop the trade. Altogether three voyages were fitted out. The profits reaped were sufficiently high to attract many of the shareholders of the Company's old Stock. But the two had no necessary connexion, and consequently the accounts of the voyages and the old Stock were separate. This involved such a confusion of accounts that at last it was resolved to turn over these voyages to the Third Joint Stock. Their valuation led to increased discussion and consequent weakness. At last, however, it was resolved to value the first Persian voyage at £160, the second at £180, and the third at £140 per cent. Moreover, as the adventurers in the first had already received their principal and £40 per cent, profit, and in the second their principal and £50 per cent. profit, the third was ordered to receive its principal, while the remains and profits of the said voyages were for the first £20 per cent., for the second £30 per cent., and £40 per cent. for the third.[4]

During the years 1629–35 the Company employed thirty-six ships to carry on their trade. Thirty-one ships arrived in the East Indies between 1629–34. Nine of the Company's vessels on their return to England were valued at £543,000. The principal lading

[1] Ib., nos. 162, 203, 250. [2] Ib., nos. 852, 857.
[3] *Court Book*, vol. xi, pp. 337–46, 2nd March 1629.
[4] *Court Minutes*, 3rd Oct. 1634, Book xv, pp. 57–64.

of six of them was pepper, cloves, and indigo, valued at £303,000. The silk contract with the Shah had resulted in large imports of that article.[1] Some light is thrown on the transactions of the Company by the following entry:—'After large debate and many arguments delivered on both sides, it was concluded to sell the whole of the pepper,' worth £150,000, 'to Daniel Harvey for transportation at 15½*d.* per lb. at 5, 6 months' time from the 1st November.'[2]

Another source of trouble to the Company was the increased demand for customs. A fresh 'book of rates' had been issued in July 1635, and came into force at the beginning of November 1636. In this new schedule the rateable price of pepper was trebled, although pepper had largely fallen in value. Its rateable price was advanced from 1*s.* 8*d.* to 5*s.* a lb., whereby the duty, being charged *ad valorem*, was raised from one penny to threepence, while the selling price had fallen from 2*s.* 6*d.* to 1*s.* 1*d.*, from which, deducting 6*d.* for freight and charges, there remained only 7*d.* as the net price, and only 4*d.*, after deducting the duty of 3*d.*, which thus appears to have been 75 per cent. of the real price.[3] A vigorous protest made to the Privy Council had no effect. To these losses must be added that caused to the Company by the Pepper Contract. This has been misrepresented by several historians. But, as Foster points out,[4] the transaction was perfectly valid, and the loan was granted on good security. The King bought 607,522 lb. of pepper for £63,283. 11*s.* 1*d.*, upon the security of Cottington, Pindar, and others. This was to be discharged by payments of £14,000 at intervals of six months. The pepper, when sold, realized only £50,626. 17*s.* 1*d.* Against this must be reckoned the interest which would have had to be paid for a loan of equal amount, and the net loss to the King on this transaction was, therefore, only £6,581. 0*s.* 10*d.* This was equivalent to borrowing the cash at about 17 per cent. It was really a good stroke of business. The security was ample, and the Company could prosecute the guarantors if the King refused to pay the amount. Only a small portion of the amount

[1] *Court Minutes*, 30th Aug. 1633, Book xiv, pp. 58-62.
[2] Ib., 20th Sept. 1633, Book xiv, pp. 86–91.
[3] Macpherson, p. 117.
[4] *English Historical Review*, July 1904.

was, however, actually repaid, and the Company had to bear considerable loss.

The East India trade received a great impetus by the decision of Charles to support it, though there is no reason to suppose that he completely severed his connexion with Courteen's Association. Even so, the Order in Council dated 10th December 1639 heartened the Company, and it tried to raise a new subscription. But owing to many discouragements, the flotation of a new Stock was hopeless. The outbreak of the Civil War rendered all charters conferred by the King liable to suspicion, nor was there any guarantee that these privileges would be respected. The Committees, therefore, fell back upon the plan of Particular Voyages, for little more than a year, on a separate subscription.[1] The response was not satisfactory, for the first list totalled only £65,000. Further subscriptions raised the sum to £80,450.[2] The Third Joint Stock was brought to a close on 14th October 1642. The remains were valued at 25 per cent. of the capital, apart from the amount which was hoped for from the Dutch, which would, if received, suffice to pay 12½ per cent. more. Adventurers were allowed to leave their division to form part of the capital of a new Fourth Stock, to which they might contribute any further sums they desired.[3] The response was fairly satisfactory.

There is a discrepancy between the total announced by the Governor on 28th August 1645 and that given by Jeremy Sambrooke.[4] The former placed it at £105,000, while the latter computed it at £104,540. The sum can hardly be regarded as satisfactory.

The years 1644–9 did not bring a return of prosperity. Courteen's Association was actively pursuing its rivalry with the older body. There were, moreover, other adventurers who traded on their own account. All that the Company could do was to launch another general voyage. The appeal met with a liberal response. The total amount actually received seems to have been £141,200.[5] Among the prominent subscribers we come across the familiar names of Maurice Thomson, Martin Noell, Andrews, and Blackman.

[1] Sainsbury, *Court Minutes*, 1640–3, pp. 187–8.
[2] Ib.
[3] Ib., pp. 276–8.
[4] Ib.
[5] Ib., 1644–9, pp. 271, 278.

The decay of the Company's trade during the period 1624–54 is the theme of a number of petitions to Parliament. A comparison of its trade in 1617 with that in 1643 will bring out prominently the low condition into which the Company had fallen. We catch a glimpse of the real difficulties by which it was surrounded in a series of papers in an Appendix to the Report of the Historical MSS. Commission.[1] The author states that the Company were resolved to divide and leave the trade. 'It is certain, as it is managed, it is a trade of loss to particular adventurers, and merchants will not prosecute a losing voyage.'[2] It is evident that the Company were quite in earnest when they declared their readiness to dissolve ('They dare not profess to dissolve, being fearful to offend His Majesty'). As regards the suggestion that the trade can be managed without a Joint Stock, the writer points out forcibly the disastrous consequence that would ensue. Another drawback from which the Company suffered was the existence of 'a rooted faction among them'. The existence of this faction is evidenced by a succession of disputes with the fantastic individual Smethwick.[3]

It was evident in face of such difficulties that the trade could hardly be carried on by the Company. It had tried to secure an ordinance from the Houses whereby exclusive trade would be guaranteed by Parliament. It is remarkable that the democratic House of Commons granted the request. On 5th December 1646,[4] it granted the Company exclusive trade in the regions extending from the Cape to Japan, provided that its membership remained open to any one willing to pay £5 for the privilege. Courteen and his partners were to withdraw their ships and goods within three years. An Act of Parliament was to be passed in due course to confirm the Company's privileges; and a new subscription was to be opened for continuing the trade. The Ordinance was, however, rejected by the Lords on 16th March 1647.[5] The Company was extremely disappointed. The

[1] *Third Report*, pp. 64 et seq. The papers are wrongly dated.
[2] Ib., pp. 64–5.
[3] See Foster's Introductions to *Court Minutes*, 1635–9, 1639–43, on Smethwick. Also Sainsbury, vol. v. And compare his petition, in Appendix to the *Fourth Report*, 1641, p. 71.
[4] *Journals of the House of Commons.*
[5] *Lords' Journals*, vol. ix, p. 81; Historical MSS. Commission, *Appendix to the Sixth Report*, p. 143 b.

Governor thought that it would be best to draw home their factors and goods, for 'if every one was to be allowed to go to the Indies, depredations would be committed for which the Company would be held responsible by the Authorities there, and great loss would result'.[1] Other petitions were sent, but they do not seem to have borne fruit, and the abolition of the House of Lords on 6th February 1649 introduced further complications.[2]

The main cause of the decline of the Company was the policy of Charles I. Civil war was, no doubt, one of the causes, but its decline was due primarily to the policy of the King himself. The Company was ready to dissolve long before the outbreak of the Civil War, and was persuaded to carry on the trade mainly because it feared 'His Majesty's dread'.[3] The history of the Company shows the disastrous effects of the inaction of the King. Mainly through his lack of support, the powerful body that was once the wonder and envy of foreigners had been reduced to insignificance.

The history of the Company enables us to appreciate at their due weight the theories of the economists of the period. The merchants desired consistent pursuit of a policy with definite, objective aims. The foreign trade could be maintained only by the protection accorded by the State. The State was called upon to represent them in their dealings with foreign powers, to exclude their rivals from a share in the English and Plantation trades, and to redress their grievances by every means at its disposal. Hence the exaggerated importance which Mun attached to the employment of various devices for the destruction of the Dutch monopoly. The movement originated by Mun was carried on by Robinson.[4] The pamphlet throws strong light on the burning questions of the day, and, while advocating many reforms desired by Mun, Misselden, Childe, and others, such as the establishment of a merchants' court, the permission to import foreign commodities, 'which we are in need of', and the institution of a State bank, on the model of the Bank of Amsterdam,

[1] *Court Minutes*, 19th March 1647, pp. 196–7.

[2] See the Papers from the Company in the *Appendix to the Sixth Report of the Historical MSS. Commission*, p. 194.

[3] Ib.

[4] *England's Safety in Trade's Increase. Most humbly presented to the High Court of Parliament*, 1641. Brit. Mus. E. 167 (5).

it strikes a completely new note. Mun had urged that the East India trade could never be carried on without the support of the Crown. Robinson's merit lies in his logical development of Mun's theories. 'If we suffer them (the Hollanders) to beat us quite out of the Indies, we must not only lose the Trade we drive in other parts with the advance of East India commodities and pay dear for what we spend ourselves, but so soon as they begin to practise, the rest of our trade in the Mediterranean will as fast decline ; the Hollanders' cheap freights being able of itself to eat us out in time, without any other stratagem or plot.'[1] The reason was that 'the Hollanders' policy of State desires nothing so much as to weary (us) out, and constrain us to abandon it'.[2] The State alone could prevent the utter extirpation of the English from the East. 'For proving there (in the East Indies) too weak, it may here be righted by His Majesty. Otherwise, nothing will certainly keep the Hollanders from attempting utter extirpation.' Nor will the opening of the East India trade, as advocated by some, be of any use. For 'if the Hollanders can countermine a whole society, so well settled, so well governed, with so great a Stock, what may be expected from ordinary private merchants? The Hollanders will have so much advantage over them, and they not being otherwise able to make a voyage, at once turn pirates, and prey one another.' Hence, the necessity for a Corporation. 'A Corporation it must be, and a powerful one too, that follows this trade, able to plant Colonies by degrees, and make head in the Indies, if need be, against the Hollanders' encroachments.' 'We must have Colonies established up and down where their shipping may be sure of relief in their distress.' Not only, however, is the conception of the East India trade widened, but the duties of the State as regards commerce are also modified. The Company may prove weak in the East, 'but it may be righted here, by His Majesty'. But this change in the king's policy towards the rivals of England must be accompanied by a change of his attitude towards the East India Company. 'There must be His Majesty's protection of the East India Company, whereby they may regain that trade, and settle another in Persia.' The king must maintain a watchful eye over the Dutch, and threaten war if they refuse to limit their

[1] *England's Safety in Trade's Increase*, p. 22. [2] Ib., p. 24.

'armaments'. 'England must procure that other States rest content with only such a number of men of war, as may not make us with just cause suspect their strength and force.' This startling proposal is followed by another equally startling. The East India trade must be made thoroughly national. If merchants cannot be found, 'then His Majesty and the nation may have a just cause to keep it up, though it were to lose at first; and if all means fail, moneys levied for maintaining it against the Dutch'. The complaint was echoed by Lewes Roberts.[1] Roberts defended the exportation of bullion on substantially the same grounds as those stated by Mun, Malynes, and Digges.[2] He thought that the decline of the Company was due to the want of timely protection and encouragement from the State. 'This had reduced them to that bad point and low pressure wherein we observe them to be.'[3]

In Robinson we find the culmination of the movement that had been carried on by Raleigh, Mun, Tobias Gentleman, Malynes, and others.[4] He carries out to their logical conclusion the theories propounded by Mun. The East India trade was to be taken over by the State, and carried on for the benefit of the nation. Its commercial rivals were not to be allowed to maintain more than a fixed number of men-of-war, and if they exceeded the number England was to declare war and reduce their ships within proper limits. Again, all the subjects of the king, 'if wronged there', 'were to be righted here by the State'. This idea of the duties of the State was not novel. It had been acted upon by the Dutch, and, to a certain extent, by James I in 1623–4. But Charles I had totally neglected to perform any one of the duties mentioned by Robinson. Mun had combined the foreign trade and the East India trade into an organic whole. Both, however, were dependent upon the State's support. Hence, in Robinson's suggestions, the State becomes the apex of the system. It initiates measures, declares war against its commercial rivals, and redresses the grievances of its subjects.

The First Dutch War would, therefore, be inexplicable without a due understanding of the above theories. The merchants

[1] The *Treasure of the Traffike*. MacCulloch's *Collection of Scarce Tracts on Commerce*, p. 105.
[2] Ib., pp. 65–8. [3] Ib., p. 105.
[4] See above on the Anglo-Dutch rivalry.

desired complete protection from the State, and called upon the latter to redress their grievances by declaring war. Charles I and James I were too weak to carry this policy into effect. Their weakness at home made a vigorous foreign policy impossible. The establishment of the Commonwealth produced a mass of literature on commerce. The victorious Republic, though still an outcast among nations, could not be ignored. It supplied, in an eminent degree, that element which was wanting in the foreign policies of James and Charles I. This element was the element of vigour. Only by the vigorous pursuit of the material interests of the nation could the rights of the English merchants be safeguarded. The economic pamphlets of the times are characterized by the same outlook. The theories of Robinson and Roberts will be quite unintelligible unless the exact condition of the East India trade is rightly understood.

The East India trade between 1640–54 supplied a very useful commentary on the above theories. The competition of Courteen's Association, and later, Assada Merchants, the depredations of the pirates, the raising of the Customs duties, and the factious opposition, had all contributed to depress the trade and the Company. Their debt in 1640 was £250,000 or over, and it was still growing. They could not raise more than £22,500 for their new Joint Stock. Nor were their petitions to Parliament of any avail. The Governor of the Company proposed to inform the King, in 1641, 'that the discouragements to the Company had so disheartened the Adventurers that the trade is likely to come to a standstill'.[1] The enormous increase in private trade arose naturally out of the loosening of the hands of authority. The Charter of the Company had been granted by the King against whom the Parliament was waging a deadly war. The Levellers would dislike its authority.[2]

[1] Sainsbury, vol. vii, p. 132. Compare also pp. 24, 32, 51, 53, 132, 178.

[2] See Firth, Introduction to *Clarke Papers*, *Cromwell's Army*, chapter on 'Politics in the Army'; Gooch, *English Democratic Ideas in the seventeenth century*, pp. 206-26. Political naturally led to social equality, and we are therefore quite prepared to find the 'Anabaptists' and Levellers as opponents of the monopoly of the East India Company. There is hardly any mention of the East India Company among the economic theories of the period. Yet what little there is seems to confirm the view. Many of the Cromwellian soldiers went out to India. Evelyn said that the refusal of some members to take the oath prescribed by the Charter was due to the 'Anabaptists', whose object was to be able to continue their private trade to the East.

Though Courteen's son had lost all his money, and was now a fugitive, his place was taken by a group of West India merchants, headed by Martin Noell and Maurice Thomson.[1] As the trade to the East Indies was now practically open, and any adventurous merchant might charter a ship and trade there, the Assada merchants had fully taken advantage of the freedom and had sent several ships. They were, therefore, opposed to the grant of a charter that would prohibit them from venturing on the Indian Ocean, and would empower the East India Company to confiscate their goods. They were, moreover, desirous of establishing plantations at Assada, as that would, in their opinion, provide them with a centre of lucrative commerce with East Africa, Asia, and even America. Moreover, they wanted to extend the sphere of the Company's activity to Guinea, China, and Japan. Nor did they regard the management of the Company as thoroughly satisfactory. 'A Joint Stock has produced neither profit nor encouragement to the Adventurers.' The liberty of trade followed as a corollary from the grant of political liberty 'and they considered that the prohibition was absolutely against the national liberties'.[2] They, therefore, advocated 'a free, well regulated trade' rather than a Joint Stock. This advocacy of the freedom of trade was not novel, and as early as the reign of Elizabeth Cecil had denounced those who would take away the Englishman's 'natural right of trade'.[3]

What was entirely novel, however, was the change in the opinion on commerce in general, and the East India trade in particular. The State now assumes the functions which were exercised with so much success by the central government under Charles II. Nor could Noell have failed to mould Cromwell's opinion on the subject.[4] The Company could hardly reject all the proposals put forward by the Assada merchants. Its trade had declined; it had lost many ships in the war; and it had, finally, some of those merchants on its own Committee. It was, however, very suspicious of the ultimate success of the rash

[1] See Andrews, *British Committee of Trade*, an account of Noell and Povey; Sainsbury, *Calendar of State Papers, West Indies*, 1570–1660. Several references to Thomson in Sainsbury, vols. viii, ix, x.

[2] *Public Record Office*, C. O. 77, vol. vii, no. 6, cited here as C. O.

[3] Cunningham, vol. ii. Compare Prothero, *Statutes*, Discussion on Monopolies, 1601.

[4] Andrews, *op. cit.*

projects of Thomson, nor was it convinced that Assada could be made profitable to the adventurers.[1] 'It desired a settled factory as much as any,' but it rightly pointed out that its successful execution would require money, which it did not possess in abundance. It was prepared, however, to concede the other propositions, and an agreement was therefore arrived at.[2]

Under this agreement, the amount of stock to be raised was fixed at £300,000, and the question of the form of government for the future Company was left to the decision of the future shareholders. The plantation at Assada was to be proceeded with, while a settled, fortified habitation 'in India was to be established as soon as possible'.[3] The amalgamation of the two Companies facilitated the ratification of the agreement by the Parliament, and the Company was secured against further attacks by the resolution of Parliament that 'the East India Trade be carried on by one Company with one Joint Stock, and the management thereof be under a regulation in such a manner as the Parliament shall think fit'.[4] Though the subscription to the new Joint Stock did not bring in more than £200,000, it may be regarded as fairly satisfactory. The United Stock thus formed, in 1650, had been heavily subscribed by the Assada merchants, and they claimed a share in the management of the Company.[5] It was now decided to appoint two sets of Committees, one for each body. The United Joint Stock chose thirteen of its members. One of them was Thomson.[6] Thomson's policy aimed at the complete transformation of the Company into a Regulated Company, planting colonies after the Dutch model, allowing every adventurer who desired to trade in the East, upon payment of a fee, and extending its commerce to Japan, China, and Guinea. He was backed up by many shareholders, and at the General Meeting held on 10th May 1654 considerable diversity of opinion was manifested on the subject. The Thomson party advocated the reorganization of the Company on a broader

[1] *Public Record Office*, C. O. 77, vol. vii, no. 8.

[2] Compare the *Agreement*, C. O. 77, vol. vii, no. 9.

[3] Ib.

[4] *Commons' Journals*, vol. vi, p. 253.

[5] Professor Scott's statement (pp. 120–1, *Constitution of Joint Stock Companies*, vol. ii) that the capital subscribed was only £125,000, is based on inadequate information. See Foster's Introduction to Sainsbury, vol. ix.

[6] Sainsbury, vol. ix, pp. 49, 113, 182, 257, 331.

basis, though the Committee appointed reported in favour of the Joint-Stock system.[1] Thomson, however, was not dismayed. The Company's petition to Cromwell, praying him to confirm the Company's charter and to prohibit interloping ships from trading to India, was replied to by the party in a series of petitions to the Council and the Protector.[2] His strength lay in the unification of the various grievances, and the utilization of the latter in his own interests. The Leveller, the city merchant excluded from the Company, the Puritan soldier who had fought against the King, would unite in condemning a Company that had been founded on a charter granted by a king, and that excluded every other English merchant from a share in the trade. A regulated trade would, on the other hand, encourage 'industry and ingenuity, and afford latitude and scope for both, every one having the ordering of his own business'. It would, moreover, increase the number of traders, and would give opportunity to all to adventure their estate at any time. 'This regulated way of trade will give some advantage over the Dutch, as going at less charge and having more opportunity to improve the industry of the managers in India.'[3] It was the Joint-Stock system that was the cause of the decline of trade. The lack of profit, the want of success, and the decay were all due to the exclusive monopoly of the East India Company.

The State was now regarded by both parties as the sole instrument whereby the East India trade could be effectively carried on. Robinson had suggested the nationalization of the East India trade. Under Cromwell the functions assigned to the State are widened. 'Without the protection and countenance of the State', says a petition of the East India Company, 'no man can promise himself safety or profit in the India Trade.'[4] This is expressed in the most thoroughgoing manner by a writer of the time. The State was to undertake the management of the East India trade. The writer thought that '£200,000 would carry it'. If it was not carried by the State, but by the Company, the result would be that 'these would serve the nation

[1] Ib., pp. 314, 324.
[2] Ib., pp. 340, 352–5, 364, 373; vol. x, pp. 122–6, 142, 143.
[3] Ib., p. 122.
[4] *Public Record Office*, C. O. 77, vol. vii, no. 85.

with what they please, at what price they please, and if they alone be allowed to trade in Spices, they can make what profit they like'.[1] 'Without assistance from His Highness and the State, nothing can do any good to the trade.'

This feature is common to nearly all the pamphlets of the period. The State is regarded as the means whereby the wishes of the authors can be realized. Perhaps the new ideas were nowhere better expressed than in Wylde's tract on the East India trade.[2] It is headed a 'Remonstrance to the Lord Protector'. Wylde urges the Protector to apply *lex talionis* to the Dutch, 'whom to turn out of those trades will be but what they have long laboured at, and had even now effected it, had not your Highness beaten them into better manners here at home'. The Dutch were to be 'beaten into better manners'. This was not all. The Portuguese, too, should be compelled to disgorge some of their ill-gotten wealth in the East. His Highness should acquire a 'commodious harbour in India; and should secure the town of Dieu from the inhabitants thereof'. The Great Mogul was to be offered an alliance, and he will 'willingly embrace an offer of aiding him by sea in his war against' the King of Bijapur. Nor should the Molucca and Banda islands be neglected, as the state of the Dutch garrisons there was little better than that of slaves. They would, asserted Wylde, be only too glad to come under Cromwell's protection. Wylde knew that the East India Company was totally unable to carry such a comprehensive scheme into effect. He therefore urged the Protector to raise a National Stock of a million sterling. All classes were to subscribe to it, and all the counties were to provide their quota. The East Indian commodities were to be allowed entry into the plantations, and 'Calicoes, and diverse sorts of stuffs, made in India, and very proper for the hot countries', were to be imported into Barbadoes.

This comprehensive scheme was not carried into effect, because the Protector was busy elsewhere. That the remonstrance of Wylde had some effect is evident from the following document: 'Having with all respect and thankfulness considered His Highness's intention to endeavour the settlement of a national interest

[1] *Public Record Office*, C. O. 77, vol. vii, no. 79.
[2] Brit. Mus., Sloane MSS., 3271, A.D. 1654.

in India, the East India Company propose, as places most convenient, the town of Bassein, with the port Bone-Bay.'[1] Moreover, a letter in Thurloe[2] says that the news of the Protector's resolution to dissolve the East India Company 'had produced consternation among the merchants at Amsterdam'.

The Company's answer to its critics was not different, so far as the protection of the State was concerned. Both parties were unanimous upon that point. The decay of trade, which the Thomson party attributed to the Joint-Stock system, was asserted by the Company to be due to the want of that system. The Company claimed that it had steadied the prices and done away with 'cut-throat' competition.[3] The results of the open trade had by no means been happy. Cloth, which was bought formerly for 10*s.*, cost 16*s.* 4*d.* at the time. The ships of private merchants were competing frantically with one another in the Eastern ports, with the result that they were being forced to sell and buy at whatever rates the Indian merchants demanded.[4] A letter from Madras[5] says that in 1656 the price of coarse saltpetre in Bengal was more than double that of the refined sort in 1655, owing to the competition of English ships, 'striving to outvy one another both in price and presents'.[6] This account is confirmed by the author of *Britannia Languens*. 'Whilst the trade was open, in the years 54, 55, and 56, our merchants sold the Indian commodities so low that they furnished more parts of Europe then since we have done, nay, Holland and Amsterdam itself.'[7] Pollexfen asserted—in 1680—that during the time when the trade was open, the prices of the East India commodities went down considerably.

The Company, therefore, were completely justified in pointing out the consequences of the open trade in the East. They asserted that if the trade were laid open, 'there will be many sellers, all anxious to dispose their merchandise, thereby cheapening the price and raising that of Indian commodities'. Again,

[1] *Public Record Office*, C. O. 77, vol. vii, no. 92.

[2] *State Papers*, vol. iii, p. 80. Compare Firth's chapters x, xv, xvi, in *The Last Years of the Protectorate*.

[3] Sainsbury, vol. ix, pp. 6, 357–60; vol. x, pp. 129–34, 137, 139, 142.

[4] Foster, Introduction to *Court Minutes*, 1655–9, p. xii.

[5] O. C. 2610, quoted by Foster.

[6] Ib.

[7] *Britannia Languens* (MacCulloch, *Collection of Economic Tracts*).

if it were not united, it would be 'subject to the affronts and oppressions of other nations, to which, having to do with fourteen sovereign princes and with the Dutch and Portuguese as competitors, it is very liable'.[1] Perhaps the most remarkable defence was that made by 'Samuel Lamb' of London.[2] The pamphlet is characterized by the breadth of view which is such a distinguishing trait of the period. The writer pleads for many reforms, and is specially enthusiastic in his description of the Dutch banks. He gives many reasons for the successes of the Dutch. The main reason, however, is the policy of their statesmen. Many of them are merchants in present trade, 'or have been bred so in their minorities'.[3] He praises their good customs, 'their care and their vigilancy'. 'The chief and considerable way, by which they have wrought themselves what they are, are banks.' Lamb then discusses the advantages that England would derive from the institution of banks and Merchants' Courts. This, however, would not remove the Dutch menace. The English merchants must be prepared to strike hard. Otherwise, 'the studious industry of our neighbours in Holland will soon overbalance us, if not timely prevented'. 'As the Spaniard aims to get the universal monarchy of Christendom, so the Hollander the universal trade, not only of Christendom, but of all the known world.'[4] This was apparent from the condition of the East India Company. The East India Company had employed in that time 15,000 tons of shipping, 'but they were so decayed, through the undermining of the Dutch, that they had hardly one ship remaining at their giving over'. Hence, the Company ought to be encouraged by the Protector and given a charter. The Joint Stock was the only organization that is suitable for the purpose. In this pamphlet we see how the various causes interacted on one another. 'The nation which hath most warlike shipping and mariners will command in chief at sea; and he that commands the sea may command in trade; and he that commands the trade will have the most money.'[5]

The policy of Cromwell has been differently stated. Hunter

[1] *Public Record Office*, C. O. 77, vol. viii, no. 46.

[2] *Seasonable Observations humbly offered to His Highness*, 1658: *Somers Tracts*, vol. vi, pp. 446–65.

[3] Ib., p. 452.

[4] Ib., p. 448.

[5] Ib., p. 462.

thought Cromwell took a personal interest in the East India Company. But the information we possess does not justify us in holding this view. He seems to have regarded it as a purely private concern, and he was not inclined to meddle with any private business.[1] He was no doubt busy at the time (1651), and the Company's tactless petitions could hardly be entertained favourably by a stranger. He was a friend of Martin Noell,[2] and was no doubt guided by his policy. Noell himself was a busy West Indian merchant, and had taken a leading part in the opposition to the Company.[3] He was a determined opponent of the Joint-Stock system, and the Protector no doubt favoured the idea of the establishment of a national interest. The authorities cited above seem to confirm the view. He may well have disliked the monopoly exercised by the Company. He certainly granted commissions to 'many private ships' with the consequence, as the Company complained in a petition to the Protector in 1656, 'that the price of native goods in India had been raised 40 or 50 per cent., while that of English ships had been lowered'.[4] There are numbers of references to the licences granted at the time to private merchants in the *Calendars of State Papers, Domestic Series*. We may conclude, therefore, that the Protector favoured the policy of Noell. His 'astounding' proposal to the Dutch Commissioners about the partition of Asia and America has been discussed by Dr. Gardiner.[5] It shows that the Protector's knowledge of those countries was, to say the least, very superficial.

The Company was, however, in a critical situation at the time. Its trade had declined; interlopers were underselling English goods in the East, and carrying on an insecure trade by resorting to questionable devices. The markets were glutted with Eastern commodities and the owners were obliged to send the surplus to continental countries, including Holland, where the cheap rates at which the goods were offered depressed the shares of the Dutch East India Company.[6]

[1] Sainsbury, vol. ix, p. 124. [2] Andrews, *British Committees of Trade*.

[3] There are several references to Noell in Andrews and *State Papers, West Indies*, op. cit.

[4] *Public Record Office*, C. O. 77, vol. viii, no. 39.

[5] *Commonwealth and Protectorate*, vol. ii.

[6] *Britannia Languens*, in MacCulloch's *Collection*.

The Company had made several attempts to obtain a confirmation of their charter from the Protector. There was, however, no sign of the Protector and his Council coming to a decision regarding the trade. At last, on 14th October 1656, the Committees of the United Joint Stock resolved to propose to their shareholders that the Company's privileges in the East should be sold for £14,000 to 'some Englishmen'.[1] It was decided, however, to make one more effort, and a fresh petition was therefore presented on 20th October. It was referred by the Council to a Committee of eight of their members, with Colonel Philip Jones as chairman. This did not, however, settle the difficulty. The year 1656 wore on, and nothing was accomplished. The Company grew desperate and resolved, at a general meeting held in January 1657, to appoint a sale on 14th February of all their rights and properties in the Indies, and bills were ordered to be set up on the Exchange notifying their intention.[2] The threat had the desired effect. Even Noell fell into line with the Company's policy, and a charter was granted in 1657.[3] 'It confirmed all privileges and immunities granted by James and added fresh ones.'[4] Perhaps this is all that we are entitled to say about it, as it was suppressed by the Company immediately after the Restoration. It had, however, one important result. The vexed question of organization that had troubled the Company for more than ten years was at last settled. The Company was granted an exclusive monopoly of the trade in the East and was allowed to fortify and plant in any of its settlements. The grant had immediate effects. The money subscribed for a new stock 'exceeded all expectation'. The total was £739,782. The amount subscribed shows the increasing popularity of the East India trade. It is, moreover, a testimony to the soundness of the Joint Stock organization in the seventeenth century. The people were not willing to invest considerably in an institution whose existence was threatened either by a domestic or by a foreign rival. The amount proved, however, to be more than the Company could immediately use with any prospect of profit.

[1] *Court Book*, vol. xxiii, 14th Oct. 1656.
[2] Ib., p. 556.
[3] For Cromwell's Charter see Foster's Introduction, *Court Minutes*, 1654–9.
[4] Foster, op. cit., p. xvii.

Consequently, after the first two instalments, aggregating 25 per cent., had been collected, it was decided to reduce the next two payments to 12½ per cent. each; and the rest of the capital was never called in. The capital of the New General Stock was therefore a little under £370,000.[1]

The Committees of the Company set to work to push the trade with vigour. In December 1657 it was agreed that the lease held by the Guinea Company should be transferred to the East India Company for £1,30c. Numerous ships were sent out to the East.[2] The Company's sphere of activity was widened. Two English vessels reached Canton in safety, and returned to England in 1659.

This wonderful revival of the East India Company testified to the vigour of the Protector's foreign policy. There is no evidence to prove that he took a personal interest therein. The East India merchants do not seem to have been consulted in the course of his negotiations with the Dutch for peace. They remained in the background. They reaped, however, the benefits that accrued from the Treaty of Westminster, 5th April 1654. The treaty provided, among other things, that the Dutch were to punish those who had been responsible for the Massacre of Amboyna, and that all claims for losses prior to the outbreak of the war were to be referred to a Joint Anglo-Dutch Commission. The English Company's claim for £2,696,000 was no less fantastic than those of the Dutch Company, who claimed £2,920,000. The English Company was ultimately awarded £85,000, and was also given back Pularoon. The Company, however, was obliged to lend £50,000 to the State. On 26th October 1656 it was obliged to lend £10,000 to the Commissioners of Customs. The total amount which the State owed has been calculated by Mr. Foster[3] at £46,000. There is no reason to believe that the money was ever repaid.

But the disadvantages of these measures were more than counterbalanced by the vigour of the Protector's foreign policy. The Company had gained what Mun desired. Its most serious rivals had been totally defeated and its trade protected by the

[1] *Court Book*, vol. xxiv, p. 114, 29th June 1658.
[2] Foster's Introduction, *Court Minutes*, 1655–9, p. xxiii.
[3] *Court Minutes*, 1655–9, p. vi.

State. Cromwell himself did not like the Dutch war,[1] yet he was obliged to carry it on for the maintenance of the material interests of the merchants. It was the merchants demanding redress for various grievances against the Dutch, grievances that had been accumulating for over half a century, that compelled him to fight the Dutch to the bitter end. The causes of the rivalry have already been mentioned.[2] The war would have been declared long ago, if a vigorous foreign policy had been possible at the time. It is for this reason that Cromwell may be called the founder of the mercantile system. It is this intimate connexion of the foreign policy of the Protector with, and its effect on, the maintenance of the East India trade that is so characteristic of the Cromwellian period. The Protector himself may not have been conscious of this.[3] He certainly disliked the Dutch because they preferred commercial advantages. Yet the bold outline of his policy is quite clear. By employing the total resources of a vigorous State against the Dutch in the interests of commerce and navigation, it facilitated the Protectionism of Charles II and the Colbertism of the Whigs.[4]

[1] Gardiner, *Commonwealth and Protectorate*, chap. xxx, p. 341.

[2] See above, on the naval rivalry and the herring fishery.

[3] See especially his speech to his Parliament, in Carlyle's *Letters and Speeches*.

[4] Compare Ranke, *History of England*, vol. iii, and Gardiner, op. cit., with Cunningham, op. cit., sections 183–4; Wolff, Introduction to Manesseh Ben Israel; Beer, 'Cromwell's Economic Policy', in *Political Science Quarterly*, vols. xii, xvii; Andrews, *British Committees of Trade*, op. cit.; Foster's Introductions to *Court Minutes*, 1650–4 and 1655–9; Firth, *The Last Years of the Protectorate*, chapters x, xv, and xvi. Compare the pamphlets cited above, on the naval rivalry with the Dutch, and on the question of the herring fishery.

II

THE COMPANY UNDER CHARLES II

THE activity of the East India Company under Cromwell had been considerably increased. It was due, however, only indirectly to the Protector. In so far as his vigorous foreign policy crushed the most serious rivals of the Company, it was undoubtedly beneficial to that body. Without it, the latter was helpless. Yet there was no direct encouragement of the East India Company and trade. Its importance had no doubt been borne in upon him by a series of pamphlets. Yet the latter do not seem to have resulted in increased active support on the part of the Government.

Under Charles II commerce and industry became the chief ends of foreign policy. The latter was influenced, no doubt, by other considerations. Charles's personal likes and dislikes could hardly be left out of account. They determined to a limited extent the course along which the foreign policy had to travel. But the main object, throughout, was the maintenance, and, if possible, extension of English commerce. This is especially noticeable as regards the two Dutch Wars. 'Upon the King's first arrival in England', says Clarendon, 'he manifested a very great desire to improve the general traffic and trade of the nation and upon all occasions conferred with the most active merchants upon it, and offered all that he could contribute to the advancement thereof.'

The Committee of Trade, and the Council for Plantations, instituted by Charles II, expressed in a concrete form the leading ideas of the Restoration period; their multifarious activity, their thoroughly representative character, their far-reaching measures, have all been ably discussed by Dr. Cunningham and Professor Andrews. It was, however, in their dealings with the East India Company that their policy is truly displayed. The low state into which the Company had been brought by the open trade under the Commonwealth, and the injurious restrictions on the exportation of bullion to the East Indies, had reduced the Company to impotence. The Council of Trade dealt with the latter in 1660. They recognized that 'there are some trades that in part cannot be driven or managed to any profit but by exporting money or bullion, as the East India do'. Nor could prohibition be justified, since the 'exportation of £100,000 per annum will purchase so much goods as do usually yield in England £300,000. One-third thereof is paid as the salary and wages, &c.; one-third serveth for the consumption of these kingdoms; the last third, as also the first third, are both exported to the Mediterranean, Spain, France, the Baltic, and other parts, where the proceeds of them serve to purchase foreign commodities for us and helps so far to the balance of our trade.' Moreover, 'if we did not follow the East India Trade, the Hollanders will derive from us at least £300,000 for the East India Commodities that we must have from them'.[1] These recommendations were carried into effect by the passing of a Statute in 1663.

The adoption of the policy which had been urged by Mun and Digges, forty years before, profoundly modified the entire economic structure of the East India Company. The prohibition of the exportation would have resulted in the loss of the East India trade, the extinction of the East India Company, and the overthrow of the English in the East. Trade without bullion was an impossibility, and the injurious restrictions imposed in the preceding reign had brought prominently into light the fatal consequences of the narrow policy.

The rapid growth of the East India trade under Charles II, and the gradual extension of the Company's influence in India, were due, to a great extent, to the wise policy initiated by the Council. The real character of this most important institution was pointed out, for the first time, by Dr. Cunningham. Professor Andrews supplied us with valuable information later on.[2] The

[1] MacCulloch, *Scarce and Valuable Tracts on Money*, pp. 130–6.

[2] *Committees of Trade and Plantations.* Dr. W. A. Shaw's masterly *Introductions to the Treasury Papers* have gone a long way towards vindicating the administrative machinery of the Government. The *Acts of the Privy Council of England*, vol. i, 1613–80, edited by Messrs. Munro & Grant, throw fresh light on many problems of Colonial administration. Dr. Percy

Council for Trade and Plantations came to an end in 1665, and for some years the Company's petitions were dealt with by the Privy Council and its Committees. In 1668 the system of Standing Committees seems to have been reorganized, and the Committees for Trade and Plantations consisted of fourteen members. In 1668 a Council of Trade was appointed, and, on 30th July 1670, a Council of Plantations. These two bodies were united in 1672. In 1674, however, their commissions were revoked by the King. This was due, perhaps, to the representations of Danby, who was instituting various economies in the Royal Household. Clarendon's account of the Council of Trade [1] can hardly be accepted in its entirety. He was certainly a biassed observer, and though he was a vigorous colonial administrator, he does not seem to have instituted any far-reaching colonial reforms.[2]

This ignorance of the work of the Council was not confined to Clarendon. Other writers of the period give us fantastic accounts of the mysterious body. We cannot rely upon them for a true presentation of the real character of the work performed by the Councils for Trade and Plantations. The best evidence of the utility of their work is to be found in the minutes of their meetings. The entries and minutes relating to the East India Company are specially noteworthy. The question of Bombay

Kaye's *Colonial Administration under Clarendon*, in Johns Hopkins University Studies, Series XXIII, nos. 5–6, discusses the effects of the Acts of Navigation. Professor Scott's *Joint Stock Companies*, vol. i, chapters xiv and xv, pp. 263–311, is full of valuable information on many important points.

The Minutes of the Committee of Trade, 1660–2, Brit. Mus. Add. MSS. 25115, ff. 44, &c., bring out the importance of many of the subjects which the Committee was called upon to decide. The *Reports of the Historical MSS. Commission* contain some of these minutes. The Appendix to the *Eighth Report of the Historical MSS. Commission*, pp. 133–4, contains minutes of proceedings of the Committee appointed to consider the causes and grounds of the fall of rents and decay of trade, 28th October 1669. The *Public Record Office*, C.O. 77, vol. xlix, contains many entries and minutes of the Committee, and is especially valuable for the period. The information the volume supplies us with is, however, insignificant in comparison with that afforded by the vols. viii–xv in the same series. Every aspect of the Company's policy is there treated with remarkable thoroughness. Nothing is more striking than a comparison of these volumes in the Record Office with the small bundle of the unbound papers that deal with the period 1689–1700.

[1] *Clarendon's Life*, Oxford, 1827: 'He erected a Council of Trade which produced little other effect than the opportunity of men's speaking together, which possibly disposed them to think more,' p. 234.

[2] See Kaye, *Colonial Administration under Clarendon*, Johns Hopkins University Studies.

was a source of constant trouble. The Portuguese claimed that the islands of Tanna and Carinjah were not included in their original grant of Bombay. They therefore levied vexatious tolls and other dues on the English ships, and annoyed them in various other ways. A dispatch to Mr. Parry, the English agent at Lisbon, requested him to make representations to the Portuguese king and to threaten him that if these annoyances did not cease, the English would be compelled to take effectual steps for their prevention. The dispatch added the following: 'They are entitled to it by law of nature.' The law of nature here referred to is not the law of nature which Rousseau praised but the law of nature which Hobbes has painted in sombre colours.

This was not, however, the end of the business. There were charges, counter-charges, replies, rejoinders to replies. Old Lord Clarendon is hunted up in his retreat to find out whether he has got the original map. Sir Robert Southwell, however, informs his Lordship that the original map cannot be found. The subject drags on. The Portuguese ambassador had referred to the case of a Portuguese, Perez, whose estate had been confiscated by the Company for desertion, and had grounded his refusal to deliver the islands mainly upon that account. We find several entries: 'On the 15th March 1677 the Lords order a letter to be written to W. Thomson, Governor of the East India Company, touching Perez as follows.' Here follows the letter. The next entry is no less interesting: 'On the 16th March their Lordships order an Account to be given to Mr. Coventry of what had passed in relation to Perez, to the end that Mr. Parry', the English agent at Lisbon, 'may be informed thereof according to the letter following.' [1]

Another feature of the Council and Committees for Trade is their influence on the foreign policy of the Crown. Foreign policy now becomes the means whereby the commercial privileges of English merchants are maintained. Herein lies its supreme importance. It embodied the demands of the English merchants for an energetic assertion of their privileges by force of arms. The conscious employment of the whole power of the State for

[1] *Public Record Office*, C.O. 77, vol. xlix; *Entries relating to the East India Company*, pp. 239, 245. Nearly half the volume treats of nothing else but the Bombay business.

maintaining the rights of the East India Company against the Dutch was effected only under Charles II. For more than forty years the East India merchants had urged upon the Central Government the absolute necessity of coupling plenty with power, of making war commercially and militarily against their most determined rivals in the East. Cromwell's war against the Dutch had been successful in the East to a certain extent. They had not, however, been totally crushed. Their supremacy in the East India Islands was no less galling to the national pride than their monopoly of the spices. The importance of the Council and Committee lie in their intimate connexion with the Executive. They were a thoroughly representative body and included the most prominent merchants of the time.[1] An essential feature of their dealings with the East India Company was their advice to the King on all subjects connected with the trade. Here, foreign policy is conceived as the best instrument whereby the trade can be preserved. If the East India Company's goods are prohibited in Spain, a petition to the Council or Committee results in a dispatch to the English ambassador there, requesting him to make a representation to the Spanish king. The English agent at Lisbon receives a series of dispatches from Coventry. Sir George Downing is requested again and again to make vigorous protests to the States-General on many of the subjects then in dispute. Childe's frequent letters to the Lords of Trade, requesting the latter 'to show more honour to the King of Bantam's ambassador', and the flowery letters of the King himself serve only to heighten the impression produced from the study of the documents.[2]

The Council and the Committee become the organ through

[1] Compare Charles's letter to the City of London. His Majesty requested the latter to give notice to the following: 'The Turkey Company, the East India Company, the Greenland, the Eastland, and the Incorporated Traders for Spain, France, Portugal, Italy, and the West India Plantations—to present the names of four of the most active members of their body, out of whom His Majesty would select two, and would join to them merchants, experienced persons, and some of the members of the Privy Council, under whose advice might be inserted in the several treaties such articles and clauses as should render the nation more prosperous and flourishing in trade and commerce.' Dated 17th August 1660. *Analytical Index to the Remembrancia*, preserved in the Archives of London, A. D. 1579–1664, p. 530, ix. 5.

[2] *Public Record Office*, C.O. 77, vol. xiv, 1678–86. This volume contains a number of letters from the Prince of Bantam, from Childe, and from the Company's factors in the East.

which the grievances of the merchants are voiced. The latter had demanded a Council of Merchants[1] and had advocated other far-reaching measures. The Council now assumes the functions which were exercised by the Merchants' Councils in other countries. Its recommendations are, so far as East India trade is concerned, invariably carried into effect. There is no instance of the rejection of the Council or Committee's report in any one of the Record Office volumes, 8 to 16. All the reports of the Council and Committee are passed by the King in Council.

It is interesting to notice the procedure of the Council. The petitions of the Company are generally considered by a sub-committee thereof. In other cases, however, they are referred by it to a number of experts, who present their reports to it. For instance, the petition of the Company against the Dutch was referred by the Council to the two Judges of the Admiralty, who presented their judgement. The Council thereupon made an elaborate report on the subject to the King. The report was, as usual, passed by the King in Council, and forwarded to Downing.[2] We find some letters addressed to the King himself, instead of to the Council or Committee. This was due, perhaps, to the fact that Bombay belonged at first to the Crown, and the governors, therefore, had no connexion with the Committee. The latter, however, wrote many letters to the East India Company's servants in the East.

The Government has now adopted a new rôle in its dealings with the foreign powers. It acts as the spokesman of the East India Company; it urges upon the foreign powers the necessity of giving satisfaction to the demands of the Company; and, finally, it threatens reprisals if its demands are not satisfied. It is this intimate connexion between the Crown and the Company which helps to explain the phenomenal growth of the East India Company. In no other trade is the influence of the Central Government so widely felt. James's peaceful negotiations end in nothing but paper-protests; Charles I's shifty policy reduces it to insignificance. Cromwell's war and his Charter to the Company go far towards re-establishing that body; yet the

[1] See above, Malynes, Robinson, Lamb, chapter i.
[2] *Public Record Office*, C.O. 77, vol. viii, nos. 148, 149, 156.

lack of energetic support hampers it in all its activities. Under Charles II the Company secures the greatest amount of royal support. Its interests are now practically identified with those of the Crown. Its cause is now regarded as the cause of the State. Its protests, negotiations, and demands are backed by the Council and Committees. Nowhere do these statements find better illustration than in its dealings with the foreign powers.[1]

Nothing is more instructive than the influence of the Council on the foreign policy of Charles II. The latter invariably carried out the policy which the Council outlined in many a report. This applies specially to the Second Dutch War. The causes of the war have been differently stated by the contemporary writers. Nothing is more interesting than a comparison of the *Life of Clarendon* with Burnet's *History of My Own Times.* The gossipy Burnet cannot see any cause at all. He is completely at a loss.[2] Not so with Clarendon. He thinks that the war was caused by the Duke of York, who was ambitious of military glory.[3] Sir William Temple hints to the same effect.[4] Others, again, blamed Downing for bringing about the war. This was the view of Burnet,[5] and James II.[6] Temple says that De Witt laid the fault of the late quarrel wholly upon Sir George Downing, 'who had a great deal of money from the East India Company, who were willing to bribe', &c.[7] It need hardly be doubted that he received money from the East India Company, and that he was not very scrupulous.[8] We cannot rely upon De Witt's account. He was naturally prejudiced against him,

[1] For the sake of brevity I have used the words 'Committees' and 'Council' as interchangeable terms. Really, as pointed out above, the two bodies were totally different.

[2] Burnet's *History*, Osmund Airy's edition. See Airy's note: 'There was no visible cause of war.' Pepys mentions, under 28th November 1663, the satirical pictures and medals that gave so great an offence to Charles.

[3] *Life*, op. cit., p. 235. Lister, *Life of Clarendon*, vol. ii, says that the reproach of having promoted it belongs chiefly to the Duke of York.

[4] *Works*, London, 1814, vol. i, p. 290: 'But others said, the Duke's military genius made him desirous to enter upon some action abroad; that the Duke of Albemarle had long had a pique to their country, upon some usage he resented during his being an officer here.' This seems to me to be nothing else but mere gossip.

[5] Op. cit., p. 366: 'Downing was a crafty, fawning man, who was ready to turn to every side that was uppermost.'

[6] *Life of James II*, vol. i, p. 401.

[7] Vol. i, p. 288.

[8] Compare Mr. Pepys's references to Downing in his *Diary*.

and, in point of morality, there is not much to choose. Both, as Lister points out in his *Life of Clarendon*, lied frequently, and it seems unjust to Downing to accept De Witt's uncorroborated statement against him.[1] He figures prominently in the Company's Court Book, No. 24.[2]

These extracts prove conclusively that Downing received money from the East India Company. It does not follow, however, that he would have acted otherwise than as he did if he had not been so bribed. We can hardly use the word 'bribe' in this

[1] Compare De Pontalis's *De Witte*, English translation, vol. i, pp. 310–11; vol. ii, pp. 131–2.

[2] 28th December 1657: The Company to draw up a Narrative of the obstructions of the Dutch at Bantam, for Downing. *Court Minutes*, 10th October 1662: 'The Governor and others were desired to meet Sir George Downing to congratulate his arrival here, and advise with him how the Company may best proceed in their business against the Dutch.' Ib., 20th March 1663: The Governor was entreated to ask Sir George Downing to appoint a time to dine with the Dutch Committee appointed by the Company, 'that they may have conference with him about their business'. Ib., 29th December 1657: 'Mr. Downing was yesterday attended in the Company's name: that a verbal relation of the business touching the Company and that of the Netherlands was made to him, who thereupon expressed a very much affection and readiness to do the Company the best service he can, when he shall be commissionated from His Highness.' Ib., 9th March 1659: 'At a Court of Committees' relating to the 'Ratification [of Cromwell] to the agreement made in Holland by the Resident Downing for the 3 ships taken at Bantam', and as it was contrary to the Company's request that no such agreement might pass which would exclude the Company, a Committee was appointed to wait upon His Highness about it, and Downing was to be written to. 27th January 1662: Sir Richard Ford was desired to draw a letter to be returned to Sir George Downing in answer of that he sent. The following are the only references to the money paid to Downing by the East India Company. On 16th January 1661 a warrant was signed for payment of '£60 to Sir George Downing'. 27th June 1662: 'The Court being acquainted that it would be necessary to disburse some money upon some occasions in the management of the Dutch business, they give that Committee with the Governor and Deputy liberty to dispose of £300 or £400, or so much thereof as . . . they shall in their discretion think fit.' It can hardly be doubted that he received a part of the sum. The same day 'Sir Richard Ford was desired to answer Downing's letter, and thank him for the pains he hath already taken in the Company's business, and promise him, when there is a good issue of the same, he shall receive their real thanks'. Note the word 'real'. The next reference to money is as follows: 29th June 1664: A petition to the King for a new accommodation of the Company's business. 15th June 1664: Sir George Downing 'desired that he might correspond about his business with one person singly. . . . Whereupon the Court entreated the Governor to correspond singly with Sir George about their damages, as occasion shall require.' They also gave the Governor power 'to act and do, and dispose of money according to his own discretion in all things relating to that business'—the Dutch quarrel—'without giving any account of his proceedings'. 18th May 1664: The Committee for the Dutch affairs to write to Sir George about an accommodation with the Dutch Company.

connexion. Nearly all who took part in the Treaty of 1619 received money from the East India Company. Nay more, some received money from both the companies. Carleton had complained of the meagre amount doled out to him by the thrifty Company. Hence, we cannot say that Downing deliberately brought about the war by presenting his demands in an outrageous manner. The real cause of the war was commerce. This was expressed tersely by Monk to the Dutch. 'Our nation must have a share (of the commerce) or peace will not be long.'[1]

Downing's grasp of the Anglo-Dutch rivalry of the period was thorough. Every page of his Dispatches in the third volume of Lister's *Life of Clarendon* and in the Public Record Office, C.O. 77, volumes viii–x, testifies to his profound knowledge, his rare versatility, and his extraordinary insight. He is unscrupulous, to be sure; but so is De Witt. In that respect, there is really not much to choose between the two men. Downing ably represented the views commonly held about the Anglo-Dutch rivalry of the times. It was the merchants who demanded war against the Dutch. Charles II himself did not want it. Clarendon says as much in his Life. He justly assigns the cause of that war to the complaints of the merchants. Sir William Temple says that some of the Lords connected with the Court were against it.[2]

We have a characteristic account of Bristol's conversation with the King on the war, and his advice to the King to follow the policy that Cromwell had been forced to follow, in Ranke.[3] It is instructive to compare the policy of Cromwell and Charles in this respect. Cromwell had been forced to wage war against the Dutch, not because he liked it, but because the commercial classes obliged him to carry on a policy in consonance with their wishes. If these causes operated so strongly on Cromwell, and if the foreign policy of the latter received a specific mould therefrom, they operated still more so under the government of Charles II.

[1] Pontalis, *De Witt*, p. 311.

[2] *Works*, vol. i, pp. 286–92.

[3] *History of England*, vol. iii, p. 419. For Downing see Professor Firth's article in the *Dictionary of National Biography*, on Downing; and his *Last Years of the Protectorate*, chapters x, xv, xvi. 'His policy was mainly dictated by commercial considerations and he looked outside Europe.' Firth, *Cambridge Modern History*, vol. v, p. 106. Compare Lodge, *Longman's History of England*, pp. 61–83.

The grievances of the merchants had been accumulating for a long time, and though they had been redressed by Cromwell, they had not died out. There is reason to believe that they increased in some respects. The question of the herring fishery had not been settled. That question has been treated in Chapter I. It is, however, necessary to emphasize its importance here, because little or no reference is made thereto in any account of the Second Dutch War. The complaints of John Keymour in about 1601 [1] that 'we are eaten out of Trade, and the Bread taken out of our Mouths in our own seas and the great Customs carried from His Majesty's Coffers to foreign princes of State', were echoed under Charles II. But, as pointed out above, the question of the herring fishery was of comparatively small importance beside the question of foreign trade. It was upon this that the quarrel hinged. We can trace it in the *Journals of the House of Commons and the House of Lords.* It is important to notice the part played by the Committee of Trade which was revived by the House of Commons on 8th November 1660.[2] Its jurisdiction is not capable of exact definition, because it treated only a limited number of subjects in the first instance. Later on, however, the petitions of 'many thousands of Merchants, Clothiers and others' are referred to it.[3] On 15th November the Committee for Woollen Manufactures and the Committee for Trade and Navigation were 'added each to other, so as to be for the future one Committee'.[4] On 11th May 1661 the House appointed the times and days of the meetings of different Committees, and the Committee of Trade. The Committee reported on various matters from time to time. It was requested to report on Bullion on 5th April 1662. A far more important point is the connexion of this body with the central Government. Besides the members appointed originally, it included 'all the members of this House of the Long Robe'.[5] The link between the Executive and the Legislature was provided by the members of the King's Privy Council. The latter were desired 'to represent the said information to His Majesty's

[1] See *Tracts on Fishery*, op. cit.
[2] *Journals of the House of Commons*, vol. viii, p. 178.
[3] Ib., p. 180. [4] Ib., p. 183.
[5] Ib., p. 178.

Council, with the desire of the House that they will consider thereof and take such order as they shall think fit'.[1]

It is important to notice various other Committees appointed by the House of Commons. The Committee appointed to prepare and bring in sumptuary Laws, and Laws to prevent Encroachment in Trade by Jews and French, produced a series of comprehensive proposals. It advised a free exportation of foreign corn; it recommended a Navigation Act, and it advised encouragement of woollen and other manufactures of the United Kingdom.[2]

Another important Committee must be noticed, as it throws great light on the trade rivalry. A Committee had been appointed 'to consider how the Trade of the Nation may be improved and advanced'.[3] Clifford made a report on 21st April 1664.[4] It was a comprehensive report and summed up all the injuries sustained by the English merchants from the Dutch. The House resolved unanimously 'That the several and respective Wrongs, dishonours, and Indignities done to His Majesty by the Subjects of the United Provinces by invading his rights in India, Africa and elsewhere, and the Damages, Affronts, and Injuries done by them to our Merchants, be reported to the House, as the greatest obstruction of our Foreign Trade; and that it is the opinion of the Committee, that the said respective Dishonours, Indignities and Affronts be humbly and speedily presented to His Majesty; and that he be most humbly moved to take some speedy and effectual course for the redress thereof, and all others of the like nature, and for the prevention of the like in the future'.[5]

The resolution deserved to be quoted in its entirety, because it shows the real character of the struggle. The stages of that struggle have been traced in Chapter I, and there is no need to recapitulate the causes mentioned there. It is essential, however, to notice the determination of the economic theories of the period by this rivalry. Economic, no less than philosophical and political, theories are really the product of their times, and it would be as unjust to criticize them without

[1] Ib., p. 178.
[2] Ib., pp. 441, 467.
[3] Ib., 6th April 1664, p. 544.
[4] Ib., p. 548.
[5] Ib., 21st April 1664, p. 548.

taking into account the conditions that brought them forth, as it would be futile to expect them to conform to a norm, set up by the followers of the classical school of English Political Economy. The whole commercial progress of England in the seventeenth and eighteenth centuries resolved itself ultimately into a struggle with her foreign commercial rivals. The political economists followed suit. The House of Lords was no less unanimous on this point than the Commons.

We glean further details from their *Journals*. The greatest sufferers from the Dutch were: (1) The East India Company, who chiefly insisted upon the depredations and wrongs done to them since 1656, to the value of £148,000 in ships and goods taken by the Dutch and of £87,000, according to a reasonable estimate, in their factories burned and spoiled by them. There were other complaints made by the East India Company.[1] (2) The Turkey Company complained of the seizure of two ships, to the value of £110,500. (3) The Royal Company complained that the Dutch had endeavoured to deprive them of their whole trade, by following their ships from port to port. (4) They had persuaded the negroes to destroy their servants and forts. (5) They had seized the island of Cabo Corso. (6) They had sent two protests to the English, requesting them to desist from settling their factories upon that coast. (7) The Portugal Merchants complained that 'a Dutch man-of-war did assault them and keep the Brazil Frigot'. (8) Likewise, 'the Traders into Africa before the incorporation of the said Company complained of the losses received of the Dutch, of at least £130,000; some of their ships sunk, burnt, their men killed and poisoned in cold blood.' The total damage was computed at £714,500. This does not include the loss of Polaroon, which was computed 'at above four million pounds'. The Lords concurred in the vote of the House of Commons, which described the Dutch as 'the greatest obstruction to our Foreign Trade'. The vote asked the King to take 'some speedy and effectual course for the redress thereof'. It is significant that both the Houses declared that 'in prosecution thereof', viz. the effectual course mentioned above, 'they will with their lives and Fortunes assist His Majesty against all oppositions whatsoever'. Charles replied that he

[1] See below.

would 'appoint His Minister at the Hague to demand speedy redress and reparation from the States-General, and also use his utmost endeavours to secure his subjects from the like violences in the future'.[1]

The grievances described above will be totally misleading unless a due sense of proportion is observed. There can be no doubt that they combined to bring about the Second Dutch War. It does not follow, however, that they were of equal importance. Most of them were local, and had little effect. They were certainly irritating, and were productive of a good deal of ill-feeling between the two nations; but they would easily have been settled. There is no reason to suppose that the Dutch were not willing. The East India trade was, however, a totally different matter. That trade had been monopolized by the Dutch for over fifty years, and they were not likely to loosen their grip upon it. Their defeat by England had been crushing, and they had promised to restore Polaroon. But the restoration of Polaroon would have involved partial abolition of their monopoly. It would, moreover, have threatened their sovereignty in the islands. Hence, we find them resorting to a succession of devices by which they could prevent its retrocession. And they eventually succeeded. Polaroon remained in their hands. Polaroon, however, was not the only cause. The ultimate cause was really the prohibition of the English Company from trading in the Spice islands. It was the old question of the freedom of trade. De Witt may speak vaguely about the necessity of 'a *règlement* of trade', &c.[2] There is no reason to suppose that he sincerely believed in it. It was really this question of freedom of trade that ultimately led to the Second Dutch War. Downing's dispatches in Lister's *Life of Clarendon* show the importance of the East India trade. Sir William Temple[3] admits that there was great jealousy between the two nations, and that the East India Company was partly responsible for it.[4] Clarendon mentions Polaroon, but his cryptic statements are no more valuable to us than the sage remarks of Bishop Burnet. Far more important are the petitions of the East India Company

[1] *Journals of the House of Lords*, vol. xiii, pp. 598–600, 22nd April 1664. See also 29th April 1664.

[2] See Downing's dispatches, in Lister, op. cit.

[3] Op. cit.

[4] Compare Ranke, vol. iii, p. 417.

to the Council; the reports of the latter thereupon; and the dispatches of Downing. All of them are to be found in the Public Record Office. They serve to bring into prominence many of the most important causes of that quarrel. The Company's petitions to the Council are perhaps the best expression of the spirit animating the East India merchants. A petition, dated 6th October 1660, refers to the 'advance of our neighbours'; shows how for many years they 'invaded the factories, and imprisoned the servants'; recalls their 'violence and murthers, as at Amboyna'. It asks the King to refer the 'legal examination for the process' to the Judges of the Admiralty, in order that they may consider the petitioners' complaints, and that the United Provinces may give the petitioners 'full and equal reparation for the losses and damages they have done'. The petition was referred to the Judges of the Admiralty, as requested.[1]

Another petition of the Company refers to the well-known island of Polaroon. The island seems to have been surrendered to the English in December 1616.[2] It may be mentioned that Courthope had been sent there on 29th October 1616.[3] The Dutch had, it seems, agreed to restore the island,[4] but, after the signing of the Accord of the treaty of 1623, they refused to deliver it up.[5] The treaty of Westminster provided for the restoration of the island to the English Company. The Company waited upon Secretary Thurloe with the draft of an instrument required by the Dutch East India Company as a condition of the surrender of the island. Thurloe asked them not to lose time in planting their new possession. It was decided, therefore, to send out ships without delay, and fresh letters were dispatched to Holland requesting the Dutch Company to give the necessary

[1] *Public Record Office*, C.O. 77, vol. viii, 16th October 1660.

[2] Sainsbury, vol. iii, pp. 52–4; *Public Record Office*, *East Indies*, vol. ii, no. 21.

[3] The following account of the people of Polaroon may be of interest: 'At your arrival in Poolaroone, show yourself courteous and affable, for they are a peevish, perverse, diffident, and perfidious people, and apt to take disgust upon small occasions, and are, being moved, more cumbersome than wasps. Their Councils are public, their resolutions tedious, and their dispositions quick to change.' Commission to Nath. Courthope. Sainsbury, vol. i, p. 479.

[4] *Public Record Office*, *East Indies*, vol. ii, nos. 53, 54, 61.

[5] Sainsbury, vol. iii, p. 194, no. 610.

orders to its servants in the East.[1] The English Company was, however, 'by the violent intrusions of the (Dutch) East India Company totally deprived thereof, and the island itself made profitless by the cutting down the Spice trees, and laying the whole island waste'. The Company, therefore, petitioned Charles to grant it a Royal Commission under the Great Seal.[2] The Commission was granted, on the recommendation of the Council for Trade and Plantations. The States-General had no doubt recommended their Governor and Council of Banda, to 'quit and deliver the above island to those that shall come to appear in the Islands of Banda', and a similar letter had been dispatched to the Governor-General and Council at Batavia; but it was hardly likely to be effective, in view of the fact that they insisted on the presentation of the King's Commission to the Dutch Governor of Banda, before delivery could take place.[3] The signing of the King's Commission would take time, and the Dutch Company was only too glad to spin out time by this means. The Company voiced its complaints through another petition. It traces the history of the Company's dealings with the natives to the imaginary treaty of Sir Francis Drake, says the Dutch have not 'forborne their wonted violence', 'but have disturbed the English commerce both by sea and land'. They had seized upon their goods at Goa, 'assaulted and wounded the factors in their own houses at Jambee', 'generally vilifying and reproaching the English nation as if they were but a degree above the slaves'.[4]

Meanwhile, the petitions of the Company about the losses it had sustained had been referred to Doctors Exton and Mason, the Judges of the Admiralty. Their judgement is highly important, as upon it was founded a comprehensive report of the Council of Plantations. They declared that 'the violent debarring of the English was unlawful by law of Nations, which allows all people in Amity the freedom of Trade and Commerce'. They declared, moreover, that their taking from them arms and ammunition, 'as also other goods', by their authority, without any just cause, 'was utterly unlawful'. So, they suggested,

[1] *Court Book*, vol. xxiii, p. 491.
[2] C.O. 77, vol. viii, no. 134.
[3] Ib.
[4] C.O. 77, vol. viii, no. 90, dated 11th December 1660.

there was just cause for His Majesty to be sensible of their losses, ascertained and duly proved, amounting to the value of £237,660, 'besides the damage and loss of two ships, which were laden homeward with goods to the value of £55,750'. The judges advised His Majesty 'to insist with the States Ambassador that full and speedy satisfaction be given unto them, and His Majesty may take into consideration how much he has been prejudiced by the loss of Customs and the English nation dishonoured by their proceedings'.[1]

Upon this judgement was founded a comprehensive report oi the Council of Trade and Plantations. The report is of the utmost importance, as it brings out all the causes of the rivalry, and suggests far-reaching measures. The Council recommended the East India trade to the King's protection and encouragement, 'in relation to the Honour of Your Majesty's Crown and Realm, and the general advancement of the Common Capital and Navigation of Your Majesty's subjects'. It is, however, in its enunciation of a definite commercial policy that its importance consists. The Council declared 'that the Holland East India Company had from their first Entrance into that Trade continually disturbed Your Majesty's subjects in the just liberties and advantages thereof, contrary to the Law of Nations, and many other agreements made with the Hollanders'. It feared that unless the King provided for the future security of his subjects, 'that whole Stock of near £800,oco, which they have engaged for the effectual prosecution of that remote, honourable commerce, is like to be extinct'. Then follows a series of measures which the Council deemed essential. These if inserted in the treaty, as recommended by the Council, would have removed all causes of subsequent friction. They were not entirely novel. Most of them had been suggested by the Lords Commissioners, but the '*règlement* of trade' was passed over, mainly through James's impatience. The Lords recommended that the East India Company should have their demands adjusted and fully satisfied, 'according to the report thereof made by His Majesty's Judges of High Court of Admiralty'. Their second proposal was much wider. They thought that the East India Company was entitled to trade at any port or place situate in the limits of their

[1] C.O. 77, vol. viii, no. 94, 19th January 1661.

Charter, and that they should not hereafter be disturbed or hindered by any of the Dutch subjects, but freely pass to and from 'the ports and islands'. Another grievance from which the Company had suffered for a long time was the refusal of the Dutch to allow 'ingress or egress' of their ships, goods, or servants in any ports that were under blockade. The Dutch contended that they had a perfect right to prevent the East India Company's men and ships from communicating with the natives of any of the besieged islands. The effects of this policy had been very injurious to the Company. The Council insisted on the right of the Company to send goods and ships to any port within its charter. Nor should the Company be disturbed or molested from 'buying and carrying any Indian commodity from any Native Indians, upon pretence of any contract that the Dutch may have made with the Natives, of the whole of that commodity'.

Another important proposal of the Council concerned the searching of ships. These were not to be molested, at sea or in port, by any Dutch ship or officers, provided they had a passport of 'this Company, or any President, Chief, or Agent of this Company'. This applied not only to English ships, but also to 'Indian Ships, Junks, Boats, or vessel whatsoever'. Nor should 'any Indian person or persons' be stopped or hindered by the Hollanders from their free passage, if they have a warrant from the commander of such a port.

These suggestions, if carried into effect, would have prevented many of the future quarrels, and might have paved the way for an accommodation with the rival Company. The Council's proposals were accompanied by 'reasons and instances offered to His Majesty', which are no less remarkable than the proposals themselves. Their importance consists in the formulation of a characteristic economic policy that underlies them. In them is to be found the best justification for the war that followed. The Council point out that the Dutch had, at most times, justified all the injuries and damages done to the English Company, and at all times palliated them. If at any time they 'have been brought to a Treaty for repairing this Company for past damages, and capitulations for future security, they have made such easy composition and partial restitution of their former robberies, as they have thought it a profitable Trade to keep the new Agreement no longer than till they might find an advantageous opportunity to break them'. Their renewed violations of articles had 'raised them up a terrible name among the Indians'.

It is interesting to compare the reasons for their first proposal with the reasons for their second and third proposals. Their appeal now is to a mysterious 'Common right'. Perhaps it is not equal to the Law of Nature in its importance. Nor can we say that the Law of Nature is meant by the Council. Though the language be that of the Council, the spirit is that of Grotius. What Grotius had claimed for the Dutch, the Council claim for the East India Company. By common right, asserted the Council, while the two nations are in amity, the Dutch 'ought not in any part of the world to impede Your Majesty's subjects from the freedom of trading with any natives that will entertain them, much less in places where the English have fixed residences and factories in their own houses', even though the Hollanders should have actual hostility against the natives. This had not been the usual practice of the Dutch Company. The latter, 'owning no other right but might', made it their common practice that where they found the natives more inclinable to trade with the English than with them, 'then to declare war against them, and to send such Naval force to those parts as may be sufficient to give losses to the English shipping there', 'to call the riding of 2 or 3 ships a beleaguring of their enemy', and on that pretence not only to impede the English trade, but to seize their ships and goods, as at Bantam, Acheen, Goa, and other places.

Their reasons for the fourth proposal are of no less importance than their reasons for the others. The Lords stated that the Dutch had not only impeded the English from many just advantages of pepper and other goods that they might have had from the East Indies, on pretence of former contracts which they had made for the whole of those commodities, but also 'when they have found the English ships lading such goods which they had bought and paid for', they had 'robbed' the English of what they had and forced the ships away 'to the loss of their whole voyage', 'as at Acheen and other places of Sumatra; yea, and in times of open hostility between the Queen of

Acheen and the Hollanders, the Hollanders destroyed the voyage of an English ship, the *Bantam*, on pretence of a former contract made with that Queen; the Queen having contracted with the English for terms of trade for pepper, gold, and all other things, as by the Queen's letters appears'. The Dutch prevented the Company's agent from lading what he had agreed for, and compelled the Queen to sign a treaty of peace and a contract for 'all the pepper exclusive of the English'.

The main cause of the quarrel was the exercise of monopoly by the Dutch. They were determined not to allow any other European power to share in the profits of the East India trade. As long as their monopoly of the spices was maintained, the price of those articles could be fixed by them at their discretion. We therefore find instances of the spices being sold as high as six shillings per lb.[1] This could be brought about only after the exclusion of every other rival. Hence we find them resorting to various devices for that purpose. In this connexion the reasons of the Council for their last three proposals are of great significance. In them are detailed the methods employed by the Dutch for the effectual prosecution of their design. In order to prevent the natives from dealing with the English merchants in the coveted spices, the Dutch 'had made it their common practice to command and force all Indian junks, and vessels coming from China, Sumatra and other parts towards Bantam and other English factors, to deviate to their throne of Batavia and sell them goods there'. They prohibited the subjects of the King of Sumatra, on no less penalty than loss of life and ships and goods, from sailing to Amboyna or the Molucca islands, so that the English, who had a factory at Macassar, might not get any supply of spices from them. They executed 'these cruel laws on the honest Indians; yea, when they met an Indian junk, deposited with the English for a debt, sailed by them in the service of the English Company from Japarra to Bantam, they assaulted and mastered the said junk, tore down the English flag most contemptuously, and destroyed the Natives which they found aboard another English ship convoying the junk'. They also seized and confiscated two junks in the English service 'going from the Bay of Bengal to the island of Scilone (Ceylon), declared

[1] For the price of spices in 1621 see Chapter I.

they would do it, though their masters pay three times the value of this, rather than to permit the English to trade to that island, to the signal dishonour of the English name and prejudice of the English nation'. The Council conclude characteristically: 'And having barbarously murdered the natives on the islands of Polaroone and Lantore, while the islands were yet in possession of the English, for the maintenance of their unjust conquest of the island of Banda, and other Eastern parts in their possession, they have made it death without mercy to any native that shall be sailing to the eastward of the Island of Bouton, by which means they desire to render the island of Polaroone, if possible, useless to the English, who are now upon planting of it, thus hindering the recourse of all nations to trade with them.'[1]

These two documents are of the utmost importance and throw a searching light on the real point in dispute.[2] It was not the question of Polaroon that led the Council to make such strong representations to Charles. It was the old question of freedom of trade in the Spice Islands. The Company were, in short, to be allowed to trade in any island, and with any native, they pleased. This is, in effect, the substance of all their reasons and advices. That question had not been settled under James and Charles I, through the incapacity of the one and the weakness of the other. Under Cromwell the Dutch had been compelled to allow a certain amount of freedom, and some of the ships captured by them had been restored. Under Charles II, however, the Council formulates the policy, and the King carries it out. That policy aims now at the maintenance of that right of which they thought they had been robbed for a long time. A comparison of these documents with Downing's Dispatches in Lister[3] is essential, if we are to form an impartial judgement on his work. Downing was no doubt imperious and unscrupulous, but he was not guilty of deliberately bringing about the Dutch War. Perhaps he did this in 1672. He certainly did not do this in 1664. The tone of his dispatches is very mild indeed in comparison with the Reports of the Council for Trade and Plantations, on the Dutch 'murders', 'robberies', 'cruelties', &c., He merely

[1] 'The Advice of the Council, and their reasons.' *Public Record Office*, C.O. 77, vol. viii, nos. 147–8, dated 3rd January 1661.

[2] It is for this reason that I have quoted extensively from them.

[3] Op. cit.

carried out a policy dictated by the Council. These, as other reports of the Council, were passed, and a copy was forwarded to Downing.

These reports were made on 3rd January 1661. Other causes of friction continued to arise, however, and to embarrass the relations of the two powers. This applies specially to the island of Polaroon. The Dutch had written official letters to the 'Governor of Banda', 'the Governor-General and Council of India', &c., requesting them to 'deliver and quit the island of Polaroone'. The Company's claim for damages against the Dutch was, however, the cause of delay. A Memorial of the Dutch seems to have declared that unless the English Company's claim were waived, the Dutch would refuse to deliver the island. A letter from the English Company to the Dutch Ambassador stated that they were confirmed in the apprehensions which they had had since they first began to address His Excellency. The Company feared that, 'after many delays, some promises and other pretended mistakes in the Secretaries in Holland', it would find its hope of right and friendship with the Dutch abortive.[1]

The letter insisted on clear and pertinent information on the part of the Ambassador. The commanders of the ships sent by the English Company to the island of Polaroon begged the Governor-General of the Dutch Indies to send a letter to the Governor of Banda, in order that the latter might deliver the island.[2] The Governor-General replied that he was quite ready to deliver the island, provided he had first a sight of their commission. The commander had probably provided himself with this indispensable instrument, and the delivery ought not, therefore, to have been delayed. A much more important point, however, was the waiving of all the claims against the Dutch on the part of the English Company. On this the Governor-General insisted. He informed the commanders that since the date of the States-General's letter to him, he had received 'further

[1] 'Pray your Excellency to consider if we can make any more favourable resentment of your paper, by which, in place of giving us letters from your States and Company for our quiet possession of our own island of Polaroone, to which you never had title but of might, you require of us to resign at once our just demands of £300,000, or thereabouts.' Desire clear and pertinent information. *Public Record Office*, C.O. 77, vol. viii, p. 158. Letter dated 1st February 1661. There is a duplicate of this.

[2] C.O. 77, vol. viii, no. 120, 23rd October 1661.

intelligence advising that the English East India Company doth pretend to have suffered much more damage from us, and withal doth renew and rip up several old sores and debates formerly enacted which have been long buried'. He therefore refused to deliver the island until he had further intelligence.[1] That it was the Dutch Government that had asked him to delay the delivery of the island is apparent from the following documents. The Ambassadors of the United Provinces requested the English Company to refrain from insisting on the insertion of their claim for damages in the treaty of 1662, but to insert the following clause instead: 'For the full taking away of all former pretences, disputes, and discontents, which are depending between the two East India Companies, to this day, or to the 20th of January, 1659 (new style), or at least all that were proved in England before that time.' This would have postponed the settlement of their claim to an uncertain period. The English Company, however, was not satisfied. In a series of petitions, it referred to the injuries sustained from the Dutch and asked the King to demand from the Dutch Commissioners a full and satisfactory account of the intentions of their 'Considerable Arming, before any Treaty of Alliance could be concluded'. They requested the King to appoint Commissioners for the adjustment and reparation for the 'vast injuries and losses they have sustained by the unjust violence of the Netherlands East India Company'. Some of them pointed out the necessity of appointing an Umpire or super Arbiter, that those necessary preliminaries might be adjusted with the Dutch.[2]

It is interesting to notice the effects produced by these petitions. All of them were referred to the English Ambassador in Holland. Meanwhile, the Dutch had been making preparations for sending out a strong naval squadron. An informant told the Company in January 1661 that the Dutch Company were setting out seven great ships 'with all expedition', and that they intended to dispatch a number of ships in April. About a month later, we find the same informant giving further details of their preparations. They had 'bought' two more men-of-war, likely to carry

[1] *Public Record Office*, C.O. 77, vol. viii, no. 122.
[2] Ib., vol. viii, nos. 176, 165, 203.

ammunition, together with 'fourteen ships, great and small, which shall carry merchandise and men'. They were reputed to have been designed for 'an island that lies near the city of Goa'. Further information was forthcoming about two weeks later. 'The East India Company go on here very vigorously in their preparations for India. There will be twenty-two ships in all, which are yet here, and in Zeeland, besides all the rest that are gone already with the last Easterly winds'.[1] The English Company was naturally perturbed at these preparations, and asked Charles to demand an explanation. They feared that they were meant for the surprise of Goa and an island adjacent to it. They feared, moreover, that by these means the Dutch 'would make themselves masters of all the trade of the Coast of India, and at once destroy it both to the Portuguese and to us'.[2]

While the Dutch were preparing for an armed struggle in the East, the English commanders of those Company's ships which had been dispatched to Polaroon were lodging protests with the Dutch Governor against their treatment there. 'The Governor persisted in an obstinate denial to surrender the said island, whether by order of the General and Council of Batavia or from the Netherlands Company in Europe.' It is clear, however, that the Governor-General was not to blame for that. He had received an order from the Company's Directors not to deliver the island unless the East India Company waived its claim for damages.[3] The Company's petition to Charles recited the various stages of the negotiations with the Dutch, and informed him that 'this Company did send two ships, the *London* and *Discovery*, with Your Majesty's Commission and Soldiers for the island', when they, arriving in Batavia in October 1661 and at Polaroon in March 1662, delivered their letters. They were, however, 'denied possession of the island and kept off'. The Company was therefore ready for a claim for damages against the Dutch. The total amount claimed was £97,000, but, as will be seen, later this was considerably increased.[4] About two months later, the Company petitioned again. It required not only the island of Polaroon, but also demanded 'satisfaction from the said Dutch for all damages which they may sustain

[1] Ib., nos. 155, 191, 206.

[2] Ib., nos. 165, 149.

[3] Ib. no. 255.

[4] Ib., no. 257, March 1662.

both of present expense, consequent loss, and disappointment that shall be given to the said Company's ships that are sent to possess the island'. The sum amounted to £157,000.[1] It need hardly be added that the sum claimed by the Company was absurd, and that they gravely risked all chances of having their grievances righted by presenting claims for damages on all occasions.

The Dutch were determined, however, not to relax their hold on the Spice Islands. The Company's informant wrote to say that 'thirty-five sail of ships arrived from Holland this year'. They had many more on the coast of India and Ceylon, and a large number in various parts of the Malayan Archipelago. There is an ominous sentence in the same letter. 'The Dutch declare they will never deliver Polaroone to the English, and call themselves masters of the South Seas, upon pain of loss of ships and lives of all such as shall trade there.'[2] These suspicions were confirmed by the receipt of a dispatch from the English Company's Agent and Council in Bantam. The writer says that the Dutch 'begin to show themselves in their height, for they have proclaimed themselves Lords of all the South Seas, and the Coast of Mallabar, from Cochin to Cape Comorin, prohibiting all nations whatsoever to trade upon the said coasts for pepper, under forfeiture of ships, goods, and persons'.[3]

The alarm excited by these proceedings of the Dutch was faithfully reflected in a letter of Charles to Downing. The King referred to the injuries done to the English Company in various ways, and added: 'We cannot but highly resent these unfriendly proceedings, opposite to the said Treaty, and we require you to make speedy applications to the States-General in our name, vigorously representing unto them both the above-mentioned wrongs, and our just sense of the same.'[4] Downing would probably have avoided the war, but it was forced on him by the unwillingness of the Dutch to comply with his requests. In this connexion his dispatch dated

[1] *Public Record Office*, C.O. 77, vol. viii, nos. 265-6. Two petitions, dated 28th and 29th June.
[2] Ib., vol. ix, no. 9. The letter is dated from Bantam.
[3] Ib., vol. ix, no. 12, 25th August 1663.
[4] Lister, vol. iii, pp. 256-8.

20th May 1664 is important.[1] He is enabled to inform Clarendon that this 'dull body doth begin to stir at last'. The Dutch attributed the war to Downing, because he was best fitted to deal with the methods they employed in their Eastern possessions. He had a thorough grasp of the main economic tendencies of the times, and was not ignorant of the harm done to the English in the East Indies. 'The Dutch East India Company', said Downing, 'are making a vast progress in the East Indies—that what they have already got is of much greater value than all Brazil.'[2] He knew, moreover, how to adapt himself not only to circumstances, but also to persons. He saw through the diplomacy of De Witt, as he had seen through the policy of the Dutch Company, and warned Clarendon of the effects that would be produced should the Dutch be allowed complete freedom in the East Indies. 'This has been the ruin not only of numbers of His Majesty's trades, but (they have) also beaten them out of mighty trades, and will certainly in conclusion utterly overthrow the English East India Company, and the Africa Company, if nothing be applied for remedy but words.'[3] Hence, 'time for words is gone by. Pay them in their kind, and get their subjects a-crying as well as His Majesty's, and you will have a fair correspondence, and they will take heed what they do.'[4] This is certainly strong language, and would hardly be imitated by an ambassador at the present day. But it is mild in comparison with that of His Majesty's Council for Trade and Plantations. The latter called the Dutch 'murtherers', 'robbers', in so many terms. Downing was merely carrying out the policy which had been urged on him by the Council in February 1661.

Other causes of quarrel arose. Downing intervened energetically in the case of two ships, *Bona Esperanza* and *Bona Adventura*, and demanded satisfaction. The Dutch advocate insisted upon the fact of having already given satisfaction to Pergen, the agent of Courteen, who had a letter of recommendation from the King. The ships had been seized and confiscated by the Dutch in 1643. Downing's demand for satisfaction was highly resented by the States-General. They asserted that they

[1] Ib., pp. 329–31.
[2] Ib., vol. ii, p. 232.
[3] Ib., vol. iii, pp. 152–5.
[4] Ib., p. 250.

could give no consent 'to the reviving and a new disputing of any cause that passed and happened before 1654'. It is difficult to see what reason they had for prohibiting the reopening of these disputes. The treaty of 1654 was not regarded as settling for ever all past differences. Moreover, the dispute had been referred to the Protestant Cantons of Switzerland and had not by any means been ended.

The two ships had been assigned to Sir Paul Pindar, who sued the Dutch Company for £75,000. Courteen, however, notwithstanding his assignment and the protest of Pindar's agent, agreed to compromise with the Dutch for 85,000 guilders. In 1654 Pindar's executors preferred his claim before the English and Dutch Commissioners for £75,000. Downing now intervened. He asserted that Courteen's agent had no right to accept the amount which the Dutch had actually paid to Pergen and another person. It was, he said, a matter of State, and he was not going to allow the quarrel to be settled privately. In thrusting himself thus prominently forward, Downing must have known that his interference would prolong the dispute instead of shortening it. His contention that Courteen had no right to the two ships, and that he could not therefore accept 85,000 guilders from the Dutch, was not at all germane to the points at issue. As the Dutch States-General replied, they relied on the letters of Charles I. The latter had, on 9th October 1647, declared that the right or title to the two ships did belong to W. Courteen, not to Pindar, and recommended that satisfaction be given to Courteen. The Dutch contended, therefore, that having paid Courteen the amount claimed, they were not bound to pay a larger sum to Pindar. Downing retorted that the King's letter could have no force, as he was 'under duress' at the time. The Dutch rejoined that the King was perfectly free at the time, and that Charles I had expressly written another letter to Boswell making the matter clearer still. Moreover, they added, Pindar, on being told that he was in the wrong, 'did abandon the cause without further prosecution, and ever since to this time is left without any pursuit in our country'. In 1654, however, he seems to have brought his case before the Commissioners.[1]

[1] *Public Record Office*, C.O. 77, vol. viii, no. 132. Letter from the States-General, dated 22nd June 1662; Lister, *Life of Clarendon*, vol. ii, pp. 248–55;

It is possible, as stated by Temple, that Downing accepted a 'gift' from Carew, and his immoderate zeal for these two ships may be explained on this hypothesis.

Downing was, however, right with regard to the two other ships that were then a bone of contention between the two powers—the *Leopard* and the *Hopewell*. The former ship really belonged to the King, and not to the Company. By the articles of agreement made the 6th December 1661, between the Navy and the Company, it was provided that the *Leopard*, having performed the outward-bound service from Portugal to Goa, then, and not before, should be at the disposal of the Company's president. The Company contended that the president was not given legal charge of the ship, and that consequently the Company were not liable for the damage done to her by the Dutch.[1]

The *Hopewell* was seized upon the pretence that she was bound for Cochin, on the coast of Travancore, which the Dutch were besieging by sea and land. The *Leopard* was seized because she was bound for Porcatt, the Rajah of which, the Dutch asserted, had submitted to them by treaty; and they therefore claimed a right to prevent all foreign ships from trading there. Downing's arguments are remarkable, not less for the thorough grasp of the subject displayed therein, than for the light they throw on the intensely logical cast of his mind.

'It was', said Downing, 'such a Conference as I never before heard of.' As to the *Hopewell*, Downing asserted that she was not designed for Cochin, but was on her way directly along the coast for Porcatt, for which she was really designed. She was there stopped by the Dutch Company's agents, and brought by force to Cochin. In proof of his statements he produced not merely a copy of the commission of the commander of the ship, and his protest, but also a copy of the Dutch commander's letter, acknowledging the receipt of the protest. The argument was crushing, and both the advocate and De Witt were reduced to say that 'if that paper were true, they must yield the Cause'. As regards the second ship, the *Leopard*, Downing denied that the Rajah had submitted to the Dutch. Supposing, however,

vol. iii, pp. 256–8, 263–70, 316–17, 330–6, 344; Temple, *Works*, vol. i, pp. 286–92.

[1] *Public Record Office*, C.O. 77, vol. xi, no. 62, dated 30th March 1668.

that the 'Rajah had absolutely given them their whole country and outed himself of all, yet that would signify nothing, for the English had at the time a settled factory there, in pursuance of a treaty; if the said Rajah had not surrendered his territory, but only made treaty with them, and that by treaty he should have allowed himself not to permit the English to trade any longer there yet, he remaining still a prince, the notification thereof must have come from him, and a competent time at least given for the removal of their effects'. Even if he had absolutely given them his whole territory, the like notification must have been made by the Dutch, and the like time given. Downing asserted that this was not a matter of civility, but of right. Their conquest was not over the English at Porcatt, but only over the Rajah and his subjects. The argument was perfectly valid, and its force could hardly be denied. 'Suppose the King of Spain should take Lisbon, should', asked Downing, 'the English and French, who are friends to both, lose their liberty and estate?' 'If there was no such thing as Neuter(al) and if this maxim were true that anything in a place or country attacked were a party,' and if this were applied, 'the States, considering how their subjects were in all kingdoms,' would be the first to suffer.

The argument was irresistible, and we are not surprised to find the Dutch advocate continually shifting his ground. Though he acknowledged that the goods did, of right, and not civility, belong to 'the English Company, yet', he asserted, 'it was in our power to say how and with what ships you should carry them away'. This was a perfectly futile reply, and it was not difficult for Downing to expose the absurdity of these reasonings. The English commanders were acting according to the orders of their superiors, and they could not allow the lading of any of their goods upon any Dutch ship. Downing then asserted that the Rajah of Porcatt, instead of consenting to the surrender of his country to the Dutch by treaty, 'was in open defiance with them'. How could, asked Downing, the English Company's ships be excluded from those parts? No notification was given to the English Company's factors at Porcatt. De Witt was forced to ask the Dutch advocate, 'if he would say no more in justification of what they had done?' The latter desired 'to have time concerning this also'. Downing retorted that the advocate had desired further time as to the *Hopewell*, 'but not for the *Leopard*. As regards the *règlement* for avoiding such disputes in the future, he declared his readiness to employ his best endeavours thereto, and to debate such propositions as should be made for the better ordering of the two Companies.'[1]

These discussions convinced Downing of the futility of negotiating with a power that was determined not to concede a single point. De Witt was no doubt anxious to settle some of the points in dispute, and 'proposed the coming to debate nearer' with him in the matter. Nay more, he expressed his readiness to discuss terms of a *règlement*, whereby the quarrels that had distracted the two Companies would have been avoided. This was due, perhaps, to their fear of the English preparations. The Dutch had started their preparations as early as 1661,[2] and had, by 1663, established complete ascendancy in the South Seas. Nor were they idle in Europe. In 1664, however, they seem to have become aware of the determination of England to enforce its demands by force of arms. 'They begin now', wrote Downing in 1664, 'to take alarm at the great talks in England, of wars in this country, especially because of the Parliament now coming to sit, and that complaints will be made against them.'[3] De Witt had talked vaguely of a project, 'a *règlement*' before. He now returned to the charge. Downing wrote in May 1664, 'De Witt agreed that we should form a project drawn into a few articles containing those maxims that are set in my several memorials, upon which I have founded the demanding of satisfaction, for the late injuries done in the East Indies and upon the Coast of Africa.' The motive is not far to seek. The Dutch were 'mightily' alarmed by news 'that the King of England was equipping might and main to get between 20 and 30 ships to sea, and that most of them were northward to look after their East India fleet'.[4] They now consented to make a *règlement* for prevention of the like in the future. This applied, however, only to the *Hopewell* and the *Leopard*. As regards the other

[1] *Public Record Office*, C.O. 77, vol. ix, f. 81, 1663–5. Downing's dispatch, 18th March 1664.

[2] See above, the letters to the Company from its factors and informants.

[3] Lister, vol. iii, p. 298, 16 March 1664.

[4] Ib., p. 317.

two ships, they were determined not to pay a single penny. They had already paid 85,000 guilders, and they were not willing to pay any more. In this respect they seem to me to be right. Downing, however, appears to have been interested in the transaction, because he was not willing to forgo any one of his claims. There were, however, other causes of quarrel. The island of Polaroon was still in the hands of the Dutch. They thought that they might induce the East India Company to waive its claim 'for a sum of money and yearly recognition of spices for His Majesty's family'. Downing's comment on this is characteristic: 'But God forbid that such a thing should take place. I know they would give any sugary words, and more, to take the place.' The *règlement* about which De Witt had talked was meanwhile suffering the fate which previous *règlements* had suffered. The Dutch had again proposed one in May 1664, and Downing thought that they were beginning to 'stir at last'. He was soon undeceived. They had continued their preparations, and 'had gone on apace with the equipping their men-of-war, and listing of seamen'.[1] Still more information was furnished by Downing in his next dispatch. He found, to his surprise, 'that the Dutch would be still justifying what they have done, and that they do absolutely claim to themselves the whole Pepper trade at Cocheene, and parts adjacent, and so continue their trade of making war with the King of those countries and keeping us from all trade with them, till they have brought them to sell all to them, and by then by virtue of such agreement for ever exclude us'.[2]

It was evident that all the talk about the *règlement* was simply a blind, which the Dutch knew how to employ. This is borne out by one of Downing's dispatches.[3] The *règlement* about which there had been so much talk is now completely discarded;

[1] Lister, vol. iii, p. 330. [2] Ib., p. 336.

[3] 'I had also much discourse with De Witt about the *règlement* for the future. He did not object against any one of the articles of what I had given in; confessed that most of them were rational, and fitting, but then added that their intent was not to make any *règlement* for matters out of Europe only, but to have Europe included also. I told them that was a new matter; that the Conference we had was only concerned with matters out of Europe; and that in former times, 1614, 1622, Treaties had been made concerning the East Indies only. As to Europe, there were so many things to be considered, that it was impossible in a year's time to bring it to any issue.' Dispatch dated 9th Sept. 1664.

De Witt now tries to shelve the whole matter and to spin out more time by his insistence on the inclusion of Europe in a settlement that was avowedly designed for the settlement of quarrels in Asia and Africa. The Parliament which the Dutch had feared, and to which Downing made a reference in his dispatch, realized their worst fears; and the war with the Dutch could not be delayed.

A review of the above transactions brings out the importance of the East India trade. The East India Company takes the lead. The Councils of Trade and Plantations, representing the English merchants, draft an elaborate report, recounting all the grievances of the Company, and insisting on the observance of freedom of trade in the East; Downing acts according to the reports, and finds his task hopeless. The negotiations drag on, and the war follows inevitably.

Hence the importance of the East India trade for a true understanding not only of the economic theories, but also of the foreign policy, of the period. The Dutch monopoly leads to the formation of economic theories which crystallize into Mercantilism. As the monopoly could be broken by the State alone, and not by the disconnected and irregular efforts of private merchants, and as, moreover, the Dutch East India Company was invested with sovereign powers, there is an increasing demand for the protection and support of the State. In a series of petitions, ranging from the petition of 1611 to that of 1686, we find the same request. The State is called upon to redress their wrongs. The Economists of the period demand the same thing.

Commercial quarrels cease to be private quarrels, but assume the character of State quarrels, and develop ultimately into the Commercial Wars of the eighteenth century. The effects of this demand on the foreign policies of James, Charles, and Cromwell have already been noted. It is more instructive to note the effects on the policy of Charles II. It does not follow that because he took a genuine interest in the English Colonies he would have been ready to go to war with Holland. His hands were, however, forced by the East India merchants, and the war which the Company had longed for was declared. The Crown, therefore, adopted a new rôle in its dealings with foreign powers. It hears the grievances of the merchants, refers them to its Council, forwards them to its Ambassador, and, when the negotiations are fruitless, declares war. It is important to notice that Mun, Robinson, and a number of economists had demanded it before.[1] This throws a vivid light on the establishment of Mercantilism in England. It was the merchants who demanded protection against the Dutch monopoly, and not the Crown. This protection assumed various forms, but the most common were wars with the commercial rival, and prohibition laws, forbidding the importation of foreign articles. Hence, Mercantilism was not imposed by the Crown on the unwilling merchants, but was imposed on the Crown by them, as the only means whereby their interests could be safeguarded. Commercial quarrels with foreign powers led to insistence on collective action against the commercial rivals. From this the step to commercial, no less than tariff, wars was easy. This is exemplified in the history of the East India trade.

It is interesting to trace the causes of the Third Dutch War. We know, of course, the secret treaties made by Charles, the monetary aid rendered by Louis from time to time, and the terms upon which the money was paid to him. The Treaty of Dover is too well known to need any mention, and, since the time of Ranke and Klopp, other treaties of Charles have become known. We cannot deny that Charles II declared war partly because he had received money from Louis. We will go further and say that without the money which Louis doled out to him the war with Holland would have been avoided. It does not follow, however, that he was actuated by this motive alone. The East India trade must again be assigned as one of the causes of the Third Dutch War. The inevitable result of Charles's dependence upon Louis for money has been that our sympathies are enlisted on the side of the 'gallant little Protestant power', which waged an heroic war with two of the most powerful nations. We not only forget the hideous monopoly of the Dutch in the East, but also exclude the possibility of Charles's declaring war against the Dutch in 1672 through commercial reasons. There is reason to believe, however, that the East India trade was one of the causes of the Third Dutch War.

The island of Polaroon, of which the Company had been

[1] See Chapter I.

deprived by the Peace of Breda, had not been forgotten, and in a petition, dated 16th March 1668, the Company referred to it. The petition traced the history of the island; the agreement of the Dutch was noticed by the English Company; it referred to the 'shuffling policy, and dubious attitude' of the Dutch. It showed that the Dutch were not willing to restore the island unless and until the English Company renounced all claim for damages. This the English Company were not willing to do. They justified their policy on the ground that the 'pretended Act of Indemnity was the grant of the usurper Cromwell, who to procure the reparation of some few particular favourites of his own, was to extinguish the just demands of this Company, who were no parties to that Treaty'. The Company concluded that, as the 'usurper Cromwell' had prevented the Company from exacting the full amount due from the Dutch, it was only just that Charles II should try to recover the amount for them. The Company's statement about Cromwell is devoid of truth; nor can we say that the Company had a just claim to £250,000. All these claims had arisen mainly out of the 'debarring' of English ships from communication with the natives. This, the Dutch asserted, they had a perfect right to do. As the question of freedom of trade had not yet been settled, and as, moreover, no *règlement* of trade had been concluded, it seems, *prima facie*, illogical to claim damages. The Company was therefore responsible for complicating the situation and rendering the position of Temple, who was then negotiating a Treaty Marine, extremely difficult.[1]

It desired to obtain several amendments to the Treaty Marine of 1668. The first amendment referred to the old question of freedom of trade. The right of trading with the natives was to be granted to both the Companies. This was reasonable enough, and might have been allowed by the Dutch. The second proposal provided that in case 'either Company made agreement with the Natives for the sole buying of any commodity, yet that shall not hinder the liberty of commerce with the other Company, and that it will apply only to the party to the agreement, and no Company shall interrupt, hinder, or injure the trade upon that

[1] *Public Record Office*, C.O. 77, vol. xi, 1668–70. *The Petition of the East India Company*, 16th March 1668, no. 19.

pretext'. The Dutch could hardly raise an objection to this proposal, and it may appear at first that both these proposals would have been granted. It is, however, very doubtful if they would have allowed the second. It was aimed at their monopoly of the spices and would have produced far-reaching effects. The third and fourth proposals were eminently rational. They proposed that 'if either Company have war, the other will not furnish the enemy with ships or soldiers'. They proposed, moreover, that the actual besieging of a place by either Company by sea or land 'shall not hinder the other Company from trading to the other places adjacent to it'.[1]

The Company's proposals were conceived in a liberal spirit. They were eminently reasonable, and, on the whole, moderate. A comparison of these demands with the report of the Council, 1661, is instructive. The Company has now receded from many of the positions which the Council had originally taken up, and is content with only an instalment. The King, as usual, lent his support to the demands.[2] He instructed Temple to insert the amendments desired by the Company. This comes out specially in the Minutes of a Council. On the 3rd of April 1668 the Company's petition, praying for 'such an agreement for settling the Trade in India as may be suitable to the weight and importance of such an affair', was referred to the Committee.[3] This was not enough, however. The Company petitioned the Commissioners appointed to treat with the Dutch, and recounted to them the history of Polaroon. That island, the Company reminded the Commissioners, was to be restored to it by the 9th Article of the Treaty in 1622. They hoped that their Lordships would remove the mischiefs and the prejudice which might

[1] *Public Record Office*, C.O. 77, vol. xi, no. 77, 9th April 1668.

[2] 'At a Court at Whitehall, the Report of the Lords Committee for Trade upon the proposals for inserting several new Provisions in the Treaty Marine, His Majesty declared his approbation of it, and the Secretary of State is to prepare the Instructions for Sir William Temple, designed His Majesty's Ambassador to United Provinces, to arrange the same to be inserted in the said instructions.' The amendments desired by the Company were substantially—not completely—approved by the Committee. C.O. 77, vol. xi, no. 85, 15th July 1668.

[3] It is noticeable that some of the petitions of the Company are referred, not to the Council or Committee of Trade, but to a special Committee appointed to deal with them. This shows that the Council and Committee were not the only bodies that dealt with these affairs, but that, from time to time, Charles appointed extraordinary Committees for that purpose.

arise by 'such dishonourable delays and braggings as offered by those Dutch gentlemen, both to the Honour of His Majesty, and the just interest of his subjects'.[1]

It is important to notice that the Company did not confine themselves to petitioning the Council of Trade. They had direct access to the Crown, and, on this occasion, 'Lord Arlington had been attended, and informed of the damages received and sustained. They desired his lordship's favour and furtherance, that things might be brought to a good understanding between the two Companies.' Arlington replied that Sir William Temple had received general instructions concerning their grievances. The Treaty Marine was a great improvement on the former treaties, and if Sir William Temple had been allowed to remain at the Hague there is no doubt that some sort of settlement would have been arrived at. This is evident from a petition of Sir John Banks, the Governor of the Company. 'Of late', he informed the Committee, 'there was a treaty for several years together, between the two nations, managed by His Majesty's direction, by Sir William Temple in order of settling of the two East India Companies.' The Treaty was a step in the right direction, and though the Company desired a number of other reforms, it does not follow that it had been a failure.[2]

The quarrel of the rival Companies was not confined to the East, but was extending to other continents. This comes out especially in a petition of the East India Company. The

[1] Brit. Mus. Add. MSS. 17, c. 18, f. 199, dated March 1668.

[2] *Court Book*, no. 28, p. 17. 21st June 1672: 'At a Court of Committees it was resolved that an humble address be made to His Majesty that the Lord Ambassador now going for Holland, may have instructions that in general it may be provided, that what unjust damages either Company has sustained by the other in the East Indies, or in their passage to or from thence, since the last Article of Peace, in the late breach, or at least from 20th June 1672, may be repaid and made good to them that shall have suffered by them that have done the wrong. And in case a treaty shall be proceeded in, then the Company may have notice, whereby humbly to present to His Majesty what shall be needful for the better settlement and carrying on of that trade.' In *Court Book*, no. 29, 16th Feb. 1676, p. 217, we find the following reference to the war: 'For as much as the Commissioners for the Dutch East India Company did in February, 1674, deliver in a paper to His Majesty's Commissioners for the Treaty, to which an answer was prepared by the Company, but before the same could be delivered in, the Treaty was concluded by a particular article, it is ordered that the said answer be transcribed, in the book of transactions touching the Dutch affairs, with a Memorandum to the purpose above mentioned.'

petition was drafted in June 1673, and is therefore full of interest. The Company's demands show no signs of abatement. All the losses sustained by the Company since the Peace of Breda were to be made good. This seems reasonable enough, but it is necessary to point out that the Company's valuation of their losses always erred on the right side. Secondly, the Company desired restoration of the island of St. Helena, which the Dutch had taken 'by force of arms'.[1]

On the whole, it may be said that the Company's demands were not excessive, and that timely removal of the various grievances from which the English Company had suffered would have gone far towards getting rid of the main obstacle to a good understanding between the two nations.

It is clear from the above that the Company's grievances had shown no signs of decline; that the Peace of Breda, instead of satisfying the Company, had intensified the rivalry; that other causes of quarrel, as, for instance, the seizure of St. Helena, had occurred in the interval; that Charles's government had made representations to the Dutch government four years before the outbreak of the Dutch War; and that, finally, Downing had been requested to protest against the policy pursued by the Dutch in October 1672. I conclude, from the above, that the East India trade was one of the causes of the Third Dutch War.

The real mistake committed by previous historians lies in their entire ignorance of the grievances under which the Company had been labouring for years. The Peace of Breda was, from the point of view of the Company, thoroughly unsatisfactory. The old grievances still remained, and to them new ones had been added. All these were known to Charles, and his government had tried to redress them. He may have been moved primarily by his secret engagements with Louis. We have sufficient evidence to justify us in regarding them as the primary cause. This does not exclude the possibility of his declaring war upon other grounds than those of dependence upon France. The possibility is converted into a certainty when we consider the nature of the pamphlets written on the subject. Some of them are very important, as they reflect the opinion of the merchants of the time. It is necessary, however, to discriminate. It would

[1] *Public Record Office*, C.O. 77, vol. xii, no. 271, June 1673.

be utterly unhistorical to regard all the rabid anti-Dutch pamphlets as our primary authorities for the period. Nor should we pay much heed to a number of absurd stories scattered through their pages. This applies, for instance, to a pamphlet entitled *A Voyage to Holland*.[1] The writer gravely informs the reader that 'the Dutch procured Oliver Cromwell to be made a Protector'.[2] There are a number of other fantastic legends in the same amusing pamphlet. The cruelties of Amboyna give him a much-needed opportunity of attacking the Dutch in the vilest and coarsest terms. Much more reliable is the next on our list. It was inspired by the government and was published to justify the Third Dutch War. The causes of the war are detailed here in a clear and luminous style. The old dispute about the herring fishery reappears in this, as in other pamphlets. The arguments employed are, however, different. The Dutch had based their claim partly on the *Intercursus Magnus*, and partly on the Law of Nations. It was not difficult for the writer to show the hollowness of their grounds. The Treaty was granted to the Belgics, and not to the Dutch. Supposing even that the Dutch people were parties to it, this cannot prevent England from resuming her ancient rights. 'What hinders us from resuming our rights, when the reasons cease for which we parted with them to the just and generous house of Burgundy, but to these Hollanders never?'[4]

As regards the Dominion of the Seas, 'this has been acknowledged[5] by foreigners, and is justified by the precedent of the Romans and others. The right is a prescription truly immemorial; we cannot tell the time we had it not, nor by what degrees we arose up to it.' Again, the three causes of dispute in the seventeenth century—the dominion of the Seas, the herring fishery, and the East India trade—which I detailed in my first Chapter, led to the war with Holland. Holland was now, as before, the most serious commercial rival. Colbert's duties on various English articles, and his 'restraint' of woollen manufactures to Dieppe and Calais, were no doubt bitterly resented by the English merchants, and had led to an imposition upon French wines and brandies in 1670, and wines and vinegar in

[1] *Harleian Miscellany*, vol. iii, pp. 1–17.
[2] Ib., pp. 10–12.
[3] Ib. *A Justification of the Present War against the United Netherlands*, vol. viii, pp. 128–71, 1672.
[4] Ib., pp. 163–4.
[5] Ib., p. 165.

1667. But the commercial rivalry with France had not begun to be felt yet, and it was not till after the end of the Dutch war that French goods were prohibited. This is evident from the statement of Davenant. Though he was a free trader so far as the East India trade was concerned, he was not a blind devotee. He thought 'that England was wanting to its own interest in the seven or eight years of Charles II's reign in not retaliating' against France 'time enough'.[1] 'If', added Davenant, 'we had so proceeded, trade would have been upon an equal footing between us.' There is no doubt that England delayed in this matter, and that prompt retaliation would have been effective. It would, however, have precipitated the conflict that raged for over a century and a quarter.

It is clear, however, from the above, that the gravity of the situation was not perceived at the time, and that it was Holland, and not France, that was the most serious rival. This is evident, not only from the statements of Davenant but also from the famous speech of Shaftesbury against the Dutch. In this speech he analyses the various elements that combined to produce the quarrel. Nothing is more remarkable than the enunciation of his 'maxim of state'. Nations, he asserted, do not fall in love with one another, as private men do. It is the material interest of the nation that is the determining factor in every alliance or friendship. England was in alliance with France, because the interests of the two powers did not clash. With regard to Holland, however, the case was different. She had hunted the English out of the East Indies; she had massacred them at Amboyna; she had deprived them of all trade in the East Indies; and she had perpetrated horrible cruelties. Was it just, asked Shaftesbury, that Holland should be allowed to exercise her sway in the East? He replied with *Delenda est Carthago.*

It has been asserted that Shaftesbury was not sincere, and that these statements were made by him mainly because he was obliged to defend the tortuous policy of his master. This may be true to a certain extent. We know, however, that he was genuinely interested in the welfare of the English plantations, and that many excellent regulations were passed by him.[2] Nor

[1] Davenant, *Works*, edited by Whitworth, vol. v, p. 368. Compare also Grey's *Debates*, vol. ii.

[2] Messrs. Munro and Grant, *Acts of the Privy Council of England*, vol. i,

were his activities restricted to the plantations. The East India Company's Minutes contain several references to him, and on several occasions Charles appointed him to a Committee charged with hearing the Company's petitions of complaint. Supposing even that he was playing to the gallery, and that he knew the causes of the Third Dutch War to be totally different, this shows all the more clearly the importance of the East India trade. The latter is now alleged as the main cause, and wars are fought with Holland for the specific purpose of extorting commercial privileges from the Dutch.

The Peace of 1674 did not end the rivalry with Holland. It could be ended only by the complete defeat of the Dutch. This would have led to the restoration of some of the Spice Islands and the grant of freedom of trade to the English Company. The failures of these two wars had momentous results. The Dutch tightened their grip on the islands, and determined to prevent all possibility of future disputes arising by extending their sovereignty to the few important places that had escaped their domination. The most important of them was Bantam. The old King of Bantam had resigned all his authority in Bantam to his son, and, 'being free from the Horrible Captivity, and glorious misery of a throne', did 'enjoy the pleasures of a retired life'.[1] 'But the Dutch, who have successfully invaded the territories of my neighbours, are now entertaining the same designs upon mine. Their progress must be highly prejudicial to' the English in those parts.

About a year later we find the disillusioned old king reporting further progress, and requesting Charles to mediate between the two parties.[2] Soon afterwards his Ambassadors arrived in London. Luttrell (*Exact Relation*) has described their entry, and the reception they met with. It seems that Charles II neglected to receive them, for we find a number of letters from Childe to the Secretary of State, requesting the latter 'to show more honour to the King of Bantam's Ambassadors'.[3] Childe

Introduction. The editors attribute the improved tone of colonial administration to Locke and Shaftesbury. This is probably true.

[1] The letter of the King of Bantam to Charles, *Public Record Office*, C.O. 77, vol. xiv, no. 37, 1678–86. Received on 19th April 1681.

[2] Ib., no. 41.

[3] Ib., nos. 61, 65; the King of Bantam desired, among other things, the following: 'some great dogs,' 'five pieces of Cannon,' 'engineers,' 'matchlocks, and firelocks.' No. 55, 24th May 1682.

found, however, that the Ambassadors had no power to conclude any treaty, nor other certain commission or credentials, 'but only to deliver their presents and letters and to request answer to them'. He, however, represented to them the advantages that would result from the lowering of their customs duties, and asked for a grant of free customs for 10 years to the Japan Seas. It is not certain whether he obtained anything in return for his labours. The hesitating policy pursued by the king proved, however, his ruin. The Dutch, taking advantage of the quarrels of the old and the new king, interfered in the dispute, and assisted the young king. They entered Bantam by force of arms 'and made conquest of that city in a few days, with the loss of not above 40 men, and having possessed themselves of that place, did prevail with the (young) King to expel the English factory' and all the Europeans resident there. They permitted the Company's estate and factors to be transported to Batavia, where they were 'remaining on 23rd September last, but were very urgent for their departure thence'.[1]

A petition of Anne White stated that 'her husband, an Agent at Bantam, had been abroad in the usual places of watching', when he was 'most barbarously murdered by some of the Natives of Bantam'.[2] Another letter stated that 'Bantam is in the possession of the Dutch, and all burnt down'. It referred, moreover, 'to the insolence of the Dutch'.[3] More light was thrown on the affair by a letter of the King of Bantam. He informed Charles that the Dutch had been invited by his son into his country, and were 'now in my fort, fighting against my people, having turned out the English, French, and Danes, and given all the pepper of Bantam and Lampoone for gratuity'.[4] Charles's letter to the States-General is characteristic. He referred to the expulsion of the 'English from their own house', 'which they had built at their own very great costs and charges, and had peaceably enjoyed for 80 years, under the colour and name of the young King, while he was but in the nature of prisoner himself, environed by Guards of your subjects in his

[1] *Public Record Office*, C.O. 77, vol. xiv, no. 117, March 1683.
[2] Ib., vol. xiv, no. 69, 23rd June 1682.
[3] Nos. 67, 75, 78-85. Charles Sweetings's *Narrative of the Affairs at Bantam*, very long and elaborate.
[4] Letter of the King of Bantam, *Public Record Office*, C.O. 77, op. cit., no. 120.

castle'. This vigorous protest was followed by a demand no less insistent. He demanded indemnity for the loss of debts due to the Company upon the Island of Java, and disappointment of their ships and cargoes of above £100,000, besides the perpetual loss of Bantam and the South Sea Islands to this kingdom. The concluding part of the petition is so important that it is reproduced here verbatim: 'This affair touches us so extremely in honour and Interest, that we cannot admit of any delay, and therefore have commanded this bearer, not to stay above 14 days, after his arrival at the Hague, for your peremptory and final answer to their Propositions. We recommend them to you as a thing of the greatest importance for the continuance of that good correspondence and friendship which we desire may be always lasting between us.'[1]

This vigorous and characteristic dispatch testifies to the genuine interest of Charles in all that concerned the East India trade, specially with regard to his representations to foreign powers. The Company is now practically identified with the State, and all its grievances are vigorously expressed, and, if possible, quickly redressed. Sunderland's letter to Mr. Chudleigh, the English Ambassador at the Hague, shows the effect produced on Charles by the 'Bantam business'. 'The King', he informed Chudleigh, 'did resent the action of Bantam and the injuries done to his subjects there.' 'His Majesty', said Sunderland, 'would have you immediately ask an audience, and deliver the same to them, and from time to time assist and Countenance the bearer, in such manner and method as he shall agree upon.'[2] The King of Denmark also protested against the high-handedness of the Dutch, and demanded satisfaction.[3]

Chardin's account of the negotiations at the Hague reveals the politic delays so successfully resorted to by the Dutch. The latter asserted that the old king was their mortal enemy, and they were therefore obliged to act in self-defence. As for the injuries and insults to the king's flag, 'these were consequences of war, no more to be imputed to them than to us'. They ex-

[1] *Public Record Office*, C.O. 77, vol. xiv, no. 131, dated 'March–April, 1682'. There is a draft of this letter in the same volume. It is numbered 129–30.
[2] Sunderland's letter to Chudleigh, *Public Record Office*, C.O. 77, vol. xiv, no. 137, dated 27th April 1683.
[3] C.O. 77, vol. xiv, 16th–20th May 1683.

cused themselves from speaking further on the plea of insufficient information, and fell back on the worn-out methods of prolonging the negotiations. Chardin concluded by saying that 'the business will take long time in sifting to compose this'.[1]

The Company had meanwhile prepared a secret expedition against the Dutch, and had secured the approval of Charles. War would, no doubt, have taken place in the East. Charles's death, however, changed their plans and the expedition was diverted to another quarter.

James II seems to have been as determined to maintain the Company in all its rights as his brother. The grant of a commission by James II to the Company and the hideous brutality which attended the trial of the rebels of St. Helena were afterwards a subject of inquiry. James II seems to have been determined to declare war against Holland, and to recover Bantam from them. Unfortunately, there is no document in the Public Record Office on the subject. Our only authority is Burnet. His statements must be taken *cum grano salis*, and must be tested and compared with some other reliable authority. He asserts that the King intended 'to make a quarrel of it as soon as his affairs put him in a condition to make a war. The French were at the same time making preparations at Toulon, and it was generally believed that the two kings were resolved again to fall upon the States.'[2] It is not necessary here to insist on the importance of Bantam to the English Company. It was the only important trading centre left to the English Company in the South Seas, and James may well have thought that the seizure of this place would be fatal to the Company's activities in the East India Islands. He may, therefore, have regarded this as a sufficient ground for war. The capture of Bantam had unforeseen consequences. The English Company had been trying to secure freedom of trade in the East India Islands for over 80 years. They had concluded many agreements with the Dutch; they had fought three wars; and, finally, they had secured the support of the State. All these efforts had been fruitless. The treaties were no sooner made than broken. The last two wars had been indecisive, and the Dutch had maintained their monopoly unimpaired. The main cause of their

[1] C.O. 77, vol. xiv, no. 150, dated 13th–23rd May 1683.
[2] Miss Foxcroft's *Supplement to Burnet*, pp. 221–2.

successes in the East lay in the exercise of their overwhelming power. This was due to their support by the State. The English Company did not secure the latter, and was consequently deficient in the former. Charles II's government identified the interests of the Company with those of the State and waged two wars. The failure of these wars sealed the fate of English trade in the islands. Nearly all the important islands were brought by the Dutch under their sway, until Bantam alone remained. With the fall of Bantam the Company concentrated all its strength on its possessions in India proper. Its energies were not distracted by the incessant demands of the Spice Islands, and it could devote itself to its proper task in a spirit of piety. Nothing is more amazing than the pious hopes, the benevolent intentions, and the fervid idealism which Childe's dispatches to his factors in India reveal. The hard, level-headed man of business sprinkles his dispatches with a liberal mixture of Biblical quotations and worthy maxims of State. There is no distraction, as there is no hurry. The Company seems bent upon enlarging its investments and establishing more factories in India. It still has a few struggling factories in the old battle-ground, but the contest is now practically over, and the Dutch are left without a rival. To the loss of Bantam may therefore be traced the foundation of the British Empire in India. Here the English factors were strong enough to keep the Dutch in check, and to oppose a formidable barrier to their ambitions. The Dutch were too weak to be able to establish their sovereignty in both places at once. Hence, their concentration on the East India Islands and their gradual decline in India.

The rivalry that had existed between the two nations gave place to Anglo-French rivalry. With the fall of Bantam and the establishment of the Dutch rule in all the important islands, all causes of rivalry disappeared. There was no rivalry in the islands simply because no rivals were permitted there. Hence the absence of anti-Dutch pamphlets. The Jacobites might write a score of scurrilous lampoons, but the Company and its defenders had their gaze fixed, not on the islands which the Dutch monopolized, but on India. There are occasional references to the Dutch 'cruelties, etc.' in the Company's dispatches. But we see no sign of that ferocious hatred which found vent in its petitions to the Charles's.

The Company, however, came face to face with another European rival in India. The Portuguese had been defeated so many times in the Indian Ocean, and had been so greatly weakened by their own misconduct in the East, that they had begun to regard them as insignificant. They certainly remained so throughout the rest of the century. But their weakness assumed a totally new form. The island of Bombay had proved very costly to the King. There were, in the first place, the difficulties that inevitably attended the surrender of the Portuguese possessions in India. It was not till 1663 that the island was actually delivered.[1] The melancholy letters of Shipman to Marlborough show that the condition of the town was not satisfactory.[2] Cooke's description of the island is interesting. He regarded it 'as a very pleasant island, wholesome air, fertile in cocoanuts and Rice, the present revenue to His Majesty but small, but will increase as trade doth and for which it is very well situated'.[3] Sir George Oxenden and others who wrote from the same place were not by any means unanimous on the last point, which Mr. Cooke had so lightly touched upon. There were a number of other difficulties. Gary had protested against 'the Impositions laid by the Portuguese Ambassador upon ships navigating in their streams', and had suggested 'that all boats and vessels should navigate freely in the streams and currents of that King, between this and the *terra firma* beyond Tanna, as far as Callian, etc.'[4]

Other difficulties soon arose. Cooke seems to have taken possession of Mahim. This was accompanied by a demand for all the rents that had been received by the Portuguese Viceroy 'from the time the Earl of Marlborough arrived to the day we took possession'.[5] For this state of things Charles himself was to blame. The English ministers seem to have had the haziest idea of Bombay. It was doubtful whether Tanna was really included in the original grant. I think that it was not included therein. Gary himself asked Charles to request the Portuguese King to grant that place. A petition of the Company throws still further light on the subject. It prayed

[1] *Public Record Office*, C.O. 77, vol. ix, 1663–5. The letter of the King of Portugal, 16th August 1663.
[2] Ib., no. 33, 18th Nov. 1663.
[3] Ib., no. 106.
[4] C.O. 77, vol. iv, no. 202, 16th Feb. 1665
[5] Ib., no. 308.

for the inclusion of Carinjah and Tanna in the treaty for the delivery of Bombay.[1]

As Charles had surrendered the whole island to the Company, Carinjah and Tanna, which the Company desired to be included in the treaty, were evidently not ceded by the Portuguese King. Only Bombay seems to have been ceded. The Portuguese seem, therefore, to have been legally justified in resisting the Company's claim to those places. These complications were hardly foreseen by Charles II at the time of the delivery of the island. They might, perhaps, have been removed if sufficient revenue had been derived from Bombay. This was, however, totally impossible. The following estimate shows clearly the difficulty of making Bombay pay for all the expenses incurred in its defence:

The total cost of a year's victuals, ships, and officers' and men's pay was calculated at	£10,498	16	0
The cost of ammunition was	1,000	0	0
Total estimate for the year will be . .	£11,498	16	0

This would have provided sixty recruits under 'some fit Lieutenant who may be allowed Captain's pay at 8/-, which, with those we support yet remaining upon, may be able to keep the island till the next year'.[2] There were, however, other troops in Bombay, and it is evident that more money would have been required for the maintenance of the garrison. The rent, however, was totally insufficient for the purpose:

The rents of various villages brought in	25,920	1	18
The rent of tobacco brought in	9,550	0	0
The rent of taverns brought in	2,400	0	0
The Customs brought in	18,000	0	0
The coco-nuts brought in	18,000	0	0
Total .	73,870	1	18
To which may be advanced	1,129	1	62
Total .	75,000 xeraphims		
The latter, when converted into English money, was equivalent to	£6,490	17	9[3]

It is evident from the above that the revenues were totally

[1] C.O. 77, vol. xi, no. 168, dated 16th Jan. 1668.

[2] *Public Record Office*, C.O. 77, vol. x, no. 35, 26th March 1666.

[3] Ib., no. 197.

inadequate, and that Charles, who was always in financial difficulties, was only too glad to sell the place for a nominal rent.[1] He surrendered all his rights in Bombay to the Company on the 16th December 1667.[2] The Attorney-General later met the Company and requested 'Arlington to move His Majesty this day in Council to order the Lords of the Committee of Trade and Plantations to meet to-morrow at 3 after dinner and so despatch this business as that it may be reported to His Majesty in Council on Friday'. This is an excellent example of the way in which the Lords of Trade worked.[3]

The Company's quarrel with the Portuguese Ambassador was due primarily to that vagueness in the original grant of the Portuguese to which I have already referred.[4] Two volumes of the C.O. 77 contain a number of memorials, petitions of the Company, and the replies of the Portuguese Ambassador. They are tedious, rambling, and uninteresting. Their chief importance consists in their giving us an insight into the administration of the Lords of Trade and Plantations. Nothing is too minute for them. They go patiently through a mass of evidence; frame their report; instruct the Secretary of State to ask Mr. Parry, the English Agent at Lisbon, to make representations about the matter, and to present their report to the Portuguese King. Mr. Parry's replies are given to us; and so are those of the Portuguese Ambassador. The Lords of Trade forward the Ambassador's reply to the Company, and wait for the reply of the Company. The Company's reply is forwarded to the Ambassador, and so the negotiations take their slow course.

Foreign policy is now dictated by purely commercial considerations, and the Lords serve as intermediaries between the East India Company and foreign powers. The Portuguese Ambassador complained of the seizure of the Port and Island of Mahim; he complained, moreover, that the Portuguese subjects had been compelled to take an oath of allegiance to the Company; finally, that though an order for the restitution of those estates which had been confiscated was carried into effect, 'there were not restituted the rents of the estate'. The Company's defence is curious. They asserted that 'Mahim is not an

[1] *Public Record Office*, vol. v, no. 226.
[2] See the Attorney-General's Draft, vol. xi, no. 40, dated 15th Feb. 1667.
[3] C.O. 77, vol. xi, no. 42.
[4] See above.

island'. Nature never made it so. With regard to the oath of allegiance, it was a sovereign privilege, and they intended, evidently, to exercise it. As regards the last point, the commands of Charles II had been punctually obeyed in restoring the land claimed by just titles to the Proprietors.[1] There is a succession of papers on the subject, containing a full account of the disputes 'lately had with the Portuguese'. An example will suffice. A petition begins thus: 'The continual Affronts, Abuses, and Injuries which the English Nation have received here in India from the Portuguese nation are innumerable.'[2] A mere assertion of right is totally meaningless without the intention of exercising that right. The Portuguese showed that they were determined to exercise it. They 'not only refused to deliver to them', the Company's factors, those islands and dependencies mentioned, but 'do on some of them so strengthen themselves as that for but passing by in the open stream, and at distance from them (they) sally out with their boats and arbitrarily lay impositions on our trade'; they forced the Company's factors and ships to pay duties for passing by those places, which were known to 'depend absolutely' on the Custom House of Bombay. Nor was this all. They claimed dominion over the Portuguese and other subjects 'remaining with the Company'.[3] Some light is thrown on the subject by a paper entitled 'Notes concerning Passages or straits of Tannah and Carinjah'.[4] The quarrel turned on the interpretation of the 11th Article of Peace with Portugal, and specially the words 'Port and island of Bombay'. The question arose whether the King of Portugal, in transferring his right and sovereignty to the Company, did not thereby transfer the same right of dominion over all the islands therein, and over all those small straits and passages which make it.

With regard to Tanna, the Portuguese do not seem to have taken any custom there, before Bombay was transferred to Charles. Moreover, the customs payable belonged as a privilege to the Customs House of Mahim. The danger lay in the Portuguese making themselves masters of Carinjah and all the islands in the bay.

[1] *Public Record Office*, C.O. 77, vol. xii, 1671–3, nos. 36, 37, 43, 54.
[2] Ib., nos. 14, &c.
[3] Ib., vol. xiii, 1674–7, nos. 47, 49, 59.
[4] Ib., no. 73.

Again, they exacted marks of sovereignty in those places and refused to pay the customs. The dispute was referred to the Lords of Trade and Plantations. Unfortunately the original map of Bombay could not be found, and the Lords therefore fell back on Shipman's commission, the drafts of which contained the following words: 'And other the Premisses.' Altogether, five copies of this commission seem to have been examined by the Lords. They relied, moreover, on one article of a memorial presented to the Portuguese Ambassador on 25th July 1663. It declared that the grant included not only Bombay proper, but also Tanna and Salsette.[1]

It cannot be denied that the Company's claim was weak. The Commission and Instructions of Shipman could hardly be produced by the Lords as evidence of the inclusion of those two places in the original grant. Their interpretation of the words in the commission was equally unfortunate. They do not refer to those places at all, but seem merely a legal superfluity. Again, it was illogical to deduce the right of the Company to those places from a memorial which desired their inclusion in the treaty. If those two places had been included in the original grant, there was certainly no necessity for the Company's petition. We cannot, therefore, regard the judgement as impartial. But impartiality was out of the question in a case which, if it had been decided in favour of the Portuguese, would have led to the strangulation of Bombay. The Lords' final report was read in Council on the 23rd of February 1677. Its recommendations might have been foreseen from their previous report. They demanded (1) the abolition of tribute for sailing

[1] *Public Record Office*, C.O. 77, vol. viii, 16th Jan. 1677, no. 125. There are five copies of Shipman's commission in the same volume. The following is an extremely interesting example of the way in which the Lords set to work: 'Upon the whole matter, their Lordships, rather than insist farther on the demand of Salsette and Carinjah, think fit to consider what is the right and extent which His Majesty has by the grant of the Port. (1) Whether it draw not with it other islands; (2) How far are the English freed by common right in the Portuguese streams, when they land not on their shores, but drive their trades with strangers, and particularly such impositions as are grown up now; (3) In Case His Majesty forbid the Company to submit to those Impositions, and write to the Portuguese, How are the Company to right themselves by the same way of Impositions on the Portuguese?' These are probably the points which the Lords discussed at their next meeting. The paper is dated 16th Jan. 1677, C.O. 77, vol. xiii, no. 143. The Report of the Lords was received by the Council on 23rd Feb. 1677.

up the river; (2) satisfaction for all that has been injuriously exacted to the 'Common Right'; (3) they advised the King to 'command his subjects to refuse payment of these arbitrary and unjust demands at Tanna and Carinjah, as prejudicial to your rights of sovereignty and contrary to the Laws of the World'; (4) they declared that if the English merchants were willing to submit to the duties and customs of each respective place, it was all that was required.[1] They added, moreover, that 'whereas the East India Company had a right to half the customs which are paid at Gombroon in Persia, as the Portuguese had the like at Cong in the same Kingdom, all the Indian Junks should be granted passes for security in their navigation to Gombroone'. The minute of the Council is instructive. 'Upon reading which clause, His Majesty was graciously pleased to approve the same, and Mr. Secretary Coventry is to take care to see the same added accordingly.'[2]

The Portuguese Ambassador alleged that the Company had given encouragement to the people to bring complaints. He asserted, moreover, that the estates of Portuguese had been confiscated, and instanced the case of an Alvaro Perez. The Company replied that Perez had been treated kindly and that he deserved the punishment meted out to him. He had been stationed to guard a post at a time when the invasion of Bombay was feared. Perez not only deserted his post, but incited others to do the same. They denied that they had confiscated the estates of the Portuguese, and asserted that 'restitution was given to all, with universal applause, and a sort of jubilee over the whole island'.[3]

The dispute was long and tedious. Mr. Secretary Coventry was requested to prepare articles for Charles's signature and to instruct Mr. Parry to solicit the effects of the Lords' Report. Mr. Parry's account of the transactions was disappointing. He

[1] *Public Record Office.* See a number of petitions from the Company on the same subject. C.O. 77, vol. xiii, nos. 168–74, 188–93, 196–202.

[2] Ib., nos. 205–6, dated 23rd Feb. 1677.

[3] The services performed by the Lords of Trade in the course of these transactions are important. The following gives us an insight into the working of this institution. 'They are sending the memorial' of the Portuguese Ambassador to the East India Company 'that you may prepare your answer thereunto, which they will be ready to receive and consider on Thursday next, being the Vth inst., at 10 in the morning'. 3rd June 1677.

pressed the Portuguese Secretary for Foreign Affairs to write to the Portuguese Viceroy in India about the matter. Yet nothing was done. The 'business has been three months before the Council of Foreign Plantations, time enough for it to give a full and particular Report'.[1] Apparently, it did not, for we hear the same complaints from the Company. There is another letter of the Lords of Trade to Coventry, requesting him to send to Parry, the English Agent at Lisbon, the papers enclosed by them, 'so that he may be able to conceive the mischief which Perez wrought in the East Indies'.[2]

We do not know what the result of these tedious negotiations was. The documents in the Public Record Office are silent. But Tanna and Carinjah remained in Portuguese hands. A review of the foreign policy detailed above brings out the importance of the reign of Charles II. The Council and the Committee of Trade and Plantations play a leading part. Their reports are acted upon by Charles; they serve as intermediaries between the Company and the foreign powers, and they mould the economic policy of the period. This conception of the duties of the State was not new. It had been urged by a succession of economic writers. What is entirely new is the effect produced by the East India trade on that policy. As we have seen, war was declared on Holland mainly because she was the most determined rival of the Company in the East;[3] the Third Dutch War is justified by Charles II on the same grounds; the capture of Bantam finds Charles ready to defend its interest to the utmost of his power. James II follows suit. The same applies to Portugal. The negotiations that ensue serve only to heighten our admiration for the essentially useful service rendered by the Lords of Trade. They give us an insight into the working of their office.

The foreign policy detailed above was dictated by purely commercial considerations. It is now conceived as the sole instrument whereby the commercial privileges of the Englishmen in foreign parts can be guaranteed. The Navy is regarded as the chief means by which this can be realized. We see here the

[1] *Public Record Office*, C.O. 77, vol. xiv, 1678–86, no. 1, 30th April 1678.
[2] Ib., no. 8. [3] See above.

fusion of the various causes of the Anglo-Dutch rivalry described in Chapter I. The political economists who had demanded State support, the seamen who had demanded expulsion of the Dutch from 'His Majesty's Seas', and the East India merchants who were never tired of pointing out the Dutch State and its intensely commercial policy as the model to which all States ought to conform—all demand energetic State action. The conception of the State has become narrow. It is now the sole instrument whereby commercial privileges can be secured. A reaction undoubtedly takes place at the end of the seventeenth century. But that reaction, as will be pointed out in the last chapter, was not a genuine reaction. The State remained the supreme organ through which the colonial, naval, and commercial aspirations of the English people could be realized. This had been due mainly to the spirit of monopoly displayed by the foreign nations. As that monopoly was backed by all the resources of an enterprising State, its overthrow was impossible without the active support of the only organ which could crush it.

Mercantilism in the seventeenth century was not, therefore, imposed from above. It supplied a genuinely felt want, and the central government did nothing else but register the decrees of public opinion. It is therefore a necessary step in the expansion of English commerce. Freedom of trade was impossible as long as other European nations exercised a monopoly of the most rigid type. Only after that monopoly had been totally crushed could freedom of trade be allowed. It is consequently entirely misleading to ignore the conditions that gave rise to the Mercantilism of the seventeenth century and to treat it as a strange phenomenon, as a classical example of perverted ingenuity and narrow selfishness.

The East India trade in the seventeenth century furnishes us with a good example of the way in which Mercantilism received its impetus. For over eighty years the petitions of the Company harp on the same theme—the absolute necessity of protection by the Crown against their rivals in the East. After the realization of its wishes by Charles and the phenomenal growth of trade that resulted therefrom, we find a characteristic change in its policy. It no longer desires 'fussy' interference with trade but advocates free trade.[1] This was due to the fact that the increased importation of Indian commodities led to fierce attacks on the Company. The latter, in self-defence, advocated freedom from restrictions on the importation of Indian commodities into England. It is necessary, however, to insist on the fact that it was the protection of Charles that led ultimately to the formulation of free trade theories by the Company. He protected the Company not only against the foreign, but also the domestic, enemies of the Crown. A series of Charters, beginning on the 3rd of April 1661 and ending[2] in 1683, conferred the most ample powers on the Company. It was allowed to make war against any non-Christian prince within the limits assigned to it, and was empowered to punish interlopers. Charles and James II's proclamations against the Interlopers and their trials in London have all been adequately dealt with by Sir William Hunter. Without the effective support of Charles the whole East India trade would have passed into the hands of the Dutch. It is this consideration that helps us to understand the exaggerated importance which the early economists attached to the support of the State and the organization of industry. Nor can we say that they were mistaken in their ideas. I have already described the fatal effects produced by the failure of the State to follow the policy which the merchants advocated.[3] It was essential that the separate traders should be organized in a Company. Only thus would they be able to deal with their enemies. Without organization there would be nothing else but confusion. This had actually happened in 1654–6. The phenomenon was repeated in 1698–1700.

The policy of Charles II forms a landmark in the history of the Company. Backed by his Government it developed into an organization wielding immense powers and exercising all the rights of sovereignty in the East. The Company, however, was not free from the constant attacks to which it had been subjected under Cromwell. With the growth of the East India trade under Charles II they increased in vigour, and assumed enormous proportions after the Revolution.

[1] See the last chapter.
[2] Shaw, *Charters granted to the East India Company*, pp. 58–119, &c.
[3] See Chapter I.

The Company's justification lay in the necessity for order and regulation. This was, contended Childe and others, the only means whereby the East India trade could be expanded. Discipline, asserted Samuel Lamb, was absolutely necessary. As an army without discipline degenerates into a mob, so commerce without discipline would degenerate into piracy. This was not all. The separate traders would be overwhelmed by the disciplined Dutch, and England would suffer. It is necessary to insist that the defenders of monopolies justified them on national grounds. No Company, asserted Childe, should exist unless it conduced to the public welfare. The arch-monopolist was the most eloquent defender of free trade. This may appear contradictory at first. Really his monopoly was the main cause of his advocacy of free trade. The end he sought was the same. 'All restrictions of Trade are nought and consequently that no Company whatsoever, whether they (it) trade in a Joint Stock or under Regulation, can be for public good, except it may be easy for all or any of His Majesty's subjects to be admitted into all or any of the said Companies.' [1] If a Regulated Company was of greater utility to the nation than a Joint Stock Company, then, said Childe, the latter ought to be abolished. But he proved that it was totally unsuitable for the purpose. 'For Countries with which His Majesty has no alliance, nor can have any by reason of their distance, or Barbarity, or non-communication with the princes of Christendom, etc., where there is a necessity of maintaining forces and Forts, such as East India and Guinia, Companies of Merchants are absolutely necessary.' [2] Freedom of trade was impossible, for 'that which is every man's business will be no man's business; the Kings and Governors of these countries will take all opportunities to make their advantage and to put injuries and hardships upon the English when they find them divided for want of Councils or strength to right themselves'.[3] In proof, Papillon cites 'the Sad experiences in 3 or 4 years of open trade, from 1653 to 1657, when the English began to lose their renown and esteem in India, and the trade in

[1] Childe, *New Discourse of Trade*, chap. iii, pp. 102–3.

[2] Ib., p. 103.

[3] *East India Trade the most profitable Trade to the United Kingdom*, by T. Papillon, 1677, Brit. Mus. 1029, g. 24. There are two editions of this in the British Museum. The other is dated 1680.

India became unprofitable'. 'There are above 100 Rajas, Kings, which are Gentu Princes, but governing with absolute power in their Dominions, and as many ports and places of Trade' with which the Company has to deal.[1] 'This could not be done but on a public charge of the nation by some General Tax, and by some United Body of Men, encouraged to undertake the same by special privileges and Immunities, granted to them and their Successors.'[2]

The arguments brought forward by the East India Company in support of its privileges harmonized with the prevailing view of the necessity of preserving the East India trade for the nation. If the private individuals had been left to shift for themselves, and to do what they liked, the trade would have been completely lost. This is what really happened under Cromwell, and again on the foundation of a rival Company under William III. The mutual recriminations in which they indulged, and the consequent weakness which flowed therefrom, opened the eyes of both the Companies to the dangers by which the two were surrounded in India. Their final amalgamation in 1708 saved the English power in India. Hence the Company were substantially correct when they foretold the disastrous consequences of the opening of the trade to the Indies. 'If the East India Company be destroyed, and the Trade left open, then all the dearly bought and valuable privileges of the East India Company will be lost.' 'Moreover, all the European nations have power to make war upon any nation in India, be it native or European. If it were known in India that they have no such power, they should be constantly affronted and abused by the Natives.'[3]

If the trade to the Indies could be carried only by Chartered Companies, the Crown had to choose between the two types of Companies then in existence—the Regulated or the Joint Stock. The Regulated type seemed to offer facilities which were non-existent in the Joint Stock. Nor were the Regulated Companies slow to take advantage of the weak points in the Company's armour. They could enlist the sympathies of the clothiers, who felt the effects of the importation of the Indian commodities; of

[1] Childe, *The East India Trade is the most National of all Foreign Trades*, 1681, India Office Library Tracts, vol. lxxxiii, pp. 30–8.

[2] *An Answer to the Two Letters*, 1676, Brit. Mus. 1029, g. 22.

[3] Childe, *The East India Trade*, p. 38.

the interlopers, who chafed at the restrictions imposed upon their 'natural right' to trade; of the lawyers, who regarded the monopoly of the Company as a glaring violation of the Magna Charta; and, finally, of the 'Country party', who viewed with the gravest apprehensions this unwarranted and unusual exercise of the King's prerogative. The latter regarded it 'as the monopoly of Monopolies. The Company's Charter creates Forfeitures of all Englishmen that dare dwell in, or trade to half the world; it gives power over their persons to imprison, and keep in Gaol during pleasure. It creates an arbitrary power in the Crown of punishing Englishmen by Discretion, after they are imprisoned and their Estates seized', &c. 'Could any man be ignorant that every Englishman hath such a property in his Estate, privileges, liberty, person, Limb, and Life, that none of them can be subject to be seized, forfeited, or anyway destroyed, but by force of Laws made by the Free Consent in Parliament. Is not this the distinction between Turkish and French vassals, and Freeborn Englishmen?'[1] If the Company's monopoly was obnoxious to the lawyers and constitutionalists, their system of trading was equally offensive to the 'true merchants'. 'The constitution of the Turkey Company being a Regulated Company, and not driven by a Joint Stock, is open and comprehensive, admitting any that are bred merchants, such as are sons and apprentices to Freemen. . . . They, upon payment of £25, or £30, are admitted into all the Privileges of the Turkey Company, and each adventures and Trades for as much as he is able, by which open way of dealing, this Company is increased, from 60 or 70 persons, to at least 500 Traders. The East India Company, on the other hand, manage their trade by a Joint Stock, confined to the narrow compass of some few persons, exclusive to all others, under the penalty of Mulcts, Fines, Seizures and other extraordinary proceedings.'[2] 'The great Companies, Turkey, Muscovy, Russia, Hamburg, are different from the East India Company in that they trade not by Joint Stock, but Regulation. The former may truly be said to be Managers, Regulators and Improvers of Trade; but the invisible East India Merchant, the Body Politick,

[1] *Two Letters concerning the East India Co.*, Brit. Mus. 1029. g. 22.
[2] *The Allegations of the Turkey Co.*, 1681, Brit. Mus. 816. m. 11 (74). Compare also Pollexfen's *Discourse on Trade*, 1696, in the India Office Library Tracts, vol. lxxxiii, pp. 49-61.

countenances some few among them to engross, buy and sell at their own Rates, and excludes all others from the great and excessive Advantage of the few.'[1]

The real weakness in the arguments of the opponents of the East India Company lay in their ignoring the fact that the trade in India could not be carried on without an authorized and definitely recognized body, supervising the Englishmen in the East. Nor could an Ambassador be sent to India. The cost of maintaining one at the Mogul's Court was prohibitive at all times. It was still more so under the needy Charles II. Only a completely centralized and co-ordinated Company could supply the place of the Ambassador. The Regulated Company, with its divergent interests, lack of control, and inefficient management was the least fitted to exercise sovereignty in a country where commercial considerations were inextricably mixed with purely political questions, where hesitation or delay involved irreparable loss, and where the disunion and mutual distrust which characterized many of the meetings of the Regulated Companies could result only in total ruin.

It is probably on this ground that 'Two papers delivered by the Turkey Merchants, including objections against the East India Company, from the Clerk attending the Lords of His Majesty's Privy Council, were now read in Court, and also a paper drawn up in answer unto the same'.[2] The Lords thereupon requested the Treasury to direct the Customs Commissioners to 'present an account of what quantity of cloth have been exported for three years past by the East India Company and the Levant Company respectively'.[3]

It is likely that the Lords desired a limited enlargement of the East India Company's Stock. 'Upon this petition the King was pleased to direct that the petitioners should propose some Methods how the same Stock and Adventurers should be enlarged, without prejudice to his Customs, and Trade; which were accordingly made, but after this Time all Endeavours of the kind were rejected.'[4] The Privy Council may have desired enlargement of

[1] *A Collection of Papers relating to the East India Trade*, India Office Tracts, vol. lxxxiii, no. 7, pp. 17–18.

[2] *Court Minute Book*, 1680–2, 19th Aug. 1681.

[3] *Treasury Book*, 1681–5, 12th July 1681, p. 241.

[4] Pollexfen's *Discourse of Trade*, op. cit., p. 57.

the Stock and may have regarded with suspicion the large amount of it held by Childe and others.[1] Yet the Joint Stock principle was maintained by the Council with rigidity and vigour. The opponents of the Company were thoroughly crushed, and did not raise their heads again till 1689. The vigorous policy of the Council aimed at the maintenance of the Company's privileges, both against the Company's internal and external enemies. The Interlopers and others who tried to evade the Company's restrictions were prosecuted; while every support was given to the Company in its negotiations with, and protests against, foreign powers. It is this combination of commerce with diplomacy, politics with economics, or, as the saying went, 'Plenty with Power', that stamps the Restoration Settlement of English Trade and Finance as the most beneficial measure of the century. The Council symbolized the ascendancy of commerce and trade, and dictated the foreign policy of the Crown for that purpose. Nor is it easy to distinguish the King from the Privy Council. We have several petitions dealing exclusively with commercial affairs addressed personally to Charles II; while others, recounting the grievances suffered at the hands of foreign powers, are addressed to the Lords of Trade and Plantations. The key to the situation is to be found in the harmonization of the policy of the two. The Committee of Trade carried out a policy with the broad outlines of which Charles II was in complete sympathy. The consolidation of the heterogeneous elements of the Company into an efficient and organized body was due not only to his desire for the extension of English trade—that was the predominant trait of the whole reign in its dealings with the Company—but also to the straightened condition in which he was placed by the actions of the Parliament.[2]

It was partly the disorganization of his finances that led to the bestowal of enormous privileges on the Company. Without it, the Company would have been shorn of many of the powers extorted from Charles. Nor did he ask in vain. The Company's address of welcome was accompanied by a present of plate worth

[1] I cannot agree with Professor Scott (op. cit., p. 142) that he owned only £17,000 stock. See next chapter.

[2] See Dr. Shaw's masterly Introductions to the *Treasury Series*, explaining, for the first time, the main causes of the poverty of Charles II. Also, his *Beginning of National Debt*, in *Owen's College Historical Essays*.

£3,000. The first loan to the King began in 1662, with £10,000. From April 1666 to July 1667 the Company lent £70,000 to the King. There is a comparatively short period of repose, but, 'His Majesty remembering with what affection and readiness they supplied him the last time, he doubts not that they will as cheerfully give their assistance in supplying him with'—money. From 1675 to 1679 the Company lent him the following sums: (1) £50,000; (2) £40,000; (3) £20,000; (4) £40,000; (5) £30,000; (6) £20,000. Total for the five years £200,000. There is a lull in 1680. But the loans of previous years are in 1681 transformed into 'voluntary contributions'. This was probably due to the inventive genius of Sir Josiah Childe. During the last four years of his reign Charles received the following: (1) £10,750; (2) £2,150; (3) £5,000; (4) £10,500; (5) £10,750. Total of voluntary contributions £39,150. The total money received by Charles in the form of loans and presents, from 1660–84, was therefore £324,150.[1]

It is this financial support on the part of the Company which helps to explain its extensive privileges. The five Charters granted by Charles enlarged the powers of the Company, decided that 'the trade can by no means be settled and carried on with such advantage as by a Joint Stock, and that a loose and general trade will be the ruin of the whole', and conferred upon the Company the invaluable right of making war with any non-Christian prince within the limits assigned to it.[2]

The Interlopers were a source of constant anxiety to the Directors. The latter's dispatches to their factors in the East are full of the negligence of their officials, the boldness of the Interlopers, and the injury inflicted on the Company by their activities. The Charters had conferred upon the Company the exclusive right to trade, and prohibited others from trading thither. But mere prohibition was not enough. What they required was the forfeiture of their goods, so as to deter others from trading there. The Company's petition was referred by the Council to the Attorney-General, who decided that the King could restrain his subjects 'from trading or trafficking with an infidel Country not

[1] I have compiled the above from the following: *Court Minute Books*, Nos. 24, 25. *Treasury Books*, 1675–9, 1681–5.

[2] Shaw, *Charters granted to the East India Company*, pp. 58, 76, 78, 119, &c.

in amity with your Majesty', and that 'the goods may justly be forfeited by the guilty party'.[1] Charles acted upon this advice, supported the Company in its struggle with the Interlopers, and issued letters patent authorizing it to set up Admiralty tribunals of its own nominees, wherewith to confiscate the ships and goods of its rivals. The campaign against the Interlopers was carried on with vigour, and the Directors wrote triumphantly that they would not be troubled by any more Interlopers.[2]

The effective aid rendered by Charles in suppressing the rebellions of Sir Edward Winter, Cooke, and Keigwin, and the promptness with which he commissioned the Company to exercise martial law at St. Helena, exemplified the co-operation of the Crown and the Company. The Directors might well write that 'there is nothing that we can modestly ask for our Company in India which His Majesty will not readily be pleased to grant us, so high an esteem and acceptance has our endeavour met with from His Majesty, who will by no means give check to the flourishing condition of our affairs'.[3]

It is this intimate connexion between the Crown and the Company which helps to explain the phenomenal growth of the East India trade. In no other trade is the influence of the central government so widely felt. Charles the First's shifty policy reduces it to insignificance; James's peaceful negotiations end in nothing but paper protests; Cromwell's war and charter go far towards re-establishing the Company, yet the lack of energetic support hampers it in all its activities. Under Charles II the Company secures the greatest amount of royal support. The Company's interests are now practically identified with those of the Crown. Its cause is regarded as the cause of the State. Charles II assigns the non-restoration of the island of Polaroon as one of the causes of the Dutch war. Its protests, negotiations, and demands are backed by the Council with favourable results. The overwhelming support of the Crown reacts on the East India trade. Without the support of the

[1] *Public Record Office*, C.O. 77, no. 49, p. 247, 16th Nov. 1682.

[2] See *Dispatches from England*, published by the Madras Government, 1916; Pollexfen's Speech, *India Office Tracts*, op. cit.; Howell's *State Trials*, vol. x, 429–36; *Calendar of State Papers, Domestic Series*; *Bruce's Annals*, vol. ii, p. 551; *Treasury Book*, 1681–5, p. 182; *Concerns the Ship 'Expectation', bound for the East Indies*, ib.

[3] *MS. Letter Book*, no. 6, p. 513. Dispatch dated 7th May 1682.

Crown the Company might have suffered the fate of many of the Joint-Stock Companies formed in the seventeenth century. With the support of the Executive the Company blossoms out into a vigorous organization, initiating experiments in colonial administration, extending commerce, developing the untapped resources of the East, and, finally, asserting its authority both against foreign and domestic foes.

The effect of this policy was felt in the East India trade; the articles most in demand were calicoes, silk,[1] indigo, pepper, lac, and saltpetre. The loss of Bantam, and the virtual expulsion of the English from the East India Islands, diminished the import considerably. 'The Spices imported since the Navigation Act have been by stealth, and without paying any Custom, being brought in by the Dutch and foreign merchants and foul traders at home. This must necessarily be because the Dutch, who have had the sole trade of them these many years, are prohibited, and the English cannot import them from Holland, because they import them not from the place of their growth, the English East India Company themselves having no capacity to do it, unless they be restored to Polaroon, or gain some of the Spice Islands, so that neither to them, nor to any other can the freedom of importing the Spices be any prejudice.'[2]

Nor did the situation improve in later years, for we find Davenant writing as follows: 'Since we were supplanted in the Spice Trade by the Dutch, and since great part of Pepper Trade is gone by the loss of Bantam, our chief investments or importations from the East Indies have been in Calicoes, Raw Silk, Cotton Yarn, Goats' Wool, or Caramine Wool, or other products of those Countries.'[3] Pepper, however, continued to be imported, but not in large quantities. In 1677 £5,000 worth of pepper was imported. Childe mentions[4] that 'the Company furnishes us with Pepper, Cowrys', &c. The gradual diminution in the importation of pepper was no doubt due to the concentration of the English on the Indian coast. This con-

[1] See previous chapter.
[2] 23rd Sept. 1662. *Treasury Book*, edited by Dr. W. A. Shaw, 1660-7, p. 432.
[3] Davenant, *Essay on the East India Trade*, Brit. Mus. 1029, b. 37.
[4] In his edition of *New Discourse of Trade*, published in 1694, Brit. Mus. 712, c. 5, p. 160.

centration had fruitful results. It paved the way for the eventual establishment of the English power in India. This, however, did not take place till about a century afterwards. What actually occurred was the enormous growth of the East India trade. The place of pepper and spices was now taken by Indian manufactures. Of these, the most important were calicoes and silk, both raw and wrought.

The Company foresaw the possibilities of the East Indian trade, and instituted a thorough organization of the Indian industry under its own management. In a dispatch dated 27th March 1668, the Directors, speaking of Bombay, say 'Encourage the natives and invite them to come thither. Invite them to bring Pepper, etc. We would also have you put the natives upon the making of such Calicoes as they are capable of, although they shall be coarse at first, that in time they may attain to the making of them better; and lest they want Cotton for that purpose, we would have you to procure the bringing of it out of the Country, or the conveying of it to them by the sea. We would willingly have some manufacture under our own Government, and the making of Calicoes is that in which people of India are most apt, and a Commodity which is most vendible in Europe.'[1] Sail-cloth was another manufacture encouraged by the Company. This was done for the increase of 'Tonnage, it being our desire to increase as much the navigation of the Kingdom in our own estates', and for that reason, the Directors sent 2 hemp dressers, one or two spinners and weavers, 'that may put them into a way of making such hempen sail-cloth as this Kingdom is wholly supplied with from France'.[2] They direct the factors to 'set their weavers' Inventions at work to make plushes, velvets, and Satins as fine as the best usually worn here'; they send patterns of 'thin silk' for the Indian weavers to imitate; and they finally send English workmen to improve the methods of manufacture. As early as 1668 the Directors had sent 'Soldiers and their wives; also one Artificer as per list'. They were followed by twelve women in 1676. 'We endeavoured to get some country girls, but have not been able to procure them.'[3] What

[1] *MS. Letter Book*, no. 4.
[2] *Records of Fort St. George, Dispatches from England*, 1680–2, pp. 21–2. Compare p. 34 (I shall cite them simply as *Records*).
[3] Ib., vol. i, p. 78.

was of far more importance was the dispatch of English weavers to teach the Indians the mysteries of their craft. This was bitterly resented by the English weavers generally. 'Before the Goods imported were Drugs, Spices, Saltpetre; and little bullion was exported. In 1672, or 73, several Artificers went over to teach the Indians how to manufacture goods for the European markets. After which began the great Trade in manufactured goods from India.'[1]

The Company was regarded as a betrayer of England, and as the cause of untold ruin. There was a flourishing woollen and silk industry before the arrival of the East India merchant. 'And now come on our East India Gentlemen. They carry away our workmen of all sorts, our Patterns and New Inventions, and promote the manufacture in the East Indies beyond any other European Nation.'[2] It can hardly be doubted that the Company sent a number of weavers to India, and that this contributed to the rapid growth of the Indian manufactures. In a dispatch to the Bay, dated December 1677, the Directors say: 'We approve of the encouragement you have given to our dyers and weavers, and note your desire for sending out a Throwster, and Throwsting Mills . . . for the better dyeing of our Taffaties, we this year send Edward Wale and Richard Smith, with those already gone, and Mr. Naylor.'[3] Two silk dyers, 'named John Pratt, an able artist in Dyeing Black, and Charles Ensall, for dyeing Colours', were sent in January 1681.[4]

This deliberate fostering of Indian manufactures had the inevitable result of arousing widespread opposition among the weavers, the manufacturers, and the landed gentry in England. The two Indian articles that competed with the English manufacturers were silk, raw and wrought, and calicoes.

The demand for raw silk was not constant, and, from 1670 to 1677, we do not note very great increase therein. In 1676, for instance, the Company required 5,000 'peeces' of mulmulls; 31,000 taffetas, and only 600 bales of silk.[5] In September 1677

[1] *Reasons humbly offered for Restraining the Wearing of Wrought Silks, &c.*, Brit. Mus. 816, m. 13 (135).

[2] *England's Danger by Indian Manufactures*, Bodleian Library, Θ. 658, no. 32.

[3] *Records*, vol. i, p. 144.

[4] Ib., p. 26

[5] Ib., pp. 36–7.

we notice a slight change. The demand for raw silk has not increased; but this is supplemented by a demand for 'ordinary Raw Silk, such as came by the "Falcon", 200 bales'.[1] There are frequent complaints of the bad system of sorting then in vogue. This applied specially to taffetas. Moreover, the colours of these goods left much to be desired. 'We being desirous to bring the Colours of our Taffaties in the Bay to perfection, and having a good character of the Ability of Thomas Reade, a dyer in all sorts of Colours, have selected him at the salary of £30. per annum.'[2] As a sample of the Bengal articles most in demand, the following list, from the Company's Records, is most instructive: '(1) Coloured Ginghams, 10,000 pieces; (2) Cassaes, 10,000 pieces; (3) Mulmulls, 4,000; (4) Silk Romalls, 15,000; (5) Nillaes, 10,000; (6) Fine Humhums of Decca, but no coarse ones, 10,000; (7) Taffaties, 30,000; (8) Raw Silk, 600 bales; (9) Saltpetre, 1,000 tons; (10) Sticklack, of the best and blackest, 50 tons.'[3] This is a typical list, and contains all the articles desired by the Directors in London from their factors in the East. There does not seem to have been any variation in the demand for silk up to 1680. After this date we notice the rapid fluctuation in the demand, and the elasticity of supply which characterized the proceedings of the Company. 'The Taffaties we received this year are better sorted than formerly, but yet there are too many bright colours.'[4] On 5th January 1681 the Directors wrote as follows: 'We are likewise informed that great quantities of several sorts of Raw Silk may be bought at Hugly, but we are not fully satisfied that it is of the same sorts that are proper for Europe, without it be such as are made at Cassambuzar, and places adjacent, and from thence brought to Hugly.' After providing for the full quantity of silk that the Directors wrote for, 'We would then have you at Hughly endeavour to buy up so much raw silk as they shall want, provided what you do there buy be of the same sorts of raw silk proper for Europe, and do not exceed in the price what it can be, or is bought at Cassambuzar, about 2 or 3 annas per seer, and buy the least proportion, or none at all, of the extraordinary finest sort, but

[1] Ib., p. 110.
[2] Ib., p. 31.
[3] *Dispatch to the Bay*, 12th Dec. 1677.
[4] Ib., dated 12th Dec. 1677.

of the middle and ordinary sorts, which turns best to account here, if it be clear wrought, and clean wound of. . . . Send us 100 Bales for a trial in all, some of each sort.'[1] Taffetas are again a subject of complaint: 'Many of the Taffaties want of their length, insomuch that we have allowed 40 or 50 yards for short measure in some chests.' These hopes were not realized, for we find the Directors writing on 22nd April 1681: 'Our Expectations were vilely frustrated last year, in that most important affair of Raw Silk. . . . We would have you send us the full quantities of every sort of Raw Silk wrote for. . . , We do lay on you the greatest charge to enlarge our Investments in all the coarsest kind of Raw Silk, because we judge it [not only] the most gainful, but the most National Commodity we can bring to England, being a commodity to be manufactured which sets our poor on Work, greatly augments our navigation, and works upon the trade of our emulous neighbours.' The Directors' demands were not confined to raw silk. It was their desire for calicoes and wrought silk that ultimately led to the prohibition of Indian manufactures. They fostered the industry by every means, and sent patterns, weavers, and mills to India, to encourage the silk industry. The following is significant: 'Set your Weavers' Inventions at work to make Plushes, Velvets, and Satins, as fine rich and as strong as the best usually worn here, and of the same breadth; there is nothing so difficult but may be effected where the material & Silk, and midwife labour are so cheap, as with you.' The demand for silk increases. 'We have heard of an excellent sort of silk Romalls to be bought cheap at Dacca; order some from thence; and some from Malda.' And on the 20th of May, 1681, they write: 'Very fine Mullmulls, finer than we have had from you of late years, would sell well.'

In the middle of 1681 the scene has shifted: we now find them asking for as much silk as they can procure. 'You should always be buying and selling in whatever quantities you can of raw Silk.' 'Buy as much raw Silk as you can possibly procure.'[2] We have the following from the Directors to their Agent in the Bay: 'Enlarge our Investments in all Sorts of Raw Silk formerly as

[1] *Dispatch to Hugly*, 5th Jan. 1681.
[2] *Dispatch to Fort St. George*, 16th July 1681.

well as now desired in our several letters, to the quantity of at least 10,000 bales of Silk of 160 seers to the Bale.'[1] They require now '10,000 bales of the kinds ordered'.[2]

The demand for the same is also felt in the request of the Directors to their Agents, to 'take up £100,000 at Interest', to be invested and 'sent us home in Raw Silks, by this year's shipping over and above the full proceed of our stock now sent out'.[3] 'Of all silk wares, take it for a certain rule that whatever is new, gaudy, or unusual, will always find a good price at our candle.' The Company have been afraid of importing thrown silk into England, but they now take courage, and request Charnock to supply them 'every year some (not exceeding 100 bales), if it does not lessen our provision of raw Silk'.[4]

In 1680 the list of enlargements testifies to the growing demand for Indian commodities in England. The list begins on the 16th July 1680. Silk romalls still maintain the former figures. The increase is most noticeable in 'raw silks of all sorts'. The Dacca products appear to enjoy an unrivalled ascendancy for a time. In January 1681 the number of silk romalls increased from 5,000 to 20,000; Dacca humhums to 8,000. Raw silk, ordinary silk, and white silk are in greater demand than ever. The Directors require 1,960 bales instead of 600 as formerly. The Cassembazaar products, which were to acquire an unchallenged ascendancy, enjoy now 'a Muster' for themselves. There is now a demand for 600 pieces of 'Satins from Cassemba Zaar'. Taffetas are as popular as ever; the Directors now require 8,300 'pieces' of them. Besides the Cassembazaar Musters, there is a Hugly Muster. There is a greater demand for articles. Silk goods predominate. The Company now invests about £200,000 in Bengal articles.

In November 1681 the demands of the Directors for silk and other goods increase. Hugly has to provide a number of silk goods. Atlasses, mulmulls, and satins are in fashion. There is greater demand for them than for any other article at Hugly. The Company demand '600 Satins of Dignagur; 1,000 pieces of Mulmulls; and 4,000 Atlasses', according to samples sent last year. 'The factories of Ballasore, Maulda, Cassemba-

[1] *Dispatch to the Bay*, 18th Nov. 1681.
[2] Ib.
[3] Ib.
[4] Ib.

zaar and Patna supply England with ever-increasing numbers of articles.'[1]

In 1677 the Company imported £5,000 worth of pepper; £24 to £30,000 worth of saltpetre; £150 to £160,000 worth of calicoes; £25 to £30,000 worth of silk; and £10 to £15,000 worth of indigo.[2] In 1681 we notice a change. The Turkey Company leads the opposition to raw silk.[3] 'They scarcely import anything but what is ready manufactured; as Calicoes and Wrought Silks, excepting lately a deceitful sort of fuzzy slight Silk, a pound whereof, being dyed, weighs at least 4 oz. more than it did before the dyeing, whereas the best Silk weighs rather one oz. or two less after dyeing.'[4] There was no objection to raw silk. The Company's importations were regarded with favour, as 'it set the poor on work'. But when wrought silk began to be imported, the Company began to get into trouble with the clothiers, and the weavers, and the Turkey Merchants. 'The reason is the Importation of better and cheaper Raw Silk touches the Turkey Merchants' profit at present, though it doth benefit the Nation. What then? Must one Trade be interrupted because it works upon others? At that rate, there would be nothing but confusion *ad infinitum.* The Italian merchants will quarrel with the Portuguese Merchants; the Shoemaker with the Cobbler.'[5] The arguments employed by Childe were very effective with regard to raw silk.

The importation of wrought silks, however, could be justified only on the plea of utility. The main part of the silks were no doubt taffetas, and other plain or striped silks; but they *did* compete with the silk manufacture of England. Childe pointed out[6] that 'a great part of the wrought Silks imported by the Company are again shipped out to France, Holland, and other foreign countries'; and that this 'benefits the King because he gets half the custom paid by strangers'. Wrought silks were, moreover, the 'strongest, the cheapest, and the most durable that come from any part of the world'. Nor did their

[1] I have compiled this list from the invaluable Dispatches of the Directors to their factors in the East, and from the pamphlets in the British Museum.
[2] *Papillon*, op. cit., p. 9.
[3] The opposition to other Indian goods arose considerably earlier.
[4] *Allegations of the Turkey Co.*, op. cit.
[5] Childe, *East India Trade*, op. cit., p. 13.
[6] Ib., op. cit., p. 18.

wearing hinder the silk manufactures in England; 'they do only hinder the importation of the like quantity from France and Italy.'[1] Yet the Company were forced to confess that 'Wrought silks, Flowered or Striped, do a little impede the growth of the silk manufactures in England'. The Company were, however, ready to forbid their Agents from sending them 'if they could be effectually forbidden from all parts'.[2] As regards wrought silks mixed with gold and silver, 'they are indeed prejudicial to the manufacture of England'.[3] The Company could hardly deny the existence of a keen competition with the English manufactures. The number of families employed at the time was 40,000. Childe himself had suggested a scheme whereby the number of families might be trebled. 'Since the East India Company have of late years found a way of bringing silk of all sorts into this Kingdom cheaper than it can be afforded in Turkey, France, Italy or any other place. Insomuch as with East India Silk we serve Holland, Flanders, and some other markets from England.'[4]

Of the existence of keen competition there is sufficient evidence to justify us in regarding the importation of silk from India as a grave menace to the English silk industry. As early as 1680 the danger began to be seriously felt. 'The result [of the importation of silk] is that masters break; Journeymen run away, having no Trade. Some fly to the Mint and Privileged places. Some to Holland; some to Ireland. Some starve to death at home with their Wives and Children. Multitudes turned upon the parishes. Houses empty. Prisons full. The Weavers petition, Pray, Wait, Use all Methods, and though Silk in India be 5 or 6 times cheaper than in England, there is no Relief. These Commodities pay Custom at the rate of 15/- per Pound Weight only, while the Foreign European Silks pay at the rate of 33/4 per Pound.'[5]

The gravest mistake of the Company consisted in sending throwsters and weavers to India. Of the unpopularity of such a step there is convincing evidence. 'The East India Company have sent over into India Throwsters, Weavers, and Dyers, and

[1] *Reply to Allegations of the Turkey Co.* [2] Ib. [3] Ib.
[4] Ib., op. cit., p. 8.
[5] *England's Danger*, Bodleian Library, Θ. 658, no. 32.

actually set up there a manufacture of silk, which not only by instructing the Indians in making these manufactures, but by importing them ready made and Dyed, into England, is an unspeakable impoverishment of the working people of this Kingdom, and to the ruin of many thousands of families here.'[1]

That the danger was real is evident from the fact that the 'Bailiffs, Wardens, and Assistants to the Company of Silk Weavers' petitioned the House of Commons against 'the Importation of Foreign Silks from France and against the East India Company'.[2]

The debate upon the petition throws a flood of light on the extent of the consumption of Indian goods in 1680. 'It will be in vain for you to endeavour to raise the Price of Wool, unless you do, in the first instance, make some Regulations for the East India Trade. For not only Silk Weavers, but most of the Trades of this Nation, are prejudiced by the consumption of goods manufactured in the East Indies and brought hither. For a great many of them are not only spent here, instead of our own manufactures, but abroad, in other parts to which we send them, they do the same prejudice; which in the end must be the destruction of our Manufactory Trade, both at home and abroad, if not looked for.'[3] 'The said trade has abundantly increased of late years, and impoverishes our own People.' Pollexfen informed the House that 'their Persian Silks, Bengalls, Printed and Painted Calicoes, and other Sorts are used for Beds, Hangings of Rooms, and vestments of all Sorts'. 'These goods not only hindered the Expense of our Wool', but also 'by hindering the consumption of them in other parts also to which we export them, and by obstructing the Expence of Linen and Silks, which we formerly purchased in return of our Manufactures.'

From 1601 to about 1675 the Company's activities were limited to the importation of raw silk. Its contract with the Persian Government facilitated the process. Nor was there

[1] *The Allegations of the Turkey Co.*, op. cit.

[2] I have not found this either in Cobbett's *Debates* or in Grey's *Parliamentary History*. A most valuable copy exists, however, in the India Office Library, *India Office Tracts*, vol. lxxxiii, containing *Debates in the House of Commons*, 9th Nov. 1680.

[3] *Debates in the House of Commons*, *India Office Tracts*, vol. lxxxiii.

any opposition to its importation. What was objected to was the wholesale importation of silk manufactures from India. The opposition at first was feeble and hesitating. After 1680 it grew in strength and in numbers. This was due mainly to the institution of a vigorous policy of the development of Indian silk manufactures in Bengal. The various silk manufactures at Cassembazaar, Patna, Malda, Hugly, and Ballasore were co-ordinated and systematized. The lynx-eyed Directors missed no opportunity of pointing out the serious drawbacks existing in some of the factories, and of trying to remove some of them. Their efforts were crowned with complete success. The imports of silk goods grew by leaps and bounds. The beginning of this growth may roughly be fixed at 1680. After that date we see a continuous increase, followed by increased opposition.

Another article that was much in demand was calico.[1] As early as 1624 we find the Directors asking for more calicoes from their Agents in the East. The rapid decline under Charles I of the East India trade was partly responsible for the reduced importation of that article. After the Restoration the imports of calicoes increased. Chintz from Surat was in great demand. In 1662 they wanted '6,000 Persian Broad Chintz'. Tapestries were also popular; 6,000 pieces of tapestries were required in 1662. There is no change in their next year's demand. The 'Bastards' are, however, very popular, and an increasing amount is required. Then follows an article that became so familiar later on: 'Several Sorts of Calicoes', altogether 24,000 pieces.

The popularity of the chintzes and quilts increased. We find the following in the Directors' Dispatch: 'The Chintz and Quilts now arrived are handsome works, and we suppose will be well liked.' The calicoes this year are reduced to 6,000 pieces. Their place is taken by the bastards, which total '35,000'.[2]

A noticeable change occurs in 1665. The Directors write, in a dispatch dated 24th March 1665, saying, 'Several sorts of Calicoes are in great demand'. Chintzes still maintain their ascendancy in 1667, though the number required is only 11,000.

[1] For the early history of calicoes see previous chapter.
[2] Compiled from the *MS. Letter Book*, no. 3, 1660-5; India Office Record Department.

In 1668, however, the Company determined to develop the calico manufacture on a large scale at Bombay. The Directors wrote in 1668 to their Agents in the East, asking them to invite the Indians to settle at Bombay. 'We would have you put the natives upon the making of such Calicoes as they are capable of, although they shall be coarse at first, that in time they may attain to the making of them better; and lest they want Cotton for that purpose, we would have you to procure the bringing of it out of the Country, or the conveying of it to them by the sea.'

Another dispatch, dated 24th August 1668, again asks the factors to encourage trade, and that especially they engage in the making of calicoes, although they be coarse. The number of calicoes required mounts up to 44,000 'pieces'. Another dispatch refers to the encouragement of calicoes, 'it being a commodity of great request in England. Cotton Yarn, Cotton Wool, and Looms should be provided for the making of Calicoes.' The manufacture of calicoes of the 'right sort' was not an easy task. 'You must observe to make our Calicoes, 18 or 19 yards long, and to improve its manufacture in Bombay.'[1]

In 1672 the demand for Bombay products was as follows: 70,000 'Bastards' and 40,000 'pieces' of chintzes.[2] Surat cloth gained favour, for we find the Directors writing, in March 1679, 'The Surat Cloth was very good'.[3] The main obstacle to the development of Indian manufactures was the neglect of the Company's factors. The cloth manufactured for the Company was 'not so good as that brought home in private trade'. We hear of four private ships, laden with various commodities, sent from Bombay. The Company, however, neglected no opportunity of extending its purchases of calicoes. They write, in a dispatch dated February 1681, as follows: 'If you shall find Calicoes procurable at Rajapur, we would have you to employ such Native Merchants for securing them from the Interlopers, and buying them for own account, as you shall think fit.'[4] A dispatch to Fort St. George, February 1681, has the following:

[1] *Dispatch to Surat*, 11th Aug. 1670.
[2] This is compiled from the *MS. Letter Book*, no. 4, 1665–72.
[3] *MS. Letter Book*, no. 6, 1678–80. [4] Ib.

'We would have you leave no place unattended where Calicoes may be had, and order 40 to 50 Thousand Pounds Sterling to be invested at Pettipolee in such proper sorts of Calicoes and other goods for this market as you judge may be had best and cheapest.'[1]

The imports of calicoes increased enormously. In 1677 Papillon reckoned them at 150 to 160 thousand pounds' worth. The amount was soon considerably increased. The efforts of the Directors resulted in an extraordinary increase in the importation of the product from India. On 9th November 1675 Papillon was obliged to defend the East India Company in the House of Commons. 'If you drive all the wool into France, they will outdo us and Holland. Some say it is the East India Company. But they send £40,000 worth yearly away to France, whither we used to carry 40 or 50 Thousand Pounds yearly; we cannot now carry 40.'[2] Two years later, however, the rapid increase in the Indian imports was forcibly described by Col. Birch. 'One commodity more ruins us, and that is Calico, which destroys more the use of Wool than all things besides. You encourage thereby trade with the Heathens, who work for a penny a day, and destroy Christians; and the French, who scarcely eat Flesh 4 times a year, and wear Linen breeches and wooden Shoes, destroy your trade by underselling you. That of Ireland is but a minute thing in comparison of the rest. You pay £180,000 a year upon account of very kitchen maids who will wear hood and scarves, and they must be of glossy silk too, made from beyond the sea.'[3] 'As ill weeds grow apace, so these manufactured goods from India met with such a kind reception that from the greatest gallants to the meanest Cook Maids, nothing was thought so fit to adorn their Persons as the Fabrick from India! Nor for the ornament of Chambers like India Skreens, Cabinets, Beds and Hangings; nor for Closets like China and lacquered Ware. The Humours and Fancies of the People thus combining with the Design of those that had the management of the Company, no Endeavours were omitted, no Addresses to the Court neglected, nor expenses valued, that might tend to

[1] *Records*, vol. ii, p. 72.
[2] Grey's *House of Commons Debates*, 1675, vol. iii, pp. 430–5.
[3] Ib., 1677–8, vol. v, p. 158.

improve this good opportunity, which soon occasioned a very great increase for the supply of all those that were fond of those Commodities, and large and Plentiful Dividend out of the Stock for those that had engrossed it.'[1]

The Parliament neglected no opportunity of investigating the matter, and their debate in 1680 testified to the expansion of the imports from India. A member beseeched the Commons to 'Cast your thoughts on this great body here by you [the Company of Silk Weavers], and the rest of the Corporations of this Nation, who must live by Trade, and consider how many thousands there are whose Lot Providence has cast on the Trade, for their Livelihood. If 3 such Charters [to the East India Company] more should be given, what would the major part of the Nation do for maintenance? The Birthright of many Englishmen is very tenderly considered in this place. By this Company, the Birthright of many thousands is prejudiced, and may deserve a serious consideration.'[2] The Company justified the importation of calicoes on the ground that it 'is a most useful and necessary Commodity, and serves instead of the like quantities of French, Dutch and Flanders Linen'. The nation saves not only '2 to 3 Hundred Thousand Pounds in its Expense; but also it hinders so far the enriching those Neighbour Nations, from whose greatness this Kingdom might fear most prejudice'. It was, it argued, 'much better for the Kingdom to expend 150 Thousand Pounds in Calicoes than 400 or 500 Thousand Pounds in French, Dutch and Flanders Linen'.[3]

The growth of the East India Company will be evident from the reply made by the Company to the Turkey Merchants. They alleged that 'the Turkey Company had not exported more than about 19,000 cloths per annum on the average during the past three years, whereas they themselves expected to send out more than that quantity in the current year, and within 7 years, if the Company be not obstructed, they may

[1] Pollexfen's speech before the Board of Trade, 1696. Pollexfen is describing here the state of Indian commodities in 1681. Included in the *India Office Tracts*, vol. lxxxiii, p. 50.

[2] *India Office Tracts*, vol. lxxxiii, p. 84.

[3] Papillon, *The East India Trade is the most Profitable Trade to the Kingdom*, 1677, Brit. Mus. 1029, g. 24, p. 10.

export more cloth yearly than ever the Turkish Company can do'.[1] Silk and calicoes were the chief articles of import; saltpetre, however, was a very important import, and we find the Directors writing again and again to their factors, asking them to get as much saltpetre as possible. The demand for saltpetre seems to have increased after the Restoration. There does not seem to have been any variation in price, for we find the following in the Treasury Book[2] under date 9th November 1678: 'Royal Warrant for payment to the East India Company, who agreed to lend to His Majesty 363 Tons 12½ cwt. 12 pounds of Saltpetre, which the said Company has agreed to furnish to the Ordnance, for £20,000.' It was, however, a most useful commodity, and the Company's advocate, Dr. Davenant, asked triumphantly whether, if the Company were dissolved, there was any other body that could supply the nation with saltpetre.

Indigo was much sought after. At Surat the demand seems to have been limited to 300 bales of Lahore indigo, and 100 bales of Sarkhej indigo. Agra indigo seems to have been popular, for we find the Directors writing, on 15th December 1676, 'contrive to get more of the Agra Indigo down the Ganges by way of Bengal, or any other way that will be most secure and cheap'. The amount varied.

Another object desired by the Directors was goat's wool from Kerman in Persia. There seems to have been great demand for this, and we find the Directors writing, in 1681, to their factors, requesting them to send as much as possible. The manufacture of sail-cloth, as fostered by the Directors, does not seem at first to have been a success. Later on, however, we notice a change. The Directors ordered 20,000 pieces of sail-cloth in November 1681.

The Company's exports were broadcloth, lead, iron, quicksilver, vermilion, and, most important of all, bullion.

The Company's Records prove decisively that it did all it could to increase the exports to India. The Directors wrote in March 1661: 'It being our earnest desire that such commodities as we send from home may find a large consumption in all parts of India'; they accordingly give their factors permission to sell at

[1] *Reply to the Turkey Company's Allegations*, Brit. Mus. 816, m. 11 (74).
[2] 1676-9, p. 1158.

cheap rates 'what Commodities you have remaining'.[1] A year later, we find them expatiating on the advantages of vending broadcloth, 'which is the chief manufacture of this nation'. They write again, in March 1668, 'We send greater quantity of Europe goods. We suppose your markets are bare, and because we desire a great vent of them, especially of Cloth and Woollen Manufactures.'[2] In spite of the heroic attempts of the Company, the export of broadcloth did not show any great increase. The following is a representative list[3] of the articles sent to Bombay:

Broad-cloths, 105 bales of 315 cloths Price	£4,162	10	4
Quicksilver	1,736	16	0
Vermilion	499	16	0
Copper	3,561	4	0
Lead, 350 pigs	1,132	11	8
Coral	3,356	10	9

In 1665 broadcloth fell to 100 bales. It increased again in 1668, when the Company sent 230 bales to Bombay. The usual number of bales of cloth on each ship to Bombay seems to have been about 190 bales. This, however, must have been liable to considerable modifications. We find the Directors sending only 114 bales of broadcloth to Bengal on three ships. The main reason for their unpopularity is to be found in the dearness of their prices. This had been pointed out before, and though the Directors tried to augment the sale, they were forced to reduce the quantity of broadcloth exported. Childe calculated that the Company 'carried out of this Kingdom about 60 or 70 Thousand Pounds in Lead, Tin, Cloths, Stuffs, and other Commodities of the production of England'.[4] This agrees with Papillon's estimate.[5]

The Turkey merchants alleged that the East India Company exported great quantities of bullion, with a small quantity of cloth, 'which they do only for a colour to gild over the Damage of their exporting money, or else to moderate the complaint which would be otherwise made'.[6] It does not seem correct, however, to say that the cloth was exported simply to 'gild over the Damage of their exporting money'. The Directors were sending

[1] *MS. Letter Book*, no. 3.
[2] Ib., no. 4, 1665–72, 27th March 1668.
[3] Ib., no. 3, 9th March 1663.
[4] Childe, *Essay*, op. cit., p. 8.
[5] Ib., p. 8.
[6] *Allegations*, op. cit.

out cloth in 1662, when the quantity of money exported was comparatively small. The second assertion, however, is founded on fact. The Directors were very desirous of exporting broadcloth so as to reduce the exportation of bullion, 'as it makes great noise here'. The controversy between the two Companies brought out some very interesting particulars about their condition. It also showed the rapid strides the East India trade had made during the twenty years of Charles II's rule. The shipments of broadcloth and woollens, from 1676 to 1680, were as follows:

(1) £48,684; (2) £52,445; (3) £24,764; (4) 32,913; (5) 51,666.

Total for 5 years	£210,472
Other goods, stores, &c.	194,646
Total .	405,118

There is a marked increase in the Company's exports after 1680. This was due to the agitation of the Turkey Company and the opposition of the clothiers. The Company were obliged to export a greater amount of broadcloth to stave off further inquiries. The progress of the Company's exports to India after 1680 was as follows:

Cloth and Woollens .	1681 . . .	£94,855
	1682 . . .	42,630
	1683 . . .	24,448
	1684 . . .	47,827
	1685 . . .	48,414
Total Cloth and Woollens 1681–5 . . .		£258,174
Other goods, stores, &c.		187,440
Total for 5 years . .		£445,614

The total of exports to the East from 1676 to 1685 was therefore £850,732.[1]

It is clear, from the above, that the Company's export of broadcloth and woollens was, on the average, very limited. Nor can we blame the Company for this. When it was forced to export a greater amount the cloth did not sell in India, and it had to dispose of it at a comparatively small price. This happened in 1693 and 1694.[2] Both Papillon and Childe were anxious to encourage the woollen manufactures: 'Without

[1] *State Papers, Domestic, James II*, vol. v, f. 102. [2] See next chapter.

doubt, it would be much to the Interest of this Kingdom to promote the manufacture of Linens in Ireland; whereby it might not only enrich that Kingdom, rather than a foreign Country, but also by diversion prevent the increase of Woollen Manufacture there, which otherwise in time, would destroy the Manufacture of Drapery in England, and thereby exceedingly impoverish it.'[1] Childe regarded wool as 'the Foundation of the English Riches; it is also generally confessed that all possible means ought to be used to keep it within our Kingdom'.[2] The real fault lay with the weavers themselves.

Another export that caused much ill-feeling was bullion. Owing to the growth of the East India trade the amount of bullion exported increased considerably. 'This practice (the practice of exporting bullion annually) having been represented by the Interlopers to be prejudicial to the interests of the Kingdom, and injurious to commercial credits, the Court adopted the decided measure of placing before the Government, a statement of facts regarding their exports of bullion and foreign coins.' The statement is very instructive:

Exports of Bullion from 1667–74.

Year	£	s.	d.
1667–8	£128,605	17	5
1668–9	162,394	9	10
1669–70	187,458	3	8
1670–71	186,149	10	11
1671–72	186,420	8	3
1672–73	131,300	5	11
1673–74	182,983	0	6
Total	£1,165,311	16	6

The total for seven years from 1667 to 1674 was therefore £1,165,311 16*s.* 6*d.*[3]

After 1674, however, the Company's exports of bullion increased considerably. In December 1676 the ships sent by the Company to Fort St. George carried bullion to the amount of £14,753 18*s.* 6*d.* The Directors write next year: 'We send you greater quantity of gold than formerly.' In December 1677 the four ships sent out to Fort St. George carried bullion to the

[1] Papillon, *East India Trade.*
[2] Childe, *New Discourse of Trade*, 1691, Brit. Mus. 712. o. 5, chap. viii.
[3] Bruce, *Annals*, vol. ii, p. 353. Bruce's total is slightly incorrect.

value of £210,084 14*s.* 1*d.* In January 1681 the total amount of bullion sent to Fort St. George and factories dependent thereupon was £323,667 3*s.* 11*d.* This does not include the bullion exported to Bombay. In 1668 the total amount of bullion exported to Bombay was £61,371 11*s.* 7*d.*[1] In February 1671 the amount totalled £19,540 16*s.* 2*d.* It increased in 1676. The estimate of Papillon seems to be substantially correct. He estimated it at £320,000. There is reason to suppose that this amount was greatly increased in 1681. The Turkey merchants accused the Company of carrying out 'immense quantities of gold and silver'. I am inclined to think that the estimate of the author of 'England and India Inconsistent in their Manufactures' is accurate enough. 'It appears by the Custom House Books, that there was entered in the Company's name, shipped out from 1675 to 1685, above 4 million pounds, which is above £400,000 per annum.'[2] Davenant calculated that the East India trade had absorbed 150 millions since the foundation of the East India Company.[3] This is, no doubt, inaccurate. Davenant's figures can hardly be relied upon, though unfortunately he has been regarded as an authoritative statistician by some historians of political economy.[4] Pollexfen estimated that the East India Company exported not less than £600,000 per annum. His estimate, however, was grossly incorrect. He was a determined opponent of the East India Company, and spoke against it in Parliament, in the Law Courts, and in the Council Chamber. We cannot, therefore, rely upon his statement. In 1681 the bullion sent to Bengal alone amounted to £320,000. This does not include the amount exported to Bombay in the same year. This was likely to be greater, as the Company were 'enlarging' their investments in India. We come to the conclusion that the amount exported, on the average, was £400,000 a year. This estimate was greatly exceeded in the following years. It could not, however, have been more than £600,000 up till 1694.[5] The exportation of £400,000 a year may not seem large now. At that time it was regarded as a heinous crime. The mercantilists looked upon it as mainly the cause of England's

[1] *MS. Letter Book,* no. 4.
[2] Ib., p. 9; *India Office Tracts,* vol. lxxxiii.
[3] *Essay on the East India Trade,* p. 13.
[4] See next chapter.
[5] See next chapter.

ruin, and the drain of gold to the East Indies was denounced in vigorous language.

Mr. Pollexfen declared in Parliament, in 1680, that 'this trade is carried on by the Exportation of 5 or 600 Thousand Pounds per annum in Bullion. The exportation of this has increased in some years from £200,000 to £600,000 per annum. This may increase to millions. Every nation ought to be very jealous of a trade carried on by the Exportation of its Gold and Silver, and to be careful how to allow it.'[1] There were, however, more serious objections to the export of bullion in 1681. Mun had contended that its export to the East brought in treasure to the country. He showed that the export of £100,000 would bring £500,000 into England, and that England gained thereby to the extent of about £400,000 per annum. In 1681 the case was totally different. The ever-increasing imports from the East competed with the English articles, and, in some cases, ruined the weavers and others. Not only, however, did the competition of Indian commodities begin to be seriously felt. The amount of gold began to be exported in greater quantity. This was inevitable, for trade in India could be carried on only by means of bullion, and as the trade grew the exports of bullion grew as well. It is this difference in the original position of the Company from that held in 1681 that explains the intensity of the attacks upon the Company. The Company's opponents now enlisted under their banners all the discontented, and the cause of the Adullamites was taken up by Parliament. The fate of the Company was sealed. This, however, did not take place till seventeen years later. In 1681 it was supported by the Crown against the Interlopers and others, and the latter had no chance of success under Charles II.

The volume of trade has been differently stated by the writers of the period. All, however, are agreed upon the rapid development of the trade under Charles II. According to Childe, 'the Trade employed more great warlike ships that may carry from 50 to 70 guns a-piece, than all the Trades of the World from England besides'.[2] The trade was, moreover, not restricted to England. From 1681 we find evidence of its extension to other countries. 'Above four-fifth parts of the commodities imported

[1] *India Office Tracts*, vol. lxxxiii, p. 83.

[2] Childe, *Essay*, p. 6.

are again exported into Foreign Parts, by which the Navigation and Trade of the World is vastly increased into Turkey, Italy, Spain, France, Holland and other parts of this Christendom.'[1] It was upon this ground that the defenders of the East India Company in 1681 justified the importation of Indian commodities into England. They argued that there was no competition with English commodities, as the greater part of the Indian manufactures were exported into other countries. There could, therefore, be no fear of competition with English articles. 'By the Returns of which more than treble the bullion is imported, and the wealth of the Kingdom is as greatly increased as by the direct Trade to and from the East Indies.' Of the large scale on which the East Indian commerce with other European countries was developed by the Company, we have many striking examples. Papillon went too far when he asserted 'There is transported from England into Foreign Countries, of goods brought from India, the value of 830 Thousand Pounds, which, with the profit arising to the Englishmen, amount to 800 thousand Pounds'. This was, no doubt, an exaggeration. It is probable that about £350,000 worth of Indian articles were exported to other European countries up to 1681. After that date the exportations no doubt increased. The East India Company were likely to exaggerate the amount, as they wanted to minimize the competition with the English articles, which had begun to be felt as early as 1675. Even so, the competition with the Indian articles in foreign countries began to be seriously felt, and this considerably reduced the demand for English manufactures in foreign countries. 'These goods from India not only hinder the Expence of our Woollen Goods, by serving instead of them here, but by hindering consumption of them in other parts also, to which we export them, and by obstructing the Expence of Linen and Silks, which we formerly purchased from our Neighbour Nations, in return of our Manufactures. This is not only a great, but a growing Hindrance to the Expence of our Woollen Goods.'[2]

The Indian commodities brought home realized, on sale in England, about 860 thousand pounds. 'So that in a plain direct way is added to the Stock of the Kingdom in one year

[1] Ib.

[2] *India Office Tracts*, vol. lxxxiii, p. 82.

430 Thousand pounds. If we deduct the charge for the maintenance of factories, Forts, &c., there will remain a clear addition to the Stock of the nation, by the Joint Trade of the Company only, of 370 Thousand Pounds.' 'If to this is added the private trade allowed by the Company to its factors, &c., there may be exported goods about 80 to 100 Thousand Pounds, which returned into England, yielded 250 to 300 Thousand Pounds, yielding a profit of about 130 thousand pounds. The total gain to the nation by the East India Trade was therefore half a million Pounds in 1677. Moreover, it employed 30 to 35 great ships, from 300 to 600 Tuns burden. Within six years there were built anew from the Stocks about 26 to 28 ships, from 350 to 600 Tuns burden. It paid the King about £60,000 per annum Custom in 1681.'[1]

The Company itself was prosperous and paid 'fat' dividends. It paid 40 per cent. in 1672, 20 per cent. in 1673, and 20 per cent. in 1674. Another dividend of 40 per cent. was paid in 1677. The balance sheet of the Company shows that the

Dead stock was	£216,483
Quick stock	£1,511,619
	£1,728,102[2]

The Company admitted that it was burdened with a debt of £550,000 'which the East India Company have never concealed, nor disowned'.[3] Their stock was alleged by them to be £1,700,000. The Turkey Company had asserted that their stock in 1681 was small, and they accused them of borrowing money at interest. The Company itself admitted borrowing £550,000, and the Turkey Company's allegations were in this respect true. With regard to the amount of stock in 1681, there is no reason to doubt the statement of the Company that it was £1,700,000. 'We are ready to make the truth of what we have asserted by a stated account verified in such manner as shall be to your lordship's indubitable satisfaction.'[4] There is reason to suppose that the borrowing was deliberately resorted to by the Company, so as to prevent the enlargement of the stock. It is

[1] Childe, *The East India Trade*, op. cit., p. 8.
[2] *Court Book*, no. 31, 12th Aug. 1678.
[3] *Company's Reply to the Allegations of the Turkey Company*, Brit. Mus. 816, m. 11 (74). [4] Ib., p. 9.

no doubt true that Childe advocated enlargement in 1681. But he did it on condition that the Charter of the Company was sanctioned by Parliament. Without that sanction it may have seemed preferable for the existing shareholders to engross the stock. £1,700,000 in 1681 was not sufficient for the purpose. The Company's trade had developed greatly since 1680, and a stock of about a million and three quarters seems to be totally insufficient for the effective conduct of that trade. Five years before a barrister had made the same charge against the Company. He asserted that the Company had only £600,000 in value. The reply was not convincing. Even if the Company possessed stock of the real value of £900,000, it could hardly be deemed sufficient. If they sent out £450,000 in 1675 the amount of the stock does not seem very large. As the Company possessed, moreover, '3 ships already arrived from Bantam, 5 from Surat, with the 6 or 7 ships expected from the Coast, amounting in all to £800,000', the total value of stock was £1,700,000. This does not include 'all the remaining goods and Debts in India and in England'.[1] If the writer's statement be true, it follows that the Company's stock decreased rather than increased within the five years. This could not have been due to a decline in trade, as the Company paid £10 per cent. dividend in 1679, 50 per cent. in 1680, and 20 per cent. in 1681. 'In seven years, from 1675 to 1681, 150½ per cent. dividend had been paid, or an average of more than 20 per cent.'[2] We are, therefore, forced to the conclusion that the bulk of the stock was engrossed not among twelve or ten persons, as alleged by the Muscovy Company, but among forty or fifty shareholders. It is, no doubt, true that the number of shareholders was 556. This does not, however, exclude the possibility of its being restricted to a few prominent men in the Company. We may well believe that about '40 persons divided the major part'. In the List of Adventurers in the East India Company for April, 1689, we find the following shareholders:

The King	£ 7,000
Sir Josiah Childe	51,000
Sir Thomas Cooke	120,000
Sir Nathaniel Herne	108,000

[1] *An Answer to Two Letters*, 1675, Brit. Mus. 1029, g. 22.
[2] Scott, *Joint Stock Companies*, vol. ii, p. 139.

At that time the Company possessed stock, after paying its debts, of the following amounts: £1,468,233 12*s.* 2*d.* The total value of an Adventurer's share of £100 in 1685 was as follows:

	£	s.	d.
	£230	5	2
'Dead stock' . . .	97	5	1
Total value .	£327	10	3

In the same year the total of all the Adventurers' Stock amounted to £736,782 10*s.* 0*d.*[1]

It follows from the above that the opponents of the East India Company had some justification for the attacks they delivered on it. We need not believe that 'they divide among themselves what they pleased, which now (1681) within these 12 or 15 months has been 90 per cent'. The controversy was carried on very bitterly, and some of the opponents soared to giddy flights of ridiculous vituperation. Their statements, however, contained a germ of truth, and their denunciations of the Directors of the Company and the 'ingrossements' which the latter resorted to were founded on well-established facts.

The rapid development of the Company's trade created many bitter enemies, and the quarrel was complicated by the fact that the King supported it against all opponents. Its importation of Indian commodities was inopportune. The woollen trade was, at that time, passing through a serious crisis. The foreign competition was seriously felt; in 1671[2] the Lords were 'bewailing the great Damage the Kingdom had' sustained 'by wearing foreign commodities, and not our own'. The situation became serious in 1675,[3] and a Bill to prevent the exportation of wool was read a second time. Colonel Birch, however, thought that 'we have more Wool than England can spend'. He attributed this abundance to the Bill for forbidding Irish cattle, 'the Irish having turned their attention from breeding Cattle to breeding Sheep'.[4]

The agitation against the East India Company roused the dour Papillon, who defended it in 1675.[5] Two years later the bill came up for consideration.[6] Colonel Birch again came to

[1] See a most interesting manuscript in the British Museum, Additional MSS. 22185, *Papers relating to East India Company*, pp. 7–8.

[2] See Grey's *House of Commons Debates*, 1667–71, vol. i, p. 434.

[3] Ib., vol. ii, pp. 430–5.

[4] Ib.

[5] Ib., pp. 430–5.

[6] Ib., 1677–8, vol. v, p. 157.

the front, and denounced 'Calico, which destroys more the use of Wool than all things besides'.

There is sufficient evidence to justify us in attributing the decline in the woollen trade partly to the East India commodities. It may, no doubt, be true, as asserted by Macpherson,[1] that the real cause was the competition of French goods. The competition of Indian commodities and the serious effect they produced on the woollen trade, as early as 1681, can, however, be proved by definite records. 'The exportation of Wool is notoriously known to all persons.'[2] 'It has been proved that many poor manufacturers being destitute of work, owing to Calicoes, have been found dead in the streets and fields where they have perished.'[3] 'An infinite number of us are already reduced to great misery.'

It is interesting to trace the stages through which the opposition to the East India Company under Charles II passed. The first petition against the East India commodities occurs under November 9, 1675.[4] Two years afterwards Colonel Birch, after denouncing calicoes, wanted to add to a private bill the following proviso: 'the sellers of brandy, Calicoes, French and Indian Silks.'[5] The Company's statement that the Indian goods did not compete with the English goods can hardly be relied upon. We have sufficient evidence to believe that the competition, though not severe, was felt keenly, even under Charles. Papillon, one of the Company's directors, admitted in 1677 that 'there may be consumed ordinarily within the United Kingdom, about 200 to £250,000 in Indian goods'.[6]

It was not the members of Parliament, however, who took the lead in this attack on the Company. Colonel Birch was merely

[1] *Annals of Commerce*, vol. ii, p. 593.

[2] *A true Case of Dyers*, Brit. Mus. 816. m. 14 (85).

[3] *A second Humble Petition*, Brit. Mus. 816. m. 14 (84).

[4] *Journals of the House of Commons*, vol. ix, p. 371. *A petition of diverse merchants, clothiers, seamen, and others, complaining of the East India Company* was also read. The petition was referred to a Committee, who were to send persons, papers, and records.

[5] *MSS. of the Marquis of Ormond*, New Series, vol. iv, pp. 405–6, 1677–8, February 23. 'This day were reported 19 heads, which are ordered to be drawn under the letter of a private Bill, and which it is presumed will afford the greatest part of the million that is voted. Colonel Birch would needs have added "Calicoes", &c., but the time was thought too precious for the new methods.'

[6] Papillon, op. cit., p. 8.

voicing the opinions of the clothiers. They had, according to Childe, complained in 1674.[1] It was stated by Childe that their complaints were directed at first against the Turkey Company, and that 'a certain lawyer' (Pollexfen ?) induced them to refrain from pursuing that course and to attack the East India Company. I have not come across any document that substantiates this assertion. It seems, in fact, to be devoid of truth. There is evidence to suppose that the Turkey merchants were generally favoured by the clothiers, as they imported only raw silk. With the East India Company the case was different. The clothiers contended that they could not compete with the Indian weavers, because, as their spokesman put it in Parliament, 'The Indians do work for a penny a day, and are not without materials at Cheap Rates. We may rather tremble to think, than easily calculate, what the Trade may in time amount to, and may conclude that it must end in the employing and enriching of the people of India and impoverishing of our own.' Another Member, Mr. Love, thought that 'it will ruin a great part of our manufactures, if not prevented'.[2]

The attitude of the Crown towards these opponents of the Company is significant. It supported the Company because it was the only body sufficiently powerful to carry on the trade energetically. All opposition to its monopoly was put down with a strong hand. Perhaps the best argument in favour of reforming the Company under Charles II is to be found in a document headed 'The East India Trade as managed by the East India Company'.[3] The writer, after describing the chief ports of India, and mentioning the commodities they yield, went on to describe the main faults of the East India Company. The Company, he asserted, never made use of their trade to the South Seas, or Japan, but 'left it to the Dutch, whose mine it is now'. Their negligence in India was also fatal. Had they but 'settled' half their force on the Coast of India, 'it would have procured them what fort they pleased; they might have commanded satisfaction for affronts, and secured themselves for the future'. The Company's fault consisted in not affording a durable stock to buy goods in the country, though their servants were forced

[1] Childe, *Essay*, p. 19. [2] *India Office Tracts*, vol. lxxxiii, p. 82.
[3] *Public Record Office*, no. 118, 1664.

to take up moneys at interest to do it at 12 per cent., when in England they might have had money at 4 per cent. The writer, after diagnosing the disease, prescribes the remedy. It is not very drastic. The Joint-Stock system is to be maintained in all its rigour; but its management ought to be conducted by 'discreet and sober persons'. 'If the trade is to thrive, it must be under a Joint Stock, though it may be for three years open.' The writer then mentions the articles that may be bought in India with profit. Many interesting proposals are made—such as the extension of trade to Japan, and the development of the Company's shipping. 'Moneys to trade, shipping and men are wanting.' The pepper trade was monopolized by the Dutch. All the important places where it was procurable—Quiloan, Porcatt and Cochin were in the Dutch hands. They would, asserted the writer, gain Karwar, Batticalla, and Mergee, if not prevented. He feared that in a few years the Company would have but little lading for shipping, but what the Dutch would afford, 'and as little of Pepper as other Spices, they resolv(ing) to gain possession of the whole coast of India'. Hence, remedies must soon be applied.[1]

The tract seems to have been written by a merchant. It shows thorough acquaintance with the commerce of India, and is admirably expressed. The manuscripts in the British Museum prove that the knowledge of India was not confined to the factors there. We have a series of tracts, monographs, &c., on the commerce of India. Sir Thomas Grantham's voyage[2] may be uninteresting now, but it was greatly significant at that time. We have also a number of tracts on the religion of the Hindus. Impartiality of judgement could hardly be expected in 1675, and we are not surprised to find ludicrous accounts of the Hindu deities.[3] The inevitable Juggernaut is there. So is Charnock, supplying the inquisitive Marshall, the writer of these travels, with information on the customs of the Hindus.[4] John Marshall's

[1] Ib.

[2] Sir Thomas Grantham's account of Keigwin's rebellion was presented to James II and bought by the British Museum. Grantham gives an interesting account of his meeting with Keigwin. *Harleian MSS.*, nos. 4763, 5101, 6245.

[3] Harleian MSS., nos. 4252, 4253, 4254, 4255.

[4] On the margin Charnock's name appears in connexion with the question as to whether the English 'had any land in the country, any woman, any children'.

account of the Indian trade is not an improvement on the document just quoted, but it is more diverting. The writer's curiosity about the religion of the Hindus overmasters him to so great a degree that in an account of the trade he cannot refrain from discussing the metaphysical points which he seems to have loved.

These accounts of the trade of India served the purpose of acquainting the people with its possibilities. It was clear, however, that the English weavers and manufacturers would not put up with the importation of Indian commodities. Their complaints never ceased. The Treasury had already asked the Customs Commissioners for an account of the quantities of cloth exported for three years past, by the East India Company. Three years later, we find the clothiers complaining again: 'The Treasury Lords recently had presented to them another petition in the name of several Clothiers, praying that the said papers may be recommended to you, the Turkey Company, the East India Company, &c.' The Commissioners forwarded the report to the Attorney General. We do not know what further action was taken upon the matter.

The opposition of the clothiers would have been totally ineffective without the support of the Turkey Company, the bullionists, the Whigs and the Interlopers. The main danger lay in the combination of the heterogeneous elements of which the opposition was composed into a united energetic party, following a constructive policy. The discontent of the Whigs was equalled only by the discontent of the Interlopers. After his *coup d'état*, Childe had declared war on the Interlopers, and was carrying on a vigorous campaign in India.[1] The opinion of the Attorney General was clear on that point.[2] Fortified by this opinion, and armed with the Proclamation which Charles issued soon after that report, the Company was victorious against the intruders. It was evident that the Whigs, who had been supporting the interlopers, were not likely to see with pleasure the

[1] *Treasury Book*, 1681–5, p. 241; 12th July 1681, p. 125.

[2] 'The King's subjects ought not to trade or traffique with any infidel Country, not in amity with Your Majesty without licence. The King may signify his pleasure therein, and require his subjects' obedience by Proclamation.' He thought that the 'penalties of forfeiture of goods may therein run upon any goods which shall be seized within the limits of the Company's Charter'. 16th Nov. 1681. *Public Record Office*, no. 14, 1678–86.

(to them) unjustifiable extension of the King's prerogative. They had denounced the Company in the Parliament of 1680, and had asserted that 'they' had 'been industrious to secure themselves by New Year Gifts.' This referred, no doubt, to the £10,000 presented by the Company to Charles II.[1]

The Whigs regarded the monopoly exercised by the Company as a grave violation of the 'natural right' of Englishmen to trade, and asserted that it was illegal. They were quite aware of the fact that 'the Corporations, Companies or fellowships of any art, trade, occupation, or mystery, or Companies or Societies of merchants within this realm erected for the maintenance of any trade or merchandise' had been expressly excepted from the Act of James I.[2] They contended, however, that the Company did not come within the scope of those exceptions. The East India Company was declared by them to be the 'monopoly of monopolies'. The Company's charter, contended the writer of *Two Letters concerning the East India Company*,[3] created forfeitures for all Englishmen that dare dwell in, or trade to half the world. It gave them power over other persons, to imprison and keep them in gaol during pleasure. 'It created an arbitrary power in the Crown of punishing Englishmen by discretion, after they are imprisoned, and their Estates seized.' No patent could restrain the liberty of the subject in anything. Every Englishman had such a property in his 'Estate, privileges, liberty, person, Limb and Life' that none of them could be subject to be seized, forfeited, or any way destroyed, but 'by the force of laws made with Free Consent in Parliament'.[4] 'Is not', asked the indignant Barrister, 'this the distinction between Turkish and French vassals and Freeborn Englishmen'?[5] It is easy to reply that the Barrister, in spite of his parade of legal knowledge, was ignorant of the exceptions to the Act of James I. This was the obvious line of argument adopted by the writer of an *Answer to the Two Letters*.[6] The writer quoted the exceptions mentioned in the Statute, and showed that the Company was excluded.

[1] Luttrell mentions it under date October 1681. Professor Scott follows him. From the above, however, it will be apparent that the New Year gifts must have been instituted considerably earlier.

[2] *Statutes of the Realm*, vol. iv, pp. 1212–14; cf. Prothero, *Statutes and Constitutional Documents*.

[3] Brit. Mus. 1029. g. 22, 1676.

[4] Ib., p. 8.

[5] Ib., p. 9.

[6] Brit. Mus. 1029. g. 22, 1676.

With regard to the monopoly of the East India Company, the word, asserted the writer, was restricted to trading within the realm only, for 'Can any subject of England lawfully trade or traffic with any foreign nation, without the allowance of the king, who hath the undoubted prerogative of making War and Peace, upon which the same depends'?[1] The king's prerogative is, moreover, wide enough to cover all the privileges conferred on the Company. The king, asserted the writer, had 'prerogative to prefer the general Benefit to that of Particulars. So sometimes to extend special privileges and grants to some Particulars for the General Benefit, though other particulars may seem to receive prejudice thereby.'[2]

In this war of pamphlets the Company must be admitted to have come off victorious. The Barrister was either ignorant of the exceptions or refrained from mentioning them. No heed could, therefore, be given to his arguments. It showed, however, the existence of an opposition to the Company gradually forming in the kingdom. The dissolution of the parliament, the increased activity of the Interlopers, and the energetic administration of the Company, brought matters to a crisis. The lawyers were intensely suspicious of this exercise of the king's prerogative. The Whigs were equally discontented. The dissolution of the Parliament, the forfeitures of the charters of many of the boroughs, and the trial and conviction of Papillon and other Whig merchants had made the Whigs desperate. They allied themselves with the clothiers. They befriended the cause of the Turkey Company. They championed the Interlopers. The alliance thus formed was to prove the ruin of the Company under William. In the time of Charles II, however, the Company was sure of the firm and consistent support of the king. The Turkey Company's contention that its 'stock was as large as the estates of many Traders' was totally beside the point. Much more serious was the statement of the Barrister[3] that the Company had been borrowing largely on the security of their seal, and that their bonds were worthless. It was easy for the Company to prove that it had sufficient funds to pay off all the debt contracted under its seal. Even so, the nervous shareholders were not likely to be encouraged to keep their shares in such a Company.

[1] Ib., p. 8. [2] Ib., p. 9. [3] Op. cit.

Another complaint that became common after the Revolution was, for the first time, voiced by the Turkey Company. The East India Company's stock, asserted the latter body, 'though it is now 24 years since it was first underwritten, and though many of the subscribers must needs (sell it), yet there is no liberty for young merchants in a new subscription'. There were 'thousands' of able and active merchants, bred up since their stock began. excluded from 'so rich and great a trade, merely because they were not born sooner, or Bred up at that time'.[1] The Turkey Company's Stock was, on the other hand, 'open and comprehensive, admitting any that are bred merchants'.[2]

The allegations of the Turkey Company had called forth an incisive reply from Childe, and the East India Company had emerged victorious from the contest, in 1681. Two years later, however, the chief opponents again mustered their forces, and fought out a sensational quarrel in the Law Courts.[3] Sands' Counsel did not commit the fatal mistake which had ruined the case of the Barrister.[4] They did not deny that the Companies were excepted. The Statute 21 Jac., Cap. 3 had expressly excluded certain types of companies.[5] They boldly declared, however, that this applied only to Companies erected for the maintenance of trade. The East India Company was not a Company that answered that description, for it restrained all but its own shareholders from trade to the Indies; it had committed many persons to prison; it had perpetrated other crimes. Again, the grant of sole trade and monopolies was against Magna Charta. Moreover by the Statute 3 E. 3 C. 1, Statute 14 E. 3. C. 2, Statute 23 E. 3. C. 2, and Statute 2 R. 2. C. 1 'the Freedom of Trade and Traffick is amply established, and all Letters Patent Grants to the Contrary are void'. The Company's opponents did not rely upon Statutes alone. They were important, no doubt, but more important was the inalienable right of Englishmen by Common Law. By Common Law trade is free and open for the king's subjects. The Company thereupon shifted their ground. They asserted that 'it had the sole trade with the

[1] *Allegations of the Turkey Company*, Brit. Mus. 816. m. 11 (74), 1681, p. 4.
[2] Ib.
[3] *Argument of the Lord Chief Justice Pollexfen upon an Action of the Case brought by the East India Company against Thomas Sands. India Office Tracts*, vol. lxxxiii, pp. 3–47; Howell's *State Trials*, vol. x, pp. 371–554.
[4] Op. cit. [5] See above.

Infidels and that such a trade the subjects had never any right to have, without the king's leave'. It was easy for its opponents to cite a number of precedents to prove the invalidity of these arguments. Englishmen had traded in Turkey; they had traded with a number of other infidels for a long time. Again, the Act of Navigation showed that 'the Infidels have the same liberty of Trade as others'. The Company's opponents were on firm ground, so far. They, however, spoilt their case by instituting comparisons between the two types of Companies—the Joint Stock Companies and the Regulated Companies.

'The Turkey Company', asserted the Counsel for Sands, 'consisted of improvers of trade. They ingross not, they admit every man that will to be free of the Company . . . and none among them makes unreasonable advantages.' But 'this invisible East India merchant, the body politic, covers and countenances some few among them to ingross, buy and sell at their own rates, and that exclude all others for the great and excessive advantages of the few'. They stated, moreover, that the Joint-Stock system was an innovation, and that 'the Companies of Turkey, Barbary, Russia, Muscovy and Hamburgh, nor any other, till of late years, did ever trade with a Joint-Stock'.

This comparison proved fatal to the opponents of the Company. The notorious Judge Jeffreys, who presided at the trial, detected the fallacy of these arguments, pointed to the large sums of money which had been expended by the East India Company, and asked whether any one was justified in demanding admission to a Company without paying for all the expenses it had incurred. 'Is it fair', asked Jeffreys, 'after they (the East India Company) have reduced it into so good a condition, at a vast expense and trouble, for other particular persons to come and say "let us have the benefit of it that have had nothing of the burden and charge?"' The argument was conclusive. It is interesting to note that this argument was employed in many of the pamphlets written on behalf of the Company.

It was hardly to be expected that these attacks on the Company would not shake its credit. Papillon's rejection at the election of 1682, and the withdrawal of many of his followers, had led to a serious crisis. They had now become 'rich interlopers who had fitted out ships for India'. Again, the jealousies raised by them and their friends in the Company 'had made a great many of the fearful members eagerly sell their Stock'.[1]

Professor Scott seems to think that the cause of the decline of the Company's stock was due partly to the indefinite postponement of the new subscription, partly to the political spirit within the Company. I think, however, that the Company's financial position was unsound, and that this was responsible for many of the difficulties under which they subsequently laboured. The Company acknowledged that it owed £550,000 in 1681.[2] This complaint of heavy borrowing had been voiced in 1677, and, with the lapse of time, the complaints increased in vigour and extent. Nor can we ignore the fact that large dividends had been paid by the Company. The Turkey Company alleged 'that last year', viz., Jan. 1681, they divided £260,000, 'though at the same time they owed about £600,000 at Interest'. That the allegations of the Turkey Company were not without foundation is evident from the Report of the Committee appointed to inquire into the Company's Accounts.[3] They found that the Company owed £613,529 7*s.* 5*d.* in 1681.

It was evident that the Company had been borrowing on a large scale, and that, combined with the dividends which they paid, goes far towards explaining their difficult situation. The decline of the Company's credit was surprisingly rapid. John Houghton's *Collections*[4] give us a useful account of the period. The most reliable information is to be found in the various appendices to the reports of the Historical MSS. Commission.[5]

That the matter was serious is apparent from the following letter: Sir John Hobart to W. Windham on the great affair

[1] *Collection of Letters for the Improvement of Husbandry and Trade*, by John Houghton, 1681–3, pp. 148–9.

[2] *The Answer to the Turkey Company's Allegations*, Brit. Mus. 816. m. 11 (74), p. 10.

[3] *Journals of the House of Commons*, vol. xii, pp. 311–12.

[4] Op. cit.

[5] We find Charles Bertie writing to his niece, the Countess of Rutland, as follows: 'The price of an "action" or share in the East India Company has gone up from the original venture of £100 to £405, so infinitely have they improved it by excellent management.' *Report 12, Appendix V, MSS. of the Duke of Rutland*, vol. ii, p. 62.

of the shutting of the East India Company, that is 'of payments until next March'; the discontent it produced, and the various reasons which caused it. Sir John says 'the great disagreements among themselves seem to me to be like a house or kingdom divided between themselves'.[1] This most interesting news is confirmed by a very valuable document. We find, on p. 156, under January 16, 1683, in the MSS. of Lord Kenyon,[2] as follows: 'The great fund of Europe, the East India Company, is shut up and will pay no more till March'. An item in the MSS. of the Marquis of Ormond, New Series, shows that[3] the shares of the East India Company had fallen to £228.[4]

It is apparent from the study of these documents that the Company's condition was not satisfactory. Nor is it quite clear whether the serious drawbacks from which it suffered later on were subsequently removed. A considerable mass of evidence seems to show that the seeds of its future troubles were sown at this time. This rendered the task of defence against the inveterate enemies of the Company very difficult. The Whigs, the clothiers, the Turkey Company, and the Interlopers were all determined to oppose it in every possible way, and to set its authority at naught. This would have proved fatal but for the fact that Charles II supported it consistently. Nor can it be said that the Company's opponents followed a truly constructive policy. Their one aim was destruction, and they did not care how they achieved their object. It was this lack of a coherent principle unifying the disparate sections of the opposition that explains their utter failure. Royal support would have been absolutely useless if the Company's opponents had succeeded in convincing the nation of the necessity of its abolition.

There is no reason to suppose that the Royal support would have availed much against universal discontent. The support accorded to the Company was due primarily to the policy sketched out by the Council in 1661. From this policy Charles never swerved. That it was sound needs no demonstration.

[1] The *MSS. of the Duke of Beaufort*, *Report 12*, *Appendix IX*, p. 186, 11th Jan. 1682–3.

[2] *Report 14*, *Appendix VI*.

[3] Vol. vii, p. 199, 23rd Feb. 1684.

[4] 'The actions of the East India Company are still at 228.' Compare Houghton's *Collections*, vol. i, p. 149; Luttrell, vol. i, pp. 210, 223, 244.

The growth of the East India trade is the best testimony to its wisdom. The Company's opponents had to contend with a powerful body, consistent in its actions, rigorous in its decrees, and impartial in its decisions. It was soon apparent that its opponents were not united on a single important point. The Whigs, who denounced the unjustifiable extension of the prerogative, had nothing in common with the Turkey Company, who arrogated to themselves the title of merchants, and who complained that 'there are thousands of able and active Merchants bred up since their stock began, which are excluded from so rich and great a trade, merely because they were not born sooner, or Bred up at that time.'[1]

The importance of the controversy lay in the fact that it led to the emergence of a truer conception of the principles of Political Economy. From 1601 to 1660 the East India Company was haunted by the spectre of the Dutch Company in the East. Its factors were insulted; its trade was greatly disturbed; it had no effective support in England; and, finally, its exportation of bullion to the East was bitterly resented by the bullionists. They charged it with taking the treasure of Christendom to the Infidels; they opposed it in Parliament, at the Court, and in pamphlets. Mun's defence of the East India trade necessitated considerable modification of the purely bullionist views of the time. Money, he argued, could be increased only by means of trade, and it was, therefore, a short-sighted policy to prevent the exportation of money, as by that means you deprive the nation of the greater amount of money that it would eventually obtain through the growth of the trade. This correct analysis of the phenomenon prepared the way for the reception of a truer theory of the functions of money. Mun may, therefore, be regarded as a forerunner of Davenant, Sir Dudley North, and others. In another sense, it is true, he may be regarded as the founder of the narrow Mercantile System so mercilessly caricatured by Adam Smith. It was, however, the competition of the Dutch and the lack of effective support on the part of the Crown, that led him to formulate theories which may well be regarded as reactionary at the present time. There is no reason to suppose

[1] *Allegations of the Turkey Company*, Brit. Mus. 816. m. 11 (74), 1681, p. 4.

that he would have advocated the measures recommended by him in his 'Treasure of the Traffique' if the conditions had been different.

It was the obstinate use of monopoly by the Dutch that gave rise to England's Navigation Act and Colbert's tariff, and attracted England and France themselves towards a like policy of pursuing mercantile objects by force of arms. Of this policy Mun became a vigorous defender. The State was to employ all the resources it could command for the pursuit of purely commercial ends. This was not possible under Charles I. Under Cromwell a start was made. Under Charles II considerable political forces were for the first time available for the pursuit of commercial and agricultural ends. The two wars with the Dutch, though not fought exclusively for commercial ends, were in the main dictated by the latter.

The State did not, however, restrict itself to the carrying on of war for commercial ends. The industries and trade were given active support. This, as pointed out above, was especially the case with the East India Company. The results of the new policy were visible in the trade with India.[1] The two things desired most by Mun were the support of commerce and industry by the Crown, and their defence against England's commercial rivals. Both were attained under Charles II. The Dutch, though not crushed, were completely exhausted, and the English industry and commerce were encouraged and fostered by the efficient Council of Trade. This explains the wonderful growth of the East India Company's trade, and shows the overwhelming importance of the State to industry and commerce in the seventeenth century. The State embodied the new spirit of commercial rivalry engendered by the monopoly of the Dutch. The effects of this policy were felt not only in the volume of trade with the East, but also in the domain of theory. Just as the actual policy of the State had affected not only the volume of trade with the East, but also the economic theories of Mun, so the effects of Charles's policy were felt not only in the trade with the East, but also in the current economic theory. The competition with the Dutch had obliged Mun to advocate a seemingly reactionary policy, while the exportation of bullion

[1] See above.

had led him to enunciate truer principles. The two views seemed difficult to reconcile. Yet they were inevitable.

Under Charles II the disappearance of the bitter commercial rivalry left the field clear for the development of a truer conception of political economy. Moreover, as the trade of the Company increased, the latter were forced to appeal from the crude bullionist views of the times to the truer principles of economics. The East India trade now acquires a national significance. 'It supplies the nation with a necessary commodity, saltpetre; it employs more great warlike English ships, that carry from 50 to 70 guns apiece, than all the Trades of the world from England besides; above 4/5 parts of the commodities imported are again exported into Foreign parts, by the returns of which more than treble the Bullion is imported'; moreover, it saves the nation 500,000 pounds.[1] It is upon national grounds that the monopoly of the East India Company is advocated. Childe states explicitly 'That all Monopolies, of what nature or kind soever, are destructive to Trade, and consequently obstructive to the increase of the wealth of our land; and that, therefore, if there be anything, either in the East India Company's Charter or any Charter of Incorporated Merchants, that hinders any of His Majesty's subjects of England, Scotland or Ireland, from coming into that Trade, upon as good Terms as others of His Majesty's subjects, it would be to the general good of the Kingdom that such Bars or Hindrances are removed'.[2] The defenders of the Company did not justify monopolies on principle. 'All restrictions of Trade are nought, and consequently that no Company whatsoever, whether they trade in a Joint Stock, or under Regulation, can be for public good, except it may be easy for all or any of His Majesty's subjects to be admitted into all or any of the said Companies.'[3] Companies of merchants possessing exclusive monopoly were, however, absolutely necessary 'for Countries with which His Majesty have no alliance, nor can have by reason of their distance, or Barbarity, or non-com-

[1] Compare Childe, *East India Trade the most national of all the Trades*; Papillon, *The East India Trade is the most profitable Trade to the Nation*, Brit. Mus. 1029. g. 24; *India Office Tracts*, vol. lxxxiii.
[2] Childe, op. cit.
[3] *A New Discourse of Trade*, by Josiah Childe, Brit. Mus. 712. c. 5, 1694, p. 104, chap. iii.

munication with the Princes of Christendom where there is a necessity of maintaining Forces and Forts'.[1] 'It is, moreover, absolutely necessary for the publick good, that whosoever gains a Trade so remote from England, and by such a multitude of Hands as the Company are forced to employ should have some extraordinary powers committed to them.'[2]

It cannot be doubted that a Regulated Company would have proved totally useless in the East. Concentration of all the materials on a definite object, and its consistent pursuit through failure and success, were the essential qualities required in an English Company in India. These could not have been supplied by a Regulated Company. It was totally unfitted for the task. It is, therefore, scarcely just to call Childe a monopolist. Macaulay gave him that appellation, and other historians of economic theory, including Professor Edgeworth, who quotes Macaulay with approval,[3] have followed suit. The real reason for his advocacy of monopoly lay in the impossibility of carrying on the East India trade by any other method.[4]

Childe developed the theories of Mun into a consistent, well-reasoned plea for the freedom of commerce from injurious restrictions. Mun had advocated the exportation of bullion at a time when the Company rarely exported more than £100,000, and never imported manufactured Indian goods. The only manufactured article imported from India at the time was calico, but in so small a quantity that it may be left out of account. English manufacturers did not fear the competition of Indian articles. From 1680 onwards the Company began to import quantities of Indian manufactured articles which raised a loud outcry among the English clothiers. Moreover, its exportation of bullion increased fivefold. The East India Company and its supporters could hardly justify these proceedings by appeal to the crude economic theories current at the time. The latter violently condemned it, and regarded bullion as the riches or treasure of the nation. 'What is termed the most useful, after

[1] *A New Discourse of Trade*, by Josiah Childe, p. 102.
[2] Childe, *Essay*. Compare *Reply to the Turkey Co.*, op. cit.; Pollexfen's Speech, op. cit.; *Answer to Two Letters*, op. cit.; *New Discourse of Trade*, op. cit.
[3] In his article on Childe in the *Dictionary of Political Economy*.
[4] Compare *Britannia Languens*, MacCulloch's *Tracts*, pp. 332-41.

what is absolutely necessary, to supply the Necessity of Nature? Some being of opinion (the writer holds the same opinion) that nothing do deserve that name or to be so esteemed, but Gold and Silver; because no other metal is so lasting and durable or so fit to receive the Royal Stamp. The trade has the worst foundation of all, because it carries from us our Gold and Silver, which we cannot well spare.'[1]

The arguments employed by the Company were substantially the same as those of Mun. Their chief merit lies in their adaptation of Mun's arguments to their altered position. Childe developed Mun's theory to its logical conclusion. 'I am of opinion that Silver and Gold, coined or uncoined, though they are used for a measure of all other things, are no less than Wine, Oil, Tobacco, Cloth or Goods; and may in many cases be exported as much to National Advantage as any other commodity.' The exportation of gold was inevitable with the growth of trade. 'No Nation, ever was, or will be, considerable in Trade, that Prohibits the exportation of Bullion.'[2]

It is this growth of the East India trade, and the consequent increase in the exportation of bullion to the East, that explains the seemingly inconsistent propositions of the defenders of the East India Company. The true view of the functions of money was forced upon them owing to the peculiar position in which they were placed. Without the exportation of bullion their trade would have come to a sudden stop. Hence the necessity for the defence of the exportation of bullion. This involved necessarily an appeal to the truer principles of economics. Nor were these views confined to Childe. Every defender of the East India Company, from Mun to Davenant, adopted them. Without their help the defence of the Company would have seemed impossible. Papillon held 'that it was a great mistake to think that the plenty or scarcity of money is the cause of a good or bad Trade'. 'Nor can the Stock and riches of the Kingdom be properly confined to Money. Gold and Silver ought not to be excluded, being merchandise, to be traded with as any

[1] *England and India Inconsistent in their Manufactures*, *India Office Tracts*, vol. lxxxiii. See also *A Reply* to it by Davenant: and *A Rejoinder* to Davenant's *Reply* in the British Museum. See below, next chapter.

[2] Childe, *East India Trade is the Most National of all the Foreign Trades*, *India Office Tracts*, vol. lxxxiii.

other sort of goods.'[1] The amount of money exported depended, however, upon the volume of trade with the East.

The growth of the East India trade led not only to the exportation of money but also to the importation of Indian articles into England. It was comparatively easy to defend the exportation of bullion. The arguments employed by Mun were used with effect by his successors. The importation of Indian commodities, however, was a direct challenge to the established Mercantile System. One of its fundamental principles had already been violated by the Company. The question raised by the competition with the Indian articles was more serious still. As will be seen later it involved the complete abandonment of the Mercantile System. For this the country was hardly ripe. The Company here, as elsewhere, broke loose from the shackles imposed by the Mercantile System. Its system of tariffs, its prohibition of the exportation of money, its imposition of injurious restraints on the freedom of trade, were denounced in eloquent words by Davenant. We see the germs of the doctrine in Childe. He acutely criticises 'the Balance of Trade', the universal test of the seventeenth century. 'This rule is fallible as regards particular Trades. The true measure of any Trade cannot be taken by the consideration of such trade in itself singly, but as it stands in reference to the General Trade of the Kingdom.'[2] 'It is true that the East India Company import much more goods into England than they export, and that they carry out quantities of gold and silver annually; yet no man that understands the Trade will affirm that England loseth by that Trade.' The dependence of foreign trade upon the Navy is well brought out. 'Though the Dominion of the Sea may be obtained by Arms, and fortunate Battles at Sea, it can never be retained, preserved and maintained, but by the excess and predominancy of Foreign Trade.'

Foreign trade, so keenly desired by Mun, is now regarded not only as a means of obtaining the treasure but also as an instrument for attaining the supremacy of the seas. Religion, foreign trade, and power 'mutually work' upon one another. 'Foreign

[1] *East India Trade is the most profitable Trade to the Kingdom*, Brit. Mus. 1029. g. 24, pp. 4–5.

[2] *A New Discourse of Trade*, op. cit., p. 152.

Trade produces Riches; Riches produce Power; Power preserves our Trade and Religion; they mutually work one upon and for the preservation of each other.' His analysis of interest is not marked by profundity. 'It is not very deep.'[1] His mistake consisted in regarding it as 'a universal cure for all diseases'. He regarded it as the 'causa causans of all the other causes of the riches of that people' [the Dutch].[2] He, however, prescribes 'this pharmacon for curing all distempers, even Exportation of Wool'.[3] The general rate of interest depends on the general conditions of demand and supply. This was not noticed by Childe, who completely ignores the conditions of demand and supply, and prescribes a flat rate of interest in all countries and for all times.

Though Childe is not free from some of the prejudices of the time, he is wonderfully acute and adaptive. His importance lies in his adaptation of the arguments of Mun to the varying phases through which the Company passed. Just as the necessity for exporting bullion had obliged him to regard it as a commodity, so the necessity for defending the importation of Indian commodities into England led him to a true analysis of the economic laws. The fundamental principles of the Mercantile System, thus violated by the East India trade, were criticized later on by Davenant, North, and others.

The keen rivalry between the English and the Dutch Companies in Mun's time had led him to demand retaliatory measures against the Dutch. The exportation of bullion had obliged him to justify the measure by appeal to the truer principles of money. Under Charles II the power of the Dutch was greatly reduced. Moreover, the East India Company was taken under royal protection. This reacted upon the East India trade. The growth of the trade led to the formulation of truer principles of Political Economy. It led to the first systematic opposition to the fundamental principles of the narrow Mercantilism so trenchantly criticized by Adam Smith. Childe, Davenant, Dudley, North, and a host of other writers[4] advocated the removal of all vexatious laws, urged the repeal of all laws

[1] Boehm-Bawerk, *Capital and Interest.*
[2] *New Discourse of Trade*, p. 8.
[3] H.R., *Interest of Great Britain considered*, Brit. Mus. 712. c. 8, 1707.
[4] See next chapter.

that restrained the freedom of commerce, and justified the exportation of bullion. This advocacy had its origin in the necessities of the East India Company. The connexion between Power and Plenty has been noticed by all the economic historians. What is not noticed, however, is the dependence of the economic theories of the time: I. On the actual course of Foreign Trade. II. And on the amount of support accorded to the latter by the State. The three—Power, Wealth, and Economic Theory—were therefore intimately connected. They acted and reacted upon one another.

The growth of the East India trade depended upon the support of the Crown. As this growth involved the importation of Indian commodities and exportation of bullion, it could be defended only by appeal to the truer principles of Economics. Hence the intimate connexion of Economic Theory, Economic Practice, and the State.

III

THE ADMINISTRATION OF SIR JOSIAH CHILDE

THE accession of James II to the throne did not affect the policy of the Crown towards the Company. There is reason to think that James's support was energetic, continuous, and prompt. He gave the Company a very liberal charter, conferring on it the amplest jurisdiction, with the right of exercising martial law and coining money. He allowed it to set up Admiralty Courts on the West Coast of India. Sir Josiah Childe would have been completely powerless in his conflict with the Mogul without James's support. It is not quite correct to say, as asserted by Professor Scott, Sir William Hunter, and others, that he 'acquired the Company's Stock'. The annual gift of £10,000 to the King was instituted, not by Childe, but 'by those who have sold themselves out, and do not complain against it'. However, 'it has since been taken off by a present of £7,000 Stock by the Company, which his present Majesty does now enjoy'.[1] The annual gifts by the Company to Charles and his brother no doubt strengthened them in their attachment to it. The Company's voluntary contributions have already been mentioned.[2] We cannot explain the warm support of the two brothers on the hypothesis of self-interest. This was, no doubt, one of the reasons for their support; yet it was not the chief reason. The chief reason for the support of James II lay in his recognition of the impossibility of carrying on the trade in the East by means of a Regulated Company. He merely carried on the policy initiated by the Council of Trade. The latter had recommended the Company, in 1661, 'to the royal protection'.[3] James did not withhold it. On the contrary, he extended it. The King's protection was

[1] *A Reply to 'Great Oppressions, etc.'*, Bodleian Library, fol. Θ. 658, no. 31.
[2] See previous chapter.
[3] *Proceedings of the Council of Trade*, Add. MSS. Brit. Mus. 22115, ff. 39, 91.

specially needed at a time when the Company was undergoing a change that may be characterized as extraordinary. This was due to the ascendency of Sir Josiah Childe. The latter's connexion with the Company dated back to 1655. He was elected a member of the Committee of twenty-four in 1674, and, with the exception of the year 1676, continued to be so elected. In 1676 the King wrote to the Company not to elect persons 'who have behaved very ill towards His Majesty'.[1] The King's dislike of Childe was due not to his opposition to the King's policy, as asserted by Macaulay and others, but to the negligence or incompetence of Childe and Papillon.

In 1672 there was a loud outcry against both the victuallers, Childe and Papillon. The beer supplied by the latter was declared by the Surveyor to 'be small, and stinking'. Childe declared that 'it was sweet, sound, and serviceable'. The next year he seems to have relinquished his office, for another victualler was appointed 'to supply the Navy with provisions'. In 1676 a warrant was issued 'for process of *distringas ad computandam* against Thomas Papillon, Childe, etc., who ought to have accompted long since'.[2] It is this failure of Childe to supply the Navy with provisions that helps us to explain Charles's letter to the Company in 1676. He was, however, elected Governor in 1681, and maintained his ascendancy in the Company's Council until the year of his death. A divergence of opinion took place among the Directors of the Company. At this time the Company's Directorate was torn by political passions, and the Whigs, headed by Papillon, suffered a complete defeat. There is no reason to suppose that Papillon wanted to reconstitute the Company on a broader basis. Papillon himself had supported the Joint-Stock Organization in 1680; and he took a prominent part in the foundation of a Company that was as exclusive as the old Company. The main cause was political. Without the consistent and staunch friendship of the King the Company was utterly helpless. Its alliance was eminently useful, and it is difficult to see what other policy Childe could have adopted. It, no doubt, proved very injurious to the Company after

[1] *MS. Court Book*, no. 29, p. 245 ff.; no. 30, p. 1 ff.

[2] *Calendar of State Papers, Domestic*, 10th Dec. 1672; ib., 23rd June 1673; ib., 1st Dec. 1673; *Calendar of State Papers, Treasury Book*, 1676–9, Parts I and II, p. 258, 1st July 1676.

the Revolution. Yet this was due as much to the opposition of the City of London, the Democrats, the defenders of the Regulated Companies, and the Interlopers, as to the hostility of the Whigs. The Crown's friendship was indispensable at the time. The comprehensive plans which Childe had sketched, and the far-reaching measures of which he was the originator, could hardly be carried out without the support of the King. Of his ascendancy in the Council there can be no doubt. The Manuscript Records, the Dispatches in the India Office, and the writings of Childe himself confirm the impression which his contemporaries had formed of his personality. A comparison of the writings given below has revealed the interesting fact that they were all written by the same person; while a deeper analysis of their contents will force one to the conclusion that their author was no other than Sir Josiah Childe.[1] The Dispatches of Childe to the Company's factors enunciate the policy advocated by him in his various books, and show his dominance in the Company's Council. Many of the peculiar turns of expression of which he was so fond reappear in the Company's Dispatches. A comparison of his Dispatches to the Company's factors in the East, in 1692 and 1693, with his letters in the Bodleian Library, brings out the interesting fact that he reproduces word for word many of the phrases employed by him in his letters to Secretary Blackborne and others. The comparison of the letters with the records preserved in the India Office Records Department would, by itself, be sufficient to convince one of the reality and vigour of his dictatorship. The impression is confirmed by a perusal of the numerous pamphlets preserved in the British Museum, the India Office Library, and the Bodleian Library, Oxford. Even in 1693 we find him dominant in the Company's Committees. He reads the reports from the Company's factors, directs the routes of the ships, rules even the Governor of the Company, recommends various persons for appointments, advises the Com-

[1] i. *New Discourse of Trade.* ii. *East India Trade,* op. cit. iii. *The East India Company's Answer to the Allegations, etc.,* Brit. Mus. 816. m. 11 (74). iv. *Answer to all the Material Objections against the present East India Co.* v. *The Humble Answer of the Governor and Court of Committees of the East India Company to a Paper of Proposals, India Office Tracts,* no. 268. vi. *The Letters of Childe,* in the Bodleian Library, Rawlinson MSS., A. 303, nos. 200–313. vii. *The MS. Letter Books,* containing Childe's Dispatches to the Factors in the East, nos. 7, 8, and 9, 1682–97.

pany upon all questions of policy, and, finally, interviews the King and the Government Departments on behalf of the Company.[1] His ascendancy remained unchallenged up to 1698, though, after the Revolution, we find him directing the Company in the background. The details of administration are left to Sir Thomas Cooke and others, while the broad lines of the Company's policy are traced out by his own firm and masterful hand. During the eight years of his dictatorship he supervised all the details of the Company. The account given by Prince Butler is substantially correct with regard to this period:

> But since the men of Gath arose,
> And for their Chief Goliath chose.
> And since that mighty giant's reign,
> Whose chiefest aim was private gain,
> This Trade was drove on by such measures,
> As soon exhausted much of our Treasure.[2]

Childe himself justified his dictatorship. He asserted that 'the more any Adventurer hath in the stock, the more he is engaged to study and promote its good by all means. A small interest will never awaken a man so often in the night.' He thoroughly despised the 'common herd', and believed in the 'wise Machiavel', who 'tells us that the State of Florence when it was commonwealth never prospered, but when someone else arrived at reputation enough to moderate the counsels of the commonwealth'. Nor did the United Provinces prosper 'unless some one man had the greatest influence upon their councils'.[3] Childe was, perhaps, unconscious of the dangers to which the Company would have been exposed if the hero whom Machiavelli idolized had directed its policy. Yet this shows all the more clearly the paramount importance of estimating the real value of his services to the East India Company. The East India trade, which pursued so chequered a course under the vigorous administration of Sir Josiah, can hardly be understood without

[1] *Letters of Childe*, in the Bodleian Library, Rawlinson MSS. A. 303, nos. 208, 212, 213, 222, 265, 266.

[2] *Prince Butler's Tale*, Brit. Mus. 816. m. 13 (127).

[3] Childe's *East India Trade*, op. cit.; *Answer to the Allegations of the Turkey Company*, op. cit.; *Answer to all the Material Objections*, British Museum; *The East India Company's Reply to the Privy Council*, 1693, *India Office Tracts*, no. 268. This argument is employed by Childe in all his important writings.

a thorough acquaintance with the leading principles which guided his policy. The latter has been regarded as a departure from the peaceful policy advocated by Sir Thomas Roe. It has been asserted, moreover, that the Company were not without occasional premonitions of 'the great destiny awaiting them'. Sir Josiah Childe has, accordingly, been hailed as the first Englishman who conceived the idea of establishing a political dominion in India. The East India Company is, therefore, regarded as the originator of that policy in the seventeenth century which bore fruit in 1746. There is no evidence for these statements at all. Of all the pamphlets preserved in the Bodleian Library, the British Museum Library, and the India Office Library, those given below are the only ones that deal, either directly or indirectly, with the Company's war with the Mogul Emperor.[1] In none of them is there the faintest suggestion of

[1] (i) *Supplement to Former Treatise*, by Childe, *India Office Tracts*, vol. lxxxiii, assigns the cause of the war to 'the necessity for recovering satisfaction for damages received, and the restoration of privileges'. There is no mention of political sovereignty in the whole book. (ii) *A brief abstract of the great oppressions and injuries which the Company have acted, &c.*, Bodleian Library, Fol. Θ. 658, no. 19, accuses the Company of carrying on war for the purpose of freeing themselves from the enormous debts which they owed in India. (iii) *The Present State of the East India Company's Affairs*, Bodleian Library, Fol. Θ. 658, no. 74, charges Childe with carrying on an unjust war with the Great Mogul. There is no reference to Childe's desire to establish political dominion in India. (iv) *Reasons against making the East India Company, &c.*, Brit. Mus. 816. m. 11 (58), denounces the Company 'for its violence and depredations' on the subjects of the Great Mogul. (v) *News from the East Indies*, Brit. Mus. m. 11 (77), reproduces the Mogul's Phirmaund, showing the low state of the Company's factors in India. (vi) *An Account of the East India Company's War with the Great Mogul*, Brit. Mus. 816. m. 11 (79), charges the Company with grave crimes. (vii) *Proposals for Settling the East India Trade*, Brit. Mus. 1029. k. 37, exposes the absurdity of levying war against the Great Mogul. (viii) *Some Remarks on the East India Company's Accompt and Propositions*, Brit. Mus. 816. m. 11 (95), shows the uselessness of Bombay, Bencoolen, &c. (ix) *The East India Company's Reply to the Petition of Charles Price*, Brit. Mus. 102. k. 40, attributes the war to the 'Insolency of the Heathen Governors'. (x) *The Company's Answer to White*, ib., ascribes the war to the Interlopers. (xi) *Some Considerations on the Nature and Importance of the Trade*, Brit. Mus. 1139. g. 4, advances good arguments for maintaining forts, but only as a precaution against the 'cruelty' of the Indian Governors. (xii) Hamilton's *Account of the East Indies*, very prejudiced. (xiii) *A Letter to a Friend concerning the East India Company*, *India Office Tracts*, vol. 268, opposes the policy of keeping forts in India. (xiv) *A Letter from a Lawyer of the Inner Temple*, *India Office Tracts*. (xv) *A Letter to a Member of Parliament*, *India Office Tracts*, vol. 268, calls the Company murderers for levying war. (xvi) *Treatise on the Coins of England* accuses the Company of robbing the Mogul's subjects. (xvii) *A Discourse concern-*

a desire of the Company for political dominion in India. The idea itself was completely at variance with the seventeenth century mode of thought. Even in the eighteenth century the Directors tried in every way to extricate themselves from the responsibilities thrust on them by Clive. How then was it possible in the seventeenth century? The mistake of Sir William Hunter and others arose through their incomplete study of the Records. This is specially the case with regard to the words 'political' and 'dominion', which the Directors use so loosely. 'Political' meant, of course, commercial to them; nor is it fair to detach a few phrases from some of the grandiloquent dispatches of Childe, and to regard them as expressing the policy to which he was devoted. As Childe himself said in 1694: 'The Dutch never thrive by Plantations. What they do in the East Indies being only by War, Trade, and building of Fortified Towns and Castles, upon the sea coasts, to secure the commerce of the places.'[1] His real policy is unfolded in the MS. Records preserved in the India Office Records Department. The MS. Letter Books, Nos. 6, 7, 8, and 9, trace the evolution of that policy. His chief aim was neither conquest nor independence, but security of the East India trade. Again, he advocated the 'Dutch method' of raising revenue in India, not their method of plantations. Again and again he insists on the absolute necessity of raising revenue in India 'by Dutch, Indian or Portuguese methods . . . to defray the charge of their protection and preservation from wrong and violence'. 'We hope Mr. Gyfford will have adventured in some reasonable way to increase our revenue there to such a degree as may fully answer the whole charge of Government, Garrison, Factory, Shops and other contingencies, which certainly is not so monstrous a difficulty as to be long hammering out. If the Dutch had had that place, they would have raised 20*s.* for every shilling raised. We should imitate their wisdom, though we hate their injustice and oppression.' 'We do require the President to increase the revenue considerably by such means as he and the Council shall

ing the East India Trade: A Reply to Childe, India Office Tracts, no. 268. 'It does not appear that forts are necessary.' (xviii) *The East India Company's Answers to the Proposals, India Office Tracts*, no. 268. Childe defends the forts on the ground 'that they are necessary for safety', &c.

[1] *New Discourse of Trade*, p. 194.

think fit.' 'If our Principal Governors and Servants in India could once arrive at the wisdom of making fortified places in India defray their cost and charge, the Dutch should have no joy of their [taking] Bantam.'[1] In practically every important dispatch we find him stressing the importance of raising ample revenue. The duties of the factors did not stop, however, with the raising of revenue. The Indians living under the rule of the Company were to be treated with indulgence. This aspect of Childe's career has never been sufficiently emphasized. Yet his dispatches from England attach as much importance to the duty of treating the Indians fairly, as they do to the necessity of raising revenue. 'Our aims are sincere, good, and politique, and we endeavour to proceed with exact truth and justice, as well as courage, and where the end is good, and the means good, it pleaseth God for the most part to give a blessing.' Though he may imitate the Dutch method of raising revenue, he is not inclined to adopt the means they adopted to effect it. 'Though we have given a hint in raising revenue to imitate the Dutch methods, yet we will not expose you to anything that may put you into the disaffection of the people.' 'This generall liberty and frank encouragement to all your inhabitants indifferently will make your place great and famous in a short time.' 'We would have you to be always most kind and indulgent to the inhabitants that observe our laws, and protect them in the same uninterrupted liberty of the several religions in which they were born and bred as you do those of our own church and nation.'[2] The piety which breathes through every page dealing with the treatment of the inhabitants is in strong contrast with the shrewd common sense, the constant scoldings, and the frequent complaints which the *Manuscript Letter Books* reveal. His ideal was a patriarchal state, dealing tenderly with the prejudices of the inhabitants, meting out prompt justice, and enacting wise laws. He wanted, moreover, to make the Company's chief factories the 'Mart of the Nations', so that they may 'flourish, and prosper exceedingly. That being the means by which God Almighty promised to make Jerusalem great.' The lofty ideals and the intense passion for toleration, which these dispatches reveal, were not alien to

[1] *Records of Fort St. George*, vol. iii, pp. 20, 26, 167, 171, 174.
[2] *Records*, vol. iii, pp. 13, 14, 38–40, 147, 167, 190–1.

Childe's nature. He had advocated them forcibly, both in his *New Discourse of Trade* and in his *Essay on the East India Trade.* It is the systematization of these disconnected and inchoate truisms into leading principles, organically connected with the minutest detail of his administration, and their application to the complex conditions of Indian life, that mark him out as the first great Englishman who pointed out the path that was trodden by Elphinstone and Monro, by Malcolm and Henry Lawrence. His administration of St. Helena has been strongly condemned by Sir William Hunter and others. They have relied exclusively upon the evidence furnished by his enemies. The following dispatches will, however, show conclusively that he was not negligent in applying the same principles to the inhabitants in St. Helena. He recognized the difference between Bombay and St. Helena, and modified his policy accordingly. Yet the broad outlines of his policy are the same. He aimed at the development of St. Helena into a self-sufficing colony, 'provided with all manner of provisions that can be raised upon the island'; he emphasized the necessity of industry and labour on the part of the inhabitants, 'so that the island may yield whatever is necessary for their comfort and subsistence'; he had 'thoughts of making the colony a large sugar plantation with mills', &c.; he 'had also thought of making it a large indicoe plantation as soon as he found a proper place'; 'the making of saltpetre there, upon discoursing with many persons for the improvement of the island,' was also regarded as practicable. His rules for the island were modelled upon those made for Bombay. Yet the island was 'very chargeable'; its turbulent inhabitants rose frequently into revolts; they supplied provisions to the Interlopers, while Mr. Church, the 'minister', was the 'first aboard the Interloper Pitt that came in last voyage, especially considering that the island hath cost us £40,000, without one penny profit hitherto more than refreshment for ourselves'. The suppression of the revolt was attended by the hideous barbarity characteristic of the times. Childe was no doubt very harsh to the rebels, and the subsequent proceedings of the Court savoured of the Inquisition. Nor can he be acquitted of tyranny. But he declared that 'there had been four rebellions in the island, and His Majesty may justly blame our conduct if there be a fifth',[1] and asked whether he had not been 'too lenient and compassionate, and never thought of the mistake of thinking that kindness and indulgence would work upon such an ill-natured and levelling constitution as those islands were founded upon'.

The extension of the Company's sphere of influence, and the development of the East India trade, could be achieved only through factories. His merit lies, not in initiating the movement for the establishment of British dominion in India, but in providing for the security of the trade. That security could be achieved only through fortified factories. His policy is best studied in his dispatch to Fort St. George, dated 22nd October 1686. 'We do think it is an excellent station for our affairs, to have one fort in every prince's dominion, with whose subjects we trade, which on the side of India are the Mogul in Bengala; the King of Golconda, where we have Fort St. George; The Gingee Country, where we have yet no fort; and that country between Trincumbar and Negapatam, where we have yet neither fort nor factory.'[2] 'The more we think, the more advantage we apprehend in having a fortified settlement for the residence of our Agent and Council of the Bay, in such a place as our great ships may lie within command of the guns of our forts, and where we may have ground enough to cultivate for the subsistence of such a body of people as we have at Fort St. George.'[3] The ideal of Childe is a strongly fortified factory, well provided with 'paddy', and capable of commercial development. The maintenance of a fort is essential, for, 'though our business is only trade and security, not conquest, which the Dutch aimed at, we dare not trade boldly, nor leave great stocks, where we have not the security of a fort'.[4]

[1] Childe's Dispatches to the Governor of St. Helena, *MS. Letter Book*, no. 6, dispatches dated 16th May 1679. Compare his dispatch dated 24th March 1680, containing the rules for the island. The rules show the paternal care exercised by the Company for the welfare of the inhabitants of the island. Dispatch dated 20th May 1681, *MS. Letter Book*, no. 7, 1682–5, p. 177. Dispatch to St. Helena. Dispatch dated 26th Nov. 1684 refers to the cost of the new settlement. On p. 417 occurs the Commission to Commissioners for the Island of St. Helena. Dispatch dated 6th May 1685. *The Deplorable Case of the Poor Distressed Planters in the Island of St. Helena, under the cruel oppressions of the East India Company*, Brit. Mus. 816. m. 11 (58).

[2] *MS. Letter Book*, no. 8, India Office Records Department.

[3] *Records*, vol. iii, p. 82.

[4] Dispatch dated 2nd July 1684.

The Directors recognized that conquest by the Company was impracticable. 'All war is so contrary to our constitution as well as our interest, that we cannot too often inculcate to you our aversion thereunto.'[1] That the Company did not follow the Dutch methods of conquest will be evident from Childe's reply to the President of Fort St. George who had asserted that 'the Dutch raised no revenue, but in conquered places'. 'It is monstrous that you should attempt to impose upon us such a fallacy.... It is only the trade and populousness of the place that gives opportunity to the Governors to create a revenue, and not the manner of their first entrance, whether by conquest, or compact, or treachery.'[2] The Dutch are no doubt regarded as the 'mirrors of the East India policy, and the only patterns to be imitated by any that would lay secure foundations for a lasting East India Trade',[3] but it is their method of raising revenue, not their policy of conquest, which the Company tried to follow. The trade could hardly be maintained without the security of the Company's forts. Childe knew it in 1681; and if he had had any opportunity for redressing the grievances of the Company, he would have precipitated the war with the Mogul. The causes of the war were many, and as they have been exhaustively dealt with by Hunter, I need not go into them here. He omits, however, the most important causes which in my opinion led to it. These are: (1) the encouragement of the Interlopers by the Moguls; (2) the Dutch activity in the East. We read of frequent complaints by Childe of the way in which the Interlopers were aided by the Moguls; and the activities of the Interlopers have been described in detail by Colonel Yule. What, however, has not been described is the effect of these activities upon the Mogul Governors. The effect was uniformly bad. Childe himself acknowledged it, in his dispatch, dated 28th October 1685. 'We have heard how shamefully our People have been abused in the late Interloping times by the Mogul's Governors and Officers at Suratt, where our servants were searched to their shirts, while the French, Dutch, and Danes pass un-molested.

[1] See the Dispatch in *MS. Letter Book*, no. 6, India Office Dispatch, dated 15th March 1681.

[2] Dispatch to Fort St. George, dated 6th June 1687, *MS. Letter Book*, no. 8, India Office.

[3] *MS. Letter Book*, no. 8, Dispatch to Bombay, 15th Oct. 1686.

They durst not have offered these insolences to our Nation, but they thought us a house divided against itself; and in consequence we could not stand long. They were in the right as to postures 3 years ago. But God be thanked, the case is now altered, and we think you will hear of no more Interlopers in India.'[1] The complaint is repeated in the Company's letter to the Mogul. 'We pray that your officers may be required to forbear searching the persons of our servants.... While the Dutch and the Danes are free, the English are searched.'[2] This difference of treatment is accounted for by the fact that the Company's conflict with the Interlopers had rendered it powerless for a time. The Mogul Governors could hardly be expected to realize the differences between the Company and the Interlopers. Moreover, it was to their advantage to keep up the feud, for by that means they could derive the greatest benefit. The Company, however, was guided by Childe at the time, and he was not likely to delay the adoption of effective measures against the Interlopers. The India Office Letter Book, No. 7, containing all his dispatches between 1682–5, gives full details of his offensive. 'Suits with the Interlopers go on well,' he says in one of his dispatches, 'the Litigations between us and the Interlopers of the last two years go on well, according to the method of proceeding in the Laws of this kingdom.' This was written in 1684. In 1686 he writes: 'Here is no interloper arrived, since Captain Day, and we question whether any of them abroad will venture in.' We find him writing jubilantly in 1687, 'you will hear *no* more of the Interlopers'.

The revival of the Dutch activity in the East, and the expulsion of the English factors from Bantam in 1682, determined the Directors to fortify their factories in India. It was this, more than any other cause, that led to the insistence of the Directors upon the importance of this point. They wrote to the President of Fort St. George, in May 1683, 'We would have you to fortify our fort and town, by degrees, that it may be tenable against the assaults of any India Prince, and the Dutch power of India, if we should appear to have any difference with

[1] Ib., India Office Records.
[2] Ib., no. 8, p. 101. No date given in the dispatch; probably 1686.

them hereafter, about the Bantam business'.[1] Childe thus tersely explains the difference between the old and the new spirit. 'It may be asked why could not the Company subsist with as small a duty as they levied formerly. The answer is, they may subsist as they did formerly, having their factories generally at the mercy of the Heathens among whom they lived, but then they shall be so weak in India, as the Dutch when they please may rout them of all India in one year, as they have already out of all the noblest parts of India.'[2] There was no change in their attitude towards the Dutch the following year. 'Our main design in sending this warlike fleet [under Captain Nicholson] and so many companies of soldiers [to Bengal] . . . we desire you to promote by all the means which lies in your power, as a matter that more eminently concerns the honour of our sovereign and his kingdom than any advantage that can accrue thereby to the Company during our lives, save the honour of preventing the Dutch from their great design of expelling the English nation from the trade of India.'[3] 'Do not quarrel with the Dutch, and don't be aggressors in any of their quarrels, but resist force by force.'[4] These were the main causes of the war with the Mogul. The Dutch and the Interlopers harassed the Company's factors, preyed upon its commerce, and intrigued against its servants with the Mogul's Governors. There is reason to think that some of them were utterly corrupt, intensely partial, and totally negligent. Their treatment of the factors could hardly be called satisfactory. Yet this was due, in the main, to the weakness of the Company itself. It was not powerful enough to crush all the Interlopers. Its servants were incompetent and dishonest. We find the Directors complaining, in a series of dispatches, of the conduct of their factors, and bringing many a charge against their servants. We are not, therefore, surprised to find that the Mogul Governors took advantage of their disunion, and consequent impotence, and treated them shamefully. The Company itself knew the cause of the other invidious distinctions about which it had complained to the Mogul. They were mistaken, however, in supposing that these distinctions could be removed by force. This was the one

[1] *Records*, vol. iii, p. 72.
[2] Dispatch, 14th Jan. 1685.
[3] Dispatch dated 14th Jan. 1686.
[4] *MS. Letter Book*, no. 8.

fatal mistake of which Childe was guilty. He had a thorough grasp of the situation in India. He had, moreover, a profound insight into the means by which the situation could be met. His insistence on the importance of fortified factories, and his determination to suppress the Interlopers at any cost, were thoroughly characteristic of his policy. The two were logically connected. Without the one the other would have been futile. Security is essential to order, and without security the East India trade would have become the prey of the pirate, the Dutch, the Danes, and others. Hence his desire for fortified towns. He did not regard them as a means whereby the English empire could be established in India, but as instruments by which 'our servants, shipping, and estate could be secured'.[1] His policy, therefore, was not the policy of Clive, but the policy of Sir Thomas Roe, with this difference, that the peaceful trade which Roe had desired could be secured only by means of forts.

Though the Company's war with the Mogul was a disastrous failure, it showed the importance of the East India trade to England. The effects of this failure on its position at home were disastrous. Childe boasted that 'such hath been God's blessing upon the company's Arms, their unavoidable necessity, and their righteous cause, that the war, beyond all men's opinions, has ended to the Eternal Honour of the English Nation in those parts of the world, and a truce concluded upon such honourable articles, that if a blank had been delivered to the Company in England, to write down their own Terms, they would not have desired more than is granted by the said Articles'.[2] His letters to his factors are pitched in a minor key. 'We received your melancholy letter of the 19th May last, with former of the 10th February, and observed the contents, which made great noise here, and raised the spirits and wings of our old Adversaries, the Interlopers, who were so elated at the first news of the Invasion of Bombay, that some of them reported that all was lost, and therefore applied for a new Company to be established by the Act of Parliament.'[3] The 'old Adversaries' were not slow to take advantage of the difficult situation in which

[1] Dispatch, April 1688. *MS. Letter Book*, no. 8.
[2] *Supplement to Essay*, p. 9, *India Office Tracts*, no. 83.
[3] *MS. Letter Book*, dispatch 31st Jan. 1690.

the Company was placed. Accordingly, 'the committee of the East India Company and their Abettors having made so great a noise, last week, of the advantageous peace they had obtained of the Great Mogul', they thought it their duty to publish a true account of the War. They reproduced not only the humiliating Phirmaund granted contemptuously by Aurangzebe,[1] but also the despairing letter of their 'wise general' to Sir Josiah.[2] The war not only disorganized the finances of the Company, but also supplied fresh recruits to its opponents. They were denounced as 'murderers', and charged with destroying 'poor innocent Banias, and other merchants'.[3] 'It is not to be hoped we shall ever gain our credit in India. Nor have we reason to believe that the Mogul and his people will be heartily reconciled to the present East India Company.' The conclusion was obvious. The Mogul's Phirmaund 'stands upon Record in the Court of that Great Prince, to the Eternal Infamy of the English Nation, whereby not only the Honour of the English, but the Interest of the East India Company, have suffered an immense and irreparable Damage, though some few, by unwarrantable and prodigious means, have gained prodigious estates'.[4] Childe's mendacious statements about the war were shown to be false. His adversaries no doubt possessed an advantage in that respect. The war with the Mogul, and the keen discussion that centred round it, were, however, insignificant, in comparison with the fundamental questions that were discussed in connexion with the East India trade. Childe's policy had aimed at the alliance of the Company with the Crown. This was eminently satisfactory up to 1689. After the Revolution the opponents who had been kept in check raised their heads again. Even the downfall of James would not have been followed by the violent attacks that were started in 1689. It was the transference of part of the powers possessed by James to the Parliament of 1689 that essentially modified the attitude of the latter towards the Company. There is no reason to doubt that William III would have supported

[1] See *News from the East Indies*, Brit. Mus. 816. m. 11 (77).

[2] *An Account of the Company's War with the Great Mogul*, Brit. Mus. 816. m. 11 (79). Proposals for settling East India Trade.

[3] Ib.

[4] *News from the East Indies. A Brief Abstract*, Bodleian Library, Fol. Θ. 658. no. 19; *Some Remarks on the Present State of the East India Company's Affairs*, ib., no. 74.

the East India Company against the violent attacks to which it was subjected. The Whigs, in 1683, quoted many precedents to prove the freedom of trade; they were powerless against the Crown. In 1689, however, the King's Prerogative was denied. Hence the Company suffered not only by the change of dynasty, but also by the change of sovereignty. Nor was this the only change effected by the Revolution. The question of Prerogative had been fought over for a long time, and it was at last decided in favour of Parliament in 1689. It was the application of the theories of the Revolution to the various elements that were the constituents of national welfare that completely modified the standpoint from which the East India trade had hitherto been regarded. It was no longer regarded as the exclusive monopoly of a tyrannical company, with ample jurisdiction, but as a source of national gain, which every Englishman ought to share. The Company was, therefore, opposed not only by (i) Interlopers, as before, but also (ii) by the defenders of the Regulated Companies, (iii) the bullionists, (iv) the Whigs, (v) the clothiers, (vi) the personal enemies of Childe. The objection of the democrats was based mainly on constitutional grounds. The monopoly of the East India Company was regarded by them as a direct negation of the principles of the Revolution. 'Freedom of Trade is a fundamental part of English Liberty, and it is surprising to me that since the Revolution Englishmen should be deprived of the liberty of Trading to any part of the known world.'[1] 'There can be no colour of reason why the Company should have £744,000 given them in that Trade for nothing, but only admitting others into a share of it, who have as much right to the trade, by the Law of the Land, as the Company themselves; nor is it reasonable the subjects of England should be forced to purchase of their fellow-subjects the admittance into a Trade at so dear a rate, when they cannot be legally excluded from it.'[2]

We do not find any trace of the 'natural right' which figured so prominently in the speeches of Cecil. A right, however, does exist, and, as 'all the subjects of England have an equal right to Trade to the East Indies, the establishing the Company would give away that right to a few men only, and thereby

[1] Wood's *Survey of Trade, India Office Tracts*, vol. lxxxiii, p. 105.
[2] *A Letter to a Member of Parliament, India Office Tracts*, vol. 268.

exclude the rest from it for 21 years'.[1] It was, said the Whigs, 'against common justice and the birthright of Englishmen to exclude any of them from so great a part of the Trade of the Nation, and that Bristol, Exeter, Plymouth, and Hull should not trade to the East Indies as well as London'.[2] 'The Establishing this Company at this time would plainly admit of the Pretended Power of excluding the subjects of England from a Freedom of Trade by Charter, to the Freedom of which they have not only a Right by Birth, but it is likewise particularly taken care of and secured to them by several express statutes, the exercise of which powers, for want of being checked by former Parliaments, has already given colour for a pretence to claim it by Prescription, the ill consequences of which no man can foresee.'[3] The importance of these statements is in the fact that the East India trade had come to be regarded as a national concern, which could be dealt with by Parliament alone. The Prerogative of the Crown had been asserted by Jeffreys in the case of Sandys.[4] It was now denied by the Company's opponents, who asserted that the King in his royal capacity could do no wrong. 'He cannot weaken the Nation by restraining, and thereby endangering, the safety of the Nation to a few, and exclude the rest of the Nation from the Benefit of it. He cannot ruin the Multitudes of his Laborious and Industrious subjects seeking a vent of their Labours in Foreign parts, if they cannot do it at home. It is dishonourable to the Nation to prefer a few and a Faction of his Subjects, above the Generality of the Nation, and Welfare of it.'[5] The opinion was shared by other writers of the time. 'The King had not by Law a power to grant the Trade to some persons exclusive of others.'[6] Again, the Whig landlords, who became dominant after the Revolution, claimed a share in the profits derived from the East India trade. We have

[1] *Reasons humbly offered against Establishing the present Company by an Act of Parliament*, Brit. Mus. 816. m. 11 (56).

[2] *Reasons against Establishing an East India Company*, Brit. Mus. 816. m. 11 (57).

[3] *A Letter to a Member of Parliament*, *India Office Tracts*, vol. 268, pp. 6–7.

[4] Howell's *State Trials*, pp. 371–554.

[5] *A Treatise concerning the Coins of England*, by R. C. (Roger Coke), *India Office Tracts*, no. 268, pp. 39–40.

[6] *An Answer to the Case of the East India Company*, Brit. Mus. 711. c. 35, p. 5.

a series of proposals, advocating the establishment of a New East India Company, with a capital of £1,400,000, 'so that the Landed Men of the Kingdom, who are the most burdened with Taxes, and who suffer so much in their Rents and Estates, may not be prejudiced, but rather advantaged'.[1] The author suggests that the Trade should be managed 'by a Number of Persons, chosen by Parliament, and accountable thereto'. 'They should be empowered to take money at Interest, not exceeding £1,400,000, for carrying on this Trade. There should be settled, for ever, one single month's Tax in a year, after the rate of £70,000 per month, as a Fund to be Perpetual Interest at 5 p.c. of £1,400,000.' It was claimed that 'besides the money employed in this Trade, there will be land security as a perpetual Fund for the Interest settled, which will give the Company such a credit, they can never want money at the lowest Interest that anywhere it can be had'.[2] The 'owners of money', however, did not think it feasible to hand over the East India Company to the tender mercies of the landlords, and accordingly we have another proposal, advocating 'the division of profit between the owners of money and land'. The latter were to subscribe £700,000 to the new Company. This, however, was not enough for Mr. Thomas Neale. Accordingly, the latter proposed that the Company should be continued, but settled by Parliament, exclusive of others. 'Its capital was not to exceed £1,400,000.' Moreover, 'all the Dividends were to be made on that footing, and that every owner of £100 stock should have a dividend of £5 per cent. in the first place yearly'. It should agree to have one single month's tax of £70,000 yearly, settled by Parliament, to ensure the said stock, and to borrow money upon.[3] The opponents of the Company claimed many advantages for their scheme. They asserted that 'it will be an encouragement for Adventurers to make new Discoveries, when every one may have the management of his own affairs, and reap the benefit of his own Benefit'. Moreover, 'there will be a larger Importation from India. This will lower the price of these goods; the many sellers at our markets give

[1] *The East India Trade*, Brit. Mus. 816. m. 11 (81).

[2] Page 2.

[3] *To Preserve the East India Trade*, by T. N., Brit. Mus. 816. m. 11 (86); *The East India Trade*, Brit. Mus. 816. m. 11 (82).

us a great advantage to surmount our European competitors in that Trade'.[1] To the objection that 'many buyers will enhance the prices of commodities in India', they replied that where there are more buyers, more goods are produced. 'For these want neither land nor people in that vast Continent, who are ingenious and civilized, great traders, and understand their business as well as any in Europe.' 'More cotton will be sowed and gathered, and made into calicoes than now is, if there be greater demand for them. Silk may be multiplied almost *ad infinitum*, as has been clearly proved by Cassemba Zaar.' 'By enlarging the Trade to India, more men and defensible ships will be employed, many unknown places discovered, the customs augmented, gentlemen's younger sons found a profitable employment, greater quantities of English goods will be exported.'[2] It was suggested, moreover, that 'all others should have liberty to trade thither, paying 20 p. c. outwards to the Company, and all who desire such a license shall be obliged to give notice to the Company'.[3] 'The revenues of the Crown and our Navigation will be very much increased.'[4] They asserted, moreover, that 'the way to prevent foreign Nations increasing their Trade to India, is to open the Trade to all British subjects, who would drive it with such vigour as to discourage other Nations, which would greatly increase the customs and enlarge the navigation of this kingdom'.[5] The weakness of the Company's opponents was due to the fact that each of them desired his own interest. The Interloper advocated freedom of trade, because without that freedom it was virtually impossible for him to contend against the authority of the Company. There is reason to believe that these adventurers became very bold, and that some of them turned pirates.[6] They plundered the goods of Europeans

[1] *Proposals for Settling the East India Trade*, British Museum.

[2] *Remedies to prevent the mischief from the late Act of Scotch Parliament*, Brit. Mus. 816. m. 11 (85).

[3] *The Heads of a Scheme whereby to Establish the present East India Company*, Brit. Mus. 816. m. 11 (54).

[4] *Proposal for a more Beneficial and Equal Establishment*, Brit. Mus. 816. m. 11 (60).

[5] A remarkable Tract in Lincoln's Inn Library, entitled *Reasons against the Bill for the better securing of the Lawful Trade of His Majesty's Subjects to and from the East Indies*.

[6] The *Calendars of State Papers, Domestic*, covering the reign of William III up to 1696, and the first volume of *State Papers, Domestic*, 1702–3, show that the Indian Ocean was infested with pirates. Pp. 343, 347, 442, 551.

and Indians, and treated them brutally. The resolution of the House of Commons declaring 'the right of all Englishmen to trade to the East Indies, unless prohibited by Act of Parliament' encouraged the Interlopers. Their numbers increased. So did the number of atrocities which they committed. Childe now allied himself with the Mogul powers, and instructed his factors to punish not only those who molested the Company's factors, but also the subjects of 'our ally, the Mogul'.[1] It can hardly be doubted that open trade was impossible in India, and the Company was perfectly right when it attributed the ill-treatment of its factors by the Mogul's Governors to the actions of the Interlopers. It especially complained of the sums of money paid by the Interlopers to the Mogul. 'It was, in their opinion, one of the principal causes of the Insolency of those Heathen Governors in denying all ancient Privileges to the Company, except they might extort from time to time what they pleased from them, as they do from the Interlopers.'[2] Childe agreed in principle that some trades might be better and more beneficially carried on by a 'General Admission of all merchants', but it must be 'where the countries traded to are near home; where little money is required at a time to carry such a Trade on; where no one Nation can be capable of engrossing the trade; where no forts are necessary, and where you can support your commerce with a strong hand. But this is not the case of the East India Company'.[3] This was, perhaps, the most effective argument employed by the Company. The freedom of trade so much desired by the theorists was, no doubt, beneficial. But this freedom could hardly be maintained in the East Indies, as the Dutch, the French, and the Danes, with their powerful companies, would

[1] *MS. Letter Book*, no. 9. 'If any Interloper, or Pirate, whatever shall offer any hostility to any of the Mogull's Subjects, or any other people of India or Persia in amity with His Majesty,' they should be seized and tried. Dispatch 29 Feb. 1692.

[2] *The Company's Answer to the Petition of Charles Price*, Brit. Mus. 102. k. 40. Compare the *Company's Answer to Two Petitions of Samuel White*, British Museum. It denounces White as a 'Great Enemy to this Kingdom in general'.

[3] *Some Considerations on the Nature and Importance of East India Trade*, Brit. Mus. 1139. g. 4. Compare Childe's vigorous defence of the Joint-Stock System, in *India Office Tracts*, vol. 268, *An Account of Transactions in the Honble. House of Commons*, 1693.

have expelled the English from the East and 'engrossed the Trade'. This had occurred actually in the Spice Islands, and the Company did not fail to point out the moral.

The agitation for open trade is typical of the period. The East India trade had come to be regarded as the source from which the different classes of society would reap enormous benefits. The landowners, the moneyed men, the King, the gentlemen's younger sons, and the English manufacturers—all were to share the profits. Hence the desire for freedom of trade to the East Indies. If, however, such freedom was impossible, the contention was that it was better to have a Regulated rather than a Joint-Stock Company for the East. The scheme had many attractive features, and in some respects it was superior to the Joint-Stock organization which was the characteristic feature of the East India Company. 'The best way to carry on trade is by the Establishing of a Regulated Company, whereby all the subjects may trade upon a legal foot.'[1] 'The way of Nations trading to the East Indies is not by incorporated Company, with a Joint Stock, but free and open to all that would follow it. The most proper means to preserve that Trade is to make it National. The people of Holland found it, for while the Trade was free they had the greatest benefit by it. The Joint Stock after arising proved an enclosure of Trade from them.'[2] Their denunciations of the East India Company's monopoly, and their constant complaints of the tyranny exercised by the 'topping men' in the Committee, were aimed, no doubt, at Childe. The latter did not find it difficult to prove the superiority of the Joint-Stock organization over a Regulated Company. He pointed out the monopoly exercised by the Regulated Companies themselves, and showed that Regulated Companies had degenerated into close Corporations. The Company had aimed at the establishment of fortified factories in India in order that it 'might secure itself against the Craft and Treachery, or open Force, of the People with which they traded'. There can be no doubt that the security of trade required fortified factories. It may also be conceded that the

[1] *Proposals, &c.*, Brit. Mus. 1029. k. 37.

[2] *A Regulated Company more National than a Joint Stock*, Brit. Mus. 816. m. 11 (71).

nature of trade required a 'variety of settlements, and factories to deal with the Indian Merchants that came thither at stated and particular times to trade'. Yet the Company was hardly in a position to carry that policy into effect. Its opponents were not slow to point out the difficulties of the task. 'If forts and castles were of any use in India, it could only be in countries of small princes; but they can never be of any use in the Mogul's Dominions, who is one of the Greatest Princes in the World.' 'As regards security, we trade in all parts of the Mogul's Dominion with as much security as Foreigners do in London.' They pointed out justly that 'the Company could not oppose the Dutch or Indians in time of War, and in Peace it must be our Strength at home that must secure us against any of their Insults abroad'. As one writer put it tersely: 'If we want Peace with the Natives, we want no forts, and if we are encouraged by the Forts to make war, the Company shall soon repent.' Moreover, the forts which the Company valued so much were useless. They showed the uselessness of Madras, 'which they had bought of a prince for £12,000, of Tonquin, built only with Canes called Bamboos, and of Bencoolen'.[1] We must, instead of relying on forts, &c., rely mainly on the goodwill and honesty of the Indians, for they are 'men of that sense and morality, that where they meet those that deal with honest and fair dealing, there is no fear of their displeasure'. The Company's forts being useless, the best course for England to adopt was the appointment of an ambassador to the Mogul's Court. Roger Coke suggested a League of Commerce with the Indian princes. By this means, 'the English trading with them will be reciprocally protected, as well by the king as by those Princes. Besides, we ought, in honour, to send an Ambassador to those princes, upon whom the Company have made such injurious wars, and whose subjects have been robbed.'[2] A convenient number of persons should be 'empowered to raise money

[1] *Discourse concerning Trade*, a reply to Childe, *India Office Tracts*, no. 268, p. 13; *A Letter to a Friend*, *India Office Tracts*, vol. 268; *Roger Coke's Observations on Coins*, ib.; *Reasons against making the Present Company the Root for carrying on the future Trade*, Brit. Mus. 816. m. 11 (58); *A Letter to a Member of Parliament*, *India Office Tracts*, no. 268, pp. 2–10; *Some Remarks on the East India Company's Accompt and Propositions for Establishing that Trade*, Brit. Mus. 816. m. 11 (95).

[2] *Observations on Coins*, *India Office Tracts*, vol. 268, p. 41.

for maintaining our Ambassador at the Mogul's Court, and Consuls at the Principal Ports'.[1] These proposals were adopted by the New Company in 1698, and an ambassador was actually sent to the Mogul's Court. But the failure of that embassy convinced the Company's opponents of the futility of the project. The policy might have proved successful under Charles II. It was completely successful under James I. In 1698, however, the appointment of an ambassador by the New Company could not but lead to disunion and strife. This had been foretold by a writer.[2] His forebodings were confirmed by the disgraceful quarrels between the two Companies in India. They were on firmer ground when they attacked Childe's policy of fortified factories. The real cause of the failure of that policy was the weakness of the East India Company. It was not able to wage a war with the Mogul successfully, as 'the Mogul was a powerful prince'. Childe, perhaps, did not know this, otherwise he would not have sent ten companies of infantry against 100,000 soldiers. His mistake lay, not in formulating that policy, but in trying to carry it out at a time when the Company's position was far from satisfactory, against a king who had unlimited resources at his disposal.

A more formidable attack was delivered from another quarter. The agitation against the exportation of bullion had died down under Charles II. The Company had secured the approval of Charles, and had satisfied the Government that the amount exported had been greatly exaggerated. After the Revolution, however, its lack of support exposed it to the fierce attacks of the bullionists. It was asserted by a writer that the 'trade carried away large quantities of money which is not only the sinews of war, but medium of trade'. For 'money in a body Politick is as blood in the Body Natural, giving life to every part'.[3] It would have been comparatively easy to silence this opposition if the Company had restricted itself to the importation of raw materials. But the conditions under which the trade was carried on rendered Mun's defence of the East India trade useless. Now not only was the bullion

[1] *Proposals*, Brit. Mus. 1029. k. 37.
[2] *Letter from a Lawyer of the Inner Temple*, *India Office Tracts*, vol. 268.
[3] *Reasons Humbly offered for the passing of the Bill, &c.*, by T. S., Brit. Mus., 1697, pp. 8–10.

exported increased in amount, but also the Indian commodities imported into England competed with the English manufactures. This was expressed concisely by one writer: 'This trade is the worst possible of all, because it carries from us our Gold and Silver, which we cannot well spare, and brings us back Toys, Handicrafts, and Manufactured Goods, which we least want.'[1]

The sentiments not only of the common people, but also of the bullionists, were expressed in the following lines:

> Whilst they promote what Indians make,
> The Employment they from the English take,
> Then how shall Tenants pay their Rents,
> When Trade and Coins (are) to India sent?
> How shall folks live, and Taxes pay,
> When Poor want work, and go away?
> Such cargoes as these ships bring over,
> In England were never seen before.[2]

It is apparent from a mass of documents that this exportation was universally unpopular.[3] There is ample reason to suppose that the bullionists would have found no hearing if the weavers and others had profited by the extension of the East India trade. This, however, was not the case. Nothing is more significant of the times than the conception of the State as an organism, in which each part serves the other, and each class and industry acts and reacts on the other. The Community is regarded as a unified body. The different classes are no doubt moved by different interests. The landlords were notoriously the most important class after the Revolution, and it would be idle to deny that their interests conflicted in many respects with those of other classes. Yet, in so far as the public welfare was concerned, all of them gravitated towards that ideal. All their

[1] *England and India Inconsistent in their Manufactures*, *India Office Tracts*, vol. lxxxiii, p. 15. 'Now let us cast an eye about the English Nation, especially those whose manufactures are opposite to India; let him reflect the total loss of so many species of manufactures, and let us inquire into the cries of the poor for employment and bread in these places,' and it will be found that the East India trade is the prime cause of all these miseries. *Profit and loss of the East India Trade stated to the consideration of the present Parliament*, Brit. Mus. 816. m. 11 (92). Printed in 1700.

[2] *England's Almanac*, Brit. Mus. 816. m. 11 (92). Printed in 1700.

[3] It will be shown in the next chapter that the complaints of the bullionists were justified; and that not only did the amount exported increase, but also the importation of Indian commodities increased.

arguments would be incomprehensible at the present day unless we place this condition prominently before us. Childe and others declared boldly that the State alone could judge whether any measure conduced to public safety. The merchants were totally unfitted to form any sound judgement on the matter, for they would naturally prefer their gains to the public right. In the controversy of the bullionists the leading idea is the same. The amount of bullion exported would have been comparatively unimportant if it had not affected the community in its totality. It was the consequences of the acts, and not the acts themselves, that were the object of the bullionists' attacks. In estimating the dire results of the measure, they made the mistake of exaggerating their importance. This was perhaps unavoidable. Only by vivid recital of all the wrongs done to the different classes could the nation be aroused to its danger. It was on this account that Pollexfen denounced the exportation of bullion. 'The original of our riches is from the labour, diligence, and industry of our people in getting out of the bowels of the earth, from our lands and seas, what may be improved and made useful for carrying on our foreign trade, upon which also depends the increase of our seamen and navigation, in which our strength consists, and the support of millions whose lot Providence has cast on trade. The great concern thus depending on trade, it may properly be said, it is to the body politic as blood to the body natural, not only to support the main, but particular members of it, and, if not allowed due nourishment, may afford too much nourishment to some, but occasion a consumption or withering of the rest. Hope of gain is the mother of trade in general, but more particularly of such as get trades incorporated in Joint Stocks, which seldom extend to relieve the meanest, but usually the richest traders, who make it their business to get it incorporated.'[1] This passage shows strikingly the importance attached by the writers of the seventeenth century to the exportation of bullion. There is no reason to suppose that gold was regarded by them as the source of all wealth. Their conception of wealth seems to have been much deeper than has been generally supposed. They attached more importance

[1] *MSS. of the House of Lords*, New Series, vol. ii, 1695-7, p. 44. Mr. Pollexfen's paper, dated 17th Feb., marked p.

to 'immaterial' wealth than to 'material' wealth; they carried the analysis of the functions of State much farther; they were sensible of the dangers of the domination of one interest over the rest; and, finally, they identified the material progress of the country with the maintenance of the Colbertism of the times.

Throughout these discussions we are struck by the frequency of their appeals to an external authority. It was the existence of this authority—the State—that made possible the composition of these differences. The ultimate foundation of all government rests on the fact that it reconciles all the divergent interests, and is not identified with a particular class. Viewed mainly from this standpoint the appeal of the bullionists possesses much more force. Why, they asked, should we send the money to employ the poor in India, when we have great numbers of poor at home?[1] The question of exportation of bullion was intimately connected with the wider question of protection of English industries. 'Would it not', asked Prince Butler,[2] in a vein of peculiar irony, 'be better that we should be at 400 or 500 thousand Pounds Charge per annum, for Indian Vanities, having such plenty of money, than for the sake of employing our own people upon our own Wool, disoblige several Maids and their Mistresses, who would then be at loss how to dress themselves in their Chamber, Parlour, and Closets?' 'Had not', asked the same redoubtable antagonist,[3] 'a hundred thousand Poor rather come to their Parishes for want of work, and all the land of England fall two years' purchase, than that the Cook-maids should not be Cloathed in India Silks, and the ladies in Callicoes?' 'Do not the East India Merchantmen know the interest of the Nation better than the country gentlemen?' It seemed to the English manufacturers a crime against the English nation that the English gold and silver should be exchanged for 'Cobwebs and Cockershells'. The Company, they asserted,

[1] *The Weavers' Twelve Queries Answered*, Brit. Mus. 816. m. 14 (122). Compare *English Winding Sheet*, Bodleian Library, Fol. Θ. 658, no. 6, p. 2. 'The East India Wrought Silks are the exportations purchased with our good, hard silver, whenas we had otherwise served those parts with silks of our own manufacturing, which had kept and increased our numbers 10 times more than they now are.'

[2] *Prince Butler's Queries relating to the East India Trade*, Brit. Mus. 816. m. 13 (128).

[3] *Querical Demonstrations*, by Prince Butler, Brit. Mus.

'debauched the nation with Cobwebs and cockershells, in return for English gold and silver'.[1] 'There needs no more to show the necessity of making a speedy Law to prohibit the Avaricious Practices of those men that would sacrifice their own country for their private Gain.'[2] To the arguments of the East India Company that silver and gold were commodities, and that the Company brought the returns of the East India goods in gold, they replied that what came back in goods to be consumed here made no amends 'for the Treasure exported, and Trades that cannot be balanced without our own Products ought to be rectified some other way, and not by sending our money to India to buy Goods for that purpose'. To some of them gold and silver were the riches or treasure of a nation. 'Though Jewels, Lead and Tin, be durable, so yet not possessing other qualifications, do not so well esteem to be Treasure. Nor can Silks and Woollen Goods be esteemed Riches between man and man.'[3] Sir William Petty admirably explained the profit derived by England from the exportation of bullion to the East. 'Question 7. Will not England be impoverished by merchants carrying out the said 100 shillings? Answer: No; if he brings home for them as much silk as will yield above 100 shillings (perhaps 200 shillings in Spain, and then the same 200 shillings into England); or, if he bring home as much Pepper as an Englishman will give him 200 of the like shillings for; so the merchants and England shall gain by exporting 100 shillings.'[4] The danger to the Company lay in the alliance of the bullionist with the clothier. The two had many things in common. Both disapproved of the East India trade; but they did it on different grounds. The bullionist regarded the drain of gold to the East as the main cause of the impoverishment of the people. He attributed the unemployment, the decline of trade in 1696 and 1697, and the consequent poverty of the working classes, to the exportation of the nation's 'Riches and Treasures' to the heathens. The English merchants, and the English weavers, ascribed the misery,

[1] *An answer to a late Tract entitled 'An Essay on the East India Trade'*, Brit. Mus. 8245. a. 15, pp. 4–11. [2] Ib., p. 22.

[3] *India and England*, &c., p. 7.

[4] Petty, *Quantulumcunque concerning Money*, in MacCulloch's *Scarce and Valuable Tracts on Money*, p. 159. This argument was developed by Davenant into a powerful plea for freedom of trade, and will be treated in the concluding chapter.

the poverty, and the wretchedness of the poor not to the war, which was really one of the causes, but to the importation of Indian commodities into England. It is very difficult to draw a hard and fast line between the complaints of the two. They have been treated here separately, for the sake of simplicity. In practice the complaints voiced by the bullionist, and those by the merchant, were fused into one loud outcry against the universal enemy. The clothiers had complained of the competition of the East India commodities as early as 1675.[1] Between 1690 and 1699 the situation became much more serious. It is not until we find the clothiers' complaints figuring prominently in the *Journals of the House of Commons* that we become aware of the serious hardship and the keen competition to which they were subjected by the increased importation of Indian manufactures. Some of their statements were no doubt grossly inaccurate. A few would convict their authors of libel in a modern court of law. Yet a careful comparison of the pamphlets preserved in the British Museum, the India Office Library, and the Bodleian Library has convinced me that the hardships they suffered were due to a great extent to the East India manufacturers. The opposition of the bullionist would have been futile without the help of the manufacturers. They would have been silenced if the Company had been able to prove that the bullion exported to India brought in greater treasure to the nation. This would have involved merely a restatement of Mun's defence of the East India trade. In 1690–1700, however, the Company could not employ Mun's arguments at all. This was due to the fact that the exportation of a large amount of bullion was followed by the importation of an increasing amount of Indian commodities. It was the competition of the latter with the English manufactures that rendered the protests of the bullionists so serious.

The price of the Company's stock is, no doubt, important. This does not, however, lessen the difficulty. The Company's stock sold at different prices in different times, and, as its price depended upon circumstances that had no connexion with the growth or decline of the East India trade, it would be totally unhistorical to treat it as the sole criterion. Hence, the profits cannot be stated exactly. Though an exact statement be impossible, a rough

[1] See previous chapter.

approximation is useful, and, for this reason, 'T. S.'s' figures are important. After stating the amount of profits that the Company derived from the East India trade, 'T. S.' mentions the loss. He could not exactly compute the 'great loss that has come to the Nation, by want of employment to so many thousands of people in London and Canterbury'. Nor could he estimate the loss sustained by the nation through the unemployment of the poor. The latter was considered by him to be 'irreparable and no equivalent to be found for it'. An equivalent is, however, found. It amounts, in round figures, to £1,200,000.[1] The figures are obviously exaggerated, and can hardly be relied upon. Yet they serve to bring into prominence the popular opinion on the influence of the East India trade. Nor can we say that these statements were totally groundless. There was a large amount of truth in the complaints of the English weavers.[2] The Indian manufactures were alleged to have directly hindered the 'Expence of our own manufactures made in London, Norwich, Canterbury, Bristol, and many other places'.[3]

[1] *Profit and Loss of the East India Trade stated*, Brit. Mus. 100. m. 46, pp. 15–17.

[2] For the effects of the East India Trade on the English industries see Chapter IV.

[3] *An Answer to the most material objections that have been raised against restraining the East India Trade*, Brit. Mus. 816. m. 11 (91), p. 3. Compare the petitions of the following to the House of Commons:—A petition of Felt Makers. 'Petitioners are an ancient Corporation, supported by many Acts of Parliament and are very numerous.' 'The East India Company have lately caused great quantities of Hats to be made in India, which they have imported into this Kingdom, which, if not prevented, would be the ruin of the trade of this Kingdom, by reason of the cheapness of materials and work in India.' *Journals of the House of Commons*, 13th Jan. 1694, p. 59. The Masters, Wardens, and Assistants of the Company of Weavers, in Canterbury, presented a petition on 11th June 1698. *Journals*, vol. xii, p. 309. 'Petitioners' trade depends on weaving all sorts of flowered, striped, and plain silks, and stuffs mixed with silk and wool, and hath, of late, been very much diminished by the importation and consumption of Indian wrought silks and stuffs.' 'If the trade is not restrained, it would inevitably destroy all this manufacture.' Ib., A petition of the Mayor and Commonalty of City of Canterbury read. 'The trade of weaving all sorts of Silks and Stuffs, mixed with Wool and Silk, within this city, hath employed and maintained a great number of poor people who have lived very comfortably, till, of late years, the trade hath decreased, and the poor sort left destitute, without Employment.' 'Prays the House to encourage the said Trade by the Bill depending for the East India Trade.' Compare the following from the MSS. of the House of Lords: Pollexfen declared that 'the East India Trade is now different to what it was'. The 'Company formerly brought home no manufactures, but since 1670, they have brought manufactures, as Cabinets, China wares, &c., and this in return of our money', vol. ii, 1695–7, p. 10. Sir Thomas Powys

'We have', asserted a writer,[1] 'already and are now inciting the Indians and Chineses that are a numerous and Laborious People, and can and do live without Fire or Clothing, and with a Trivial Expence for Food.' 'It is', declared the writer, 'impolitick and utterly destructive of our own manufactures.' We find a succession of writers denouncing the East India trade upon this ground. 'The Indians', asserted Pollexfen, 'will take any nation's money that come to them. They exclude none.' In this controversy the manufacturer and the bullionist were in complete agreement. It seemed to the latter to be unworthy of a Christian to enrich the heathen at the expense of the English. As one acute writer pointed out, 'It was the English that first put the Indians on that great excess they now are, of throwing, dyeing, and weaving, when both they and the Indians could not do less than laugh in their sleeves at the Act that prevents

(for the linen drapers, calenderers, upholsterers, and persons who have lent money on the Customs) acknowledged that 'there never was so much cloth exported from the Indies', p. 238. John Andrews, dealer in India and English silks, declared that, during the last four years, 'there has been more consigned than in any years before'. 'The English cannot nearly supply the nation.' Mr. Dodd, for the Bill, declared that the Bill was for the advantage of the people of England. Englishmen were as competent as foreigners. 'We can outdo the Dutch and French Silks. We can make them as cheap as they can.' A very interesting account of the Norwich trade is to be found in the same volume. A Mr. Lamb, 'employed by his friends and relations at Norwich', declared that several sorts of stuffs were made in imitation of Indian goods. 'We are forced to go 40 or 50 miles for looms, &c. We want hands to work.' 'The trade is gone to other places.' 'We have lost the whole trade.' It is very interesting to estimate the influence of the East India commodities on Spitalfields, the home of the silk industry. A Mr. Smith, 'who had lived some time in Spitalfield', declared that 'when the East India ships come in, half our weavers play'. 'For two or three years we have increased and employed French refugees, and can employ more if further encouraged.' Compare the testimony of Mr. Medcalf, the factor at Canterbury, 'the East India goods are prejudicial to us'. Compare the evidence of John Mennel, linen-draper, ib., 'I never knew such a consumption of East India goods before'. Compare the petition of the Churchwardens of Bethnal Green, ib., pp. 509-11. 'The poor of our hamlet are grown extreme numerous amongst us, in regard many weavers and others employed in and about the silk and woollen manufactures, have entered His Majesty's service.' 'The weaving trade and several other trades depending thereon are extinguished among us, which formerly used to be the chief maintainer and support of the necessities of our poor; the importing of wrought Silks, Bengals, and printed and stained calicoes from India and Persia being the chief occasion thereof.' 'A great number of weavers are out of work, who formerly used to contribute to the necessities of others.' Petitioners pray their Lordships to restrain the India silks, &c.

[1] *An English Winding Sheet for the East India Manufactors.* Bodleian Library, Fol. Θ. 658, no. 6.

throwing and dyeing'. 'It was', bewailed the writer, 'the English that sent over artists of all these trades and patterns that might suit the European humour.'[1] They argued that, if the increase of woollen manufacture in Ireland was judged prejudicial, because the Irish could underwork and so undersell the English weaver, the East India manufactures ought to be regarded in the same light.[2]

Wool had hitherto been regarded as the staple manufacture of England. Childe and Davenant were, probably, the most thorough-going Free Traders of the time. Even they were unanimous upon that point. The staple commodity ought, they thought, to be developed by England, and every means tried to make the manufacture perfect. This had been voiced in a well known broadside[3]:

> The Loom, the Comb, the Spinning Wheel,
> Do all support this kingdom's Weal.
> If you will wear your own silk and woollen,
> You will keep your coin, your poor, your bullion.

The complaints of the competition of East India manufactures are repeated in a number of pamphlets. 'Finding', asserted the petitioners, 'that the late great Importation and Wear of their Indian Manufactures are increasing and have already, in a great measure, ruined the Canterbury Trade, and obliged the weavers to fall upon all sorts of woollen manufactures, to the prejudice of several places where such manufactures have long been established, we are therefore come again, to represent our deplorable case, and pray the consideration of this Parliament.' 'It is worthy of consideration', asserted another writer, that 'abundance of particular weavers and Traders that are destroyed both in Canterbury and Norwich, do employ more numbers of people than any country or Corporation Workhouse'.[4] By these means, 'thousands of Broad Looms, and hundreds of Throwsters' and Twisters' Mills stand to spoil, and burn, and many thousands of people forced to transport themselves, or beg, or steal, or starve, while the Mogul's subjects are encouraged and employed, and

[1] *English Winding Sheet*, op. cit.

[2] *A Short Abstract of a case presented to Parliament*, circa 1700. Bodleian Library, Fol. Θ. 658, no. 11. Compare an *Answer to the most Material objections that have been raised against restraining the East India Trade*, Brit. Mus. 816, m. 11 (91), p. 3.

[3] *England's Almanac*, Brit. Mus., op. cit.

[4] *English Winding Sheet.*

multitudes of Looms and Mills made to imitate those Silks and Stuffs lately exposed at Skinner's Hall'.[1]

The effects of this competition would, in the opinion of the writer, be disastrous. In the end the East India trade must produce 'empty purses, empty Houses, empty Towns, a small, poor, weak, and slender people'. Another result would be a fall in the value of lands. 'As things are, nothing can prevent ruin.'

Nothing is more instructive than the arguments by which the prohibition of the East India trade was defended. The weavers justified it mainly upon the ground that the increased imports would result, not only in the ruin of the woollen manufactures, but also in the impoverishment of the nation. It is extremely doubtful whether the opposition of the weavers would have had any effect if the other classes of community had held aloof. The ladies seem to have been the greatest offenders, so far as the wearing of Indian silks was concerned.[2]

The above documents show the nature of the opposition to the East India trade. The woollen manufactures were considered the staple commodity of England, and any trade that competed with them was regarded as highly injurious. It is, however, doubtful whether the weavers' representations would have had any effect, apart from the aid which the opposition of the joiners and other classes rendered them. The joiners complained of the dispatch of English workers, 'and models and Patterns of all sorts of Cabinet goods to the East'. They returned from thence such quantities of Cabinet wares manufactured there, after the

[1] Ib. Compare the following: 'The Parish of Bishopsgate, whose many By Lanes and Alleys being chiefly inhabited by workers of silk and their dependents, doth so abound with Poverty that for the maintenance and prevention thereof, though their Assessment is doubled upon most of their Inhabitants of what they used to pay to the Poor Rate, they are nevertheless obliged to pay 34 months' Assessment thereto, to pay former debts.' The parish was indebted to the amount of £300.

[2] An interesting pamphlet addressed to the ladies says: 'It has been proved that many poor manufacturers being destitute of work, and consequently of subsistence, have been found dead in the streets and fields, where they have perished. An infinite number of us are already reduced to great misery. The Poor Rates have doubled, and in some cases trebled.' Brit. Mus. 816. m. 14 (84). A Scheme for preventing the export of wool proposed, among other things, 'to reduce the vast quantities of Indian Commodity lately worn, which appears a great prejudice to the Traders and Dealers in Woollen Manufactures, and this Nation especially, the ancient and famous artists in the City of Norwich and County of Norfolk'. *To the Rt. Hon'ble the House of Commons.* Brit. Mus. 816. m. 14 (107).

English fashion, that 'the said trade is in great danger of being utterly ruined by the ingrossment of the said merchants'.[1] I have not been able to trace any other complaint by the Joiners' Company. This may be due to the fact that cabinet and lacquered goods from Tonquin, &c., proved very costly. We find the Directors requesting their Factors at Tonquin not to send any more goods, 'as they were very costly'.[2]

Perhaps the best testimony to the existence of a keen competition is to be found in the Manuscript Letter Books in the India Office containing the dispatches of the Company's directors to their factors in the East. The history of the progress of the Indian commodities in England can be traced by following the dispatches of the directors. They supply us with minute information on all the Indian manufactures that were in demand in England at the time. From them we know the quantity and quality of the articles required, while the best method of packing them is shown us in an unconsciously humorous way. The strength of the Company's opponents rested mainly upon the way in which they pointed out the inner connexion among the several industries. They attempted to show that the question was of a far more significant nature than the Company had supposed. The ultimate consequence of this trade would, in their opinion, be disastrous. 'The

[1] *A Case of the Joiners' Company against the importation of Manufactured Cabinet-work from the East Indies*, Brit. Mus. 816. m. 13 (2). Compare the following: 'It is visible now, how the Fancy and Humour of the Female Sex, with the advantage the Late Law hath given them, inclines several men of great stocks, and many of them out of necessity, and against their judgement, merely for the employment of their Estates to advantage, to strike into this pernicious India Trade; so that the vogue and cry is like our Watermen with "a hye India, hye India, hye" to almost a total neglect and Disrespect of the good and welfare of the Turkey and other more advantageous Trades of England, with a subversion of our most profitable manufactures.' *English Winding Sheet for East India Manufactors*, Bodleian Library, Fol. Θ. 658, no. 6, p. 3. Compare the following, ib., p. 4: 'As they have already almost swallowed and engrossed the Silk weaving, Throwing, and Fan-making of England, brought all our Cabinet-making into contempt; they will by the same ways and means ruin all Trades and Manufacturies.... The very mercers they strive to spoil by their setting up Retail Warehouses; and if not prevented, they will if possible effect it.... Their plenty of Copper and Tin will give them opportunity to ruin both our Braziers, and Pewterers, Tin-men and Mines. The Joyners and Carvers they have pretty well encroached upon.' India was, I presume, to take the place of Paris as a dictator of fashion. 'Though Modish Garments from France was always accounted grievous to us, yet from East India, multitudes of them are brought to the great prejudice of the Tailors.'

[2] *MS. Letter Book*, no. 9.

nation would be impoverished; the population will decrease; if the people falls, the Rents will do also'; and, 'as the woollen and worsted manufactures depended on the silk and stuff manufactures, and as, moreover, other allied trades, Upholsteries, Iron, Steel, Cabinet-making', &c., had begun to suffer, the total English trade would receive a shock from which it would be difficult to recover. National ruin would follow. The English weavers attacked it therefore, on national, and not on sectional grounds. The whole fabric of the Colbertism would have collapsed if the theories of the defenders of the East India trade had been carried to their logical conclusions.

Of the numerous pamphleteers of the period three stand out prominent. Prince Butler attacked the Company with a vigour that is still unsurpassed.[1] 'Had not', asked Prince Butler, 'a hundred thousand poor rather come to their Parishes for want of work, and all the land of England fall two years' purchase, than that the Cookmaids should not be cloathed in India Silks and the ladies in the Calicoes?' 'Would it not', inquired that merciless critic, 'be better if we send for the corn to the East Indies, for theirs is much cheaper than ours? And employ the Dutch Shipping, for they always sail much cheaper than we do, and then we may send our own ships to all foreign nations that either want or hire them?' Carey was another opponent who figured prominently at the time. In a series of pamphlets he traced the history of the East India trade; replied to the arguments of the Linen Drapers; and effectively silenced the latter. Finally, 'T. S.', a weaver, defended the Mercantilism of the day against the assaults of the Free Traders of the time. The cogency of his arguments, combined with the directness and brilliancy of his style, rendered him a formidable opponent. In a succession of pamphlets he controverted Davenant's figures; defended the position he had taken up in his first pamphlet; and showed the extent of the influence which the East India trade exercised upon English manufactures. Davenant can hardly be said to have come off victorious. His statements were questioned; his honour was brought into question; while his Jacobite leanings were made an excuse for a rabid attack upon his integrity.

[1] Compare *Butler's Tale*; *Querical Demonstrations*; *Prince Butler's Queries*, op. cit.

Davenant's feeble replies do not seem to have produced much effect.[1]

The attacks continued without a pause, and the ranks of the Company's opponents were now joined by the merchants of London. They complained specially of its methods of disposing of its goods by private contract among shareholders. 'They monopolize those commodities in best demand at rates to their own use.' There was, moreover, 'manipulation of the sale by the alteration of the Lots on the part of the Managers, even though Publick Notice has been given in Printed Books of an intended Sale'.[2] We are not surprised to find the merchants taking a leading part in the foundation of a New East India Company. Their opposition to the Company was due mainly to their desire to partake of the riches of the East. They had always protested against their exclusion from the Company, and regarded with unconcealed dislike the policy which it had inaugurated under Childe, while their grievances were intensified by the losses which they had suffered during the war with France. We find Somers writing to William III as follows: 'The London merchants, as well as other merchants of the greatest estates, being joined in opposing the Charter, they say that in such an unhappy junction, when they are deprived of the Mediterranean trade, and are such losers everywhere else, they ought not to be excluded from the trade of so great a part of the world.' They pressed 'to be permitted to send out 5 ships to the East, promising to export Commodities to the value of £100,000'.[3]

The opposition of the English manufacturers was directed

[1] See below, Chapter IV.

[2] *The Grounds of Complaint of Several Merchants and other Traders of the City of London*, Bodleian Library, Fol. Θ. 658, no. 23. Compare the following letter of Somers to William III: 'There are several other petitions from clothiers in diverse countries, and from traders representing the deplorable condition they are in by interruption of the Turkey trade,' and praying to be allowed to trade to the Indies. *State Papers, Domestic, William III.* Compare the following petition of 'diverse merchants and traders in and about the city of London', against the East India Company: 'The trade to the East Indies is of great importance, yet by the manifold abuses of the present East India Company, both at home and abroad, it is like to be utterly lost to this Kingdom, and to fall into the hands of Foreigners, unless timely prevented by some better Regulation,' *Journals of the House of Commons*, vol. x, 28th Oct. 1691, p. 541.

[3] Somers to William III, *State Papers, Domestic, William III.*

against the East India trade. There is no reason to suppose that they joined the ranks of the Company's opponents mainly because they disliked the Joint-Stock organization. It was immaterial to them whether the trade to India was carried on by a Joint-Stock or by a Regulated Company. Their object being the prohibition of the importation of East Indian Commodities into England, they were ready to ally themselves with any power that would render them effective aid in their campaign against the East India trade.

The opposition to the foundation of a Scotch East India Company exhibited all the characteristic features of a commercial war between the two countries. Not only was the Parliament moved to seize the papers of subscribers to the Scotch Company resident in England, and to impeach the leading members of the Company of high crimes and misdemeanours,[1] but also the leading English Companies and manufacturers joined with the English East India Company in a bitter attack on the promoters of the Company. The English East India Company pointed out the dangers that would arise from the formation of a Scotch Company. If the Scotch Company paid no taxes on Indian articles Scotland would be made a free port for all East India commodities, and, consequently, several articles formerly supplied from England would in the future be sold by the Scotch Company. The danger pointed out by the Company paled into insignificance in comparison with a far more serious danger. If the Scotch Company were allowed to carry on its trade with the stock and assistance of the English, 'little or none of our English provisions will be made use of by them in carrying on their trade, but they will immediately endeavour to set up all our manufactures in Scotland, and thereby not only supply India, but other markets with them, and inevitably lessen our exportation of the English manufactures'.[2]

The other English Companies were no less hostile to the Scotch Company. The Hamburg Company advocated effectual prohibition of all Englishmen 'from being concerned in the Scotch Company'; the Royal African Company feared that

[1] *Journals of the House of Commons*, vol. xi, p. 407. Compare an interesting pamphlet in the Lincoln's Inn Library, entitled *The Case of the Late African and Indian Companies of Scotland.*

[2] *MSS. of the House of Lords*, New Series, vol. ii, 1695–7, p. 14.

the Scotch Company would 'engross the whole trade to Africa from the English'; the Commissioners of Customs thought that the Scotch Company 'must have a very fatal influence upon the trade, navigation, revenue and Customs of England'; the Leeward Islanders advocated 'the prohibition of all Englishmen from dealing with the Company'. The Levant Company was of the opinion that 'all English subjects, and Jews, should be prohibited from dealing with the Scotch Company'. It thought that 'mariners, artificers, shipwrights, and others should be discouraged from all employment or assistance to the Scotch Company'. The situation was believed to be so dangerous that the Commissioners sent a letter to the Governors of Carolina, Pennsylvania, Rhode Island, and Jersey Island, in which, after referring to the mischiefs likely to be brought on the English trade through the Scotch Company, they urged them 'to a vigorous execution of the several laws made in England for the security of the plantation trade, and making this kingdom the staple, both of the Commodities of other countries and places for the supply of the said plantations'.[1]

The protests of the English Companies show that the danger to the English manufactures was real, and that, though the Turkey Company might oppose the English East India Company, it was not unaware of the importance of the trade to the Indies. The pamphlets that poured in at the time showed the influence exercised by the East India trade. They discussed every aspect of it with a minuteness and industry that are hardly surpassed. They show the intensity of the passions engendered by the quarrel. They show, moreover, the deep interest taken by the public in the East India trade. It is doubtful whether, without the aid of the weavers and others, the opposition of the Company's opponents would have proved effective. It is certain, however, that the difficulties of the Company played into the hands of its opponents. The latter would have achieved no success whatever if the position of the Company had remained sound. This was unfortunately not the case.

The Company's opponents had a certain amount of justification for the attacks which they made on the disorganization of its

[1] *MSS. of the House of Lords*, New Series, vol. ii, 1695–7, pp. 14–24.

finances.[1] It is not quite clear whether it recovered completely from the shock of 1683. We find that the Company's stock continued to fall in the following year.[2] In 1681 the Company was indebted to the amount of £61,352. 7*s.* 5*d.*[3] They paid four dividends of £25 per cent., between 11th October 1685 and 20th April 1688. Another dividend of £5 was paid on 2nd April 1689, the last was paid on 8th April 1691, so that the dividends from 1657 to 1681 amounted to 440½ per cent., while those from 1681 to 1691, after doubling the same, as the stock was doubled, amounted, according to that nominal duplicate, to 400 per cent. Altogether, dividends of £840½ per cent. had been paid from 1657 to 1691 on the original stock of £369,891. 5*s.*[4] It is instructive to compare the return which the Company presented to Parliament. It estimated its stock in England at £564,603. 17*s.* 8*d.*; its quick stock in India at £828,860. 0*s.* 5*d.*; total £1,393,463. 18*s.* 1*d.*[5] It acknowledged that it owed £525,702. 9*s.* in England. Deducting the debt, it arrived at a balance of £867,761. 9*s.* 1*d.* This included its stock in England and India. The debt in England seems, however, to have amounted to about £675,732 on 31st March 1698.[6] Moreover, the Company had neglected to mention their debts in India. White declared that when the Company's general 'gave them the go-bye, the Company was indebted to the merchants there at £300,000'.[7] This statement is difficult to accept, as George White was not an impartial critic of the Company. We know, however, that it was indebted to the amount of £230,000 at Surat in 1695.[8] Nor did the Company deny its liabilities in India. It asserted that it had been able to borrow money in India because 'it had also

[1] Professor Scott has investigated this aspect of the Company's history with admirable thoroughness and lucidity. I think, however, that his treatment of this period is not altogether satisfactory. In my opinion, the finances of the Company were in a disorganized state at the time. I am convinced that a deeper study of the Journals of the House of Commons would have led him to modify some of his conclusions. Compare Scott, *The Constitution and Finances of the Joint Stock Companies*, vol. ii.

[2] See the authority cited in the preceding chapter.

[3] *Journals of the House of Commons*, vol. xii, 1697–9, pp. 311–12.

[4] *Journals of the House of Commons.*

[5] *Public Record Office*, C.O. 77, vol. xvi.

[6] See *Journals of the House of Commons.*

[7] White's paper in the *Public Record Office*, C.O. 77, vol. xvi, no. 3.

[8] Brit. Mus. Add. MSS. 5540. f. 111.

great credit at Surat, and that the Indian merchants lent the Company between 40 and 50,000 Rs. cheaper'. It declared that it owed, in January 1691, 200,000 at Bombay and Surat. This may have been true. If so, it is difficult to reconcile this statement with its assertion that 'most, if not all, its debts had been paid' by 1691. We know that it owed £230,000 in 1695 at Surat.[1] We are therefore forced to conclude that it deliberately deceived the House of Commons by presenting a false return.

Another account of the East India Company's finances is instructive. Its debts at Surat amounted, in 1694, to £257,062. 10*s.* It owed in England £817,127. 3*s.* 7*d.* The total debt was, therefore, £1,110,981. 9*s.* 0*d.* This account was presented on 12th March 1696. Its stock was, however, valued at £2,336,483. The amount was undoubtedly exaggerated. It included various doubtful items in its accounts. Many of the items included in the Company's account were struck out by the Committee of the House of Commons.[2] It is difficult to see what other course it could have followed. The Company valued all their forts, &c., at £370,000. It can hardly be said that the valuation was reasonable. The Company had valued all their forts in 1657 at £20,000, and as, since then, they had lost several forts, it seems unreasonable to demand such a large sum for the remaining forts of the Company. It had no doubt spent large sums on Bombay and other factories in India, but the total amount expended could hardly have been higher than £100,000. Nor is it certain that the forts of the Company were justly valued by its opponents. George White regarded the proposal of the East India Company to remove the mart of trade from Surat to Bombay as but a 'dream'; 'at Madras, the Company had driven away many, and put a general Damp and Discontent on all'; as to the Company's forts on the West Coast of Sumatra, Bencoolen, and Indrapura, 'they are notoriously unhealthy'; with regard to its fort at 'Carwar', it was 'still more Romantick in

[1] *Answer of the East India Company to certain Heads of Complaint exhibited against them*; the Company's *Answer to thirteen Articles delivered by their Adversaries*, Bodleian Library, Θ. 658, no. 31; *Public Record Office*, C.O. 77, vol. xvi. This volume contains three bundles of unbound papers, 1689–1700, 1701–25, 1726–44.

[2] *Journals*, vol. xi, 12th March 1696.

talking of a Fort and Town at Retore in the Queen of Attinga's country, where all the Company have is a mean, slight house, made of Cajans, that half a dozen men would pull down to the ground in an hour'; the same applies to 'forts' in the Gengee country, &c.[1]

After taking the above facts into consideration, and comparing the different documents, I have come to the conclusion that the Company's financial position was unsound. The war with the Mogul had cost it £400,000; the capture of a number of the Company's ships during the war with France added to its difficulties. Moreover, a large amount of money had been spent on bribery in 1693. Hence, we are not surprised to find it decline quickly. In their petition to Parliament on 10th June 1698 [2] they returned their stock at £1,574,608. 10*s.* 1*d.* They were, however, 'willing to submit to a valuation of 50 per cent. for their Stock, 20 per cent. for their Dead Stock and 30 per cent. for their Quick Stock'. This petition shows the extent to which the Company's stock had fallen. It is necessary, however, to remind the reader that this was the price they had set themselves, and that others were by no means agreed upon the point. They had acknowledged that dividends had been paid out of capital, owing to the inability of their factors in India to buy Indian goods through the Mogul's war with Golconda. 'The Company's stock lying dead, both in England and India, the said Dividends were made.'[3] The Company's opponents asserted that their stock 'was not worth 20 p. c.'; while 'their quick stock was not worth 3 p. c.'[4] The new Company asserted that their accounts 'could not be relied on', and that, though they estimated their quick stock in 1696 at £1,600,000, it was not clear whether they could actually be credited with that amount. They declared these statements to be false, and showed that two ships included in their returns had been captured by the French, and that the cargo of the

[1] George White, op. cit; compare also *The Pretence of the present East India Companies Property stated and considered*, Bodleian Library, Θ. 658, no. 34; *Sam. against Sheperd*, ib., no. 62. I content myself with citing only two pamphlets here. Nearly all the pamphlets of the time refer to the Company's forts.

[2] *Journals of the House of Commons*, p. 308.

[3] *A Reply to the Brief Abstract of Great Oppressions, &c.*, Bodleian Library, Fol. Θ. 658, no. 31.

[4] *An Answer to the case of the East India Company*, Brit. Mus. 711, c. 35.

Thomas, worth £61,875, which they had included in their estimate, was employed by the factors.[1]

I conclude, therefore, that the Company's stock had fallen considerably; that in 1698 it was much less than 50 per cent. in value; that it would have subscribed a larger amount to the New Company if it had had more money at its disposal; and that, during the years 1689–1700, its finances were in a disorganized state.

It seems probable that its difficulties were enhanced by the curious devices to which Childe resorted in order to raise the price of the Company's stock. The 'pernicious art of Stock Jobbing' may not have been new to England, but it seems to have been perfected by the fertile mind of Childe. That astute operator took steps to reap the full benefit of his enterprise by instructing brokers, who were known to act for him, to sell when he had just received favourable information, while, on a reaction being established, other agents purchased quickly.[2] These practices seem to have passed unnoticed up till 1695. However, from 1696 onwards we hear a series of complaints on the subject. *England's Almanac*[3] denounced this race of harpies, while another declared that 'the trade had degenerated into a Trick; and instead of employing a stock in honest adventures abroad, there is lately set up a new Society of Artificers, who blow the Price of the Stock up and down, as best suits their design, and encroaching themselves by the ruin of others; and this Legerdemain is managed by a strange sort of Insects, called Stock Jobbers, who devour men on our Exchange, as the Locusts of old did the Herbage of Egypt'.[4] This explains the startling

[1] *Some Considerations on the proposals of the East India Company*, Brit. Mus.; *Some Remarks upon the East India Company's Accompt and Propositions*, Brit. Mus. 816. m. 11 (95); *A Reply to Popular Arguments*, Brit. Mus. 816. m. 11 (61); *The Old Company's Complaints Answered*, Brit. Mus. 816. m. 11 (69); *The Clauses in the Act of Parliament*, Brit. Mus. 816. m. 11 (67); *An Extract of an Act for raising two millions, with Observations*, Brit. Mus. 816. m. 11 (66); *An Act for raising two millions*, Brit. Mus. 816. m. 11 (65). Compare the following interesting pamphlets on the hard lot of the separate traders in the Lincoln's Inn Library: *The Case of Persons concerned in the separate Trade*; *The Case of John Powell. The Case of the English Company trading to the East Indies*, Bodleian Library, Fol. Θ. 658, no. 33, gives a very interesting account of the negotiations that preceded the formation of the New East India Company.

[2] Compare Scott, vol. ii, p. 258; Defoe, *Villany of Stock Jobbers Detected.*

[3] Brit. Mus., op. cit.

[4] *An Account of the Trade to East Indies, Public Record Office*, C.O. 77, vol. xvi.

fluctuations in the price of the Company's stock. Defoe asserted that 'within ten years or thereabouts' the Company's stock sold from £300 per cent. to £37 per cent.[1]

These devious ways of Childe do not seem to have produced any good. It is highly probable that the fall of the Company's stock was due partly to this cause.

It will be apparent from the above that the Company's position was not invulnerable. Its disorganized finances rendered it comparatively weak to foil all the attacks of its adversaries. It is doubtful whether it would have succeeded in silencing the opposition. The alliance of the English manufacturers with the enemies of the Company lacked stability and coherence. It had been brought about mainly because both disapproved of the Company. Their opposition to the East India Company was based, however, on totally different grounds. The English manufacturers attacked the Company chiefly because it was responsible for the importation of Indian manufactures into England. This would, they asserted, ruin the leading English industries. The Interlopers disliked it mainly because it restricted their freedom of trade. It was, they declared, a 'pernicious contraction of trade'. 'The subjects of England', stated another writer, 'have the undoubted right to trade to all parts, not prohibited by Act of Parliament.' It is significant that the writer does not mention the various proclamations of Charles II, prohibiting all outsiders from trading to the East, and lays emphasis on the 'Act of Parliament'. This freedom of trade is confirmed (1) by 'The several Statutes', which assert the 'Right to Freedom of Trade'; (2) by the opinion of judges; (3) by His Majesty's message sent to the House of Commons last Sessions; (4) by the several petitions of the Company to Parliament, 'praying to have it established by an Act of Parliament'.[2]

The Interlopers were joined by a new type of opponents. As Papillon and others were no less determined to get rid of the Company, and to establish a new one, an alliance between the two sections was easy. Nor was it impossible to cement the

[1] *Villany of Stock Jobbers Detected.*

[2] *Reasons Humbly Offered*, Bodleian Library, Fol. Θ. 658, no. 2; *Reasons Humbly proposed for securing the Rights of Subjects to Freedom of Trade*, Bodleian Library, Fol. Θ. 658, no. 2b; *The Pretence of the present East India Companies Property stated and considered*, ib., no. 34.

bond between the English weavers and the personal enemies of Childe. The bond, however, was weak and was liable to break at any moment, owing mainly to the divergence of their interests. The Interlopers and Papillon's followers could hardly sympathize with the grievances of the English weavers. If these grievances had been attended to, and the Indian manufactures prohibited, the trade for which they had been fighting would have disappeared from England. It is evident that the foundation of this alliance was insecure, and that a calculating and shrewd merchant would have found it easy to dissolve it. It was not, however, possible at the time, mainly because the designs of the opponents of the Company were not disclosed till the foundation of the New East India Company in 1698. It was only in that year that the various elements of which the opposition was composed began to fall asunder, and to reveal the inherent weakness of that alliance. The eyes of the weavers were then opened, and they demanded the prohibition of the East India manufactures, against the interest of their quondam allies. 'The proposal of advancing two millions', complained the weavers, 'for the supply of the Government, was the great inducement for the establishment of the new Company, and the reason the manufacturers did not complain, and solicit against the establishment, as they had formerly done, proceeded from the fair promises given by the New East India Company men, and the hope of more favourable opportunity, being unwilling to disturb the loan.'[1] Accordingly, 'the manufacturers, being deceived by the New East India Company's fair promises, are therefore come again to represent their deplorable case'. The complaint was echoed by other merchants. 'The restraining the (East India) manufactures is no more than what Mr. Sheppard, Mr. George Heathcote, and many more of the chief promoters of the subscription (to the New Company) oftentimes declared to them was absolutely necessary to be done, but desired it might then be postponed, for fear of discouraging the Loan. By which fair speeches they gained a good opinion, which we hope they will study to preserve for the good of the Nation.'[2] Accordingly,

[1] *A Short Abstract of a Case which was last Sessions presented to Parliament*, Brit. Mus. 816. m. 11 (93).

[2] *The Answer to the Most Material Objections that have been raised*

'the manufacturers being deceived by the East India Traders' Fair Promises, and finding that of late great Importation and Wear of their Indian Manufactures are increasing, and have already in a great measure ruined the Canterbury Trade, and obliged the London weavers to fall upon all sorts of Woollen Manufactures to the prejudice of several places where such manufactures have for a long time been established', they had come to lay their petitions before the Parliament.[1]

It is necessary to insist here that the manufacturers did not become conscious of the divergence of their interest until 1698. The alliance formed in 1690 might have dissolved sooner if the Company had been able to answer all the charges that were brought against it with success. There is no evidence to show that it accomplished this. We cannot dismiss all the charges against it as unworthy of serious attention. This has been done by several historians. I cannot follow in their footsteps. I think that the Company was guilty of serious errors, and that some of its actions were indefensible. This is specially the case with regard to its war with the Mogul. Childe's mistake had consisted in the declaration of war at a time when the Company was in financial difficulties. It may, no doubt, have been forced upon it by the action of the Mogul Governors. Even so, the Company was not justified in committing acts of gross dishonesty. It was charged with borrowing large sums from the Indian bankers, and with failing to pay its debts. It is evident[2] that it owed £257,062. 10*s.* at Surat in 1694. It will, therefore, be safe to conclude that the debt was larger before the beginning of the war than in 1694. Nor can we deny that the seizure of the Indian vessels in the Indian Ocean, before the declaration of war, was unjustifiable. The Company's statement 'that no ships were taken before the war' can hardly be accepted. It admitted the seizing of Indian goods on freight in their own vessels, but asserted that they had been paid for.[3] Nor can we rely upon

against Restraining the East India Trade, Brit. Mus. 816. m. 11 (91), pp. 3–4.

[1] *A Short Abstract of a Case which was last Sessions presented to Parliament: Being a true Relation of the Rise and Progress of the East India Company*, Bodleian Library, Fol. Θ. 658, no. 11.

[2] See above.

[3] *The Answer of the East India Company to certain Heads of Complaint*, 13th Nov. 1691, *Public Record Office*, C.O. 77, vol. xvi; *Reply of the East India Company to thirteen Articles*, *Public Record Office*, ib.

the statement of the Company that the Indian ships captured by them were small in number. The seizure of the vessels seems to me to have been the chief inducement for the precipitation of the war. It had taken ships in prizes to the value of £1,500,000. This was proved in the Exchequer Court upon a Bill brought by the Attorney General for the King's Tenth.[1]

The Company's treatment of the rebels of St. Helena left much to be desired. It was undoubtedly cruel.[2] It admitted that seven persons had been put to death in the island. Of these seven, five were executed on the authority of the King's Commission, and two by a jury. With regard to the King's Commission, 'it is a matter of law'; with regard to the jury they asserted that 'the Company are in no way guilty of it, since it was done without any order or direction from them'. It seems clear that the Company was forced to adopt these measures, owing to the fact that by this means alone could they maintain discipline on the island. Though we cannot approve of the proceedings of the Commissioners, we cannot deny that the rebellion required firm handling. They were charged, moreover, (1) with raising the customs duties in their factories; (2) with 'seizing the goods and ships of our fellow subjects'; (3) 'with multiplying the votes in order that particular persons may engraft themselves'. It was asserted, moreover, (4) that they had made dividends out of their capital; and that they had 'expended great sums of money under the title of secret service money'.

With regard to the first charge the Company admitted that they had raised the customs, but defended it on the ground that the cost of the enlargement of their forts had to be borne by somebody. 'They have in a small measure raised their Customs, but so far from oppressing the English or Natives, that in all but 5 per cent. Customs and 18 pence ground rent for a large house, 12 pence for a middling house, and 9 pence for a small one, together with some ordinary port charges (were imposed),

[1] *Case of the Mariners which served the East India Company in the Wars in the East Indies*, Bodleian Library, Fol. Θ. 658, no. 21.

[2] Compare the *Petition of the Islanders of St. Helena to James II, Public Record Office*, C.O. 77, vol. xv, no. 180. Refers to 'that monster of rebellion, Oliver (Cromwell)', and asserts that the Company's Governor followed the same principles. *The Mournful Cries of the Planters of St. Helena*, Brit. Mus., op. cit.

and the inhabitants of the house were well contented.'[1] As regards the second charge the Company asserted that the Joint Stock was the only form of organization suitable in the East, and that the Interlopers were really the main cause of the war. As regards the third and fourth charges the Company's reply was not conclusive. They admitted that they had paid dividends out of capital, but defended it on the ground that capital was lying idle at the time, as the factors could not buy commodities in India owing to the Mogul's war with Golconda.[2] This may probably be true.

The most serious of all the charges was that relating to the fortifications of the Company. A succession of pamphlets denounced that policy.[3] White asserted that 'many hundreds of our seamen have been sacrificed to the irrational obstinacy and wicked designs of those who have assumed an Arbitrary Predominancy over the Company's affairs'. He predicted that 'blood will certainly be required at their hands in another world, however much they may escape with Impunity in this'.[4] The Company defended the policy of fortifications upon grounds of security. It is difficult to see what objection could have been taken to that policy. It was absolutely essential to the maintenance of English trade in India. The main grounds for the construction of forts were nowhere more lucidly stated than before the House of Lords. The Company put forward with prophetic foresight the following reasons for the introduction of a new policy. 'Though at this time the Mogul has subdued a great part of India, yet, whenever he dies, it is very probable that that great Empire will break into several pieces, and great wars will arise, and certainly our fortifications will, in such cases, preserve our trade and factories, and hinder them from being overrun by one party or other, especially if it be considered that Bombay did hold out a siege of 16 months against 16,000 of the Moors.'[5] The prophecy was fulfilled to the letter, after the death of

[1] *Answer of the East India Company, Public Record Office*, C.O. 77, vol. xvi.

[2] Ib.

[3] See the pamphlets cited in the beginning of this chapter.

[4] *An Account of the Trade to the East Indies, Public Record Office*, C.O. 77, vol. xvi.

[5] *MSS. of the House of Lords*, N. S., vol. ii, p. 40.

Aurangzebe, when the Company was forced to rely upon its forts for defence.

A review of the above charges leads us to the conclusion that many of them were frivolous and were dictated by unworthy considerations. It cannot be denied, however, that some of them were true, and that the Company's defence against these charges was weak and unconvincing. This explains the apparent solidarity of the two wings of the opposition. Their union depended upon their opposition to the Company. They were sustained in their opposition by the conviction that the public would support them in their crusade, and that Parliament would render them effectual aid in their assaults on the Tory Company. The prospects of the opposition to the Company were considered so hopeful that by 16th January 1690 £100,000 had been subscribed to be used as a campaign fund, and soon afterwards £180,000 was raised.[1]

It was rumoured as early as 16th June 1689 that the Company was likely to be dissolved.[2] A 'list of all those persons who have taken a great deal of pains, and lost much time to discover the iniquity and Evil Practices of the East India Company' was drawn up, and the persons named therein were recommended as fit persons for the Committee of the New East India Company. In the list we find the familiar names of Thomas Pitt, Sir Basil Firebrace, Sir John Houblon, Sir John Banks, and Gilbert Heathcote. They had already presented to Parliament in September 1691, *Heads of Complaint against the Company*. There are sixteen heads in all, and each of them contains proofs of complaint, by prominent men, such as Pitt, Dr. St. John, Mr. Johnson, &c. The paper is full of the usual complaints against the Company. They reappear in a *Speech delivered in the House of Commons.*[3]

The main object of the opponents was the dissolution of the existing body, and the establishment of a new Company. 'Grafting on the Remains of the present Stock' would be meaningless unless it were known beforehand 'whether there is anything left to Graft upon'; nor was it easy to ascertain the 'Debt

[1] Luttrell, vol. ii, pp. 7, 8; Bruce, *Annals*, vol. iii, p. 83.
[2] *Evelyn's Diary*.
[3] *Public Record Office*, C.O. 77, vol. xvi. The list of persons is dated '1693'. Brit. Mus. Add. MSS. 22185.

and Engagements' of the old Company.[1] The stock of the Company, asserted its opponents, was only an 'imaginary sum', as it had not any real stock of its own to carry on the trade. The Company was, moreover, guilty of 'Rapine and Impiety, and it would not consist with the honour of the House, who had voted them guilty of Murdering the subjects of England, to maintain the present Company'. The establishment of a new and the dissolution of the old agreed, moreover, 'with the genius of the Nation'.[2] The old Company were regarded as 'beggars', who were unable to carry on the trade. 'Moreover', asserted its opponents, 'Forts and Garrisons were a perfect Lumber and Trumpery, and absolutely useless to the Trade.'[3] A more serious loss was that of the invaluable jewel, 'our Reputation and Honour', nor could the Mogul be expected to tolerate a Company that had committed such heinous crimes in India.[4]

I cannot accept Professor Scott's[5] view that the Company's opponents did not want to dissolve the existing body. The authorities cited above will prove my theory. In fact, the opponents could never have succeeded in enlisting the English manufacturers under their standards unless the latter had been assured that a new Company would be formed, and that that Company would import fewer Indian commodities. It was this that led the manufacturers to support Heathcote and Papillon. If they had known that their object was amalgamation with the existing body, or the creation of a new Joint-Stock Company, they would certainly have refused their aid. Nearly all the pamphlets—and they were many—that were written against the Company demand the dissolution of the old Company. Moderate men were disgusted with the violence of both parties. They admitted that the Company was guilty of some fault, but asked 'is this the reason that the whole Company should be dissolved and innocent Adventurers severely punished?' 'The expulsion of the Fellows of Magdalen College was as nothing in

[1] *Reasons Humbly offered against Grafting upon or confirming the present East India Company*, Bodleian Library, Fol. Θ. 658, no. 22.

[2] *Reasons humbly offered against Grafting or Splicing, and for dissolving this present East-India Company*, Bodleian Library, Fol. Θ. 658, no. 69, January 16⁸⁸⁄₉₀.

[3] *Sam. against Sheperd*, Bodleian Library, Fol. Θ. 658, no. 62. A very interesting pamphlet; it contrasts the views held on the above before, with those held after, 1699.

[4] George White, op. cit.

[5] Op. cit., vol. ii.

comparison with this attempt on the present East India Company.' The former concerned only twenty or thirty men, 'while the breaking of the Company will divest at least a 1,000 people of their Rights and Properties. Among the Adventurers of the Stock are great many Widows and Orphans.'[1] It is rare to find such a moderation of language expressed in the pamphlet literature of the period.

The quarrel was now transferred from the printing presses to Parliament. The attitude of the House of Commons towards the East India Company has been discussed by Macaulay and Hunter. Professor Scott has also devoted attention thereto. I think, however, that their treatment is not satisfactory. They assume that the House of Commons was determined to dissolve the East India Company, and that its request to William was the inevitable outcome of the causes that had operated since 1689. It is undeniable that just after the Revolution the Commons formed a Committee to inquire into the state of the East India Company, and that all petitions against the Company were referred to it. Nor were the petitions few in number. They poured in, almost from every quarter.[2]

The House referred these complaints to a Committee; and it cannot be denied that on that Committee sat some of the most determined opponents of the Company. This does not, however, invalidate the theory that there was no thought of dissolving the Company. Nor does it prove that the East India Company found no defenders in the House. The dispatches of Childe reveal a totally different state of things. He remained very hopeful of getting his charter confirmed by Parliament.[3]

[1] *A Letter to a Friend concerning the East India Company, Public Record Office*, C.O. 77, vol. xvi. It is signed *J. B.* and is undated.

[2] *Journals of the House of Commons*, vol. x. Compare pp. 92, 120, 167, 363, 397, 541, 560–1, 592, 617, 637, 642, 643 (important), 652.

[3] Compare his dispatch dated 11th Sept. 1689. 'You will receive many particulars of bustle and noise that the Interlopers and their adherents made in the last Sessions of the House of Commons' in *MS. Letter Book*, no. 9. In October 1690 we find him more hopeful: 'We will begin no new settlement in any place in India until our Charter be established by Act of Parliament with the same powers and authorities as the Dutch Company have exercised in India', *Fort St. George General, MS. Letter Book*, no. 9. The hope is expressed in the following dispatches as well: 19th Dec. 1690 and 18th Jan. 1693. In April 1693 we find him writing gleefully to the President of Fort St. George 'His Majesty has ordered a new Charter to be granted to the Company, which is now a-drawing, and we hope may pass

It is apparent from a study of his dispatches that he expected the confirmation of the Company's charter, and that he was certain of success. It is clear that if the House had acted honestly by the Company, and if the agreements entered into on 18th December 1691 had been carried out, the subsequent troubles from which the Company suffered would have been avoided. The House agreed on that date that the assets of the Company were to be written down to £774,000, and that a new subscription should be taken so as to bring the capital up to a million and a half. No person was to hold more than £5,000 stock. The Company agreed to these terms, and promised to furnish security for the amount. Sir Josiah Childe became a security for £100,000, and it seemed as if the matter was settled, and that the new subscription would result in the removal of all opposition to the Company.[1] The House ought now to have acted honestly, and to have brought in a Bill for establishing the Company. A Bill was actually brought in, but it provided for the establishment of '*an* East India Company'. The substitution of the indefinite for the definite article in the above has not been noticed by the historians, and they have charged the Company with obstinacy. Their view is based mainly upon the *Account of some Transactions in the Commons*, 1693, in Somers' Tracts, vol. x. The account leaves out the above detail. This fact seems to me to be essential for a right understanding of the position of the Company. Up till 8th January 1692 the negotiations had been conducted smoothly. The Company had promised to find security, and it seemed that a Bill would be brought in. On 8th January 1692, however, a motion was made to 'bring in a Bill to establish *an* East India

the Great Seal time enough to send you a copy. In the meantime, His Majesty has been pleased to cause the Interlopers that were creeping out to be effectually stopt, so that we have reason to hope that neither we nor you shall ever again be troubled with any of those kinds of mischief-makers': *Fort St. George General*, 10th April 1693. He is not dismayed by the resolution of the House of Commons, declaring the right of all Englishmen to trade to the East Indies. 'This, we hope, brings us nearer to our desired Parliamentary Settlement.' 'Yet, peradventure some ill-minded persons that love to fish in troubled waters may shelter themselves under this vote, and may be creeping out,' the President is instructed to take the necessary action, *Dispatch to Fort St. George*, 2nd Feb. 1694. A dispatch of a later date says, 'We have reason to hope that the Lords and Commons will soon confirm the Charter'. These hopes were never realized.

[1] *Journals of the House of Commons*, pp. 592, 617, 642, 643.

Company'. An amendment was proposed to substitute 'the' for 'an' East India Company. The House divided, and there voted for the amendment 85, against 115. Hence, the amendment was rejected. It is not too much to say that the rejection was primarily responsible for the subsequent troubles by which the Company was harassed for over nine years. The Company was completely right when, in a letter to the Commons,[1] it pointed out that the resolution of 8th January 1692 was inconsistent with its agreement of 18th December 1691. The Bill had been read a second time and passed by 171 votes to 116.[2] The Company, therefore, declared that if the House passed it, then they desired to be excused 'from presenting security'.

We cannot withhold our sympathy from the Company for the trick that had been played upon it by the Commons. Yet Macaulay and those who came after him have repeated the well-known tale. The Commons thereupon requested William to dissolve the Company.[3] William seems to have tried to accommodate the differences between the Company and its opponents. It is instructive to compare the eight volumes of State Papers in the Public Record Office dealing with the Company under Charles II, with the beggarly volume for William III's time, that contains little or no State document, but a collection of pamphlets, &c., against the Company.[4] Under Charles II every side of the question is treated with patience and wisdom, and important matters are discussed with calmness. Under William III the scene has shifted. The Parliament now takes a leading part, and all the party passions are let loose. There is no restraining influence. William's voice is lost in the roar of the battle. He tries to bring about a settlement, but he is powerless. The question, instead of being tried by experienced merchants and well-known statesmen, is now a subject of dispute among the two parties. The enormous mass of pamphlet literature of the period testifies to the absence of any controlling hand that could mould the opinions and shape the policy of an unorganized assembly of 500 men. After the rejection of the Govern-

[1] *Journals of the House of Commons*, p. 652. [2] p. 637.
[3] Ib., vol. x, p. 652.
[4] There is only one volume that deals with William's reign, C.O. 77, vol. xvi. It is unbound.

ment's proposal the Company began the favourite policy of *divide et impera.* It was not difficult for Childe to see that the creation of divisions among his opponents was the safest course to adopt. Accordingly, we find him employing his tools for this purpose. He himself remains in the background. 'Sir Josiah Childe being examined, said he never disposed of £10 of the Company, to his Remembrance, and always affected ignorance in that matter.'[1] His ignorance did not prevent him from recommending Acton, 'as being an honest man, who ought to do service to the Company in Parliament, because of his Acquaintance'.[2] As regards the Company's opponents, he asserted that 'there was a Committee of twenty-five who sat *de die in diem* to destroy the Company'. He therefore told Sir Thomas Cooke, the Governor, 'that he thought Sir Basil Firebrace the fittest to divide them'.[3] Sir Basil seems to have been thoroughly fitted for the task. About half the Interlopers came to terms on the basis of receiving a bonus of 25 per cent. on their respective expenditure, and half the profits. Others refused to take part in the accommodation unless they were given 30 per cent. bonus.[4] Sir Basil himself was rewarded with a gratuity of £10,000, and a further sum of £30,000 to make up the difference in the price of the stock.[5] The subscription of 1693 amounted to £1,220,314. 13*s.* 3*d.*, of which £593,605 was subscribed by the old Adventurers, and £626,709. 2*s.* 10*d.* by the new Adventurers.[6] From a printed list in the Public Record Office[7] I find, after calculation, that the number of old Adventurers was 494, and that of new 730. This speaks volumes for the enterprise of Childe. He had overcome the fierce agitation in the Commons, and had succeeded in maintaining the privileges of the Company against its rivals. The inquiry into bribery and corrupt practices seriously damaged the Company's reputation.[8] Yet Childe escaped without a word of censure. He was too wary to fall into the trap. The Company weathered the storm of 1695.

[1] Childe's *Examination*, in *Collection of Debates in Parliament*, 1694–5, op. cit.

[2] Ib.

[3] Ib.

[4] *Examination of Sir Thomas Cooke*, India Office, vol. 268.

[5] Ib.

[6] *Journals of the House of Commons*, Report of Committee, 14th July 1698.

[7] C.O. 77, vol. xvi.

[8] *Collection of Debates*, in 1694–5, op. cit.

Nor is there any reason to doubt that it would have weathered the storm of 1698 if its financial condition had been sound. It had sufficient time to subscribe the total amount, and thus to assume complete control over the new Company. The Company expressed its readiness to supply the Government with the amount required, provided that its present stock, worth £1,574,608. 10*s*. 1*d*., were valued at 50 per cent. They were ready to open books for new subscription and to make up the present stock, reduced to £787,304. 5*s*. 3*d*., not exceeding two millions. They were, moreover, prepared to raise 'so much money upon the whole, as the Fund of the eight per cent. shall amount to, not exceeding two millions, provided they are settled by Act of Parliament'.[1] They brought in another proposal, and expressed their readiness to raise £200,000 as the first payment (for two millions).

The House seems to have received the proposal favourably, but no further action was taken by the old Company. On the 14th July books were opened, 'when it was still in the Power of the Company to have subscribed the greater part of the two millions, and so have had the charter if they pleased'.[2] They could not do so, chiefly because they had not got sufficient capital. Hence they contented themselves with subscribing £315,000.

The existence of two rival Companies would have jeopardized the interests of the Englishmen in the East. The disunion that resulted, and the discreditable quarrels that took place between 1698–1700 would, if carried further, have led to the expulsion of the English from India. Both parties were conscious of the dangers of the situation, and the negotiations, begun almost immediately after the establishment of the new Company, for the union of the two Companies, were completely successful. The two Companies were united in 1709. The principle for which Childe had fought was maintained. He had asserted the superiority of the Joint-Stock System over the Regulated

[1] *Journals of the House of Commons*, 10th June 1698.

[2] *The Case of the English East India Company Trading to the East Indies*, Bodleian Library, Fol. Θ. 658, no. 33; *An Act for raising two millions, with Observations*, Brit. Mus. 816. m. 11 (66); *An Act for raising two millions*, Brit. Mus. 816. m. 11 (65). Compare a very interesting pamphlet on the hard lot of the separate Traders, in the Lincoln's Inn Library, *The Case of Persons concerned in the separate Trade; The Case of John Powell*.

System. It was comparatively easy for his opponents to combine together and attack a common enemy. When, however, they were allowed to form a Company, the divergence of interests became manifest. The opposition soon fell to pieces. The failure of the opposition testified to the superiority of the Joint-Stock System. Without the latter there is no reason to doubt that the expulsion of the English from India would have followed. Without the ceaseless energy, the indomitable courage, and the remarkable dexterity of Childe, the trade would have been lost to the nation. It was he who faced the storm, and piloted the Company through enormous difficulties.

IV

THE EAST INDIA TRADE, 1680–1702.

THE progress of the East India trade after 1680 was unusually rapid. The importation of Indian manufactures showed a phenomenal increase, while the exportation of bullion showed no signs of decline. The two were intimately connected, and the Company could hardly import an ever-increasing number of Indian manufactures without increasing the export of bullion to the East. The latter step was rendered inevitable by the fact that English cloth did not sell very well in the East. Otherwise, the returns of English cloth might have been made in Indian silks and calicoes. This would have prevented the agitation against Indian manufactures from assuming dangerous proportions. As will be shown later on, the Company did their best to increase the sale of English cloth in Persia and India. All their efforts were, however, fruitless. The high prices charged by the Company for its cloth forbade its purchase by any but Royal households and Imperial Viceroys. The exportation of bullion was, therefore, necessary. The latter policy did not conciliate the Company's opponents. Even the exportation of bullion might have been allowed, and was actually allowed, if the importation of Indian manufactures had not followed in its wake. It was the increase in Indian imports that aroused a storm of protests. The prohibition of Irish wool has diverted the attention of the economic historians from the serious consequences of the growth which the Indian manufactures attained at the time. That growth had been very slow at first, and had passed unnoticed. But the last twenty years of the seventeenth century saw an unusually rapid development.

The Indian manufactures were greatly increased; they vitally affected the silk industry of England; they threatened the staple industry so much prized by the English landlords; and, finally, they competed with the English manufactures abroad. The data for the history of that conflict exist in abundance. The

British Museum and Bodleian Libraries contain a collection of pamphlets and broadsides that is probably unsurpassed in the United Kingdom. We cannot, however, form an impartial judgement without a comparison of those documents with the Company's dispatches to their factors. The latter give minute information on everything connected with the trade in Indian manufactures. They detail the quantity and quality of goods required in England; they criticize the investments made by the Company's factors in undesirable articles; and they enable us to state the volume of that trade with a preciseness and a certainty that is unattainable in the case of any other industry. Hence the necessity for a comparison of the two types of original authorities.

The chief articles of export from the East were: (1) raw silk; (2) silk manufactures; (3) calicoes; (4) coffee; (5) indigo; (6) Kerman wool; (7) saltpetre; (8) pepper; and (9) drugs.

Of these exports silk goods and calicoes were by far the most important. The former had been brought to a high state of perfection by the eminently wise policy of the Company. That policy aimed at the utilization of Indian talent for the purpose of developing the industries for which the Indian workmen were specially fitted. For this purpose the Company invited workmen from all parts of India, and encouraged them in their industry by every means in their power. The needy workmen were lent money on good security; the Company guaranteed complete religious liberty to all who worked for it; it urged its factors to treat them with kindness and 'even indulgence'. All the manufactures that England wanted from abroad, or that could be cheaply produced in India were to be encouraged. 'You are to encourage all you can the Natives to plant Indigo and Cotton, and to make Saltpetre, if there be any proper grounds for it near Chyttegam [Chittagong], which we cannot doubt, as also the planting of Mulberry Trees for Silk Worms.'[1] Twelve years later we find them pursuing the same policy with zest.[2] The

[1] *Instructions for Agent and Council of Bengal*, January 1686.

[2] 'We resolve to have you set upon the manufacturing those goods, and do order that you give encouragement to the Painters by taking off their hands all they make, and giving them full employment.... If you could produce fine Indigo, it will be a very noble Experiment, and yield good profit here.' *MS. Letter Book*, no. 10, p. 22, 26th Jan. 1698.

Company (as pointed out in Chapter II) had embarked on the policy of encouraging the Indian manufacturers, and had sent out a number of English instructors for the purpose. This policy was pursued down to the end of the seventeenth century. The war with France necessarily lessened the volume of trade, and produced great hardships among the merchants. The Company's homeward bound fleet of five ships was taken by the French during the season 1695–6.[1] The greatest sufferers were, however, the Turkey merchants. The destruction of the Smyrna fleet brought ruin and misery to the homes of many merchants, and paralysed the commercial activity of the metropolis for a time. The calculating Childe looked, however, with great satisfaction at the ruin of the Company's opponents. The Turkey merchants, 'who had assaulted and battered perpetually at the Company', were to be completely displaced from their privileged position in Turkey, and their place was to be taken by the East India Company.[2]

The interruption of trade to Turkey had very important results. The Turkey trade was so much interrupted by the French war that raw silk had become 'an extraordinary commodity' in England. Its price had risen considerably owing to the limitation of supply. Childe propounded a novel scheme to his factors in Persia. The Company was obliged, by the new Charter, to export at least £100,000 worth of English cloth. The amount stipulated was undoubtedly large; the Indians had never bought the commodity in large quantities, and its sale was confined within narrow limits. This point could hardly be noticed by the English weavers, nor is it certain whether the Company's own statements did not mislead the public at the time. Evidence leads us to suppose that the Company exaggerated the quantity of woollen goods exported to the East, and that the government, urged by the weavers, inserted this provision with a view to warding off all future attacks from that quarter. It was plain to Childe that, unless a market could be discovered for the sale of English cloth, the Company would suffer a loss. He had suggested the proposal to his factors at Gombroon as early as

[1] Bruce, *Annals*, vol. iii, p. 179.

[2] *Dispatch to Lt. General, Surat and Bombay*, 27th Oct. 1693. *MS. Letter Book*, no. 9, p. 294.

May 1691.[1] The Persian Empire bought nearly 30,000 (clothes?) annually from the Dutch and the Venetians. Childe, therefore, could not 'apprehend' why the English Company should not be able to afford cloth cheaper than any other nation in Persia. The Company would, moreover, pay no Customs, and their freight standard would be little different from that of Bombay.[2] It looked, therefore, a profitable transaction, and he hastened the conclusion of the contract with feverish energy. This was due, in no small measure, to his desire to employ the Armenians under the Company's rules. They were considered by him to be 'profoundly skilful, as well as careful, diligent, and exceedingly frugal'. He urged his factors to 'encourage the Armenians in lading Indian goods', and asked them to treat them with kindness and to persuade them to settle in the Company's factories. By these means the Company hoped that their forts and garrisons would be made marts of nations, 'which will, in a few years, aggrandize our revenue and with that our strength'.[3] The Armenians were not the only nation to which the Company extended its protection. The Jews were in the same category, and it followed the same enlightened policy with regard to them. The Company's defence of their policy is characteristic. It is not based on a clear-cut, logical theory of religious toleration. They were nothing if not practical, and in their defence of the policy they exhibit the same utilitarian tendency. As to the Armenians' contract, 'they are the only persons that can increase the vent of English cloth, by carrying it into the Upland and Northern parts of Persia and Tartary, whereby new markets for the same can be obtained; the factors and agents never being able to penetrate so far into the country, and by permitting them to carry out foreign commodities as well, which always used to go with the Caravans, it would in-

[1] 'It would be of mighty advantage to this Kingdom if the Court of Persia could be persuaded and prevailed with to let the Armenians bring all their silk for Europe by sea in our English shipping.' A dispatch, dated 25th Sept. 1691, says, 'We have not for many years past been served by any of the Agents, but if it please God to preserve the life of your own honest Agent, Mr. Gladman, we hope highly to improve that trade for the Publick Good of this Kingdom especially the trade of English Broad-Cloth'. *MS. Letter Book*, no. 9, *India Office Record Dept.*

[2] *MS. Letter Book*, no. 9, dispatch to Persia dated 25th Sept. 1691.

[3] Ib., p. 306.

crease our Navigation, and may, in time, bring all the fine calicoes expended in Italy that used to go overland by the caravans, to the increase of our Trade in India'. With regard to the Jews, the Company observed that it was 'no more than what is done in England, and they may as well accuse the Government as the Company thereof'. As for their 'being part of government', 'it was admitted to them, as to all other nations, thereby to encourage persons of all persuasion to settle among them, for the increase of Trade'.[1]

The defence of the Company brings out the importance of the contemplated contract with the Shah. Sir Thomas Roe had suggested it before, and the Company, as we have seen, had actually brought over a large amount of silk from that country. Owing, however, to various causes, the silk trade was not carried on with vigour, and it was not till 1691, when the interruption of the Turkey trade had increased the demand for silk, that the Company's eyes were opened to the advantages of that policy. Two years later the grant of a charter, providing for the exportation of £100,000 worth of woollen cloth, hastened the negotiations. 'Owing to the war', wrote Childe, 'Raw Silk had become an extraordinary commodity.'[2] 'It is', wrote the directors in a dispatch dated 3rd January 1694, 'absolutely impossible to dispose of so great a quantity as we are now obliged to send ... except we should send over quantity of Cloth to India, sell part of it, and give away the rest, or suffer it to lye in the Godowns till it be eaten by white ants, and other Insects, by which we have exceedingly suffered in India heretofore.'[3]

The Company aimed at turning the ancient course of trade between Persia and Aleppo. The Persians had, for hundreds of years, bought vast quantities of silk in the province of Ghilan; had carried it to Aleppo, to truck it off there for cloths and other European goods. The Company now proposed to bring the silk from Ghilan to Ispahan, to 'truck' there for English cloth and stuffs, and to bring the Persian silk to England. This

[1] *Reply on behalf of the East India Company to a Paper of Complaints, commonly called Thirteen Articles, delivered by their Adversaries, to Members of House of Commons*, *Public Record Office*, C.O. 77, vol. xvi, Bundle 1, containing documents of the period 1689-1700.

[2] *MS. Letter Book*, no. 9, 24th May.

[3] Ib.

would, explained the directors, 'increase the English navigation and greatly augment His Majesty's Customs here'.[1]

It is evident that the Company expected to derive great benefits from the proposed contract. A certain Choja was the agent of Childe, and it seemed that the contract would be signed within a short time. But unforeseen events occurred, and the negotiations were broken off. The price of Persian silk was regarded by the directors as prohibitive; the quantity too seems to have been limited. 'It has been', wrote the directors, 10th March 1698,[2] 'a great omission that you did not soon inform us of the great unlikelihood of procuring silk in Persia, and that the king suffered none to be exported out of his kingdom, except the Dutch Quota, and at best that it would cost 2 or 3,000 Tomands to purchase that liberty, which we are not so fond of as to procure it at so great an Expence, because we can buy silk at half the Rates in Bengal, and as much as we can want.'[3]

The failure of the negotiations was a great blow to the hopes of Childe. The contract, if successful, would have revolutionized the silk industry of England; would have increased considerably the English trade with Persia; and would, eventually, have led to the extension of British influence there. The failure of the Persian contract exercised great influence on the development of the East India trade. The Company was enabled to buy raw silk at a comparatively low price in Bengal and to import a large amount into England. The influence of Bengal silk had begun to be felt as early as 1686. The gradual fall in the price of raw silk was due to the 'importation of great quantities of Bengall Silk, and some considerable increase in the product of Italian silk'.[4] The demand showed no decline after that date. 'Raw Silk and Taffaties', wrote the directors, in 1685, 'are always the most noble and staple Commodities your Agency affords. Provide all you can possibly of both kinds, and of the specified sorts which you have often been informed by our Lists do turn best to account here.'[5] In the list of goods to be provided at the

[1] *MS. Letter Book*, no. 9, *Persia*, *General*, 6th June 1694, p. 375.
[2] Ib., no. 10.
[3] Ib.
[4] Ib., no. 8, September 1686.
[5] *Dispatch to Bengal*, 13th Feb. 1685.

Bay for the year 1686 the silk goods of Bengal maintain their supremacy. Silk Romalls seem to have been then popular, as we find the directors requiring 50,000 pieces at a time.

Another article that is frequently to be found in the lists is Mulmulls. The exquisite Bengal Mulmulls found no difficulty in beating out the rival silk fabrics of England. Another important silk manufacture exported from Bengal was Taffetas. The directors required 17,000 pieces of Mulmulls and 40,000 pieces of Taffetas in 1686; while the amount of raw silk exported from Bengal was 1,400 bales.[1] Three years later the number of bales of raw silk had increased to 1,560. In 1692 an entirely new situation arose. The Turkey trade being practically at an end, the East India Company utilized the opportunity. Sir Josiah Childe was not unaware of the advantages of the situation. With characteristic impetuosity he threw himself heart and soul into the project of importing large quantities of Indian goods. 'It is', wrote that calculating merchant, 'good to strike while the iron is hot.'[2] 'Every ship that arrives while the markets are so high for the East India goods, is as profitable as three in the ordinary times of peace.' (Letter quoted above.) We find the directors urging their factors in 1692 to send as many Indian goods as they possibly could. 'You can', they wrote, 'send us nothing amiss this time, when everything of India is so much wanted.'[3]

It seems clear that Indian goods were in great demand from 1691 onwards. They had, as shown in Chapter II, competed with the English manufactures during the reign of Charles II. During the last ten years of the seventeenth century, however,

[1] *MS. Letter Book*, no. 8, dispatch, January 1687, p. 245.

[2] Childe's *Letter*, dated 22nd July 1692, Bodleian Library, Rawlinson MSS. A. 303.

[3] *MS. Letter Book*, no. 9, dispatch, 18th Jan. 1691. Compare the following: 'You cannot send too many goods.' They required 100,000 Romalls of all sorts in 1693. Coloured Ginghams were as popular as ever. 'You cannot send us too many goods. At this time, you can send us nothing that will not turn to very good account, and therefore send us all you can meet with of any kind or sorts, named before, or others.' *Dispatch to Bengal*, 10th April 1693, *MS. Letter Book*, no. 9. The popularity of Bengal Silk, and the remarkable increase in the sale of Indian commodities in England, come out strikingly in a dispatch to Bengal: 'Bengal silk is the very best commodity that can now be sent from India, it being at an excessive rate, by reason of the obstructions which the present war hath given to the Turkey trade.' Ib., *Dispatch to Bengal*, p. 297.

their progress was more rapid. We find the Directors still urging their factors to send as many Indian goods as possible, 'as everything of India' was in great demand at that time. The silk goods of Bengal are prominent in all their lists. They figure in the Company's dispatches, in the memorials of English weavers to parliament, and in the pamphlet literature of the time. The name of Cassimbazaar seems to have been familiar to English weavers. The delicate Atlas of that place, 'made very good, very well covered with Satin, with all sorts of Stripes', was no less popular than the Cassimbazaar Taffetas, of which the directors wanted large quantities.

We have a very interesting account of the East India trade in about 1695, from the pen of one Samuel Baron.[1] Baron seems to have resided in the East for a considerable period, and to have thoroughly explored the Company's trade there. He thought that Bombay was a most 'excellent harbour, able to contain a fleet of ships, and a fit magazine of all warlike stores'. Surat, however, was regarded by him as the 'Mogul's Chamber, and Seaport to Agra, Lahore, Brahampore', &c. The goods yearly exported from Bombay and Surat seem to have been 'Baftas of all sorts, brown, blue and white; Cotton Yarn and Woollen atlases, Niconees, Braules, Cambayes, Guinea Stuffs', Indigo, Drugs of several sorts, besides Diamonds that 'came overland from Vizapore and Golconda, and Pearls that are brought from the Gulf of Persia, and Straits of Manar'. Baron was sanguine about the Persian trade, and thought that if factories were established at Ispahan and Shiraz 'and the abuses committed by the Armenians in some measure prevented', the trade in Persia would prove 'very considerable'. It is, however, in his account of the Bengal Presidency that the importance of this manuscript lies. As far as trade to England was concerned, the presidency of Bengal was the 'most considerable to the English nation of all their Settlements in India'. Baron then describes the usual freight and price of Bengal goods. Mulmulls, 'fine piece goods', and Taffetas are the most important. It is instructive to compare the Directors' List of Goods desired in England with this List. The similarity between the two lists is

[1] Brit. Mus. Add. MSS. 34123, ff. 30–40.

striking. Another document in the same series[1] furnishes us with a very full account of silk manufacture in Bengal.[2] There seem to have been three main types of silk at the time. The silk bought at the best hands must be bought in the 'Putta or short Skean', which was first wound off from the 'Bag of the worm'. Its price seems to have varied from 15 to 19 annas the half seer, 70 Tolas each. This was commonly turned into three kinds, viz., head, belly, and foot. The head and belly seem to have been the only valuable sorts. There was a better kind, called Puttany, which was priced from 5¼ to 6¼ rupees per seer. The third type was procured from Agra and was called 'Dolleria', which was 'head, belly, and foot mixt together'. It is interesting to notice the mutual influence of Cassimbazaar and Agra. 'According as this silk sells in Agra, so the price of Silk in Cassimbazaar riseth or falleth. The exchange of money from Cassimbazaar riseth and falleth as the said silk findeth a vent in Pattana or Agra.'

This interesting account gives us a glimpse into the condition of the silk industry in Bengal in the years 1678–95. The Company's policy of fostering the Indian industries in Bengal had resulted in an unusual increase of the Bengal silk trade. The demands of the Directors show no sign of decline, and we find them asking for large quantities of silk goods to be sent.

The Company was not the only body that carried on trade with India. Any account of the East India trade would be totally misleading unless the activities of the Interloper were duly emphasized, and their place in the progress of the trade clearly recognized. Unfortunately, we cannot arrive at any conclusion on the subject. The documents which illustrated their several voyages, their wonderful resource, and their unfailing courage are gone. Gone, also, are the accounts of their dealings with the Indians. A few of them exist, however. We come across many a reference to them in the Company's dispatches. These, however, are not sufficient for our use, and we have consequently confined our attention to the Company's trade. The silkworm, stated the Leeward Islanders in 1696, produces

[1] Ff. 30–40.

[2] *Trade Reports from Fort St. George*, 1678–95, Brit. Mus. Add. MSS. 34123.

hundreds, and hundreds will produce thousands if the inhabitants can find their account with them, 'as has been clearly evidenced by Cassimbazaar, a town in Bengal, which some years since made but 4,000 bales of silk a year; (but) upon merchants buying at what price they brought to market have now multiplied their silk to 18,000 bales a year'.[1] The Directors' Lists of Articles desired in subsequent years exhibit the leading features of this progress.[2]

The demand for Indian silk goods seems to have considerably risen during the years 1697–1702. The *MS. Letter Books* in the India Office do not supply us with an exact account of the total quantity of silk goods imported into England in any one year. We cannot calculate the total amount of silk goods in, say, 1698. The *MSS. of the House of Lords* and some of the pamphlets in the Bodleian Library contain, however, extremely interesting information on the subject. No survey of the East India trade would be complete without them. According to an Account laid before Parliament on 13th January 170¾, by Davenant,[3] there were exported in 1698–1702 from England, Indian manufactures, mixed with Silk, Cotton and Herba to the value of £487,896 *6s.* 10¼*d.*, while Wrought Silks were exported to Ireland and the Plantations as follows:

To Ireland	£18,491	2	7
Plantations	29,823	7	3¼
Total .	£48,314	9	10¼

We derive interesting information on the quantity of Indian goods from Lloyd's printed lists of Cargoes. These famous lists contain a good deal of interesting information, and are valuable for our purpose. 'It was commonly said', said the writer of the *English Winding Sheet*, 'that one ship, the *Rising Eagle*, had brought ninety-seven Chests of Wrought Silk and not one pound of Raw'.

Further information is supplied to us by another writer, who said that the *Rising Eagle* had brought about 11,000 pieces of

[1] *Manuscripts of the House of Lords*, New Series, vol. ii, 1695–7, Paper e. *The Leeward Islands Papers*, p. 20.

[2] 'Sindi and muslin goods are in the greatest request, and will turn to great profit here, if you can procure quantities of them.' *MS. Letter Book*, no. 10, 6th April 1697, p. 567.

[3] Bodleian Library, Fol. Θ. 658, no. 3.

wrought silk, 'and not one pound of Raw Silk', valued at £40,000. This had 'put a great damp upon the few silk weavers that are left, and will, no doubt, cause many to be turned out of work'. It appears from a printed list, 'sold by Mr. Edward Lloyd in his Coffee House in Lombard Street', that from 20th May 1699 to 4th September 1699, there arrived from East India and China, ten ships, which brought 500,000 pieces of manufactured goods, computed at a million pounds. The 'Cassimbazaar' silk goods seem to have been the most popular of all that came from India. Nor did the exquisite workmanship displayed by the Cassimbazaar weavers pass unnoticed at the time. Up to 1698 muslin goods seem to have passed unnoticed in England. A change, however, occurred in that year. 'Thin shadow muslins of the slight sort are grown into use and fashion again. Send us 20,000 pieces.'[1] The demand was not, however, limited to muslins. Every variety of Bengal goods was required. The effect of this increase in the Company's Indian imports upon the silk and woollen industries of England will be shown later on. Here it is only necessary to point to the enormous increase in the importation of Indian silk goods.

Another commodity that was extremely popular in England was calico. The popularity of Indian calicoes had been commented upon by Pollexfen in 1680. There is reason to believe that this popularity was maintained during the years 1680–1702. We find the Directors writing to their factors in 1683 as follows: 'We resolve to drive our trade through, having the markets here to ourselves, especially in Silks and Calicoes, which we would have you be always providing of, upon the very best terms, and in the cheapest seasons of the year.'[2] The demand showed an immense increase in 1687. 'Bafts, broad, white and blue are the best commodities you can send us of Calico, which we note to you that you may exceed our former order therein, as also in Chintz of all sorts, whereof some to be of grave and cloth colours with the greatest variety you can invent, they being become the wear of ladies of the greatest quality.' Accordingly, we find the Directors requesting their factors to dispatch as many pieces of calico as they could procure. In the Company's Lists for 1689 and 1690 calicoes figure

[1] *MS. Letter Book*, no. 10, 1698, p. 115. [2] Ib., no. 7, p. 154.

prominently. The main drawback from which the manufacture suffered was their shortness. The Company had to pay the same duties for long and short pieces, with the result that short pieces were disliked by the Directors. We find them complaining frequently of this serious defect. This, however, does not seem to have affected their popularity in England. On the contrary, their extraordinary sale in England excited the wonder of the Directors themselves; they request their Agents to send us by every ship: 'Some bales as well of Silk as of Calicoes.' The demand for calicoes was, however, greater in 1692 than in 1686. We find a marked change in the quantity demanded. The Company write, in a dispatch to their Surat Agent: 'The very best commodities for this market are measured Calico goods of all sorts, white and coloured.'[1]

In the Company's List of Goods to be provided at Surat for the year 1695, the quantity of chintzes of different types, which the Company wanted, reach the high figure of 50,000. Quilts formed another popular manufacture. The Company's demand for quilts and chintzes from Surat and Bombay showed no great fluctuation. The quantity of chintz required in 1696 was 50,000 pieces.[2]

Scind goods became popular in England. For the first time we come across a list of goods to be provided at Scind for the year 1696; the quantity and quality required in England depended, no doubt, upon the condition of English trade at the time. Even so, the absence of any violent fluctuation in demand, together with the steady increase in the demand itself, force one to the conclusion that the Indian manufactures in England had attained a measure of popularity that may justly be called unrivalled. Nor was the weaving trade of Bombay neglected. A letter to Bombay, dated 1st July 1696,[3] says 'We cannot but commend the beginnings which our General has made to promote the weaving trade on the island of Bombay, wherein we would have all manner of encouragement given'. The popularity of Agra and Ahmedabad goods is evidenced by the following dispatch: 'We would have you send as much indigo as you have money to procure. The same applies to all other sorts of Agra

[1] *MS. Letter Book*, no. 9, dispatch to Surat, 20th May 1693.
[2] Ib., no. 9.
[3] Ib., no. 9.

and Ahmedabad goods, which are in great request here and would be welcome to us.'[1] It is clear that calicoes maintained their ascendancy during the period preceding their prohibition. Nor is it difficult to account for their popularity. It was due mainly to their cheapness. It is difficult to state the price of the calico, and other Indian goods, at the time. Probably the most reliable information is to be found in the Court Minutes. Even so, a number of influences co-operated to render the price of those goods uncertain and indefinite. Some of the pamphlets of the time contain, however, prices of several goods, and it would be better to compare them with some other source, in order that we may arrive at an approximation to truth. A writer complained that 'from 1678 to 1685 many ships were sent to India, and returned hither with commodities of those countries, upon private accounts'. He thought that the cargoes that several of the ships brought were better in shipment and quality than the Company's. During the period the price of long cloth varied from 20*s.* per piece to 32*s.*, 34*s.*, and even to 50*s.* per piece.[2] The rise in prices was due, no doubt, to the increase of demand, consequent on the dislocation of foreign trade by the war with France. Even so, the price of calicoes was only one-third of that of woollen manufactures. The demand for printed goods showed no decline. 49,000 pieces of Betteloes were required in 1698.[3] The directors urged their factors to send as many coloured goods as possible. 'Your chintz Ahmedabad, Chintz Seringo, and in general all the printed coloured goods are profitable commodities, whereof send large quantities, taking care the cloth be good.'[4] The quantities of chintz required in 1699 reached still higher figures. The list of goods to be provided at Surat and Bombay included the following: cotton yarn, 400,250 bales; quilts, 25,000; chintz of all kinds, 46,000. Scind goods of all the sorts that could be had were to be sent. Bombay and Surat seem to have been the principal sources from which the Company secured the supply of these goods. Attempts had no doubt been made to develop the industry at Fort St. David. The directors had urged their President to 'get as many goods,

[1] *MS. Letter Book*, no. 9.

[2] *Reasons Humbly Offered against establishing by Act of Parliament*, &c., Bodleian Library, Fol. Θ. 658, no. 2.

[3] *MS. Letter Book*, no. 10.

[4] Ib., no. 10, p. 55.

and as good of their kind, to be yearly sent us, and to put off as much of your own manufacture as you can'.[1]

It seems that Fort St. David's had exported very little 'Painting', for we find the Directors complaining as follows: 'Of late years, you have scarcely had a piece of Painting sent us from your parts of India, but understanding that the clay and water about Fort St. David's is much better for that purpose than either Fort St. George or Vizapatam, we would have you set upon the manufacture of these goods, and do order that you give encouragement to the Painters by taking off their hands all they make and giving them full employment.'[2] The advice seems to have been faithfully followed, and we find consignments of goods from Fort St. David's. It is clear, however, that the exports from the Fort were not popular with the directors. 'Your Indigo', say the latter, in a dispatch, dated 28th October 1698, 'from Fort St. David's will not do at all here, except you can have it made full as good as the best you sent for a sample, at half the cost you paid for it; and if you can have it so, the gains will be very inconsiderable, because the worst of Indigo pays as much freight and as high duties here, as the best Lahore or Agra Indigo.'[3] They go on to say, 'Encourage others to raise Silk-worms, and lend them 2 or 300 pagodas or more upon good security, but not upon the Company's Account'. It is evident that the policy pursued by the Company under Charles II had been followed consistently in the succeeding years. Indian industries were encouraged by every means; Indian workmen were lent money by the Company's factors, in order that they might start their trade; and, finally, religious and political liberty was guaranteed to them by Childe. The lists of cargoes of the Company are interesting reading. They supply us with unique materials for the construction of the history of foreign trade during the period, and they express in a brief form the progress of Indian manufactures in England. The following gives a bird's-eye view of the nature of the East India trade during the last years of the seventeenth century. 'A particular of the Silks and a specimen of the Toys and Handicraft Wares, which came from the East Indies, in the ships *Martha*, *Sarah*, and *Dorothy*,

[1] *MS. Letter Book*, no. 10, 26th Jan. 1698, p. 22.
[2] Ib., no. 10, p. 22.
[3] Ib., no. 10.

according to the Book of Sale of those ships and printed Cargoes.' (1) On the ship *Martha* the price of goods made of silk, herba or mixed, was £117,225; (2) on the *Sarah* the total amount of silk was valued at £11,422; (3) on the *Dorothy* £30,000. The total amount, £158,647, may not seem a large sum now, but it must be borne in mind that this refers to three ships only, and that the Company possessed about fifty ships at the time. The most remarkable toys and handicrafts were as follows: china ware pieces, £150,000; fans, £38,557; lacquered sticks for fans, £13,470; lacquered trunks, bowls, cups, dishes, &c., £10,500; lacquered tables £189; shells, painted, double gilt, £286; pictures, £669. I have left out a number of smaller articles.[1]

Another article that was in great demand was indigo. We find the Directors urging their factors to send as much indigo as they could get. 'Indigo', they said in a dispatch of 1686, 'is now a great commodity here.'[2] We do not find much evidence of decline in demand; in later years they frequently ask their agents to send as much 'Lahore Indigo as can be got'. The two main varieties were Circas indigo, and Lahore indigo. Agra indigo took, later on, the place of Circas indigo. The usual quantities required seem to have been 100 and 200 tons. About the end of the seventeenth century Indian indigo seems to have suffered in competition with indigo from Jamaica and New York. During the years 1697–9 the former exported three hogsheads and 914 barrels to England; while the latter sent, in one year, eight hogsheads and forty-six barrels of indigo.[3]

Saltpetre was another useful article imported from the East. The average quantity does not seem to have exceeded 800 tons. This applies only to times of peace. During the war-time demands were made by the Government for a larger amount, and its price was fixed by Godolphin in 1693. The quantity of saltpetre imported was not adequate to the demand, and we

[1] Bodleian Library, Fol. Θ. 658. Compare: 'The cargoe of *Sarah Gally*, arrived from China, July 1700; it contains a number of Lacquered Wares, and 16,005 Bales of Raw Silk.' 'The cargo of 4 ships, the *Nassau*, the *London Frigatt*, the *Armenian Merchant*, and the *Amity* in 1696 contained a number of Bengal goods.' Brit. Mus., *Sloane MSS.* 2902, Fols. 146, 149.

[2] *MS. Letter Book*, no. 8.

[3] *MSS. of the House of Lords, Inspector General's Account*, vol. iv, New Series, p. 444.

find several writers complaining of the Company's inability to supply the nation with saltpetre. The need for that article was so greatly felt that a Bill was brought in Parliament to license its importation from Holland. 'Though', asserted a writer in 1693, 'most sorts of East India Commodities are, and have been sold, some double, some treble, and some four times as much as formerly, for saltpetre they have had scarcely any of late, so that for want thereof a Bill is now brought into Parliament, to license the importing of it from Holland, that Commodity being now sold for £8 per cent., which was formerly sold for little more than 40/- per cent.' The writer's statements are confirmed by another writer. In his *Reasons Humbly offered*, &c., the author states that the price of saltpetre had risen from 32*s.* to £8 per cwt. Another writer, referring to the desire of the London merchants for freedom of trade to the East Indies, declared that 'if they could have obtained the same, they would have paid £60,000 for Customs at the return of those Ships, in less than 2 years' time, and have furnished His Majesty with 500 Tons of Saltpetre at £50 per Ton, which by the Company's hindering the others from Trade is now sold at £160 per Ton'.[1]

The Company declared in 1694 that they had more than 100 tons of saltpetre in their warehouses; that one of their ships on her way from Barbadoes had 200 to 300 tons on board; and that there were four more ships expected from India, by which they were to receive about 1,000 tons of saltpetre. In reply it was denied that they possessed more than seventy tons. Moreover, several traders were ready to take up 300 tons a year if the Company were willing to supply them. Another trader could use 2,000 tons a year. The price was raised from £40 per ton to £120 per ton. Nor was it quite clear whether the Company could supply the total amount required. They had been asked to supply 3,000 tons of saltpetre at £4 1*s.* per cwt. for the brown, and £5 per cwt. for the white saltpetre. The General Meeting of the Company had already rejected the terms of the proposed contract, and demanded a higher price.[2]

[1] *Reasons Humbly Proposed for Asserting and Securing the Right of the subjects to the Freedom of Trade*, Bodleian Library, Fol. Θ. 658, no. 2[b].
[2] *Public Record Office*, C.O. 77, vol. xvi, 11th Oct. 1692.

Childe followed up the attack in 1693, and trenchantly criticized the proposals of the Government. By their New Charter, however, the Company was obliged to supply the nation with 500 tons of saltpetre at £45 per ton in times of war, and at £38 10*s.* per ton in times of peace.[1] There is reason to believe that the amount which the Company had promised fell considerably short of the effective demand. A number of persons asked for a patent for making saltpetre.[2] Moreover, a bill was brought into Parliament to license the importation of saltpetre from abroad. The Company opposed it on the ground that it could supply 1,000 tons. It is extremely doubtful whether it was in a position to do so. Even if it could furnish 1,000 tons, there were still 1,000 to 2,000 tons to be provided. The quantity required could hardly have been less than 2,000 in times of war. The author of *Reasons Humbly offered against a Saltpetre Bill*[3] declared that the Company and the Interlopers had given out larger commissions for saltpetre than they had done before, and that several gentlemen had laid out £5,000 a piece in order to make it in Europe. 'By this', he concluded, 'the Kingdom has a Expectancy and Security for Petre.' But expectancy of private persons must give way to national welfare, and, as it was conclusively proved before the Lords that the supply was unequal to the demand, the Saltpetre Importation Bill became law on 2nd April 1694.[4] The passage of the Bill into law deprived the Company of one of its strongest grounds of defence. It had repeatedly urged that, as it was the only body that supplied the nation with saltpetre, any diminution in its authority would make it incapable of supplying that indispensable article. Many of the attacks made upon it had been warded off in this ingenious manner. Its most eloquent champion, Dr. Davenant, put forward the same line of argument in its behalf. It is doubtful whether this dexterous device was completely successful. The replies of its opponents teem with references to its negligence to supply the Government with a sufficient amount at a reasonable

[1] *Reply to Childe's Discourse of Trade, India Office Tracts*, vol. 268, pp. 8–9.

[2] *Calendars of State Papers Domestic, William and Mary.* There are several petitions.

[3] Brit. Mus. 816. m. 13, no. 112.

[4] *MSS. of the House of Lords*, Historical MSS. Commission. *Appendix to the Fourteenth Report*, part vi, vol. I, p. 370.

price. We may therefore conclude that the Company was not altogether successful in its line of defence. It must, however, be said in its favour that it had sustained serious losses during peace times, and the Directors had complained again and again of their inability to sell the article. They informed their agents in 1678 'that Saltpetre was at present a very Drug in these times of Peace, and can hardly be sold on any terms'.

Another article that was in great demand was Caramina, or Kerman, goats' wool. The amount demanded can hardly be stated in exact terms, as the materials at our disposal are insufficient for the purpose. It is apparent, however, that the Company needed a large amount. In practically every dispatch that contains a reference to the subject the directors ask their agents to send as much Caramina wool as possible. This applies to the years 1680–1702. The supply of the Caramina Wool seems, however, to have been limited, and it is doubtful whether the Company's factors were able to satisfy the Directors in this respect.

Two interesting articles figure frequently in the list. These were opium and coffee. I have not come across many references to tea in the Letter Books. Coffee, however, seems to have been in great demand at certain periods. Up till 1686 the amount of coffee required hardly varied. From that time, however, the demand increased. The directors mentioned in a dispatch dated the 6th of December 1686 that 'Coffee begins to rise. Indigo and Coffee are the most profitable bulky Commodities you can send.'[1] After the Revolution the number of coffee houses considerably increased. The Company were never behind the times. Their chief merit consisted in adaptation to novel circumstances, and they increased their demand for coffee. They imported 100 tons of coffee in 1698. The figure is not, however, a representative one, as the New Company and private traders imported about 100 tons more. Opium does not seem to have been popular in England. A number of MSS. in the British Museum show that during the period a large trade in opium was carried on between India and China. The Englishmen do not seem to have been fond of the commodity, as the average amount of opium imported did not exceed 2 to 3 tons per annum.[2]

[1] *MS. Letter Book*, no. 8, dispatch to Bombay.
[2] Ib., no. 9, List of Goods to be provided at the Bay for the Year 1696.

The last place in our list is taken by the pepper, spices, and drugs from India. The Company had been founded mainly with a view to securing a share in the spices. Eighty years of strife with the Dutch had resulted in the expulsion of the English from the Spice Islands, and their concentration on the Indian Coast. The trade in spices might have flourished if the Coromandel Coast and other places in India had been suitable for their cultivation. This does not seem to have been the case. The pepper imported from the Coromandel Coast appears to have been poor in quality and very dear in price. The Directors are found complaining of this in their dispatches. 'The pepper provided by you from the Inland Country has proved so very dear to us, being invoiced from 5d. to 6d. per pound at the Fort, that we forbid them sending more, unless it comes to us at 4d. per pound.' The Company had tried to cultivate pepper at Sumatra. They hoped to get sufficient supplies from thence 'and better Regulation of our Officers there'.[1] The same applies to drugs. A limited quantity of Persian and other kinds of drugs was still imported. No considerable trade was, however, possible, either in drugs or in spices. The Company could not compete with the Dutch, who had the monopoly of the whole commodity; nor was India suitable for the cultivation of the spices. Hence, it concentrated itself mainly on the exportation of manufactured articles from India. Their opinion with regard to drugs was well expressed in their dispatch to Fort St. George, 'Make it a rule that a little of any Druggs may probably come to a good price, but a great deal of any Druggs generally damps the market'.[2] It was this inability of the Company to content itself with the importation of spices into England that explains the complaints of the weavers and bullionists. If it had restricted its activities to the importation of spices and drugs, there is no doubt that the fierce agitation which began immediately after the Revolution would have been totally ineffective.

The above were the chief articles of import from India. The exports of the Company were usually tin, lead, copper, swords, cloth, quicksilver, vermilion, and bullion. During the years 1680–1702, however, there was no change in the quantity of any of the above exports, with the exception of cloth and

[1] *MS. Letter Book*, no. 10, p. 120, 28th Oct. 1698.

[2] Ib.

bullion. As regards cloth, the Company had made many attempts to increase its sale in the East. All these were, however, fruitless. The cloth was offered at a prohibitive price, and the Indian workmen could not afford to buy it. It met with the same fate in Persia. A dispatch to Bombay dated 28th July 1686 refers to the limited sale of cloth in Persia, and provides that cloth should not remain unsold for more than six months. It adds: 'For the like purpose of venting great quantities of English cloth, though but at our Invoice Price, and for one third truck in Legee or Ardos Silk, by which trade we know we shall get nothing at present, but, however, to please His Majesty, and for the good of our country, and to turn the course of that trade from Aleppo, we shall be content to carry it on upon such mean terms for 2 or 3 years, in hopes that we may make our Markets hereafter.'[1]

The Company's later dispatches tell the same tale of unsold cloth. To remedy this defect it tried to enter into a contract with the Shah, whereby the Persian silk could be exchanged for English cloth. This had been mooted in 1686. In 1691 we find the Company recurring to the same subject in their dispatch to Persia. 'We hope highly to improve that trade for the Publick Good of our Kingdom, especially by the Trade of English Broadcloth, of which there is provided One thousand whole Pieces dyed into Proper Colours for Persia with great Care, and with the advice of the Armenian Merchants here. . . . We can see no reason why We should not another Year send five times so many. We know the Empire of Persia spends near thirty thousand Clothes annually.' The Company were, however, disappointed. The contract was not concluded, as the Shah of Persia demanded 500 Tomands. Moreover, the Company was obliged by the Charter granted to them in 1693 to export at least £100,000 worth of English cloth annually. The Company did its best to comply with the regulations. We find the Directors writing as follows: 'The obligations laid upon us . . . have made us supply your side of India not only with more Broadcloth than usual, but also to enlarge in serges, says and other like sorts of Woollen goods, different from our usual Sortment.' They are to clear their

[1] Dispatch dated 28th July 1686, *MS. Letter Book*, no. 8, India Office Records Dept.

cargoes of all old remains every year, and to make room for new ships.[1]

There is no reason to doubt the Company's statement that they sustained loss by the export of cloth to the East. We find this confirmed by several dispatches in the Company's Records at the India Office. One to Bombay, dated the 1st of July 1696, refers to the 'unhappy circumstances our affairs were in Persia, by reason of our Cloth lying unsold there. We hope our Agents have retrieved, as much as in them lay, the misfortune of that great mismanagement, and not suffered our Cloth to lie rotten by.'[2] The misfortune to which the Company referred was not local in its effect. We find the Company bewailing the loss on cloth not only in Persia, but also in India. Its dispatch to Fort St. George has the following: 'We are sorry you should have so great a quantity of woollen goods lying upon your hands, and undisposed of, which, that it might not be burdensome to you, we sent but little last year, and none this.'[3] There was no visible improvement in 1698. The Company urged their factor 'to sell our Cloth, or perishable goods, as well as you can at Invoice price, or under, rather than keep them in your Warehouse'.[4] The Company, however, still urged their factors to 'Endeavour the consumption of woollen goods by selling at low rates, if you can thereby advance their wear'.[5] This was due mainly to the fact that the Government required a full account of the total cloth exported to the East. At the back of the Government were the English weavers. The latter had been clamouring against the importation of Indian commodities, and had insisted upon the necessity of exporting at least £100,000 worth of cloth. The Government had inserted this provision in the Company's new charter, and had obliged it to export £100,000 worth of cloth every year (see above). Nor was it content with mere promises on the part of the Company. Whenever the clamour against the Indian commodities was louder than usual, it had recourse to the Company for information on the quantity of woollen manufactures exported by it. The following example will suffice: 'On reading a letter

[1] *Surat General*, *MS. Letter Book*, p. 415, dispatch dated 6th March 1695.
[2] *MS. Letter Book*, no. 9.
[3] Dispatch dated April 1697, *MS. Letter Book*, no. 9.
[4] Dispatch to Surat, 10th March 1698, *MS. Letter Book*, no. 10.
[5] *MS. Letter Book*, no. 10, dispatch dated 20th Dec. 1699.

from the Secretary to the Lords Commissioners of the Council of Trade, it is ordered that the Accountant should forthwith draw up particulars of what woollen Manufactures of this Kingdom have been exported by the Company, in pursuance of their Charter.'[1] It is clear that the Company complied with the conditions imposed by the Government, and that an enormous amount of cloth was annually exported to Persia. I have already cited the extracts from the Company's records on that matter. They show conclusively that much English cloth lay unsold. The amount of cloth exported to Persia seems, however, to have deceived the contemporaries. They testified to the efforts of the Company to develop the trade in cloth. They were mistaken, however, in thinking that all the cloth exported to Persia was actually sold there. Nathaniel Harley wrote to his father from Aleppo that 'the Turkey Company may thank themselves, who, not content to enjoy the trade themselves, complained that the East India Company carried out no cloth, and thereby gave themselves a mortal blow not to be recovered. For now they do it with that success that they supply Persia, which was wont to be done from Smyrna and this place; and I suppose Parliament so well understands the interest of the nation, as not to alter what is so happily begun, which in time may grow to a vast trade, and beat out the Dutch from thence, as it is from hence.'[2]

It was not Harley alone who held that belief. The Commissioners of Trade and Plantations reported in January 1698 'that it would be inconvenient that the East India Company should send any greater quantities of draperies into Persia than they had done formerly, and that they ought, therefore, to vend the draperies they are obliged to export, either in India, China, Japan or elsewhere, at such distance from those places where the Turkey Company have usually traded as may not cause an interfering between the two Companies'.[3] It may be admitted that large quantities were imported into Persia, and that if all the cloth exported to Persia had been capable of being sold, the East India Company would have proved a very serious rival

[1] *Court Minute Book*, no. 37, 30th April 1697, India Office.
[2] *MSS. of the Duke of Portland, First Appendix to the XIIIth Report, Hist. MSS. Commission*, vol. ii, p. 246, 20th Oct. 1696.
[3] *Report of the Commissioners of Trade and Plantations, to the House of Lords, MSS. of the House of Lords*, New Series, vol. iv, 1699-1702 pp. 450-1.

to the Turkey Company. There is, however, no evidence to show that the total amount exported had been sold. The Commissioners were deceived by the statements of the Turkey Company, and they assumed that as the exports of cloth had enormously increased, all of it had actually been bought by the Persians. It seems clear that the Company sustained serious loss through the inability of its agents to sell the cloth, and that all its efforts to increase the sale were fruitless.[1] The Company can hardly be blamed for this state of affairs. It had done everything possible, and had sustained serious loss through the transaction. All, however, was of no avail. 'I have it', asserted a writer, 'from known persons that before our cloth was carried directly by sea to Persia, great numbers of Caravans used to come through a long tract of land, many hundreds of miles, with Silk and other commodities to Aleppo, and buy our cloth of our factors that reside there; and in their return in great towns and villages, as they passed, they used to sell our cloth to the inhabitants of those countries in very large numbers; and that since the India merchants have supplied the Persians, these Caravans have ceased to come, and though we have kept the Persia Trade, we have lost the trade in those countries through which these carriers have formerly passed, which is a loss to our Export of Cloth, and employment of the Poor.'[2]

It is essential to a true understanding of the position of the Company that this should be kept prominently in mind. The Company's opponents were unscrupulous in the use of their weapons, and every means was adopted to make it odious to the nation. The woollen manufacturers were, according to Davenant, 'the nourishment of our Body', and, if it could be shown that the Company neglected to increase the sale of cloth in foreign parts, the object of the opponents would be attained. The Company would become odious to the Whig oligarchs, the

[1] Compare the following dispatch: 'Their Majesties have obliged us, by the New Charter, by which we are obliged to send out greater value in Woollen Manufactures than we formerly did, and it is absolutely impossible to dispose of so great a quantity as we are obliged to send, considering the market that there is for these commodities in Persia; except we should send over quantity of cloth to India, sell part of it, and give away the rest, or suffer it to lie in the Godowns till it be eaten by white ants, and other insects, by which we have exceedingly suffered in India heretofore.' *Dispatch to Persia*, 3rd Jan. 1694, *MS. Letter Book*, no. 9.

[2] *The Profit and Loss of the East India Trade considered*, Brit. Mus., op. cit.

English weavers, and, generally, to the nation. It is hardly necessary to add that they partly succeeded in accomplishing their object.

Another commodity exported by the Company from England was bullion. I have already traced the history of the exportation of bullion to India.[1] It had aroused a storm of opposition, and had led to the production of valuable pamphlets on the subject. But the trade had not then assumed the serious proportions which it did during the years 1680–1702. It was during the last twenty years of the seventeenth century that the East India trade expanded enormously, and threatened many of the English industries. But the increase of that trade was scarcely possible without an increase in the amount of bullion exported. The trade could be maintained only by the exportation of bullion, and as the trade increased so did the amount of bullion. The amount exported by the Company during the years 1681–91 could hardly have been less than £400,000 a year. It is difficult to state exactly the total amount exported during the period, as we possess very few accurate materials for the period. The most reliable authority seems to me to be the MS. Letter Books. The latter contain, in their Lists of Cargoes, &c., the amount of bullion exported. During the year 1681, as shown in Chapter II, about £300,000 was shipped to one Presidency alone. As, however, great quantities of bullion were exported to other parts of the East as well, it will be safe to assume that in exceptional years the amount exceeded that figure, viz. £400,000. As, moreover, the trade continued to develop under James II, it is highly probable that more than £400,000 a year was exported during the period 1681–91. Davenant asserted that 'the Silver and Gold brought from America and the Silver produced from European mines during the last 200 years, amounted to 800 million pounds. I cannot find what is become of the 800 millions dug out of the earth unless 150 millions of it be carried away and sunk in the East Indies.' It is difficult to accept this statement. Davenant was certainly unscrupulous in the use of some of his materials, if not all. His first two reports on the Public Accounts[2] are a model of lucidity and clear exposition.

[1] See Chapters I, II, and III.

[2] Davenant's *Complete Works*, by Whitworth, vol. v, pp. 347–643. Whitworth's edition seems to me to be unsatisfactory. A number of pamphlets

Yet his egotism seems to pervade nearly every page. He cannot refrain from criticizing Mr. Culliford, his predecessor in office, while his own merits are vaunted in a number of pages of the Reports. The same applies to his account of the East India trade. The figures supplied are obviously exaggerated, and it would be unsafe to rely upon them. He was, however, correct in estimating the average annual export of bullion by the Company at £400,000. This is confirmed by the statement of Pollexfen and a number of other writers. Leaving aside the obviously absurd figures supplied by some of them, the total amount of bullion stated by the majority seems to me to have been correct.

After 1691, however, the amount of bullion exported increased greatly. The average amount annually exported during the years 1697–1702 was hardly less than £800,000. There is reason to believe that during the years 1698–1700 not less than a million pounds was annually exported to the East. It is instructive to compare the different types of authorities for the statement. In the Company's Records we find that £309,264. 1*s.* 4*d.* was exported in 1698. This was in eleven ships only. The amount sent by the two other ships is not mentioned; but it could hardly have been less than £100,000. There is a considerable increase in the following year. The following is the amount sent from England to Surat, Bombay, and Persia in 1699. Total sent out: £659,802. 12*s.*, total received back: £314,716. 9*s.* 3*d.*

Much more accurate information is to be gleaned from the Bodleian and British Museum Libraries. According to an account laid before the House of Commons in January 170¾ by Charles Crisp, there were exported to the East, during the years 1698–1703, the following:

	£
Silver	3,392,158
Gold	128,229
	3,520,387 [1]

From another source we learn that the bullion exported from

by Davenport have been left out, while the edition suffers from a lack of necessary notes, &c.

[1] Bodleian Library, Fol. Θ. 658, no. 3.

5th October 1697 to January 1699 amounted to £1,530,527. Besides this the East India traders took £765,263 into foreign parts. Again, the Company's captains took out about £52,000 to the East Indies. It was asserted that 'there has been exported to the East Indies in two years almost one-third part as much silver as has been coined in England since the Recoining of our Money'.[1] The most noticeable feature in this enormous increase of bullion is the demand for silver. Sir Isaac Newton informed the Parliament in his Third Representation to the Lords Commissioners of His Majesty's Revenue[2] that 'when ships are lading for the East Indies the demand of Silver for Exportation raises the price to 5*s.* 6*d.* or 5*s.* 8*d.*, though at a medium the Bullion of Standard Alloy is valued at 5*s.* 4½*d.* per oz.' The Company frequently gave 3*d.* an oz. for exportable silver above its value in coin, which was above 5 per cent. 'This tempted our people to send all our Foreign Silver to London, to take the benefit of an advanced price, and also to melt down ours.'[3] 'Our people' means, of course, the Irishmen. The latter took advantage of the increased demand for bullion, and reaped profits from it. Prior estimated the average amount of bullion exported to the East at a million pounds a year. He feared that 'if so much treasure shall flow for any considerable time in the same channel, it will put an end to that trade. For such large Remittances in Silver must in time make this Metal empty in those parts, and as its quantity increases, its quality will lessen. So that, by Degrees, Silver may come to bear the same proportion to Gold in the East Indies, as it does in Europe, and their Commodities will rise in proportion.'

The prophecy does not seem to have come true. The exportation of bullion to the East increased rather than diminished in the eighteenth century. Yet none of the phenomena which the author had forecasted actually occurred. This does not detract from the merit of his essay. His analysis is wonderfully suggestive, while his anticipation of the quantity theory of money is remarkable. His figures are confirmed by other authorities.

[1] *England's Almanac*, Brit. Mus. 816. m. 11 (92).
[2] Printed in MacCulloch's *Scarce and Valuable Tracts on Money*, p. 247.
[3] Thomas Prior, author of *List of Absentees of Ireland*, in *Observations on Coin in General*, in MacCulloch's *Tracts on Money*, pp. 391–8. A very remarkable pamphlet. It is vigorous, lucid, and accurate.

The old Company exported, from Michaelmas 1698 to February 1699, £917,772. 1*s.* 6*d.*; while the new Company exported, during the same period, £500,782. 19*s.* 6*d.* Moreover, the private traders exported, during the period, £215,701. 2*s.* The total amount of bullion exported by the three bodies was, therefore, £1,634,256. 3*s.* This does not include the money shipped from Cadiz. We find many dispatches to the English bankers at Cadiz requesting them to ship a stated amount to the Indies. A writer says that during the period 'about £600,000' was shipped. The total of money exported by the New and the Old Companies and Private Traders during 1698-9 was, therefore, £2,234,256. 3*s.*[1] This is certainly a stupendous figure, and, at first sight, may appear to be inaccurate. There is, however, no reason to doubt its accuracy. This is evidenced by the Reports of the Inspector-General. He estimated that from Michaelmas 1697 to Christmas 1699, £1,459,033. 9*s.* 11*d.* worth of Indian goods had been imported into England. These figures are misleading, because, as pointed out by Davenant, he does not include in them the large quantities of goods that were re-exported to foreign countries.[2] He is much more reliable in his calculation of the quantity of bullion exported to the East. He stated that 'by the entries in the Custom House books, it appeared that we had for several years exported to the East Indies above £400,000 per annum in bullion, besides what was carried out privately or shipped from Spain. Such trades had occasioned the exportation and decrease of our silver coin.'[3] It appears that from Christmas 1698 to Christmas 1699 there was exported to India, in (1) silver, £841,881; (2) in gold, at £4 per oz., £29,228. The total amount exported in one year was therefore £871,109. This does not include the bullion exported by the new Company, the private traders, or the Spanish bankers. Adding a proportionate amount for each of these bodies, and comparing our total with the total given above, we find that there is really not much difference between the two authorities. The figures supplied by both the authorities substantially agree. The Inspector-General's remarks on the above are worth notice:

[1] Bodleian Library, Rawlinson MSS. A. 303, no. 134.

[2] *MSS. of the House of Lords*, New Series, vol. iv, p. 431; Davenant, *First two Reports on Public Accounts*, op. cit.

[3] p. 455.

'The exportation of bullion for India has much increased upon us, which has occasioned a greater consumption of silver; and our increasing expense in the consumption of some foreign Commodities at home has hindered the importation of it.'

Another account of the amount of bullion exported is interesting. It appears that during the years 1697–9 there was exported 4,177,859·13 oz. of silver and 4,027·3 oz. of gold.[1] Another report of the Inspector-General informed the Lords that the amount exported by the new Company during the years 1698–1700 was £564,845. 13*s*. 6*d*., and that the United Company had exported £600,000 in nine months.[2]

This was an enormous amount for the times and excited keen opposition. The opposition of the bullionists, sketched in Chapter III, would be totally unintelligible without a due examination of the data on which their conclusions were founded. The above account shows conclusively that their complaints were not without foundation; that the 'drain of gold' to the East which they denounced in forcible terms was not a fiction of their imagination; and that the amount of bullion exported to the East increased *pari passu* with the increase of the East India trade. There is no reason to suppose that the amount of bullion exported decreased in the eighteenth century. It was proved in the House of Lords that in 1717 the East India Company had exported nearly 3,000,000 oz. of silver.[3] The Goldsmiths' petition asserted in April 1690 that 'Since last October, the entries had been made of 286,102 ozs. of silver in bullion, and 89,946 dollars and pieces of eight by divisions'; they doubted not 'but it would appear that not only the East India Company, but also Jews and merchants, had of late bought up great quantities of silver to carry out of the Kingdom, and had given 1½*d*. per oz. above the value, which had encouraged the melting down of much plate and milled money'.[4]

The Company's shipping exhibited the same tendency during the period. In 1689 it had thirteen ships consigned to Fort St. George, the Bay, and the Coromandel Coast; seven ships to China and the South Seas; and fifteen ships consigned to Bombay

[1] *MSS. of the House of Lords*, vol. iv, p. 91, 12th Feb. 1700.
[2] Ib., vol. v.
[3] Shaw, *History of Currency*, 1896, p. 231.
[4] Shaw, op. cit., p. 22.

and the Coast of India. Since 1681 sixteen new ships had been built, besides 'a number of smaller ones now in their service'. All of them were three-decked ships, and were of 'burthen, according to the King's Tonnage, from 900 to 1,300 Tons each'.[1] The Company's war with Aurangzebe seems to have increased its tonnage, as a number of Indian junks and vessels were captured. The war with France and the disorganized state of the Company's finances paralysed its activity for a time. The Company lost several ships during the war, while the increase of piracy in the Indian Ocean added to its difficulties. The famous Captain Kidd's exploits have been preserved to us in a series of interesting accounts, but, as they are beyond the scope of this work, no notice can be taken of them here. In December 1692 it was alleged that no funds were available to equip twelve ships, which it was proposed to send to India in the following January.[2] This is confirmed by the petitions of the Clothiers of Gloucestershire, of 'Several merchants and others trading to the East Indies', and of divers merchants of the City of London.[3] All of them declared the trade to 'be lost'. The East India Company, asserted the clothiers, 'had bought none of their manufactures, nor of other counties'.

This inactivity of the Company was due, as explained above, to its financial weakness. Moreover, the war with France had rendered its voyages to India extremely dangerous, and five of its ships had been captured by the French. A letter of the Company, addressed to several persons, refers 'to the disappointment the Company sustained in the loss of their 4 ships, which made them apply to the King, who has supplied them with 2 vessels to carry orders and not disclose to any person'.[4]

The King wanted ships for his own use, and the Company could hardly deny the absolute necessity of utilizing every ship for the purpose of defence against foreign foes. Nor is it clear whether the Admiralty was efficient at the time. Internal evidence goes to show that the losses incurred by the Company

[1] Childe, *Supplement to the East India Trade*, 1689.
[2] *Reasons for the East India Company's sending out Twelve Ships to India, about the 15th of January next*, 7th Dec. 1692, Bodleian Library, Fol. Θ. 658, no. 37.
[3] *Journals of the House of Commons*, vol. x, pp. 541, 710, 711.
[4] *MS. Letter Book*, no. 9, p. 439.

could easily have been avoided if a little more care had been exercised by the Admiralty. The *Calendars of State Papers, Domestic, William and Mary*, leave one with an impression of naval maladministration. This reacted on the disorganized state of the Company, and we are not surprised to see it inactive for a time. Characteristically enough, it was encouraged by the destruction of the Smyrna Fleet, and from that time may be dated the unusual progress of the East India shipping. Childe had urged them in 1692 to send '4 ships'. This showed a great falling off. In 1693, however, the grant of a charter encouraged the Company, and no less than twelve ships were sent to India. In 1694 the number increased to thirteen. The total number of ships during the years 1697–1702 is not capable of exact calculation. It is clear, however, from the MS. Letter Books that the Company's tonnage was greatly increased. A dispatch, dated 15th December 1698, reckoned the number of ships bound for the East at nine.[1] The total was probably fifty. This figure occurs in several pamphlets of the time and seems to me to be accurate.[2]

The Company exported comparatively large quantities of Indian goods to the plantations. As the Indian silk goods became popular in England, the Colonists followed the laws of fashion ordained by the upper classes in England. The cheapness of the Indian calicoes was the strongest ground for their popularity in the colonies. Accordingly, we find evidences of the general use of Indian calicoes. 'Our West Indies', bewailed an English writer, 'that used formerly, and still might be clothed with our own manufactures for the Female Sex, will now touch none, unless such as are very cheap at 8*d.*, 10*d.*, or 12*d.* per Yard;

[1] *MS. Letter Book*, no. 10.

[2] Compare *England's Almanac*, Brit. Mus., op. cit.; *A Short Abstract of the Case*, &c., Bodleian Library, Fol. Θ. 658, no. 11. 'There are now gone to the East Indies and China 50 ships, computed at near 400 tons per ship, by a modest computation, reckoning to have carried with them 2 million sterling or £40,000 per ship.' Compare the following with regard to the crews: 'We have for many years had great complaints of the miscarriage of persons employed in your country ships, and others in the Permission Trade from Bombay, Surat, to Bengal. Your Country Commanders and other officers paying no respect to our Agent and Council, quarrelling and fighting with the Natives in their drink, giving great disturbance to our affairs, and raising the prices of goods.' Dispatch to the Lt.-General of Bombay, 1st May 1693. *MS. Letter Book*, no. 9.

and to that Degree is that Trade lost, that of all these several species of fine goods, that used to be exported out of England, there is not now 100 looms at work in the whole Nation upon Stuffs for Women.'

Another writer argued that if the English nobility used Indian manufactures, the West India islands would do the same, 'as all persons know that they will imitate the gentry of England, and those Merchants' commissions run for fashionable commodities'.[1] The weavers feared that 'if the East India Silks be the mode here, they will be so in our Plantations and Ireland, and where the orders sent being generally to send over such Manufactures as are most fashionable in England, and we would, therefore, in a great measure much lose what we have now'.

That these fears were not groundless is proved by the reports of the Commissioners of Trade and Plantations to the House of Lords. 'For the better preventing other more general inconveniences from the East India Trade', they proposed that 'the wearing or consumption of the manufactured goods of India, Persia or China, made of silk or herb, or mixed with other of these materials, as also of painted or stained Calicoes, of all handicraft wares, imported from these parts should be discouraged and lessened in these Kingdoms, and in His Majesty's Plantations'.[2] The prohibition of the East India goods in the plantations seems to have produced the desired effect. Reliable materials for the construction of a history of those commodities are difficult of access. It is clear, however, that the amount of silk exported to the plantations was not large. During the years 1697–1702 wrought silks were exported to the plantations to the value of £29,823. 7*s.* 3*d.*; and to Ireland, £18,491. 2*s.* 7*d.*[3] The Accounts do not state the quantity of

[1] *The Profit and Loss of the East India Trade Compared*, Brit. Mus. 100. m. 46, pp. 10–12; *Reasons Humbly offered for the passing a Bill*, &c., Brit. Mus., 1697, p. 7. Compare the following: 'As to our Exportation, it has been a great hindrance of our Exports to Holland and our West India Colonies, that we have enjoyed the one for 100 years, and the other for a long time. We had a very considerable Trade to those places in commodities made of Wool, Silk and Wool for Women's Wear and Use, and that no European Merchant could ever get this trade from us, these being natural to England.'

[2] *MSS. of the House of Lords*, New Series, vol. iv, *Report of the Commissioners*, pp. 450–1.

[3] *Accounts Laid before House of Commons on Thursday*, 13th Jan. 170⅔. Bodleian Library, Fol. Θ. 658, no. 3.

calicoes exported to the colonies. It is reasonable to suppose that the amount was a large one, as the calicoes were generally preferred to the English woollen goods, owing to their cheapness. The Company's activities were not confined to the plantations. It exported a large amount of Indian goods to Germany. Davenant asserted that 'for Indian goods we could purchase at a better rate the Linens of Silesia, Saxony and Bohemia'. Moreover, 'in times of peace, we did and may gain Traffic with France for our India goods against the things of luxury which will always be brought from thence'.[1] It is clear that the Indian commodities were exchanged for the German linens and that the English weavers suffered by this method. They had exchanged their linens for English cloth and the transaction seems to have proved profitable to both parties. Now, however, the importation of Indian commodities interfered with this trade. As the German linens were no longer exchanged for the English woollen goods, the former developed the woollen manufactures in their own country. 'By reason of the great wear of Muslin and Calicoes, we have lost the greater part of our woollen cloth to Germany, Silesia, etc., from whence we had formerly great quantities of Linen. But when we would no longer take off their Linen', owing, of course, to the popularity of calicoes in England, 'they were forced to set up manufactures of woollen, by reason of which we have wholly lost that profitable trade.' The same complaint is echoed by other writers.[2]

The Indians showed a regrettable liking for the German swords, and it is evident that the returns of Indian manufactures were made sometimes in that weapon. They were highly prized in India, and the astute Armenians, with the traveller Chardin at their head, contracted to supply them with that instrument of destruction.

Another European country to which the Company exported large quantities of Indian goods was Spain. There is evidence to show not only that Spain was well supplied with calicoes, but also that her plantations were regularly furnished with Indian

[1] Davenant, *Essay on East Trade*, p. 22.

[2] *An Answer*, &c., Brit. Mus., 816. m. 11 (91), no. 2; *A Reply to a Paper delivered to the Rt. Honble the Lords*, Brit. Mus. 816. m. 13, no. 142; *An Answer to the Most Material Objections of the Linnen Drapers*, Brit. Mus. 816. m. 13, no. 139.

goods. Mr. Thompson informed the House of Lords that when he was in Spain, 'a great many Calicoes came thither, and bullion came back for them'. In one ship 2,000 pieces had been sent to a Bilbao factory, 'in a year'—'more ships go'. They are, he concluded, of general use in Spain. Captain Dorrell informed the Lords that he had carried calicoes to Spain, 'and brought bullion for it'.[1] These are not the only references to Indian commodities in Spain. Owing to the scanty materials at our disposal it would be dangerous to dogmatize. It is safe, however, to conclude that the Indian commodities were well known in Spain and that the Spanish colonies were generally supplied with comparatively large quantities.

The rapid strides made by the East India trade during the last ten years of the seventeenth century could hardly be ignored by the English weavers. The competition of Indian manufactures with English industries was, as pointed out in my former chapters, at first hardly recognizable. From 1675, however, the competition began to be seriously felt. By the end of the century the English weavers had organized a systematic opposition to the importation of Indian calicoes and silks. The opposition ceased only with the utter defeat of the Company. The forces arrayed against it proved too strong. The chief English industries affected by the Indian manufactures were wool and silk. The exquisite workmanship of Indian weavers proved serious to the English silk weavers. It became popular in England, and was used by ladies of quality, by gallants, and by the gentry. Of the serious injury inflicted on the silk industry there can be no doubt. 'The Silks do us a further mischief by being spent directly in the room of our Stuffs made of Wool, Hair and mixed with Silk and worsted, and that no other Silks made abroad did ever serve for these uses, and are therefore most dangerous.'[2] They were used for the same purposes as 'our Manufactures are, and so discouraged Tradesmen from driving larger Trades, it being uncertain when these ships will come in and uncertain what sort of Commodity they will bring. Every Tradesman is liable to be undone, if he ventures to inlarge his

[1] *MSS. of the House of Lords*, vol. ii, New Series, pp. 242–3.
[2] *England and India Inconsistent in their Manufactures*, *India Office Tracts*, vol. lxxxiii, p. 11.

Trade, as is plain by many hundred Instances in 20 years space. These Foreign Manufactures have spoiled our Foreign Trade for Fine Stuffs made in Norwich and London.'[1] London, Canterbury, Gloucester and other counties seem to have suffered most from this competition. 'In Spittlefields, there has been a very large manufacture settled, which long struggled with Italy, France and Holland, but kept its head above the water for a long time. Now come our East India Gentlemen. They carry away our workmen of all sorts, our Patterns and New Inventions, and promote the manufacture in the East Indies. The result is that Masters break, Journeymen run away, having no Trade. Some fly to the Mint and Privileged Places; some to Holland, some to Ireland, some starve to death at Home with their Wives and Children.'[2]

The clothing trade of Gloucestershire was similarly affected. 'The poor Clothiers come to London, expecting a Market for their Cloth, but the Merchant can neither pay the old score nor buy more.' Canterbury, however, seems to have been the greatest sufferer. The instances given by the writer illustrated the difficulty, and the resulting uncertainty of the weavers. 'Last year they ran into debt, so as to keep on their Trade, and provide quantities of Goods for the English West Indies, but being no prophets, could not foresee the effects of the unmerciful cargo of Indian Damask, and they had to sell from 30 to 40 p. c. loss. By which means, half the working men of the Town of the Weaving trade are now running up and down the Nation, seeking Bread from Canterbury to London, from London to Norwich. Their families are left to the Parishes.'[3] There is no reason to doubt the statements of the writer. He himself suffered severely from the competition, and had to leave his trade. We are told by Prince Butler[4] 'that the East India Trade had in a great measure ruined the Canterbury Silk trade, and obliged most of the London Silk Weavers and Throwsters to give over their several Trades and employment. Many have gone to Ireland, and set up Trade there; others fallen to comb, card, and spin; others

[1] *Reasons Humbly offered*, British Museum.

[2] *England's Danger by Indian Manufactures*, Bodleian Library, Fol. Θ. 658, no. 32.

[3] Ib.

[4] *Queries*, Brit. Mus. 816. m. 13 (128); *Querical Demonstrations*, ib. (129).

make cloth, stuffs and serge.' The dreadful consequences of the wearing of East India silks were vividly stated by a writer. 'It will destroy our woollen Manufactures, fall the value of our land, cause us to abandon our Duty to God and Nature, by lessening the poor's wages and Employment, and thereby depopulating our Country, forcing our People away to foreign parts.'[1] The English silk weavers, however, did not deny the excellence of the silk goods imported. They admitted that, by various means, great encouragement had been given to the manufacture of silk, half-silk, and worsted, 'which have been very much improved in a great variety of figure, striped and other Sorts of Stuffs'.[2] This is clear from the evidence of other writers. It was no doubt true that the importations from India hindered the sale of silk goods from Holland, France, and Italy. The quantity of Italian wrought silks imported into England was limited to 2,630¼ pounds; it increased, no doubt, two years later, but, even so, it did not exceed 9,828½ pounds in 1698–9.[3] The diminution is accounted for by the competition of Indian silk goods. This is confirmed by Mr. Sheldon's paper. In it he informed the House of Lords that, having no sarsenets, ducapes, taffetas, or plain silks for linings made in England, they formerly had them from Italy and France; 'but those we have of late years brought from Bengal are found to be more durable and useful, and are sold here in England for little more than half the price of those brought from Italy and France'.[4]

It was the perfect workmanship of the Indian goods and their comparative cheapness that rendered them a formidable rival to the English silk goods. The Company admitted before the House of Lords that nine-tenths of the Indian silk goods imported into England were consumed here; nor is there any reason to doubt the genuineness of their statement.[5] They

[1] *Considerations relating to a Bill for Restraining the Wearing of India Wrought Silks*, Brit. Mus. 816. m. 13 (134).

[2] *Reasons Humbly offered for Restraining the Wear of Wrought Silks*, op. cit.

[3] *MSS. of the House of Lords*, vol. iv, p. 48.

[4] Mr. Sheldon's paper, marked Q, *MSS. of the House of Lords*, New Series, vol. ii, p. 49, 1st April 1696.

[5] The Silk Weavers were specially bitter on the advantages the Company derived by its privileged position. It was, said a writer, the English that first set the Indians on that vast increase of Silkworms 'and to that great excess they now are of Throwing, Dyeing, and Weaving, when both they and

pointed out that if the Indian silks were prohibited, the French, Danes, and Dutch would furnish the same articles at a far greater price, and that the strictest prohibition could not hinder them from purchasing Indian goods at extravagant rates. The Company's defender showed, in a masterly treatise, the folly of propping up infant industries, and pointed out the benefits derivable from the concentration of energy on the production of a single manufacture. He advised the silk weavers to leave their trade in order that more hands may be employed on woollen manufactures. In his opinion the English soil was not fitted for the development either of silk manufactures or of the linen trade. His opponents were not prepared to follow this advice. If the silk industry had been confined to a few score of men the advice would have proved useful. This was not, however, the case. The silk weavers could point to 'the vast numbers employed at Spittlefield and Canterbury, who had their sole dependence upon them. This would have convinced him that our English weavers showed themselves able to contest the French, Dutch, and Italians.' Nor could the prosperity of the silk trade before the invasion of Indian silk goods be denied either by the Company or its defender. The Company, however, when pressed upon this point, changed their tactics. They argued that, as the Indian silk goods took the place of Dutch and Italian silks, they performed a national service by supplying the nation with those articles at half the prices charged by the foreigners. Was it fair, they asked, that East India goods should be prohibited? Why are not the Dutch and Italian silks prohibited as well? Otherwise, the Dutch and Italians will find opportunity to increase their silk trade with England and to engross the Indian silk trade in their own hands. Why should the East India silk goods be prohibited when they are three times as cheap as Dutch, Italian, and French silks? Nor did they see any reason why we should raise some industries to oppress others. These invidious distinctions were in their opinion calculated to strike at the very root of national well-being. 'If spinning and weaving be English Manufactures, so is Dyeing, Glazeing, and Printing.'[1]

the Indians could not do less than laugh in their Sleeves at the Act that prevents Throwing and Dyeing, the profit whereof is wholly lost to us, and Gain to India'.

[1] Davenant, *Essay on East India Trade; Eleven Queries Humbly*

Some of the questions asked by the Company were remarkably acute. They were, however, unskilfully framed, and it was quite easy for their opponents to prove the inaccuracy of their figures and the hollowness of some of their arguments. Their argument that we should buy in the cheapest market was sound. Nor can we say that it was seriously challenged. Their opponents, however, pointed to the misery that the importation of Indian commodities had wrought; brought forward figures to show that the importation of Dutch and Italian silks into England was insignificant, and that it was the Indian silk manufactures that threatened the English silk industry. There can be no doubt of the genuineness of the English silk weavers' grievances. Nor can we doubt the statement that the Dutch and Italian silks were not exported in large quantities at the time. The statement is verified by a series of documents. We cannot controvert it.[1]

The prohibition of Indian silk goods was only a matter of time. It might have been averted if the injuries inflicted had been confined to one industry. The silk industry was, after all, a manufacture that had been developed only recently, and if it could have been shown that the nation derived more profit from the Indian trade than from that industry, the Prohibition Act might not have been passed. It was the damage to the woollen trade of England that intensified the opposition. The woollen industry was regarded as the national industry. Even Davenant regarded the woollen manufactures as the 'Nourishment of our Body'. 'As Bread is called the Staff of Life, so the Woollen Trade is truly the Principal Nourishment of our Body Politick.'[2] The Whig landlords were intensely jealous of the competition of foreign

Tendered, Brit. Mus.; *An Answer to Mr. Carey's Reply*, Brit. Mus. 816. m. 13, no. 143; *The Linnen Drapers' Answer*, Brit. Mus. 816. m. 13, no. 141; *Reasons against Prohibiting*, &c.; *Five Queries Humbly Tendered Relating to the Bill*, Brit. Mus. 816. m. 13, no. 133; *The Weavers' Twelve Queries Answered*, Brit. Mus.

[1] *England and India Inconsistent in their Manufactures*; *Reasons Humbly Tendered*; *A Brief State of the East India Trade, as it relates to other Branches of the British Commerce*; *A Reply to an Essay* (by Davenant); *Considerations relating to the Bill for Restraining, &c.*; *A Reply to a Paper*; *An Answer to the Most Material objections of the Linnen Drapers*; *The Linnen Drapers' Queries Answered.* All these pamphlets are in the British Museum.

[2] *Essay on the East India Trade*, p. 9.

articles with woollen manufacture. They had prohibited the French goods and the Irish woollen goods. They were not likely to tolerate the Indian calicoes, and other goods, in England. No serious danger arose from the calicoes until about 1675. After that their imports increased rapidly. Pollexfen may denounce them; Wood[1] may despise 'the Effeminate luxuries from the East'. The East India merchants went on increasing the importation of calicoes. Within the years 1697 to 1702 no less than £1,053,725. 0*s.* 5¼*d.* worth of calicoes were imported into England.[2]

The effects of this increase were serious. The Indian goods were asserted to have been 'directly opposite to the Employment of 250,000 Manufacturers, and to the consumption of 16 or 18 thousand Packs of Long Fine Wool in one year, of the growth of the largest sheep that feed in the Pasture Ground. Employment of these people is the only way left to give a value to the Land in those parts where they inhabit.' We find the calicoes condemned in several petitions and pamphlets of weavers. *The Languishing state of our Manufactures*[3] condemns the 'Painted Calicoes, Soft Muslins and the Curious Landskips of an Indian fan, brought home with our bullion'. Another writer complained of 'the grave inconveniences of India Cotton Yarn, which will be as obstructive to our Manufactures as Calicoes were'.[4] Some of them seem to have been reduced to the greatest straits. 'An infinite number of us are already reduced to great misery; the Poor Rates have doubled, and, in some cases, trebled.'[5]

The progress of the East India trade is attested by the increase in the customs duties on East India goods. From August 1685 to August 1687 the Company paid in customs £225,326. 10*s.* 1*d.* In 1688 the war with the Mogul reduced the Company's trade considerably, and the duties did not realize the same amount. In 1690, however, the Company paid £100,074. 19*s.* 10*d.* From Michaelmas 1691 to March 1692 'New Impositions on East

[1] In his *Survey of Trade.*

[2] *Dr. Davenant's Accounts laid before the House of Commons*, Jan. 1703.

[3] Brit. Mus. 816. m. 14 (83).

[4] *A True Representation of the Manufacture of Wool*, Brit. Mus. 816. m. 14 (83).

[5] *A Second Humble Answer from the Poor Weavers to Ladies*, Brit. Mus. 816. m. 14 (84).

India Goods' brought in £141,968. 11*s.* 7*d.* The following year, only £92,518. 4*s.* 5*d.* was realized. The grant of a Charter restored the Company's prosperity. This is visible in the customs duties paid by the Company, which amounted to £130,571. 4*s.* 1*d.* In 1695 the customs duties were £161,546. 14*s.* 3*d.* The following year showed a slight decrease: £157,146. 2*s.* 6*d.* The following were the amounts realized in 1698, 1699, 1700, 1701, and 1702 respectively: £137,369. 18*s.* 11*d.*; £173,909. 17*s.* 4¾*d.*; £191,472. 8*s.* 5½*d.*; £173,982. 14*s.* 3½*d.*; £145,322. 16*s.* 2*d.*; £139,278. 5*s.* 2½*d.* Total for the years 1689 to 1702 £1,801,906. 2*s.* 9¾*d.* The duty of fifteen per cent. on India wrought silks and muslins yielded the following amount. From 1699 to 1700 £11,793. 12*s.* 4*d.* From Michaelmas 1700 to 1701 £80,268. 6*s.* 9½*d.* The effect of the Act of 1700 is shown in the amount realized the following year. It did not yield more than £11,793. 12*s.* 4*d.* Total for the three years £116,767. 18*s.* 6*d.*[1]

The agitation against the East India goods supplied an instructive example of the way in which the Mercantilism of the day affected the different industries. The woollen manufactures were regarded as the staple commodity of England, and a system of bounties and subsidies was granted solely with a view to the preservation and development of woollen goods. The calicoes, asserted a writer, were prejudicial to the traders and dealers in woollen manufactures, hence 'the staple commodity of England ought to be upholden and encouraged'.[2] This idea runs through all their complaints. The development of a national industry was, in their opinion, a sufficient reason for the prohibition of all competing manufactures. They called upon the State to protect them from the attacks of the Linen Drapers, the East India merchants, and other rival manufactures. It is clear that the State had a very difficult part to play at the time. At first sight it may appear that the prohibition of the Indian goods would have been cordially approved by the Whig landlords and the demands of the weavers satisfied. This would, no doubt, have taken place if the East India trade had benefited the Company alone. There is no reason to suppose that such

[1] Compiled from a *SUPPLEMENT* by Childe, to his *ESSAY*, Brit. Mus. Add. MSS. 10122, pp. 3-49; Egerton MSS. 518.

[2] *To the Rt. Hon. the House of Commons and Lords*, Brit. Mus. 816. m. 14 (107).

was the case. It seems clear from a letter of Vernon to Shrewsbury that, as early as 1696, it had been decided to bring in a bill prohibiting the wearing of East India silks. It was ordered on 7th March 1696 and passed on 31st March 1696.[1] It was read in the House of Lords on 2nd and 3rd April 1696.[2] In Committee the Lords inserted several amendments, extending the operation of the Bill to all wrought silks exported, and all calicoes printed or stained out of the realm.[3] The Commons, however, disagreed with these amendments. They thought they would injure the export trade, and that as the amendments imposed additional penalties, and as all impositions ought to originate with the House of Commons only, the action of the Lords was unconstitutional. This was followed by numerous conferences between the two Houses. The Lords, however, insisted on their amendments and the Bill was lost.[4] The Act prohibiting the calicoes, &c., was not passed till 1700. The delay in the passage of the Bill showed the difficulties of the Government. It had to deal not only with the Indian merchants, but also with a host of industries that were dependent upon that trade.

Nor was this divergence of interest confined to calicoes. Other Indian goods employed a number of people and maintained flourishing industries. The controversy exemplifies the difficulties by which the Parliamentary Colbertism of the day was beset. It was on the horns of a dilemma. If the Government prohibited the wearing of Indian goods, it would entail misery on thousands of men engaged in printing calicoes. If, on the other hand, the importation of Indian calicoes were not prohibited, the woollen industry might be seriously affected. This was the inevitable result of the Mercantilism then in vogue. The grant of a bounty to, or the imposition of a tax on, a manufacture

[1] *Journals of the House of Commons*, vol. xi.

[2] *Journals of the House of Lords.*

[3] Ib., 20th and 22nd Feb. 1697.

[4] *Lords' Journal*, vol. xvi, pp. 116, 128, 129, 132. *Commons' Journals*, vol. xi, pp. 720, 742, 752, 755, 756. Compare the following account by William Fleming: 'There is a Bill depending in our House for prohibiting the wearing of East India Silks, which should have been read yesterday, but the House being engaged in the Capitation Bill, it was put off till Monday week, too long a day if all our House were hearty for it, but many are not.' 21st Jan. 1697. *MSS. of S. H. Fleming, Appendix to the 12th Report*, part vii, p. 346.

could be justified only on national grounds. It was very difficult, however, to separate the purely personal from a truly national industry. Every industry called itself national, and justified its existence mainly on that ground. The chief cause of the failure of the Mercantilism of the day lay in its neglect to strike a mean between the two and to abstain from surrounding particular industries with bounties and tariff walls. The question whether bounties were necessary is totally irrelevant to the issue. They were probably necessary at the time, and, considering the state in which the chief English industries then were, essential. This does not, however, prove the necessity of imposing differential duties. There is evidence to show that this was done, and that particular industries suffered thereby. The case of Linen Drapers furnishes us with a classical example of the system, or want of system, that was in operation at the time. The divergence of their interests is revealed in a number of documents. The weavers asserted 'that the printing and dyeing of linens doth alter the use thereof, and the very intention for which they are profitably brought into England, which is for inside wear only'.[1] 'They ought not', opined another, 'by their Gaudy Show be converted into outside garments.' The Linen Drapers replied that the linen industry was as much a national industry as the woollen manufactures; 'that it was the interest of the nation that the Home Consumption should be little, of a Cheap and Foreign Growth, and that our own manufactures should be sent abroad.' This was but a development of Davenant's argument, and implied a fundamental change in the economic policy of the times. It is interesting, however, to examine the grounds on which they based their opinion. They declared that 'by all that is spent at home, one loseth what another gains; the nation is not the richer'. They thought that if the Indian calicoes were prohibited, the Dutch, Italian and German linen would take their place.[2]

[1] *The Case of several thousand Poor of the Wool Manufacturers, ruined by the Printing and Dyeing of Linnens in England*, Brit. Mus. 816. m. 14 (87).

[2] Compare *A Reply to a Paper*; *Answer to Mr. Carey's Reply*; *Linnen Drapers' Answer to Mr. Carey*; *an Answer to the Material objections of the Linnen Drapers*; *Weavers' Twelve Queries Answered*; *Answer to some of the Linnen Drapers' objections.* All of them are in the British Museum series known as 816. m. 13.

England, they asserted, sent to Germany wool, tin, copper, &c., and returned from thence whatever was fit for her purpose; if she bought smaller quantities of German linens, the balance would be returned in money. It would, they argued, be better to send one-third part of that money to buy calicoes if the latter were three times cheaper than German linens. England would, therefore, keep two-thirds of that money, 'instead of taking it out in Linens from Germany at treble the price'. Carey's answer is characteristic. He did not deny that calicoes were cheaper than linen. He asserted, however, 'that our goods will be cheap in time. They would have us wear their slight shadows and rotten Calicoes in England, and send our own manufactures abroad.'[1] To the objections of the Linen Drapers that if calicoes were prohibited, Dutch and Italian silk goods would take their place, Carey replied that the additional duty of twenty per cent. on Dutch and Italian silks had so hindered them from sending them to England 'that there has been not so much as one case of these (Dutch) goods imported for six years; nor is it possible for them to do so'. Moreover, the Scotch and German linens to which the Linen Drapers had referred were not absolutely necessary. Hence, the calicoes would not be replaced by German linen at all, 'as we now make such variety of things in England, with Silk and Worsted, and with Cotton Yarn from our Plantations, that do in a measure supply the uses of linens'.[2] Consequently, the prohibition of Indian calicoes would not result in increased buying of German linen. Even if German and Scotch linen were bought, it would be better to spend money on them rather than on Indian calicoes, as the former were exchanged for English wool, and, therefore, 'German and Scotch linnen when purchased for our manufactures are much cheaper to us than calicoes, though bought for Bullion in the East Indies at one third part'.[3]

Even such a specialized trade as the East India trade was related to so many industries in England, and the influence it

[1] *An Answer to some of the Linnen Drapers' Objections*, Brit. Mus. 816. m. 13 (143).

[2] *An Answer to the most material objections of the Linnen Drapers*, Brit. Mus. 816. m. 13 (139).

[3] *A Reply to a paper delivered to the Rt. Hon. the Lords*, Brit. Mus. 816. m. 13 142).

exercised on Linen Drapers and others was so far-reaching, that the prohibition of calicoes, &c., was effected only after years of bitter controversy. There is reason to believe that Linen Drapers suffered severely. Thomas Kettle informed the House of Lords that 'if Calico is prohibited, we must starve—thousands are employed in dyeing and calendering, 2 or 300 employed in dyeing and stiffening'.[1]

Nothing is more remarkable than the evidence furnished by the petitions of thousands of workers against the Bill. The Linen Drapers prayed to be heard before the Second Reading; a petition, signed by 50 Calico Printers, requested a hearing; another petition, signed by 141 Dyers of Wrought Silk, pointed out 'that the Bill will ruin the petitioners'; while another petition, signed by 281 'Gentlemen's sons and Apprentices', said 'that the greater part of their money will be lost if the Bill pass'; a petition of Packers and Clothmakers informed the Lords that if the Bill passed, the greater part of the woollen goods bought by the Company would remain unsold; there were further petitions from the Calenderers, Glaziers, and Buckram Stiffeners in the City of London; while the 'Shopkeepers and Warehouse keepers trading in East India, Persia, and China Silks, Bengal and Painted Calico, in the City of London' thought that 'the Bill will utterly deprive them of the greatest part of their Livelihood'.[2] The petitions that poured in testified to the existence of serious alarm among the traders who depended for their livelihood upon the East India trade. It was impossible for the Lords to ignore either the intensity of the feeling or the existence of the serious competition that resulted from its expansion. They tried to settle the dispute by compromise. They prolonged the time for three years—allowed printed, stained, and dyed calicoes from India to be imported without any obligation to transport them; and, finally, they omitted the Bengal goods altogether. The Lords' amendments were certainly comprehensive and far reaching, nor can it be denied that they altered materially the Bill sent by the Commons. Even the Commons were not unanimous on the point, 'and many were not hearty for it'. The weavers were, however, determined to enforce their will and to compel them to

[1] *MSS. of the House of Lords*, New Series, vol. ii, p. 242.
[2] Ib., April 1696.

pass the Bill. The weavers' wives were irritated by the long delay, and were under the impression that the Bill was going to be dropped.[1] They invaded the House of Commons and threatened the members who had voted against the Bill. Soon afterwards a mob of 3,000 weavers assembled to attack Childe's magnificent mansion; the East India House also was attacked, and the Company's treasure nearly got possession of. It was not till after the militia and the press-gang had been called out that they dispersed.[2]

The weavers' activities were not confined to attacks on the Parliament House and the East India House. The Linen Drapers had advocated the rejection of the Bill in a series of masterly pamphlets and broadsides, and pleaded the cause of free trade with great acumen and insight. The weavers concentrated all the forces at their disposal for an attack on their dangerous rivals. The inhuman treatment of the wearers of printed calicoes and linens 'hath so terrified them that the commodity has stagnated in the hands of the Dealers therein. They are not only mobbed out of their trade by the Artful Management of weavers, but they still continue their Riotous Practices and pursue them with Clamour and Complaints.' Owing to this systematic persecution, 'there remained unsold of printed calicoes in the hands of Drapers and Dealers in London to the value of £250,000, near half of which has been paid in Custom'.[3] The Act of 1700 was due mainly to this agitation. The weavers had their reward, and 'all Silks and all Calicoes, except such as are entirely White, as also almost the whole China Trade', were prohibited by that sweeping measure.[4] Its immediate effects were disastrous. Amsterdam

[1] '4, or 5,000 weavers' wives, and great many joining with them,' went down to the House of Commons on 21st Jan. 1697. Mr. Fleming called Massam, 'who was coming behind him, to shut the door, which he did. Three,' continues the narrator, William Fleming, 'got by me, and two by him, but the rest I stopped, and satisfied to return. So we stopped their passage that way, and locked the lowest door. But they being got into the lobby, pressed so hard to go into the House that they had much ado to keep them out; the doors were forced to be locked up. . . . Those Members that had been against the Bill were in great fear, but those that were for it might pass and repass at pleasure.' *MSS. of S. H. Fleming*, *Appendix to 12th Report Hist. MSS. Comm.*, part vii, p. 346.

[2] Luttrell, *Brief Relation*, vol. iv, p. 200; Macpherson, p. 158.

[3] *Observations on the Bill*, Brit. Mus. 816. m. 13.

[4] *A List of several sorts of Silks and Calicoes usually imported from the East Indies and prohibited by Parliament*, Brit. Mus. 816. m. 13 (132).

and Rotterdam became the magazines for the wrought silk, Bengal stuffs, calicoes, and other East India goods.[1] Such goods were bought cheaper in India, and sold by the shrewd Dutch for very high prices in Europe. England, lamented Davenant, sent out its bullion, ran all the hazard of the sea and by capture, and maintained forts and castles[2]; yet she derived no advantage thereby. The Dutch took full advantage of the Act of 1700, and, by a medium of four years, the prohibited and unprohibited goods of the growth of East India carried to Holland were valued at £250,317 per annum. They would, asserted Davenant, continue to be sharers in the profit of the East India trade, as long as prohibition continued in England. It was, thought Davenant, better for the public to impose a duty of about thirty per cent. upon the Indian goods, as 'the taking off of the prohibition will encourage the Company to enlarge their trade in the Indies, viz., by making new settlements and engaging deeper in the Coast trade'.[3] He was confident that an experiment of four or five years would plainly demonstrate that their use in England 'would not so much hurt us at home in the consumption of our Woollen Manufacture, as the vent of them abroad interferes with the sale of our woollen goods in foreign markets'. It is clear that the Dutch utilized the opportunity and flooded Europe with Indian goods. Nor is it quite certain whether this produced any effect on the sale of English cloth in foreign countries. England sustained a double loss through the Act. Not only did she lose the benefit which the East India Company had derived from the sale of the prohibited goods in England, but she also felt keenly the competition to which her woollen manufactures were subjected in European countries. Though the immediate effects were harmful, the ultimate effects were, in my opinion, beneficial to English commerce. It has been shown in this and the third chapter that nearly all English industries were threatened by the Indian goods. The silk industry was seriously affected; the weavers were in distress; the fanmakers were intensely hostile; while other classes of traders were indignant at the freedom allowed to the East India merchants. I have tried

[1] Davenant, *Complete Works*, by Whitworth, vol. v, containing his priceless *Reports on Public Accounts*, pp. 347–463.

[2] Ib., pp. 430–1.

[3] Ib., p. 33.

to show that the grievances of all these classes were real, and that the competition to which they referred in mournful tones operated harshly on all of them.

The significance of these complaints has been lost sight of, and the Act has been cited as a classical example of the fatuous policy of the Mercantilists. A careful perusal of the last two chapters will convince the reader of the utter absurdity of the charge. It was not the Government, but the weavers who dominated the Government, that desired the Act. The House of Commons was not enthusiastic. We have evidence to show that 'many of them did not like the Bill and voted against it'. The same applies to the House of Lords. It was the agitation of the English weavers that led to the passing of the Act. Nor is this confined to the period under consideration. The Government merely carries into effect the wishes of the people and registers its decrees during the seventeenth century. There is no imposition of tyrannical economic law on the devoted heads of a long-suffering people. The economic measures which figure in the Statute books of the seventeenth century did not take their origin in the capacious brains of the statesmen, but were placed on the Statute book mainly because they expressed the desires by which all the classes affected by the laws were animated. It is, therefore, totally misleading to choose the Executive in the seventeenth century as a scapegoat, and to heap upon it all the blame of the economic measures of the times. If any one is to blame for the follies of the Government which Adam Smith so trenchantly exposed, it is the people. It was they who desired these measures, and who attacked the Government if it failed to carry them out. Mercantilism was not an alien system, imposed on the unwilling shoulders of a deluded people, but the expression of a common desire for participation in the commercial progress of the times and defence against foreign commercial rivals. It is this conception that helps to explain the seemingly inconsistent laws passed during the period. The East India trade had determined, to a certain extent, the economic and foreign policies of James I, Cromwell, and Charles II. It was the merchants who had compelled these rulers to follow a consistently national policy, and to defend them against the attacks of the foreign powers. The policy of the East India merchants had aimed at the utilization of the State for the purpose of defending their privileges in the East. The complete protection and the unlimited support which Charles II's government conferred on the Company had resulted in an enormous expansion of the East India trade. The State, which the Company had worshipped until the time of Charles II, was now regarded in a totally different light. Its importation of Indian goods had been allowed up till that time, partly because they did not seriously compete with English goods, and partly because Mun's argument that the bullion exported by the Company ultimately brought in a greater amount of money, still held good. After the Revolution, however, the scene was totally changed. Not only was the amount of gold and silver exported to the East greatly increased, but also the Indian goods vitally affected the chief English industries. The English Parliament could hardly remain indifferent to the serious injury inflicted on English commerce. The instinct of self-preservation is no less strong among nations than among individuals, and the Parliament would have abdicated its primary duty if it had remained indifferent to the protests of the English merchants. Hence, the Parliament cannot be blamed for prohibiting the Indian manufactures. It had done the same with regard to the French and Irish manufactures, and would have followed the same policy with regard to any other foreign industry that showed signs of driving an English industry out of existence.

The full significance of the controversy will be totally lost on us unless we pay careful attention to the evolution of the stock argument of the Company into an eloquent plea for freedom of trade. Mun's argument had lost its force, as the Company itself admitted that a large part of the Indian goods were not exported, but 'consumed' in England. It was fixed as high as nine-tenths. The defenders of the Company had to show not only that the exportation of bullion was ultimately beneficial to England, but also that the Indian goods imported into England did not compete with English industries. Both these actions of the Company cut at the root of the fundamental principles which were the basis of the modified Mercantilism of the day. The Company could defend the increased exportation of money only on the ground that it brought in more money to the kingdom. This was true up till the time of Charles II. The Indian goods were undoubtedly exported to foreign parts during the period, and England therefore gained by the transaction. After that time, however, the policy was reversed. Nine-tenths of the Indian goods were used in England, and the Company was therefore forced to defend its policy on Free Trade principles. Hence the importance of the East India trade in the seventeenth century economic thought.

The Company had advocated commercial war against Holland, and had insisted on the necessity of State support. It had, moreover, shaped the economic and foreign policy of Charles II, and had, generally, been the most consistent advocate of the Mercantile System. After the Revolution, however, it was forced to rely upon Free Trade principles for the defence of its policy. This advocacy of Free Trade was not confined to Davenant or Sir Dudley North. It has really obscured the issue, and has induced Professor Ashley to treat the 'Tory Free Traders' as isolated beings, who spun out their theories without any reference to the commerce about which they were supposed to be theorizing. Nor is it accurate to label all Free Traders as Tories, and to treat them as being friendly to France, and as advocates of peace. The division of the economists of the last years of the seventeenth century into Whig and Tory, according as they advocated Free Trade or the reverse, seems to me to be illogical. The *fundamentum divisionis* is vitiated by a fallacy, and the result is that we are liable to concentrate our attention on the unessential points of the controversy. It was not the love of Free Trade in the abstract that compelled some of the economists of the time to advocate freedom of trade. The theories were really due to the progress of the East India trade during the last ten years. We find the Company defending in a series of pamphlets the importation of the East India goods on the grounds that we must buy in the cheapest markets, and that all laws that restrict this freedom of buying are prejudicial to trade. Not merely Davenant and the author of *Considerations on the East India Trade* defended the Indian manufactures on that ground. We find the same defence employed by the Company in a series of broadsides, pamphlets, answers, &c. The Company was, in fact, bound to have recourse to Free Trade principles for the defence of the policy. In doing this it prepared the fall of the Mercantile System.

Nothing is more misleading than to describe the economic

theories of the time without any reference to the causes that gave rise to them. Economic, no less than political and metaphysical, theories are the outcome of a series of events, linked together by a few leading conceptions. In this lay the mistake of Adam Smith. The 'Smithsianism' which the Germans condemn is bad, not because it is pernicious in its effects, but because it is misleading. It leaves out the important contribution that the seventeenth century economic thought made to the theory of the State. To Machiavelli the State is everything, and in it he realizes himself. To it he sacrifices morality and law. To the seventeenth century economist the State is the only means whereby the nation can realize its commercial greatness. The economist of the times combines two seemingly inconsistent characteristics. His idea of Sovereignty is borrowed from Hobbes, while his passion for what may be called 'practicality' is the gift of Bacon. He has an intimate acquaintance with the minutiae of commerce, and an unlimited faith in the wisdom of State action. These are the main features which strike a student of the seventeenth century economic literature. The Baconian love of analysis is conjoined with the Hobbist fondness for the omnipotence of the State.

Adam Smith has ignored this national aspect of the theories, and treats them merely as curious specimens of the absurdity of the Mercantile System. The East India trade had, as shown in previous Chapters, played a prominent part in this development of the Mercantile System. It became now the most determined enemy of the very system which it had helped to develop.

The leading idea that runs through all the pamphlets written by the opponents of the Company is that of the development of national resources for the acquisition of power. To them, 'power' is more important than 'plenty', and labour of greater importance than money. 'The original of our riches', said Pollexfen, 'is from labour, riches and industry of our people in getting out of the bowels of the earth, from our lands and seas, what may be improved, and made useful for carrying on our foreign trade, upon which also depends the increase of our seamen and navigation, in which our strength consists.'[1] It was the loss to the productive powers of the nation in general,

[1] *MSS. of the House of Lords*, New Series, vol. ii, p. 44.

rather than the injury inflicted on a score of private persons, that was frequently emphasized. 'For', said another writer, 'the case of a Nation is like that of a private person; if he be inclined to good husbandry and prudently direct his affairs, he may thrive and grow rich, without any laws to limit or circumscribe the methods thereof.'[1] Hence, a nation's trade was to be carried on mainly with a view to increasing this power. 'These advocates for Free Trade are gentlemen of the same kidney with those private Tradesmen who supply our Extravagant Gallants with whatsoever his luxurious fancy directs. If his stewards warn him, he replies that he is a Free Agent, and ought not to be circumscribed or restrained.'[2]

The same aspect of the question was grasped by Prince Butler with unrivalled foresight. He showed the consequences of the theories advocated by the Company, and asked them whether they were prepared to carry them to their extreme limits. As cheap labour was so beneficial, would it not, asked Butler, be better to send for corn to the East Indies, 'as theirs is much cheaper than ours?' Would it not be better, asked the same opponent, to employ the Dutch shipping, 'for they always sail much cheaper than we do, and then we may send our own ships to Foreign Nations that want to hire them?'[3] Would it not, asked another writer, be better 'to clothe the English nation in the Mogul's Livery?' The English weavers did not deny that the calicoes were cheap. But, said they, 'Consider the price of provisions in England, and the goodness of our work, and we shall see who will work cheaper. Our Cloth Weavers work only for 5*s.* per week in the country; our Dressers are tied to 1*d.* per hour; our Serge Weavers the same. Even silk weavers get only 12*s.* a week, and pay two boys out of it.'[4] This was really the main ground of their attack. The Company had pointed out the benefits that England would derive from wearing cheap Indian goods and exporting all her dear woollen goods to foreign countries. If this were acted upon, then, said Pollexfen, the Indians being ingenious and being able to secure material cheap and live 'on half pence or a penny a day', 'what costs there 1*s.* will cost to be made here at 20*s.*' This would

[1] *Reasons Humbly offered*, pp. 20–1.
[2] *The Answer to the Most Material objections*, op. cit.
[3] See the Works of Butler cited in Chapter III.
[4] *Reasons Humbly offered*, pp. 20–1.

naturally disable the Europeans from competing with the Indians on equal terms, and as the trade was free, the ultimate result would be that the people would starve, and the English industries would be driven out of the market. Such freedom of trade was not to the liking of the English weavers. A writer, after relating his own experiences of the fatal effects of this freedom of trade, concludes thus: 'Yet though these calamities are upon us, and many more in view, yet trade must be free; though French, Italian, Holland, and Ireland Trades must be curbed, yet this trade to the Indies must not be touched.'[1] The Company's advocates had pointed out that Holland had pursued the same Free Trade policy, and that her commercial greatness was due mainly to that cause. The Mercantilists denied that there was any analogy. Holland, they replied, was a small country, and was obliged to leave trade free. 'But we that are blest with a large tract of fruitful land, rich mines, productive and laborious cattle, convenient ports, and navigable rivers, must with the manufacturing our own Productions improve our land by feeding our people, Support our Trade and Traffick, Navigation and Land Carriage, and by all lawful means increase our people.' The time for Free Trade was not come yet; 'when the other parts of the world can agree on a Free Trade, it will be time for us to consider; and till then, make the best improvement of the Almighty God'.[2] Davenant's theory 'that trade is in its nature free, and finds its own channel', was not congenial to the Mercantilists. They pointed out that all trading nations had put a restraint upon trade, 'according as their circumstances required; the French have, since many years, prohibited our woollen manufactures, and by that means have set them up in their own country'. The Dutch had also prohibited dyed woollen manufactures, and had by this means 'gained a profitable employment'. The Venetians too had prohibited the English cloth. The same applied to Sweden and Denmark. They asserted that the cheapness of an article did not always prove its utility, and quoted Childe to prove that 'wherever the wages are high, it is an infallible Evidence of the Riches of that Country, and vice versa'. It is, said they, the multitude of people and good laws that principally enrich any country.

[1] *England's Danger by Indian Manufactures*, Bodleian Library, op. cit.
[2] *Reasons Humbly offered*, Bodleian Library, Fol. Θ. 658, no. 2.

Their reply to Davenant's argument in favour of exportation of woollen manufactures, and consumption of the Indian goods in England, took the form of a denial of the existence of a foreign market, where English goods could be exported. 'If we could find a Foreign Market for our manufactures, this objection would be of force, but this is impossible.'[1] It followed that Free Trade was impossible, and that England could thrive only after the prohibition of the East Indian goods. The leading idea underlying nearly all the statements of the Mercantilists is admirably expressed by the following: 'If by Free Trade be meant absolute Free Trade, without any limitation or qualification at all, but every man to do what he likes, then we may as well transport Corn, Wool, and Fuller's earth out of the Nation, as any other Commodity. And the rich men may engross the Corn and other things of livelihood, into their own hands, and no man may say, Why do you so? But it is hoped no man will desire to have such freedom. Free trade must have its interpretation, or limitation and bounds, which is the Nation's Good. Such freedom we plead for.'[2]

This passage brings out the prominent characteristics of the Mercantilism of the later half of the seventeenth century. Its supporters took a far deeper view of the effect of the growth of the East India trade and other foreign trades on English national life than has generally been supposed. Their gaze was fixed not upon the money that would flow into the pockets of the East India merchants, but upon the miseries that the trade would inflict upon the nation in general. They regarded the State as an instrument which would rectify all the abuses that had crept in through the unlimited freedom accorded to the East India merchants. It need hardly be added that some of them identified the interests of the nation with the maintenance of their own supremacy, and that Davenant was substantially correct when he denounced the weavers for perpetrating such a fallacy. This does not alter, however, the fact that their appeals had effect mainly because they expressed in a vigorous and terse language what the majority of the English manufacturers were

[1] *An Answer to the Most Material objections against the Bill restraining the East India Wrought Silks*, Bodleian Library, Fol. Θ. 658, no. 54.

[2] *Reasons showing that the Desires of the Clothiers will not be prejudicial to the Grower*, Brit. Mus. 816. m. 14 (92).

feeling at the time, and that their arguments proved successful only because they were in harmony with the prevailing conception of the theory of the State.

The East India Company were not, however, without adequate representation, and their cause was championed by a series of remarkable writers. The Company's advocacy of the freedom of trade was not accidental, but logical. As long as it was menaced by the Dutch it clung to the skirts of the Government, and advocated commercial war. The growth of that trade, however, led to attacks upon it under Charles II. Childe and Papillon, as shown in Chapter II, had replied to its critics with considerable effect, and had reduced its opponents to silence. When it was attacked after the Revolution the Company employed the previous arguments of Childe, and deduced freedom of trade from the necessity of importing large quantities of cheap Indian goods into England. They showed that England gained considerably by using cheap Indian goods. They admitted that the Indian goods 'interfered with the Woollen, Silk, and linen manufactures of this Kingdom'. Nor did they deny that a great part of the Indian goods were consumed in England. But they pointed out that in that case, 'it may as much be argued that all foreign commerce is prejudicial to the common interest of England, for that without it we should have wherewithal to feed and clothe ourselves, and thereby keep our own people in full employ'.[1] It was, they declared, to the interest of England to have silks and linens from the cheapest markets, 'whereby we impoverish our neighbours by supplying ourselves and them with such goods as work against and beat out their manufactures'. Hence, nothing ought to be done to limit the freedom of trade. 'For it is an undeniable maxim, and what is the general practice and policy of all trading countries, that trade ought not to be limited or restrained, but left to its free current. Nothing being more visible than that, if it be stopped or dammed up in one part, it will overflow in another.'[2]

The freedom of trade which the Company desired would, said a writer, make all manner of commodities cheap; 'the cheapness

[1] *MSS. of the House of Lords*, New Series, vol. ii, p. 52.
[2] *East India Company's paper delivered to the House of Lords*, New Series, vol. ii, p. 52.

of commodities empowers our people to work cheaper; the cheapness of work encourages foreign trade; Foreign trade brings wealth; that raises the price of land.'[1]

The cause of the Company was defended in a series of broadsides, pamphlets, &c., and it is difficult to come across a document of the period dealing with that trade that does not discuss the advantage or disadvantage of Free Trade. It was not an abstract theory, discussed with touching impartiality by 'men of speculation', but a burning question of the day, involving thousands of people, and shaping the destinies of many a person in manifold ways. This illustrates strikingly the interest taken by the people in the East India trade. It has been said that at the election of 1700 the two Companies were fought for by many a candidate at the polling booth. Of the writers, however, Davenant was probably the ablest. There is no evidence to suppose that he was a thoroughgoing champion of Free Trade. He asserts again and again in his classical *Reports on Public Accounts* the necessity of levying impositions upon those foreign articles that competed with English articles. Nor does he deny the efficacy of prohibition in particular cases. He thought that French goods ought to have been prohibited earlier than they actually were, and that the Dutch goods could be prevented from injuring English manufactures only by the imposition of heavy duties upon their importation into England.

As regards the East India trade, he justified the exportation of bullion by the Company on the ground that 'the returns from India of £200,000, when exported to other countries, must increase the first sum at least fourfold, and perhaps £800,000'.[2] He estimated that the Returns of £200,000 in times of peace might probably yield abroad £800,000 and that the Returns of £200,000 at home would yield £800,000. Accordingly, by the exportation of £400,000 to the East, the country would derive a profit. From this have to be deducted various charges. The net profit from the Trade will be £600,000.[3] The profit did not all accrue to it, but was national and divided among many thousands of people. Davenant's line of defence was the same as that of Mun. His figures were naturally different. The

[1] *An Answer to Mr. Carey's Reply*, Brit. Mus. 816. m. 13 (143).
[2] *Essay on the East India Trade*, p. 16.
[3] Ib., p. 53.

accuracy of these figures was brought into question by several writers. His statement that the Nation increased in riches from '1656 to 1688' 2 million pounds per annum, can hardly be accepted without further evidence. Nor are we prepared to say that, of this increase, '£900,000 was due to the Plantation Trade, £500,000 to our Products and Manufactures and £600,000 to the East India Trade'. An opponent asserted that he had 'never seen a collection so generally mistaken. If he had consulted only with men of Speculation, who gather from Paper, he might well run into such mistakes.'[1] Davenant's reply that by the 'yearly increase of 2 millions a year', he meant only 'average increase', was not conclusive.[2] More important is his defence of the exportation of bullion to the East Indies. Childe and Papillon had asserted that 'money is a commodity, and may in many cases be exported as much to National advantage as any other Commodity'.[3] Davenant developed this proposition, and asserted that 'silver and goods serve as the measure of other commodities and are valuable only in proportion to them. Money is not the Riches of the Nation, for you are not sure you shall purchase with that whatever you have occasion for'.[4]

To the Mercantilists, however, bullion seemed to be the 'sinews of war'. 'For money in a Body Politick is as Blood in the Body Natural, giving life to every part.'[5] 'As our Treasure doth ebb and flow,' said the author of *Interest of Great Britain Considered*, 'so doth our strength, Money being the sinews of State and War.' John Carey asserted that the 'Wealth of the Nation was not a bit greater than at the beginning of the century'.[6] The East India Company were therefore forced to treat money as a commodity. They could hardly agree with the idea of the Mercantilists that money was treasure. Their

[1] *An Answer to a Late Tract*, Brit. Mus. 8245. a. 15. See also the following replies to Davenant: *England and India Inconsistent in their Manufactures*; *Reasons Humbly Offered for the Hindering the Home Consumption of East India Silks.*

[2] *Some Reflections on a pamphlet entitled 'England and India Inconsistent in their Manufactures'.*

[3] See Chapter II of this Thesis. For a discussion of the function of money, see my treatise on 'Indian Banking and Currency', 1920.

[4] *Some Reflections on a pamphlet entitled 'England and India Inconsistent in their Manufactures'.*

[5] *Reasons*, op. cit., pp. 8–10; *India and England*, op. cit.

[6] Carey, *Discourse concerning the East India Trade*, Brit. Mus. 8245. b. 14.

increasing exports of money could hardly be defended upon any other ground. Money came to be regarded, therefore, as a measure of exchange. 'What would happen if a country were isolated, even though it possessed enormous riches.' The country would be in a miserable condition with respect to its neighbours, who have free commerce.[1]

North pointed out the absurdity of the idea that money ought to be hoarded and preserved so that the Nation might not get bankrupt. 'Let not the care of money torment us so much. For a people that are rich cannot want it, and if they make none, they will be supplied with the Coin of other Nations.'[2] The main characteristics of money and the various functions it performs were pointed out with a vigour and directness that is still unrivalled. Simon Clemens's acute analysis of Money, in his *Discourse of the General Notions of Money, Trades and Exchanges*,[3] and his adoption of the historical method, were no doubt an immense improvement. He mentioned the advantages derived from the exportation of bullion to the East. He did not, however, go further. The writer of *Some Considerations on the Nature and Importance of the East India Trade*[4] brought out the essential features of money. The Mercantilists, he asserted, 'considered Money as the Ancients did the Blood, that all that came in must necessarily be kept in the Body, vainly fancying a perpetual Addition without any Decrease of Circulation.' 'But of late men have regarded Silver not only as the measure and stand of Trade, but really as much a Commodity, and as much the subject of Stock Exchange and Traffick, and like them continually fluctuating in its Price, according to the Quantity and demand of it. No Laws can restrain its outlet, no more than they can the circulation of the Air, or the Course of the Tide.'

If gold and silver were commodities, the East India Company were justified in exporting large quantities of bullion. The Company asserted that exportation of bullion resulted in a net profit to the nation. The Company defended its exports of gold and silver on the ground that the amount exported either brought more merchandise in return, or this could be

[1] North, *Discourse on Trade*; MacCulloch's *Early English Tracts*, 1691.
[2] *Essay*, &c., p. 53.
[3] Brit. Mus. 8224. c. 24.
[4] Brit. Mus. 11399. g. 4, pp. 16–31.

sold in foreign countries for three times the amount of money exported. The nation was, therefore, a gainer by this trade. It was, asserted the author of *Considerations upon the East India Trade,* an exchange of less for greater value. The export of bullion for Indian manufactures was an exchange of less for greater value. 'It is to exchange Bullion for Manufactures more valuable, not only to the Merchants, but also to the Kingdom.' The principal riches, whether of Private Persons, or of whole Nations, 'are Meat, Bread, Clothes and Houses, &c'. Money itself, thought the author, is secondary and dependent. Clothes and manufactures are real and principal riches. Hence, 'to exchange Bullion for more manufactures is to exchange the Secondary for more of the Principal Riches than are elsewhere to be had on the same terms.'[1]

The chief merit of the writer consisted in his extension of the theory propounded by Childe, Clemens, and Barbon. If money is a commodity, as asserted by Childe and others, then, argued the author, it is only a secondary commodity. The principal commodities are houses, meat and clothes. As the East India trade involved the exchange of secondary for principal riches, the nation was a gainer by the trade. Even Simon Clemens would not go so far. He was content to say that 'if that business (East India Trade) were well managed, we should be able to send so much of the goods brought from thence to our Neighbour Markets as would return us more money, and Money's worth than what we first sent out for India'.[2] His eyes are still fixed on the money that England would get by the exchange. He does, however, consider the possibility of the exchange of Indian goods for foreign goods. The returns of Indian goods sold in foreign countries may be made either in bullion or goods. Clemens defended the sale of Indian manufactures on the ground that the returns were made in bullion. The writer of *Considerations* argued in its favour for the reason that the exchange led to the acquisition of 'principal Riches'. The Mercantilists, however, were not satisfied. They argued that the exportation of Indian manufactures to Germany,

[1] *Considerations on the East India Trade*; MacCulloch's *Collection of Economic Tracts*, pp. 549–629.

[2] Simon Clemens, *General Notions of Money, Trades, and Exchanges*, Brit. Mus. 8224. c. 24, p. 15.

though it led to the increase of bullion, did not benefit the nation, as the Germans no longer required English cloth, and had, according to Davenant, built up a large industry of their own. Hence, as the balance of trade with Germany was unfavourable, increase in the amount of bullion through the exportation of Indian commodities was detrimental to the kingdom.

The Company opposed the general balance of trade to the particular balance of which the Mercantilists were so fond. Childe had acutely criticized the methods employed at the time, and had pointed out the difficulty of forming a right judgement. 'The True Measure of any trade', said he, 'cannot be taken by the consideration of such trade in itself singly, but as it stands in reference to the General Trade of the Kingdom.'[1] He had pointed out that it was impossible to take a true account, as the Custom House books were not true guides. He showed that a number of accidents, as losses at sea, bad markets, increased demand abroad, &c., might render the Custom House books totally unreliable. Nicholas Barbon amplified this statement of Childe, and exposed the dangers involved in the fallacy. He asserted 'that there is nothing so difficult as to find out the Balance of trade in any Nation'.[2]

The merit of Davenant lay in his organization of these disparate and disconnected statements into a closely-reasoned plea for freedom of trade. This freedom was not advocated by him either because he recognized its importance in the abstract, or because he was a fervid enthusiast for commercial liberty. He was quite willing to see the Dutch manufactures prohibited, nor was he averse to the prohibition of French manufactures. His advocacy of the theory had its origin in his perception of the impossibility of carrying on the East India trade without freedom of trade. It was the actual state of the East India trade that compelled him to advocate Free Trade measures. The Company had advocated it before, and it had become so familiar that in nearly all the pamphlets written on either side freedom of trade was discussed. Nearly all the economists of the time would be totally unintelligible to us unless we have a thorough grasp of the conditions that occasioned those theories. This is

[1] *New Discourse of Trade*, chap. ix, p. 152.
[2] *Discourse Concerning Coining*, p. 34.

the main cause of the misrepresentation of the seventeenth-century economists by Adam Smith and his followers.

The multiplicity of facts in which these theories are embedded are separated off by watertight compartments from the theories, and the latter are treated either to point out a moral, or to serve as examples of misdirected energies and crude fallacies. Nothing could be more unhistorical and unjust. Their authors were eminently practical men, and their theories summed up the results of their own experiences. Davenant was probably an exception, and was therefore reviled by his opponents as 'a mere man of speculation'. It is, probably, this quality in Davenant that saved him from the fate which has overtaken his critics. He possessed in an eminent degree just those qualities which the economists so sadly lacked—a charming literary style, breadth of view, deep insight into the relation of the various trades to one another, and fertile imagination. All these qualities were exhibited in his exposition of the fundamental principles underlying the prominent commercial phenomena of the day.

The criticisms of Childe and Barbon of the balance of trade theory were skilfully transformed into a cogent plea for freedom of trade. He showed that it was difficult to rely on the well-known statistics of Sir William Petty, 'as the farmers, in their several contracts, had never been obliged to give in a real statement of the Accounts, and a true produce of their respective Counties'.[1] But the calculation of a balance of trade was far more difficult than 'political arithmetick'. 'It is', he said, 'utterly impossible exactly to state the balance between one country and another.' He then showed the dangers of prohibition and imposition. He agreed that 'we might safely prohibit, or put a clog upon, the traffic of that country where we think ourselves the losers', but this was to be done with the utmost caution, as high duties and impositions not only broke 'some of the links in the chain of trade', but generally ended in a war between those nations where they were made use of frequently.[2] Hence, laws to compel the consumption of some commodities and prohibit the use of others may do well enough where trade is forced and artificial, as in France, but in England they are needless and artificial. It was admitted by Davenant that the

[1] *An Essay on Ways and Means*, part I, chap. i, pp. 127-50.
[2] *Two Reports on Public Accounts*, vol. v of *Complete Works*, pp. 379-80.

East India trade hindered the consumption of English manufactures. Nor did he deny that the exportation of bullion to the East proved injurious to Europe. He asserted, however, that it was the interest of Englishmen to be the carriers of the world. 'There is no trade so advantageous as that of buying goods in one Country to sell them in another, and it is the original and chief article of great wealth in Holland.'[1] He denounced injurious restrictions on trade, and declared that the natural way of promoting the woollen manufactures was not 'to force its consumption at home', but by wholesale laws to the contrary, that it might be bought cheaper. 'Trade', said Davenant, 'is in its nature free, finds its own channel and best directs its own course, and all Laws to give it Rules and Directions, and to limit and circumscribe it, may serve the Particular Ends of Private Men, but are seldom Advantageous to the Nation.'[2] Hence the necessity of freedom of trade. Davenant thought that England should concentrate on the exportation of her manufactures to foreign parts, because her geographical position and her 'Dominion of the Seas' eminently fitted her to perform that rôle. This advice remained a counsel of perfection for about a hundred years, and it was not till the Industrial Revolution that England assumed that rôle which she has maintained since, and which Davenant had urged nearly a hundred years before. Sir Dudley North carried out the ideas of Davenant to their logical conclusion. He had revolutionized the theory of foreign trade by showing that it was nothing else but a barter of commodities. He now showed in his *Considerations on the East India Trade*[3] 'that England was fitted by nature to be the greatest carrying nation in the world'. He developed these ideas with characteristic thoroughness. He bade England concentrate on the exportation of her manufactures to 'foreign parts'; showed the loss sustained by the nation through wasteful employment of a number of persons; and proved the advantages of the division of labour with a vividness and insight which even Adam Smith might have envied.

[1] Davenant, *Essay on the East India Trade*, p. 35; *The Weavers' Twelve Queries Answered*, Brit. Mus. 816. m. 14 (122). Compare the following: 'The Encouragement of English Trade could be effected only by leaving the Trade free, and sheltering it against all Prohibitions.' *The Linnen Drapers' Answer to Mr. Carey*, Brit. Mus. 816. m. 13 (141).

[2] *Essay*, p. 23.

[3] MacCulloch, *Collection*, op. cit.

An Abstract of the Number of ships and tonnage set out by the of ships sent each year to the East Indies. The Rawlinson MS.,

Year	Total value sent each Year.			Bombay, Surat, and Persia.			Fort and Bay.		
	No. of Ships	Ton-nage	Total value	No. of Ships	Ton-nage	Total value	No. of Ships	Ton-nage	Total value
			£			£			£
1689	3	1,878	21,404	2 B	1,218	15,896	1 F	660	5,508
1690 } 1691 }	5	1,078	801	1 B 1 S & F	348	165	Blank		
1692	6	3,285	180,925	2 S	1,080	82,591	1 F	200	701
1693	6	3,380	193,473	1 S 1 B	1,400	79,591	1	670	38,665
1694	11	4,073	450,394	4 S 2 P	1,363 940	105,255 108,573	1 F & B 1 Coast	750	127,114
1695	4	1,585	212,786	1 S	210	41,032	1 F	720	90,062
1696	10	3,975	398,992	4 S 1 P	1,550 780	218,788 47,229	1 F 1 for Spices	575 90	61,558 1,766
1697	12	5,355	494,416	4 B 1 B & Mocoo }	2,060	177,717	2 F	920	56,177
1698	14	5,465	624,414	1 B 2 B S 1 C & S 1 P	1,720 450	200,619 40,653	Blank		
1699	13	5,130	601,531	3 B	1,600	169,744	2 F & St. Helena	730	80,693
1700	12	4,600	682,898	3 B	750	77,960	4 Fort Bengall 2	1,975 975	282,444 194,979
1	2	3	4	5	6	7	8	9	10

Notes: Blank means no ship sent in the year.
Contractions: B, in column 5, means Bombay; S, Surat; and P, Persia.
The same applies to columns 8 and 11.

ıst India Company in each year from 1689 to 1700, showing the number
302, ff. 297ᵛ and 298ʳ, Bodleian Library, Oxford.

Coast and Bay.			China.			Bencoolen.			St. Helena.		
o. of hips	Ton-nage	Total value	No. of Ships	Ton-nage	Total value	No. of Ships	Ton-nage	Total value	No. of Ships	Ton-nage	Total value
		£			£			£			£
	Blank			Blank			Blank			Blank	
	Blank			Blank		1	350	636		Blank	
						2	380 Madagascar and Bombay			Blank	
C & B	2,005	97,633		Blank			Blank			Blank	
C & B	1,310	75,217		Blank			Blank			Blank	
1 B	700	73,554	1	200	33,189		Blank		1	120	2,709
C & B	655	81,692		Blank			Blank			Blank	
F & B	860	66,051		Blank		1	120	3,600		Blank	
C & B 1 B	975 7,501	142,189 53,574	2	650	64,759		Blank			Blank	
C & B 1 B	2,345 450	291,366 36,299	1	280	37,554	1	220	7,925		and St. Helena	
4 B 1 C	1,550 400	222,911 45,677	2	600	76,206	1	250	6,300		Blank	
	Blank		3	900	127,517		Blank			Blank	
11	12	13	14	15	16	17	18	19	20	21	22

CONCLUSION

THE history of the East India trade in the seventeenth century is important for several reasons. In the first place it exemplifies the close connexion of economic theories with the commercial and industrial activity of the times. Mun, the Director of the East India Company, advocated the exportation of money, because without it the Company's fate was sealed. Childe, its Dictator, treated money as a commodity, and disliked restrictions on the freedom of trade because, otherwise, the importation of large quantities of Indian manufactures into England, and the exportation of more than half a million pounds a year to the East, would have been impossible. Lastly, Davenant and others defended the East India trade because it was impossible for them to defend the trade on any other ground. They wanted to buy in the cheapest market, and consequently disliked all regulations that prevented them from exercising their choice. It was purely a business question; and it must be confessed that the East India Company completely ignored the national aspect of the agitation against the importation of Indian manufactures during the last ten years of the seventeenth century. It could hardly be expected to acquiesce in the virtual prohibition of a trade that had been acquired only after numerous difficulties had been encountered; nor is it surprising to notice its determined opposition and ruthless treatment of its rivals. Its advocacy of Free Trade theories has prevented us from analysing objectively the policy of its opponents. In justice to them it must be said that the thoroughly national and truly valuable advice tendered by the representative Mercantilists was based upon conceptions whose logical force we cannot deny, and their consistent application, under suitable conditions, and with proper safeguards, has invariably resulted in striking improvements in the state applying it.

It would be easy to prove that the Company was inconsistent

in the advocacy of the Free Trade theories, for Mun had advocated, and the Directors had insisted, up till 1680, upon the necessity of vigorous action and commercial war. The Company had, as shown in Chapter I, really been the most important instrument in the development of Mercantilism during the periods Mun has been called the truest representative of Mercantilism in the seventeenth century. To one, however, who has gone through the data of the period, it will be clear that Mun merely expressed in a different language what every one connected with the East India Company felt. When we compare Mun's theories with the voluminous data from which he deduced, and which are preserved in the archives of the Company, we are irresistibly forced to the conclusion that Mun summed up in a few connected sentences the leading features of the Company's policy.

This leads us to our second conclusion. The existence of the Company depended ultimately upon the energetic and consistent support of the Executive. It could succeed only after its rivals had been crushed, and this postulated complete harmony between the interests of the Crown and those of the Company. There was no inherent reason why there should be any conflict of interests, and the actual practice of all the European powers throughout the eighteenth century exemplified strikingly this identification of interests. In the seventeenth century, however, it was only with difficulty that such an identity of interests was established. James I, no less than Charles I, constantly treated the Company as a private concern, whose quarrels were to be separated from State quarrels. A deeper analysis of the function of the State necessarily brought about fundamental changes in this conception. Charles II's support of, and his action in, the Company reversed the position which the Company had occupied under his father and grandfather. The comparative neglect from which the merchants suffered under the latter was one of the most important causes of the growth of demand for State action.

In the third place, the support of the Company by the Crown under Charles II led to an enormous expansion of Indian trade. The Company was on the horns of a dilemma. It had been foremost in demanding State action; and when the latter resulted in increased trade, it led to the Company's opposition by the followers of the same theory which it had done its best to enforce.

It had done its best to multiply Mercantilists; when its trade developed, and Indian manufactures competed with the English manufactures, the Mercantilists attacked it in no measured terms.

There was, consequently, a complete change in the rôle it had performed from the beginning of the seventeenth century. During the last ten years of that century the original position of the Company was reversed, and the Company advocated Free Trade with the same passion, it championed the importation of Indian manufactures with the same vigour, under which it had advocated Mercantilism under James I and Charles II. It is essential that we should notice this change, as this helps us to explain the two most characteristic features of seventeenth-century English economic theory—the Mercantilism of Mun, and the Free Trade theories of the time of William III. They were the result, not of any elaborate chains of abstract reasoning on the part of their advocate, but of the profound changes which the ever-increasing commerce and trade with India produced during the period. In other words, they merely sum up the characteristic features of the commercial progress of the seventeenth century, and Mun no less than Sir Dudley North merely expresses in an abstract form the vital changes through which the Company passed during the period.

The seventeenth-century English economic theory is but an expression of the manifold changes wrought by the English East India Company on the national industries, and no other trade supplies a better example of the vital connexion between the Executive, the Industry, and the Economic Theory of a Nation. The three are mutually dependent.

I need hardly point out the effects of the increase in the importation of Indian manufactures into England. I have tried to show that the competition of Indian manufactures was severely felt, and attempted to prove that some of the English industries were seriously affected. The Parliament could hardly avoid passing the law of 1700, for the destruction of some of the English industries would have followed in the train of Indian imports, and it is as illogical to blame the Parliament for preserving what was deemed to be the life-blood of the nation, as it is foolish to expect it to remain impervious to the appeals of thousands of weavers, and manufacturers.

Its position would really have been greatly weakened if the fervid appeals, passionate arguments, and genuine sufferings of the English weavers had been ignored. That some sort of compromise was actually suggested has been made clear, above; but its failure testified alike to the intensity of feeling among the English weavers, and to the severity of the competition to which the English manufactures were subjected by the Indian manufactures.

INDEX